A
GENEVA SERIES
COMMENTARY

JUDGES

A CRITICAL AND

EXPOSITORY COMMENTARY

ON THE

BOOK OF JUDGES.

BY

REV. A. R. FAUSSET, M.A.,

SOMETIME SCHOLAR AND GOLD MEDALLIST IN CLASSICS, TRIN. COL., DUBLIN,

Editor of Bengel's "Gnomon" in English; Author of "Studies in the CL. Psalms;"
and Author in part of the "Critical and Experimental Commentary."

THE BANNER OF TRUTH TRUST

THE BANNER OF TRUTH TRUST
3 Murrayfield Road, Edinburgh EH12 6EL
P. O. Box 621, Carlisle, Pennsylvania 17013, USA

*

© Banner of Truth Trust 1999

Previously published as
A Critical & Expository Commentary on the Book of Judges
by James Nisbet & Co., London, 1885

First Banner of Truth Edition 1999
ISBN 0 85151 762 5

*

Printed and bound in Great Britain
by Cromwell Press,
Trowbridge,
Wiltshire

PREFACE.

THE Bible holds a unique position in relation to the Sacred Books of the world, in the fact that it alone connects its spiritual and moral teachings with a framework of history and chronology capable of being tested. The explorations of modern discoverers in Palestine, Moab, Egypt, Assyria, Babylonia, Asia Minor, Greece, and Rome, have been continually bringing to light fresh confirmations of the trustworthiness of our Sacred Records. At the same time, the histories in Holy Scripture are so wonderfully framed by their Divine Author as to set forth spiritual and everlasting truths for all ages, and especially to typify Him in whom all history, type, and prophecy find their centre—"Jesus Christ, the same yesterday, and to-day, and for ever." For "the testimony of Jesus is the spirit of prophecy" (Rev. xix. 10).

My aim in this Commentary on the Book of Judges has been—First, to examine critically the original Hebrew, and to give to the English reader the results of reverent modern scholarship, so that he may know accurately the meaning of the sacred text: Secondly, to give the fruits of modern research in relation to the topographical, historical, and chronological references in the book: Thirdly, to endeavour, in dependence on the Holy Spirit, to draw forth from the narrative and the inspired Word the spiritual lessons designed by the Divine Author. The Synopsis of Contents will afford to the student, the teacher, and the preacher, a comprehensive view, at a glance, of the whole and of each particular history, and their spiritual lessons.

May our God use this work for His own glory and the edification of His Church!

AND. ROB. FAUSSET.

St. Cuthbert's Rectory,
York, *October 5, 1885.*

SYNOPSIS OF CONTENTS.

INTRODUCTION.

CHAPTER III.

CHAPTER XXI.

A CRITICAL AND EXPOSITORY COMMENTARY

ON THE

BOOK OF JUDGES.

INTRODUCTION.

I. THE TITLE AND THE SUBJECT: THE SPECIAL OFFICE OF THE JUDGES.

THE name of this book indicates its subject, namely, the
doings of those Judges whose office it was to judge, or
rule righteously, in Israel in the period extending from the
death of Joshua to the time of Samuel (ch. iv. 5, x. 2). The
Hebrew term for Judges, *Shophetim*, answers to that of the
chief magistrates in the Phenician colonies, *Suffetes*. Judging
was the only royal function which was entrusted by God the
Heavenly King to man, under the Israelite theocracy. Moreover, as it was in the hands of the people's natural leaders, it
ranked very highly in the feeling of the nation. But the
distinguishing feature in the functions of the Judges, from
whom this book takes its name, is that these were not the
ordinary rulers of the people, but were raised up by the special
providence of God, not only to administer justice in Israel,
but to be the "saviours" of His people from the oppression of
their enemies (marg. ch. ii. 16–19, iii. 9, 15; Obad. 21).
These extraordinary Judges, in delivering the chosen people
from their oppressors, were not arbitrarily sent forth to their
work, but were chosen to vindicate Jehovah's righteousness,
that is, His faithfulness to His covenant, in behalf of Israel.
His eternal principle is, when His people return to Him in
penitence, He returns to them in mercy. His salvation and

A

His righteousness go hand in hand (Isa. xlv. 8). Thus they were Judges of righteousness not only in, but for, Israel: and accordingly Deborah and Barak, in their hymn of thanksgiving, dwell upon the manifestation of the divine righteousness in the deliverance just vouchsafed: "Speak ye that *sit in judgment*—They that are delivered shall rehearse *the righteous acts of Jehovah*, even *the righteous acts towards the inhabitants of His villages in Israel*" (Judg. v. 11). The Lord raised them up to save Israel, at intervals, as need required. They were the vicegerents of Him who was at one and the same time the civil, as well as the spiritual, King of Israel.

There were in all fifteen judges between Joshua and the Kings —Othniel, Ehud, Shamgar, Deborah and Barak (counted as *one*), Gideon, Abimelech (an usurper), Tola, Jair, Jephthah Ibzan, Elon, Abdon (probably the same as the Bedan in 1 Sam. xii. 11), Samson, Eli, Samuel. But Eli and Samuel were of the priestly order; and as such were *officially* judges. Eli was not a *Deliverer* or *Saviour*, and Samuel inaugurated the *Prophetic* dispensations (1 Sam. iii. 19–21; Acts iii. 24), and delivered the Lord's people, not by the sword, but by the word and by prayer (1 Sam. vii. 3–10); whereas the 'Judges,' specially so called, were not of the priestly family, but were *extraordinary* ministers called forth by God to deliver Israel, and forming in their rule a kind of distinct dispensation. The Lord raised them up (ch. ii. 16), and qualified them for their ministry by causing His Spirit to come upon them (ch. iii. 10, vi. 34, xi. 29, xiii. 25). Barak was called by a prophetess, Deborah. The providence of God overruled the people's choice in Jephthah's case. Throughout the book God appears as maintaining His own glory against the idols of the surrounding heathen, and not sparing even His own people whenever they apostatised from Him, and conformed to the vanities of the world, and always hearing His people's cry and delivering them, when they turned penitently to Him.

II. DESIGN OF THE BOOK.

Keil truly remarks, Israel's unfaithfulness punished by the foe's oppression, and Jehovah's faithfulness in raising up

Judges to deliver them at their cry, are the two hinges upon which the history turns. It may be further observed, that God's eternal principle in His dealings with the Church in relation to the world is, that of righteous retribution in kind. When Israel forsook the Lord, her rightful King, to conform herself to, and lean upon, the surrounding world-powers of heathendom, justly He paid her in kind, by making the instruments of her sin to become the instruments of her punishment. The inspired writer of this book everywhere views Israel's history in the light of God's law. The Judges were the vicegerents of God in carrying out part of that particular providence, which characterised His moral government of Israel, in contradistinction to the Gentile nations, whose idols were utterly unable to help them. The state of Israel at the time, wherein each did what was "right in His own eyes" (xvii. 6), gave scope, as no centralised government could equally do, to the operation of that extraordinary and special Providence, which assigned prosperity or adversity according to the obedience or disobedience, not only of the nation, but also of each tribe and each family (ch. i. 1–19, 21–23).

Thus the aim of the book is not to give a continuous history of the period between Joshua and Samuel, but to illustrate in particular striking deliverances the divine principle of dealing with Israel, which is laid down in ch. ii. 16–19: "Nevertheless Jehovah raised up judges [the first introduction of the term which designates the book], which delivered (*saved*) them out of the hand of those that spoiled them: and yet they would not hearken unto their judges, but they went a whoring after other gods, and bowed themselves unto them; they turned quickly out of the way which their fathers [Joshua's generation and the elders that outlived him] walked in, obeying the commandments of Jehovah; but they did not so. And when Jehovah raised them up judges, then Jehovah was with the judges, and delivered them out of the hand of their enemies all the days of the judge; for it repented Jehovah [Jehovah *had compassion: yinnacheem:* compare Ps. cvi. 44], because of their groanings, by reason of them, that oppressed them, and vexed them. And it came to pass, when the judge was dead, that they returned, and corrupted themselves more than their fathers, in following other gods to serve them, and to bow down unto them ; they ceased not from their own doings, nor from their stubborn way." The Psalmist (cvi. 34–45), just before the close of the Babylonian captivity, embodies the leading thoughts of this passage in his spirited closing Psalm of the Trilogy (civ., cv., cvi.), which rests the hope of restoration upon Jehovah's everlasting ' covenant,' inasmuch as it engages deliverance when Israel shall return to the Lord.

Causes of Israel's Apostasy.—The causes were manifold which inclined the Israelites to *add* to the worship of Jehovah the idolatries of heathendom ;—for they had too cogent and palpable proofs of the truth of the divine law to renounce it *wholly.* Such causes were—intermarriages with their heathen neighbours, Gentile associations, the beauty of the Canaanite women, the pomp, gaiety, and voluptuousness of their rites, the hope of learning the future by idolatrous divination, and superstitious fears of the supposed gods of the localities where they settled. Severe chastisements of God executed by those very nations whose sin they copied, and the succeeding rule of judges who were raised by God in answer to their cry, and who saved them out of the hands of their oppressors, were just the kind of discipline which they needed.

Imperfection of the Judges.—The Judges themselves imperfectly realised the divine ideal. The possession of inspired gifts was not always accompanied by a right use of them : just as the miraculous gifts at Corinth were abused (1 Cor. xiv.). This is analogous to God's way of dealing in the bestowal of natural gifts. Being pleased to create men free agents, He lays upon them the responsibility of using aright, or otherwise, the faculties and opportunities which He bestows. Gideon introduced the golden ephod. Jephthah made a rash vow, and gratified his own violent spirit in taking vengeance on Ephraim. The history of Samson, the last Judge, illustrates at once the strength and the weakness of Israel, whose representative he was : strength in being separated to Jehovah, utter weakness, when the consecration became severed, as Samson's locks, by lust.

The deliverances partial.—Each Judge delivered only part of Israel,—Shamgar, the district in the Philistine direction; Deborah and Barak, Northern Israel (ch. iv. 10; so also Gideon, ch. vi. 35). Jephthah saved Eastern Israel; Samson, Judah and Dan. Historical facts which did not subserve the spiritual purpose of the book are not specially detailed, as Ephraim's victory over Oreb and Zeeb (ch. viii. 3; Isa. x. 26). Samson was the last extraordinary Judge, and was born during Eli's priesthood. At that time the Philistines ruled Israel: and the Divine promise concerning him was, "He shall *begin* to deliver Israel out of the hand of the Philistines" (ch. xiii. 5). The deliverance so *begun* by Samson was completed by Samuel. Only the tribes suffering at the time under the enemy's oppression are noticed, whilst the rest who observed the law of Jehovah, and therefore had peace, are not alluded to.

Jehovah's threats and their fulfilment.—The Lord three times threatened Israel for unfaithfulness:—(1) at Bochim, ch. ii. 1–4; (2) at the Midianite invasion, ch. vi. 7–10; (3) at the Ammonite and Philistine oppression, ch. x. 10–14. These threats came to pass in Israel's ever-deepening oppression by the enemy without, and in the mutual severance of the tribes within. Under Othniel and Ehud, all Israel combined against the oppressor. Under Barak, Reuben, Gilead, Dan, and Asher took no part (ch. v. 15–17). Gideon with difficulty appeased the sensitive jealousy of Ephraim (ch. viii.). The further decay of the nation betrays itself in Abimelech's usurpation of kingship at Shechem (ch. ix.). Ephraim fought with Jephthah and the Trans-jordanic tribes, to its own grievous hurt (ch. xii.). Judah was so degenerate as to seek to give up the nation's deliverer Samson to the Philistines (ch. xv. 9–14).

God's epiphanies and Israel's apostasies and servitudes.—On four occasions the Divine Angel appeared, and the Spirit of God followed qualifying the Judge for the saving of Israel:—(1) ch. ii. 1–5, iii. 10; (2) vi. 11, 34; (3) x. 10–16, xi. 29; (4) xiii. 3–25. But the epiphanies of God, which revived the nation for a time, were followed by ever-deepening apostasies. So, consequently, the people's servitudes increased successively in

length, for the most part. They served Cushan-Rishathaim
for eight years; Eglon for eighteen years; Jabin for twenty
years. The servitudes increased also in the degree of humiliation. First, they served a distant king; next, a neighbouring
king; then, a king in Canaan itself. Jabin disarmed them
(ch. v. 8), as in 1 Sam. xiii. 22, the Philistines subsequently
did. It is remarkable that the three nations which first
brought Israel into bondage, were the same which proved to
be her scourge in subsequent history—Mesopotamia, Moab, and
Philistia. The fourth, fifth, and sixth servitudes, namely, those
to Midian, Ammon, and the Philistines, rise in progressive
severity, lasting as they did for seven, eighteen, and forty years
respectively.

Peaceful times under the Judges.—At the same time we must
remember, as Jahn observes (*Heb. Commonw.*), the book is a
record of the exceptional diseases of the body politic, whilst
the years of health are passed over in almost total silence.
The servitudes occupy only 111 years; the time of peaceful
independence, 319 years, if we take the whole period as 430
years. Jair's time is a sample of one of those peaceful
intervals, of which it has been said, a people is then happiest
when it has the least to record (x. 4). The recurring phrase,
" the land had rest 40—80—40—40 years," is another
illustration of the general tranquillity which characterised the
period of the Judges, notwithstanding the sad interruptions
which occurred (iii. 11, 30, v. 31, viii. 28). Hence, in the
coming millennial restoration of Israel, Jehovah promises
(Isa. i. 26, compare xxxii. 1), " I will restore thy judges as at
the first," namely, as in Israel's happiest days of the theocracy,
when the Lord Himself was king, and princes ruled in
judgment (Isa. xxxii. 1; compare Matt. xix. 28).

Israel's degeneracy entailed an earthly monarchy.—But the
general decline of Israel rendered the succeeding establishment
of an earthly king a necessity, for a carnal people who had not
the faith to appreciate the blessings of a theocracy : " From
him that hath not, even that he hath shall be taken away
from him." Repeated successive declensions, after frequent
revivals, degrade the impenitent lower than ever (Matt. xii.

45). Samson was left by the degenerate people to resist the foe single-handed; yet in his death, he, under God, accomplished more than what previous Judges had effected by their lives. Thus the last spiritual lesson taught in the book before the appendix (chs. xvii.–xxi.) is, life for the elect people resulting from death, the prophecy in type of Messiah who "through death was to destroy him that had the power of death, that is, the devil" (Heb. ii. 14).

III. HISTORICAL TRUTHFULNESS.

The age in which the Judges lived was not like the heroic age in Greece, mythical and prehistoric. Though the Judges were heroes, they lived in a settled community, which was illuminated by the Mosaic code of laws, and enjoyed the knowledge of the art of writing (compare ch. viii. 14.). It was no age of ignorance or semi-barbarism. There are no traces of an attempt to glorify Israel, such as are the glorifications of Greek heroes in the Iliad of Homer. The faults of Israel are too faithfully recorded to admit of the theory that the story is a patriotic fiction. None else but the Spirit of truth could have dictated the record which vindicates God's righteousness, at the cost of exposing to view the sin, shame, and suffering of the writer's own nation. Moreover, the mention of the Canaanite chariots accord with the Egyptian hieroglyphical records, which make the chariots of the Cheta or Hittites their main strength. An inscription of Rameses II. agrees with ch. ii. 11–13, in making Ashtaroth the goddess of the Hittites. The Shasous in the Egyptian monuments correspond to the Midianites and Amalekites of chs. vi.–viii. The decline of the contiguous empire of Egypt at this time synchronises with the rise of the Philistine power, which otherwise would have been hardly possible. The period of the Judges was probably from 430 to 450 years. Jephthah's express assertion, that 300 years had elapsed since Israel's settlement in Heshbon (xi. 26), suffices alone to disprove the supposition in Speaker's Commentary, that 150 years cover the whole period of the Judges.

Pember (*The Great Prophecies*) beautifully harmonises S. Paul's 573 years between the exodus and the building of the Temple (Acts xiii. 18–21 : 450 under the Judges, 40 in the wilderness, 40 under Saul, 40 under David, 3 of Solomon before his beginning the temple building) with 1 Kings vi. 1, which gives 480, by distinguishing the *mystical* from the *ordinary* chronology. Paul has the *ordinary* chronology : 1 Kings vi. 1, the *mystical*. The latter omits the 93 years (exactly : 8 under Cushan Rishathaim ; 18 Eglon ; 20 Jabin ; 7 Midian ; 40 the Philistines) of God's formal rejection of Israel during the times of the Judges :

$$\frac{\begin{array}{r}573\\480\end{array}}{93}$$

IV. DATE OF AUTHORSHIP.

This cannot be earlier than the close of that deliverance from the Philistine oppression, which Samson 'began' (ch. xiii. 5), and Samuel completed (1 Sam. vii. 9–14). Again, it was before David's taking Zion from the Jebusites (i. 21; 2 Sam. v. 6); for these dwelt with the Benjamites in Jerusalem down to the time of writing the book of Judges. Zidon oppressed Israel during that period (x. 12), and it was to Zidon that the Canaanites then looked for protection (xviii. 7). In David's days on the other hand, Tyre took the lead, and was his ally, instead of being, like Zidon, Israel's enemy. By the time when the book of Judges was composed, Israel had a king, and was enjoying a more organised government, as is proved by ch. xviii. 1 : "In those days there was no king in Israel, but every man did that which was right in his own eyes " (compare xvii. 6, xix. 1). Probably Samuel, or one of the school of the prophets, was the writer, in Saul's reign, or early in that of David. It was written after the Philistine capture of the ark, and its return and setting up at Nob in Saul's reign (1 Sam. xxi.), as appears from ch. xviii. 30, 31 : "Until the day of *the captivity of the land* (*i.e.*, the captivity of the ark ; for the ark was regarded as the very heart of the national theoracy, and its capture as the captivity of the people), they set up Micah's image, all the time that the house of God was at Shiloh;" the last words brand them with the stigma of perverse wickedness, in face of the Divine testimony close by them in Shiloh.

v. DIVISIONS.

I. *The Introduction* (ch. i.–iii. 6). This consists of two parts. (1) *Israel's relations to Canaan*, geographical and political: the doings or failures in duty of the tribes and families severally, in subduing the land (ch. i.). (2) *Israel's relations to Jehovah* (ch. ii.–iii. 6); apostasy accounting for Israel's failure to drive out the Canaanites utterly, and for Israel's consequent chastisement by the enemy. Jehovah left those nations in order to prove whether Israel would obey Him. The events in ch. i. and ii. 1–6 occurred before Joshua's death, which is narrated in ii. 7–9 by repetition from Josh. xxiv. 29–31. Therefore the introductory words in ch. i. 1, "Now after the death of Joshua," must refer to ch. ii. 11, "The children of Israel did evil in the sight of the Lord," and all that follows. The general facts and lessons of the book are briefly set forth in ii. 11, iii. 6, namely, the high calling, and the apostasy of Israel, notwithstanding God's distinguishing favour: Jehovah's consequent chastenings, and His subsequently raising up Judges, because of His compassion for their groanings and cries to Him; then upon the death of each judge, their relapse into idolatry.

II. *The body of the work* (ch. iii. 7–xvi.). Ch. iii. 7 resumes the opening formula from ii. 11: "The children of Israel did evil in the sight of the Lord." Political events are treated as secondary; the spiritual truths of the history occupy the foreground. Out of the thirteen Judges, seven are very briefly noticed; the record of the remaining six is full, viz., Ehud, Deborah and Barak, Gideon, Abimelech, Jephthah, and Samson. Othniel is the only representative of Judah. Most of the Judges belonged to Northern and Eastern Israel. Gideon is the only one whose son's career is detailed; and the reason doubtless is, because it illustrates the spiritual lesson of the whole. Gideon's sin in making the ephod resulted in the destruction of all his family except Jotham; and this, by the son of his concubine, Abimelech, aided by the men of Shechem;

then these in turn, Abimelech and the men of Shechem, were made by God the instruments of punishing one another. Such was the fatal issue of the first effort to substitute an earthly king for Jehovah the Lord of the theocracy.

III. *The Appendix* (chs. xvii.–xxi.). (1) *Micah's idolatry in Mount Ephraim, and the adoption of it by the Danites on their way to the conquest of Laish.*—This was at a time "when there was no king in Israel" (chs. xvii., xviii.). It was before the days of Samson, as appears from comparing ch. xviii. 12 with xiii. 25. It must have been also before that Jabin established his kingdom so firmly in Northern Israel; for after its establishment Dan could not have taken Laish in the north. A comparison of ch. xviii. 1 with i. 34, and Josh. xix. 47, leads to the inference that this history occurred at the earliest part of the period of the Judges. Moreover, no mention of the Judges occurs in the appendix. But the writer notices "the day of the captivity of the land," *i.e.*, the carrying away of the ark by the Philistines; for the sanctuary was "the kernel and essence" of the land (Hengstenberg); and the Psalmist (lxxviii. 60, 61) describes the capture of the ark in similar language: "God forsook the tabernacle of Shiloh, and delivered His strength into *captivity*, and His glory into the enemy's hand"; and the completeness of Israel's prostration under the Philistines is indicated in 1 Sam. xiii. 19–23.

(2) *Gibeah's awful wickedness, and Benjamin's defence of it, and consequent punishment almost to extermination by the rest of united Israel* (chs. xix., xx., xxi.). The unity of the tribes, and the mention of Aaron's grandson, Phinehas (ch. xx. 28, compared with Josh. xxii. 13, xxiv. 33) point to a date just after Joshua's death. These two histories depict the spirit of the age. They are intimately connected with the account of the Judges, to which they are appended at the close, so as not to interrupt the historical sequence. They were not isolated events, but exercised a permanent influence for evil in doctrine and practice. Micah's idol, apparently the first introduced after, and in spite of, Joshua's charge and the people's solemn protest of faithfulness (Josh. xxiv. 15, 16, 20, 21), was permanently set up, with a regular priesthood, by Dan (ch. xviii.

30, 31). Gibeah's moral filthiness, the invariable associate of idolatry, was not eradicated by the terrible punishment of Benjamin, but affected the tribes ever afterwards, as the prophet Hosea testifies, ix. 9 : "They have deeply corrupted themselves, as in the days of Gibeah "; x. 9, " O Israel, thou hast sinned from the days of Gibeah."

Connection of his book with the preceding and the succeeding books of the Canon.—Finally, the connection of Judges with Joshua appears in the repetition from Josh. xxiv. 28–31 of the account of Joshua's death (ch. ii. 6–9). The book, though having as its subject events after Joshua's death, yet narrates, at the beginning, events preceding it, as being spiritually connected with those following it. Thus the statements in ch. i. 10–15, 20, 21, 27, 29, are identical with Josh. xv. 14–19, 13, 63, xvii. 12, xvi. 10; also ch. xviii. with Josh. xix. 47. Moreover, the book of Judges prepares the way for the books of Samuel and Kings. Thus the tributary state of the Canaanite remnant under Solomon (1 Kings ix. 13–22) harmonises with the statements in ch. i. 28, 30, 33, 35. The kindness of Saul and David to the Kenites (1 Sam. xv. 6, xxx. 29) is accounted for in ch. i. 16. And allusion is made in 2 Sam. xi. 21 to the death of Abimelech recorded in ch. ix.

CHAPTER I.

THE CONCERT OF JUDAH AND SIMEON AGAINST THE CANAANITES
AND PERIZZITES COMBINED (VER. 1–8).

*The captor caught, and the measure which he had meted to
others, meted to himself.*

(1) *Now after the death of Joshua* [see Introduction. The
clause anticipates ch. ii. 8, 9. From i. 1 to ii. 8 *is a continuous
narrative of events just before Joshua's death,* but told here as
being spiritually connected with the events *after* his death], *it
came to pass that the children of Israel asked the Lord* [*i.e.,*
inquired His will through the Urim and Thummim of the
high priest (ch. xx. 23, 27 ; Numb. xxvii. 21). The omission
to ask counsel thus at the mouth of Jehovah, led to the unwise
league with Gibeon (Josh. ix. 14). Joshua so consulted Eleazar
on the very same subject, *the assigning of inheritances* (Josh.
xiv. 1, xviii. 1, 10, xix. 51)], *saying, Who* [*i.e.,* which tribe, as
ver. 2 proves] *shall go up for us* [which of our tribes shall go
up] *against the Canaanites first* [Heb. *in the beginning,* to open
the campaign] *to fight against them?* (2) *And the Lord said,
Judah shall go up* [viz., from the plain about Gilgal (ch. ii. 1 ;
Josh. xiv. 6), up to the hill country of Judah]; *behold I have
delivered the land* [the portion of Canaan falling to him by lot ;
a pledge and an earnest of the occupation of the rest by the remaining tribes] *into his hands.* (3) *And Judah said unto Simeon
his brother* [both being sons of Jacob by the same mother (Gen.
xxix. 33, 35) ; and therefore associated in their inheritances, so
that Simeon's land was within Judah's (Josh. xix. 1). Judah
took the lead, having been given the pre-eminence above his
brethren of being forefather of the Shiloh 'Prince of Peace,' in

Jacob's blessing (Gen. xlix. 8–12)], *Come up with me into my lot* [the inheritance allotted to me], *that we may fight against the Canaanites ; and I likewise will go with thee into thy lot.* (4) *And Judah went up ; and the Lord delivered* [fulfilling His promise in v. 2; compare Numb. xxiii. 19 ; Heb. x. 23] *the Canaanites* [fulfilling the curse on these descendants from Ham. They were *lowlanders* dwelling by the Jordan and the Mediterranean (Numb. xiii. 29; Josh. xi. 3)] *and the Perizzites* [living in the woods and mountains (Josh. xi. 3, xvii. 15). Bochart derives their name from *Perazoth*, ' hamlets '] *into their hand : and they slew of them in Bezek* [mentioned also in 1 Sam. xi. 8 ; where it gives its name to a *district*. Eusebius mentions two villages so named 17 Roman miles from Shechem, on the road to Bethshean. Before they could attack the Canaanites in their tribe-land, they must first turn their arms against the Canaanite forces- which Adoni-bezek had collected to oppose them in the north] *ten thousand men.* (5) *And they found* [came by surprise upon] *Adoni-bezek,* [*i.e.*, Lord *of Bezek;* his official title] *in Bezek; and they fought against him, and they slew the Canaanites and the Perizzites* [evidently another slaughter besides that in ver. 4]. (6) *But Adoni-bezek fled ; and they pursued after him, and caught him, and cut off his thumbs* [disabling him for bearing arms; our word *poltroon* means one who maims himself of his thumb, to escape military service, *pollice truncus*] *and his great toes* [disabling him for running against or from a foe(ch. iv. 15; 2 Sam. ii. 18)]. (7) *And Adoni-bezek said, Threescore and ten kings* [Canaan was then parcelled out among a number of petty chiefs, whose intestine wars were overruled by Providence to facilitate their conquest by His people Israel. Joshua smote 31 kings (Josh. xii. 24). The king of Bezek was not among them, being in a quarter where Joshua did not go. He did not venture to attack combined Israel, but waited till they were separating to go to their several inheritances. If Adoni-bezek's statement was not an exaggeration, the *seventy* were probably conquered by him at successive times, and some of them were successive chieftains over the same towns or clans], *having their thumbs and their great toes cut off, gathered their meat* [fragments or crumbs;

treated like dogs, Matt. xv. 27; Luke xvi. 21] *under my table.
As I have done, so God hath requited me.* [Retribution in kind,
the *lex talionis* (Lev. xxiv. 19, 20; 1 Sam. xv. 33; Isa. xxxiii. 1;
Matt. vii. 1, 2; James ii. 13)]. *And they brought him to
Jerusalem* [the northernmost city of Judah's allotment, though
in Benjamin; so the men of Judah began their campaign with
it. They brought Adoni-bezek with them thither, as a proof of
God's retributive righteousness, and of their victory through
His might. Probably a king of Jerusalem had been one of
his victims; thus the same place that witnessed his cruelty
witnessed his punishment; so Ahab, 1 Kings xxi. 19], *and there
he died* [anguish of mind, through the stings of conscience, aggra-
vating his wounds, which were not of themselves fatal]. (8)
*Now the children of Israel had fought against Jerusalem, and had
taken it, and smitten it* [rather, "*And* the children of Israel
fought against Jerusalem, and *took*, and *smote* it," viz., at this
time, not previously. The *king* of Jerusalem was early conquered by Joshua (Josh. x. 23, xii. 10); but not the city, which
only *now* fell before the children of Judah, somewhat before
Joshua's death. After its people were smitten, and the city
"set on fire" (a phrase only in xx. 48, marking that the appended
last chapters were earliest in point of time), the Jebusites
returned, and "dwelt with the children of Judah (and the
children of Benjamin) at Jerusalem," as these "could not drive
them out" (Josh. xv. 63; Judg. i. 21). Hence the city was
called Jebus, or the city of the Jebusites, till David's time
(Josh. xviii. 28, xv. 8; Judg. xix. 10–12; 2 Sam. v. 6)], *with the
edge of the sword, and set the city on fire.*

I. *Concert of Judah and Simeon against the combined forces
of the Canaanites and Perizzites.*

1. *Consultation of Jehovah; His answer; Judah's obedience.*—
When the children of Israel had to face a hazardous enterprise,
they sought council of Jehovah. It is well when even perils
and difficulties to be encountered drive us in simple faith to
the Lord, with the cry of David (Ps. lx. 11, 12) "Give us
help from trouble, for vain is the help of man. Through
God we shall do valiantly, for He it is that shall tread
down our enemies." They not merely offered general prayers,

but sought the Divine guidance in every detail, ' Who,' that is, "Which of our tribes shall go up against the Canaanites first?" Compare David's prayers for special direction, and the consequent success (2 Sam. v. 19–25): also see Phil. iv. 6, " In *every-thing* by prayer let your requests be made known to God." By the counsel of Jehovah, and relying on His promise of victory over the foe, Judah went up. God's promise of giving the heavenly land into His people's hand guarantees His delivering also the foe who obstructs them, into their hand (compare ver. 2 with 4 ; Rom. viii. 37–39, xvi. 20). Judah was first in dignity, so he must be first in duty. As it was he whom his brethren should *praise* (as his name means, Gen. xxix. 35, xlix. 8), so must he lead in the service of danger ; for the post of honour and the post of labour must be one. But this must not discourage us ; for whosoever the Lord calls to work, He also qualifies for the work (Josh. i. 2–9 : Acts xviii. 9, 10). The service and the success go together : Judah must do his part by going up, and he shall find Jehovah faithful to His promise of delivering the land and the enemy into his hand (Phil. ii. 12,˙13).

2. *Judah associates Simeon with him in the enterprise.*—The lot of Simeon fell within that of Judah, and was assigned out of it. Simeon was one of the least important of the tribes, and Judah one of the most important ; yet Judah does not hesitate to solicit Simeon's alliance and help against the common foe. We Christians cannot afford to despise the aid and sympathy of even weaker brethren, in our spiritual conflict for the goodly land, against the prince of darkness. God can bring forth strength out of even the most humble (Rom. xiv. 3, 4 ; 1 Cor. i. 27) ; so that he that is high as the head, cannot say to those who are low as the feet, I have no need of you, seeing that all believers are members one of another (1 Cor. xii. 21 ; Acts xi. 17, xv. 8, 9, 11). As Judah and Simeon combined, though different tribes, so should real believers co-operate in the good fight, though called by different names. And those that render help to their brethren, shall receive help in turn from brethren, as Judah promised Simeon, " Come up with me into my lot and I likewise will go with thee into thy

lot." Then both the helpers and the helped shall be together crowned at last with victory from the God of love, and shall alike share for ever the heaven of his love.

II. *Their success by Jehovah's help. The captor caught, and the measure which he had meted to others, meted to himself.*

1. *Conquest of the Canaanites and Perizzites.*—Judah was valiant, and Simeon loyally supported his ally; yet the victory is ascribed not to their valour, but to the Lord: "Jehovah delivered the Canaanites and the Perizzites into their hand." So the redeemed, who have "overcome because of the blood [so the Greek, διὰ τὸ αἷμα, Rev. xii. 11] of the Lamb," attribute their victory wholly to Him, "casting their crowns before the throne, and saying, Thou art worthy, O Lord, to receive glory, and honour, and power" (Rev. iv. 10, 11).

2. *Capture of Adoni-bezek, and retaliation upon him of the cruelties which he had practised on his captives.*—He had been a great king and conqueror, so that no fewer than seventy petty kings were subdued before him. What were the occasions of his wars with them, we know not; but ambition never wants a pretext to cloak its self-aggrandisements. True greatness he was utterly destitute of; for God, who alone is infinitely great, shows His greatness in mercy; whereas this monster in human form insulted over the fallen. Instead of pitying them in consideration of their former dignity, he cruelly maimed them, and degraded them to the level, not merely of slaves, but of the very dogs gathering the crumbs under his table; thus making their agony and shame the instrument of his fancied greatness and cruel pride. How little man can be trusted with power! The so-called great men of the earth again and again have sought to magnify themselves by spreading desolation on all sides without remorse, and to gratify their insatiable ambition at the cost of the sufferings and humiliation of thousands of their fellow-men. Yet let us not forget, whilst we stigmatise such selfish and cruel pride, that the seeds of all these hateful dispositions are in ourselves by nature. Hazael little suspected the cruelties he was capable of, till he was tried (2 Kings viii. 12, 13). The love of lording it over our fellow-men is common to us all: and, if we are preserved from such outrages

against humanity as Adoni-bezek was guilty of, it is to the grace of God alone we owe it.

But though the prosperous sinner's day be prolonged, and vengeance be delayed, yet it will come at last (Eccl. viii. 12, 13 ; Isa. iii. 11). The longer it be deferred, the heavier it will be when it comes. The heathen classics (Horace, Carm. iii. 2, 31) represent "Divine Retribution as lame of foot, yet sure to overtake the guilty one who flees before." Not only so, but vengeance comes in a form corresponding to the sinner's transgression. God warns the offender, " Be sure your sin will find you out " (Numb. xxxii. 2, 3). Not merely the punishment, but the sin will find the sinner out : " Thine own wickedness shall correct thee " (Jer. ii. 19). Punishment, in God's righteous government, is not a mere arbitrary penalty having no direct connection with the offence, but follows by a law of necessary consequence, as surely as the fruit is the natural offspring of the tree. This was the spiritual lesson taught in the Mosaic law, which required " an eye for an eye, a tooth for a tooth "—not indeed as an act of private revenge, but of magisterial authority. Adoni-bezek was made to learn this eternal truth by bitter experience. To have imitated his cruelty, as a mere insult of the victors over the vanquished, would have been inconsistent with the law of the God of love. But to make him an example of God's retribution of sin in kind, was only a vindication of the majesty of the law of the God of justice. Maimed of his limbs, his own sin in maiming seventy others was brought to his remembrance ; and he was led to confess, " As I have done, so God hath requited me." Thus not only he, but his conquerors especially, were taught at the outset a principle which is the keynote of the whole book of Judges, namely, that transgressors " shall eat of the fruit of their own way, and be filled with their own devices " (Prov. i. 31).

3. *God is still known by the judgments He executeth.*—Though now God's moral government is more secret than when the Theocracy existed, and when reward and punishment palpably followed obedience and disobedience respectively, yet it is no less real now than then. As Jacob's lie to Isaac, his father, was repaid in kind by his sons' lying to him, causing him

B

bitter and life-long anguish, and as David's secret adultery and murder were followed by the open taking of his wives, and the continued unsheathing of the sword against his house; so still for the most part the spoiler is spoiled, and the treacherous dealer is dealt treacherously with. If it be so even in the case of the godly, as Jacob and David, how much more will God give retribution in kind to the wicked? (1 Pet. iv. 17, 18). If men will not hearken to the Lord's voice, He gives them up unto their own counsels (Ps. lxxxi. 11, 12). Those who *judge not right* to retain God in their knowledge, God gives over to a mind *incapable of judging right* [καθὼς οὐκ ἐδοκίμασαν, παρέδωκεν, εἰς ἀδόκιμον νοῦν: Rom. i. 28].

4. *The cases wherein God requites not the good and the evil now, are a token that He will do so in the world to come.*—His present judgments upon *some* are a proof that even now He governs the world in righteousness. His omitting to judge in *all* instances now is a proof that He will judge the whole world hereafter. Meantime, when afflictions come, they have a voice to us from God, calling us to self-examination, that repenting of, and forsaking all sin, and abiding in Christ, we may have confidence, and not be ashamed before Him at his coming. Not merely the sinner, but "the righteous shall be recompensed in the earth" (Prov. xi. 31); just as not only Adoni-bezek's sin, but also Judah's faithfulness, was requited in Canaan. Righteousness shall be the righteous man's eternal reward: and he that has been faithful here over a few things shall be ruler over many things, in the heavenly and abiding joy of his Lord (Luke xix. 21; Rev. xxii. 11).

THE REWARD OF WHOLE-HEARTEDNESS AND THE PUNISHMENT OF INDECISION.

JUDGES I. 8–II. 5.—*Now the children of Judah had fought* [since the capture of Jerusalem, here recorded, evidently was just before the events which follow in ver. 9, as the word 'afterwards' proves; translate, not "*had* fought" but

'fought'] *against Jerusalem, and had taken* [rather 'took']
and smitten [rather 'smote'] *it with the edge of the sword,
and set the city on fire* [Joshua had slain the king of Jerusalem,
Adoni-bezek, after the battle at Gibeon (Josh. x. 3, 18–26,
xii. 8, 10), but had not taken Jerusalem itself. In Josh. xv.
63, we read, "As for the Jebusites, the inhabitants of Jerusalem, the children of Judah could not drive them out; but
the Jebusites dwell with the children of Judah at Jerusalem
unto this day;" and here (ver. 21), "the children of Benjamin
did not drive out the Jebusites that inhabited Jerusalem, but
the Jebusites dwell with the children of Benjamin unto this
day." Probably, then, Jerusalem was taken now by Judah,
in Joshua's life time, for the first and last time before David's
taking it (2 Sam. v. 6–9). After Judah the conqueror left
the city to war with the Canaanites who dwelt "in the
mountains, and the south, and the valley" (ver. 9), the Jebusites
returned and rebuilt it, and neither the Judæans, the original
conquerors, nor the Benjamites to whom it had been allotted
(Josh. xviii. 28), could drive them out, but were content to
live with them in the lower city, whilst the Jebusites remained
masters of the upper city and its stronghold, and gave their
name to the whole city (ch. xix. 10, 12), so that it is described
as "the city of a stranger not *Israel*"]. (9) *And afterward*
[following up the success in smiting the capital] *Judah went
down* [from the heights of Jerusalem to their own allotment]
*to fight against the Canaanites that dwelt in the mountain, and
in the south* [the Negeb, 'the *dry* region' or 'south land,' consisting of soft chalky limestone, extending from the Jeshimon
or desert on the east, to 'Anab on the west, and Beersheba on
the south], *and in the valley* [*the Shephelah, the low rolling hills
between the mountain and the plain ;* not as the English version
'the valley.' The three natural divisions of Judah's territory
(compare Josh. xi. 16). This summary includes the conquests
given in detail subsequently; Hebron and Debir in 'the
mountain' (ver. 10, 11); Arad and Zephath in 'the south'
(ver. 16, 17); and Gaza, Askelon, and Ekron in the 'plain'
(ver. 18, Josh. xv. 33, 45–47)]. (10) *And Judah went against
the Canaanites that dwelt in Hebron* (*now the name of Hebron*

before (was) Kirjath-arba): *and they slew* [smote *Yakku*, ʻdrove thence,ʼ *Yoresh*, in Josh. xv. 14], *Sheshai, and Ahiman, and Talmai* [*Caleb* being Judahʼs leader (Josh. xi. 21, xv. 13, 14). The mention of *Judah* here in Judges accords with the plan of the book, which is to describe the conflicts of the *several tribes* with the Canaanites. ʻAnakʼ means ʻlong-necked.ʼ As Sheshai, Ahiman, and Talmai, the children of Anak, are mentioned forty-five years previously (Numb. xiii. 22), they must be, not individuals, but three *tribes* of Anakim. The Anakim had been driven away from Hebron or Debir by Joshua. But they only withdrew to Philistia, and returned whilst Joshua was campaigning in the north against Jabin (Josh. xi. 16, 21, 22). Caleb, who as spy first brought tidings of them, was eventually their destroyer. As in Numbers xiii. 22, it is abruptly stated that " Hebron was built seven years before Zoan in Egypt," Knobelʼs conjecture is reasonable that the two cities had a common founder or else rebuilder, viz., one of the Hyksos or Shepherd race (probably Hitites), which for a long time ruled Egypt, and to which the Anakim probably belonged. Hebron was the original name, meaning ʻjoining together,ʼ akin to the Hebrew *habru* (Gen. xiv. 3, xiii. 18); and perhaps alluding to Abramʼs ʻjoiningʼ the Amorite Aner, Eshcol, and Mamre, as confederates with him against the confederate kings Amraphel, Arioch, Chedorlaomer, and Tidal. Arba, the ʻgreat manʼ (Josh. xiv. 15) of the Anakim subsequently to Abrahamʼs time, settled there, and called it Kirjath-Arba, "the city of Arba" (Gen. xxiii. 2, 19, xxxv. 27). Caleb, who led the men of Judah, on conquering it, restored the old name ʻHebron.ʼ Evidently the writer of Gen. xxiii. 2, " Kirjath-Arba-Hebron, in the land of Canaan," was not then in Canaan ; an undesigned propriety which confirms Mosesʼ authorship. In a valley surrounded by hills, on the way from Jerusalem to Beersheba ; now *El-Khalil*, ʻthe friend of God,ʼ Abrahamʼs designation. Close to the cave of Machpelah, his burial-place, over which is a mosque]. (11) *And from thence he went against the inhabitants of Debir ; (and the name of Debir before (was) Kirjath-sepher)* [the Debir here is that in the mountain region south of Hebron, distinct from that in Josh. xv. 7, between

Jerusalem and Jericho, and the Gadite Debir, Josh. xiii. 26. It was afterwards assigned to the Levites (Josh. xxi. 8, 15). Debir means 'oracle;' Kirjath-sepher, 'city of books:' called also Kirjath-sannah, 'city of palm-branches,' or else 'of sacred learning' (Bochart). It was probably an ancient seat of Canaanite learning]. (12) *And Caleb said, He that smiteth Kirjath-sepher, and taketh it, to him will I give Achsah my daughter to wife* [compare 1 Sam. xvii. 25, xviii. 17. The greatness of the reward offered implies the difficulty of taking the city]. (13) *And Othniel the son of Kenaz* [*i.e.*, son of Jephunneh *the Kenezite* (Josh. xiv. 6)], *Caleb's younger brother, took it, and he gave him Achsah his daughter to wife* [the law did not forbid marriage to a niece. Othniel showed himself an equally brave warrior subsequently, when as Judge under the Lord he saved Israel out of their bondage to Cushan-rishathaim (ch. iii. 8–11)]. (14) *And it came to pass, when she came (to him)* [to live with him as wife], *that she moved him to ask of her father a field* [Hebrew '*the* field,' *i.e.*, the well known field, which had become historical by the time that the book of Judges was written: but in Josh. xv. 18, '*a* field,' *i.e.*, an open unenclosed country; *sadeh*, a land that could be cultivated]; *and she lighted from off* [a rare Hebrew word, *tzanach*, 'to leap forth:' with eager impulse she 'sprang off'] (*her*) *ass* [in token of reverence (Gen. xxiv. 64; 1 Sam. xxv. 23)]; *and Caleb said unto her, What wilt thou?* (15) *And she said unto him, Give me a blessing* [a gift, in token of goodwill, accompanied with prayers for a blessing on the receiver (Gen. xxxiii. 11). When her husband hesitated to ask Caleb, the daughter, who knew the large-heartedness of her father, asked for a large gift. Spiritually, our Father delights in being asked for large blessings (Ps. lxxxi. 10; John xv. 7, xvi. 23)]; *for thou hast given me a south land* [*hanegeb*, rather 'the dry' or 'barren land:' as in Ps. cxxvi. 4]; *give me also springs of water. And Caleb gave her the upper and the nether springs* [Conder, in the Quarterly Statement of the Palestine Exploration, identifies Debir with *El-Dhoheriyeh*, a corruption of Deberah, meaning in Arabic "the village on the ridge." Exactly at 3000 (6 inches) cubits on the south

road is a large stone which formerly marked the suburban
bounds assigned to Debir as a Levitical city.   A similar stone
stands on the western side.   " It is truly the dry land."   But
at 6½ miles northward are fourteen springs, divided into three
groups, in the valley *Seil-el-Dilbeh*.   These doubtless are 'the
upper and nether springs.'   No other such are found in the
Negeb or south country of Judah.   The dwellings at Debir
are mostly caves in the rock with rude arches carved over
doorways.   ' Rock excavation,' the primitive mode of Canaanite
habitation, marks its great antiquity].   (16) *And the children
of the Kenite* [Kain, the tribal patriarch], *Moses' father-in-law*
[rather " brother-in-law (Numb. x. 29–31).   Hobab, whom
Moses had entreated that he should be to Israel ' instead of
eyes' in the wilderness, as being better acquainted with
life in the desert, its tracks, passes, and places fit for encampment.   His father-in-law Reuel was probably too old to
have been such a guide.   Moses had urged his brother in-law
to share in Israel's promised blessing, 'We are journeying
unto the place of which the Lord said, I will give it you
—Come thou with us, and we will do thee good—What goodness the Lord shall do unto us, the same will we do unto
thee.'   The Kenites complied, and so partook in the Divine
goodness to Israel, down to the Assyrian captivity.   As
Balaam prophesied (Numb. xxiv. 22, Hebrew), 'Kain shall
surely not be for destruction until Asshur shall carry thee
away captive' (1 Sam. xv. 6; Judg. iv. 11).   Spiritually,
compare 1 John i. 3; Ruth i. 16, 17: If we suffer with the
Israel of God in the wilderness, we shall reign with them in
the heavenly Canaan (2 Tim. ii. 12; Luke xxii. 28, 29)];
went up out of the city of palm-trees [Jericho: ch. iii. 13;
Deut. xxxiv. 3; 2 Chron. xxviii. 15]; *with the children of
Judah into the wilderness of Judah, which (lieth) in the south
of Arad, and they went and dwelt among the people* [when
Israel advanced into Canaan, and destroyed Jericho, the
Kenites, as nomads, pitched their tents amidst its palm-groves;
then accompanying the Judæans southwards, they settled on
the south-western edge of the desert of Judah, south of Arad,
now Tel-Arad, with the people of Judah].   (17) *And Judah*

went with Simeon his brother [fulfilling his promise to his brother in ver. 3], *and they slew the Canaanites that inhabited Zephath* [in the allotment of Simeon (Josh. xix. 4, xv. 30); the pass *Es-Sufa*, from the Arabah to the south country bears trace of the name], *and utterly destroyed it. (And the name of the city was called Hormah)* [called so in Numb. xiv. 45, by anticipation : there the Amalekites discomfited Israel, after the people's unbelief (because of the unfaithful spies' report), and subsequent presumption. Returning after thirty-eight years' wandering (Numb. xxi. 3)—the period briefly noticed in Numb. xv., xvi., xvii., xviii., xix.—the Israelites, by God's favour in answer to prayer, defeated *the king of Arad* (for so the Hebrew ought to be translated), who had at first taken some Israelites prisoners ; next they destroyed Hormah. But on their leaving the place, the Canaanites reoccupied and restored it, under the old name Zephath. Joshua slew the king (Josh. xii. 14) ; but it is not said that he took Hormah. To Judah and Simeon was granted the honour of now executing the *ban* pronounced by Moses upon this town, from which it was named permanently henceforth Hormah, *i.e., banning.* This explanation sets aside the objection to Numb. xiv. 45, and xxi. 3, as if these passages were post-Mosaic. The only spy besides Joshua, faithful among the faithless, Caleb was (ver. 29) doubtless with Judah at the destruction of the very town which witnessed Israel's discomfiture because of heeding the unbelieving spies]. (18) *Also Judah took Gaza with the coast thereof, and Askelon with the coast thereof, and Ekron with the coast thereof* [the *order*, Gaza southernmost, then Askelon, then Ekron the most northerly, indicates that Judah and Simeon advanced into the *Shephelah* from the *Negeb* or south. Ashdod and Gath, the other two of the five Philistine cities, are not mentioned as conquered. Nor did Judah long retain the three mentioned (ch. iii. 3, xiii. 1, &c.; compare Josh. xi. 22, xiii. 3, xv. 45–47)]. (19) *And the Lord was with Judah* [the secret of his success : compare Josh. i. 5, 9]; *and he drove out (the inhabitants of) the mountain* [rather 'he seized upon the mountain' vacated by the foe's expulsion]; *but could not drive out the inhabitants of the valley* [*ha-emek*, distinct from *Shephelah* in ver. 9]; *because they had chariots of iron, i.e.,* of wood tipped with iron. [But it was not so much these, as their own defect of faith, which caused their failure. Compare Josh. xi. 6, 9, xvii. 16, 17; Judg. iv. 3; Ps. xx. 7, 8]. (20) *And they gave Hebron unto Caleb, as Moses said* [Numb. xiv. 24. Caleb, at the close of the campaign, came with the children of Judah to Joshua in Gilgal, and reminded him of Moses' promise at Kadesh Barnea, in the second year after the exodus: " Surely the land whereon thy feet have trodden, shall be thine inheritance, and thy children's for ever, because thou hast wholly followed the LORD my God." Thirty-eight years subsequently, Caleb entered Canaan with Joshua; seven years more passed in war in Canaan, so that now Jehovah had kept him alive 45 years, since the promise given when he was forty years old. Caleb, said " Now, lo ! I am this day fourscore and five years old. As yet I am as strong this day as I was in the day that Moses sent me; as my strength was then, even so is my strength now, for war, both to go out, and to come in. Now therefore give me this mountain, whereof the Lord spake in that day; for thou heardest how the Anakims were there, and that the cities were great and fenced; if so be the Lord will be with me, then I shall be able to drive them out " (Josh. xiv. 6–15)]; *and he expelled thence the three sons of Anak* [see ver. 10, and Josh. xv. 13, 14. This proves that the campaign recorded here in Judges was in Joshua's lifetime, not after his death]. (21) *And the children of Benjamin did not drive out the Jebusites that inhabited Jerusalem* [for Judah had taken it not for himself alone, but for Benjamin: compare Josh. xv. 63]; *but the Jebusites dwell with the children of Benjamin in Jerusalem unto this day. (22) And the house of Joseph* [*i.e.,* Ephraim and Western Manasseh: the record of events here (ver. 22–36), answers to that in Josh. xvi., xvii., xviii., xix.]. *They also* [as Judah and Simeon went to obtain their allotment, ver. 2, 3] *went up against Bethel* [Josh. xii. 16, xvi. 2. It had been assigned to Benjamin (xviii. 22), but lay on the southern boundary of Ephraim, so that the house of Joseph felt obliged to expel the Canaanites from it.

It had an importance in relation to the northern tribes, somewhat like what Jerusalem had in relation to the southern. Now *Bcitin*] ; *and the* LORD (*was*) *with them* [so ver. 19]. (23) *And the house of Joseph sent to descry Bethel* [to *explore* a way of entrance into it, as the people had shut themselves within its fortification]. (*Now the name of the city before* (*was*) *Luz*) [Gen. xxviii. 19. Probably an old Hittite city, see ver. 25 ; and Numb. xiii. 29]. (24) *And the spies* [*or watchers*] *saw a man come forth out of the city* [by some unobserved passage], *and they said unto him, Show us, we pray thee, the entrance into the city, and we will show thee mercy* [as in the case of Rahab at Jericho (Josh. ii. 12–21, vi. 22–25)]. (25) *And when he showed them the entrance into the city, they smote the city with the edge of the sword; but they let go the man and all his family.* (26) *And the man went into the land of the Hittites* [the most widespread and powerful of the Canaanites; proved to have been a great empire, which disputed the supremacy for a time with Assyria and Egypt ; a striking confirmation of Scripture : the Chata on the Egyptian monuments (see Josh. i. 4; 1 King x. 29)], *and built a city, and called the name thereof Luz, which is the name thereof unto this day.* (27) *Neither did Manasseh drive out* (*the inhabitants of*) *Beth-shean* [or Bethshan, 'house of quiet'; allotted to Manasseh though within Isachar. Now *Beisan*, 14 miles south of the Sea of Galilee, and on a height over the Jordan Valley] *and her* [dependent] *towns, nor Taanach* [*sandy soil*, south-east of Megiddo], *and her towns, nor the inhabitants of Dor* [*Dandora or Tantura*, near the foot of Carmel, assigned to Manasseh, though within Asher] *and her towns, nor the inhabitants of Ibleam* [belonging to Manasseh, yet in Asher], *and her towns, nor the inhabitants of Megiddo* [*el Lejjun*] *and her towns, but the Canaanites would dwell it that land* [nearly all these towns were in the plain of Jezreel or Esdraelon, which runs south-west from the Mediterranean, above Carmel, almost to the Jordan ; on the north it is bounded by the hills of Galilee, on the east by Mount Gilboa and Little Hermon ; near the great roads from the Mediterranean coast to Damascus and Central Asia. The Canaanites naturally brought all their force to defend these roads, and their war chariots

could act effectively against Israel in the plain (ver. 19).
But it was Israel's want of *resolute faith* that disabled
them from overcoming the *resolute will* of the Canaanites who
"*would* dwell in the land" (Josh. xvii. 12). Tannach, Megiddo,
and Dor were of the thirty-one royal cities enumerated in
Josh. xii., of which list Conder (*Palest. Explor. Quart. Statem.*)
remarks, that it 'precedes all the other topographical lists, and
forms the key of the whole system ']. (28) *And it came to pass,
when Israel was strong, that they put the Canaanites to tribute, and
did not utterly drive them out* [in disobedience to God's express
command (Exod. xxiii. 32, 33, xxxiv. 12, 15). Compromise,
indifference to the honour of God which idolatry insults,
indolence, and love of gain, made Israel content with imposing
tribute, even when strong enough to have extirpated them. So
far was the extermination from being the effect of Israel's
blood-thirstiness, that whenever terror of the immediate punishment was withdrawn, they disobeyed God by sparing the
Canaanites. The law to do so was evidently from God, the
righteous judge, not man; and the Divine aim was to exterminate
idolatry, and its attendant pollutions. Humanity in other
cases breathes throughout the Mosaic law (Exod. xxiii. 4, 5, 9,
11, xxii. 22–24). The putting of the Canaanites to tribute
was effected gradually, in the period of the Judges and Kings,
(1 Kings iv. 12, ix. 20–22)]. (29) *Neither did Ephraim drive
out the Canaanites that dwelt in Gezer* [Ganneau discovered an
inscription in Greek and Hebrew at *Abou Shushah*, on the
plain between Jaffa and Jerusalem, "the boundary of Gezer,"
thereby identifying the site with *Tel el Djezir*. This was its
eastern limit of suburbs as a Levitical city (Numb. xxxv. 5). A
similar inscription exists on the south-west. The sacred
boundary was a square, having its four angles at the four
cardinal points. Identical with Gob; compare 1 Chron. xx. 4
with 2 Sam. xxi. 18. An important fortress as lying on the
coast road to Egypt] ; *but the Canaanites dwelt in Gezer among
them.* (30) *Neither did Zebulun drive out the inhabitants of
Kitron* [Kattath, Josh. xix. 15], *nor the inhabitants of Nahalol;
but the Canaanites dwelt among them, and became tributaries.*
(31) *Neither did Asher drive out the inhabitants of Accho*

[Ptolemais; now St Jean d'Acre, called from the Knights of St John, 'the key of Palestine'; the chief seaport of Syria, 30 miles south of Tyre. Carmel is on the south side of the river Belus, on which it lies], *nor the inhabitants of Zidon* [called 'great,' as the metropolis of the Phœnicians (Josh. xi. 8). Now *Saida, i.e., 'fishing* town,' 20 miles north of Tyre, which is called her 'daughter' (Isa. xxiii. 12). Tyre is not mentioned in the Pentateuch, but first in Josh. xix. 29; but Zidon, as early as Gen. x. 15. Not till David's time is Tyre represented as the *chief* Phœnician city. A coincidence with secular history confirming the truth of Scripture, for Homer mentions Zidon, but not Tyre; and old Egyptian inscriptions give Zidon the first place], *nor of Ahlab, nor of Achzib* [10 miles north of Accho, on the Mediterranean: now *Ez-zib*], *nor of Helbah, nor of Aphik* [near Zidon, Josh. xix. 30], *nor of Rehob.* (32) *But the Asherites dwelt among the Canaanites, the inhabitants of the land* [seven out of the twenty-two towns of Asher, including the great towns Zidon and Accho, remained in the Canaanites' possession ; therefore, it is said, not as in ver. 30, "the Canaanites dwelt among" the Asherites, but *vice versa*, implying that the Canaanites had the upper hand; for it is said that they "became tributaries"]; *for they did not drive them out.* (33) *Neither did Naphtali drive out the inhabitants of Beth-shemesh* [*i.e.*, house of *the sun*], *nor the inhabitants of Beth-anath* [Josh. xix. 38]; *but he dwelt among the Canaanites, the inhabitants of the land: nevertheless, the inhabitants of Beth-shemesh and of Beth-anath became tributaries unto them.* (34) *And the Amorites forced the children of Dan into the mountain; for they would not suffer them to come down to the valley* [Josh. xix. 40–48. The allotment to Dan was almost all in the plain. Being forced out of it, they were shut out of most of their inheritance]. (35) *But the Amorites would dwell in Mount Heres,* [*the sun :* answering to Ir-shemesh, *city of the sun* (Josh. xix. 41). Now *Ain Shems.* called *Beth-shemesh,* in Josh. xv. 10] *in Aijalon* [or Ajalon, 'the place of gazelles.' Now *Yalo,* north of the Jaffa road, on the hillside bounding the valley *Merj-ibn-Omeir;* alluded to in Joshua's apostrophe to the sun (x. 12)], *and in Shaalbim* [*place of foxes* or *jackals*], *yet the hand of the house of Joseph prevailed, so that they became tributaries.* (36) *And the coast of the Amorites was from the going up to Akrabbim* [Maaleh-Acrabbim (Josh. xv. 3); "the ascent to Akrabbim" (Numb. xxxiv. 4); *i.e., The Scorpion pass;* the same Hebrew in all three passages. The cliffs intersecting the Ghor below the Dead Sea, abounding in scorpions; the southern boundary of the Holy Land], *from the rock* [*Ha-Selah,* not as in 2 Kings xiv. 7, *Petra;* as the object is to explain how the Amorites were, by their position, able to force the Danites out of their inheritance. To refer to Petra, south-east of the Scorpion pass, and so considerably south of the Holy Land, would not be in point. ' *The* rock' here is that in the *south-west* corner of Palestine, in the desert of Zin, on the southern edge of the Rakhma plateau; its notoriety was due to the events which took place at the waters of strife (Numb. xx. 8, 10). As the Amorites extended to the Scorpion heights on the *south-east* boundary of the Holy Land, so to ' the rock ' on the *south-west* boundary (Numb. xiv. 24, 44, 45); Deut. i. 44)], *and upward* [*i.e.,* northward].

CHAPTER II.

(1) *And an angel of the* LORD [Translate, ' *Then* THE angel of JEHOVAH': the Second Divine Person: for THE ANGEL identifies himself with JEHOVAH in His words and deeds, as no prophet does. Hag. i. 13; Mal. ii. 7, iii. 1, are no objection; for ' messenger,' *Maleach*, is shown by the context to be appellative in meaning. Sixty times the phrase expresses the angel of God's presence (Gen. xvi. 7, xxii. 11; Exod. xiv. 19, xxiii, 20, 21; Numb. xxii. 22; Judg. vi. 11, 12, 21, 22 ; Isa. lxiii. 9)], *came up from Gilgal to Bochim* [not so much a geographical, as a spiritual intimation. As the Angel Prince of Jehovah's host at Gilgal assured Israel of the fall of Jericho, directly after their *rolling away* the reproach of Egypt by their circumcision, whence the place was named Gilgal, which means ' rolling '—so here at Bochim, which means *Weepers*, and is *geographically unknown*, He declares that, by their having broken the covenant in making leagues with the Canaanites, and not throwing down their altars, they incur the penalties of its violation, to be inflicted by those very Canaanites. So 'from Shittim to Gilgal' is not geographical, but reminding Israel of God's favours at those places (Mic. vi. 5)], *and said, I made you go up out of Egypt, and have brought you unto the land which I sware unto your fathers ; and I said, I will never break my covenant with you* [Gen. xvii. 7; Ps. lxxxix. 34]. (2) *And ye shall make no league with the inhabitants of this land* [Exod. xxiii. 32, xxxiv. 12; Deut. vii. 2]; *but ye have not obeyed my voice* [so by breaking their covenant with Him, they forfeited His covenant with them, referring to Exod. xix. 4-8], *why have ye done this?* (3)

Wherefore I also [in retribution for *your* unfaithfulness] *said* [I *now* declare my *fixed purpose*], *I will not drive them out from before you; but they shall be* (*as thorns*) *in your sides* [as God threatened, Numb. xxxiii. 55, and Joshua reminded them, Josh. xxiii. 13], *and their gods shall be a snare unto you* [Exod. xxiii. 33]. (4) *And it came to pass, when the angel of the* LORD *spake these words unto all the children of Israel* [*i.e.*, unto representatives of all the tribes and leading families, probably *the same general assembly at Shechem as that which Joshua addressed* (Josh. ẋxiv. 1, 2, 27), "All the words of the LORD *which He spake unto us*," answer to 'these words' which 'the angel of the LORD *spake unto all the children of Israel'*], *that the people lifted up their voice, and wept.* (5) *And they called the name of that place Bochim* [*weepers*];' *and they sacrificed there unto the* LORD [Jehovah's manifestation there warranted their sacrificing (ch. vi. 20, 26, 28; 2 Sam. xxiv. 25). Besides if, as seems likely, the assembly be that recorded in Josh. xxiv. 1, 26, 27, the place was Shechem, between Mounts Ebal and Gerizim, where the covenant had been recited on Israel's first entry into Canaan, where also first God promised the land to Abram's seed (Gen. xii. 6), and where Jacob consecrated his house to the Lord, at *the oak under which Joshua set a great stone*, and with *the very directions which Joshua quotes* (xxiv. 23, 26: compare Gen. xxxv. 1–4). Joshua mentions "the sanctuary of the Lord" as close by, perhaps the very altar of Abraham and Jacob still remaining. Lastly, what confirms the identity of the assembly here and in Josh. xxiv., is the identity of the particulars which follow here and there, Joshua's dismissal of the people to their several inheritances, Joshua's death and burial in Timnath Heres, and the people's serving the Lord all Joshua's days, and those of the elders who outlived him, and had seen all the works of the Lord for Israel (compare Josh. xxiv. 28–33 with Judg. ii. 6–10)].

I. THE REWARD OF WHOLE-HEARTEDNESS.

I. (1) *Caleb's faith and reward contrasted with the faint-heartedness of the spies and its fatal issue.*—The men of Judah began well. Having taken and destroyed Jerusalem, full of

spirit because of their success, they went down to expel the
Canaanites from the inheritance allotted to Judah. That faithful and valiant veteran, Caleb, was at their head, as we learn
from the book of Joshua (xv. 13–19). He who forty-five years
previously represented Judah in spying out the land of promise
(Numb. xiii. 6), now at Judah's head enters the same goodly
land as its conqueror. He who had seen at Hebron the giant
sons of Anak in possession of its high-walled fortifications,
lived to drive thence those giants whom his fellow spies had
so much feared; and he received the city as the reward of his
faith (Numb. xiii. 22, 27, 28, 31, 33; Josh. xv. 13, 14). The
unreasonableness of unbelief appears in the self-contradictions
of the report of the ten spies. In one and the same breath they
said, " Surely the land floweth with milk and honey," and yet
" It is a land that eateth up the inhabitants thereof "—"We
saw the giants—and we were in our own sight as grasshoppers,
and *so we were in their sight.*" How could they know, what
they were *in the sight of the Anakim ?* But faithlessness breeds
fear, and fear hath torment. So, according to their unbelief it
was unto them. A lion was in the way, and they had no
sword wherewith to slay him; so they never entered the land
of rest. On the other hand, Caleb had 'another spirit with
him,' and 'followed the Lord fully' and 'wholly' (Numb. xiv.
24, xxxii. 11). His language corresponded to his name, which
means *All-heart,* "Let us go up at once and possess the land,"
not merely let us *attempt* it, since faith in Jehovah's promises
assures him of success, "for we are well able to overcome it."
His sole and firm dependence was on Jehovah: "If so be the
Lord be with me, then I shall be able to drive them out ;"
he believed God's word to Judah (ch. i. 2), "Behold I have
delivered the land into his hand." According to his faith
it was unto him. Jehovah's promise to him by Moses was
fulfilled to the letter: "Surely the land whereon thy feet have
trodden shall be thine inheritance and thy children's for ever,
because thou hast wholly followed the Lord thy God" (Josh.
xiv. 9, 12).

(2) *The believer's trial and triumph, the scene of trial being
the appointed scene of his reward.*—In a spiritual point of view,

we are in the wilderness. Jehovah's word is pledged to bring
us into the heavenly inheritance, if only we believe. It is
true there are mighty adversaries in the way; but difficulties
disappear before resolute trust in the power and the faithfulness of Jehovah to His promise. Jehovah's word to each is,
" Only be very courageous to do according to all the law : turn
not from it to the right hand or to the left, that thou mayest
prosper whithersoever thou goest " (Josh. i. 7). As the scene of
Caleb's trust became the scene of his triumph, so that very earth
wherein the saints have witnessed for Christ in the face of an
unbelieving world, shall be reigned over by them as kings and
priests unto God (1 Cor. vi. 2; Rev. v. 10, xx. 4–6; Matt. v. 5;
Luke xix. 12–19). Half-heartedness gives only enough of religion
to make one uncomfortable, not enough to make one blessed either
here or hereafter. Whole-heartedness brings with it peace now,
and a share in the promise of the inheritance to come, when
the " kingdom and dominion, and the greatness *under the whole
heaven* [marking *this earth* to be the scene of the kingdom],
shall be given to the people of the saints of the Most High,
whose kingdom is an everlasting kingdom " (Dan. vii. 27).
With such an inheritance in view, we can afford, though it
tarry long, to wait for it; because it will surely come, it will
not tarry (Hab. ii. 3). Caleb in his eighty-fifth year, after
forty-five years of waiting, was richly repaid in the end for
his long-tried faithfulness. "*Our* lightness of affliction, which
is but for the present passing moment, worketh out for us more
and more exceedingly (literally, *in excess and to excess*) an eternal
weight of glory " [τὸ παραυτίκα ἐλαφρὸν τῆς θλίψεως ἡμῶν
καθ᾽ ὑπερβολὴν εἰς ὑπερβολὴν αἰώνιον βάρος δόξης κατεργάζεται
ἡμῖν, 2 Cor. iv. 17]. Compare for illustrations of heartiness for
God, 2 Chron. xxxi. 21; Gal. iv. 18; Col. iii. 23.

(3) *Achsah and the power of prayer.*—As was the father,
so was the daughter, the worthy offspring of a worthy
sire, no degenerate child, but large-hearted, like the whole-
hearted Caleb. Her father gave her in marriage to the
victor of Kirjath Sepher, a stronghold of the enemy.
Othniel, though urged by Achsah, was too bashful to ask
anything more from his father-in-law, having received from

him the best of earthly gifts, a devoted wife. But Achsah
knew her father's generosity and readiness to give, and that
he only needed to be asked. Caleb did not even wait to
be asked, but observing her eagerness, anticipated her
with his question, "What wilt thou"? "Give me a blessing,"
was her reply ; "thou hast given me a dry land, give me also
springs of water." So he gave her the upper and the nether
springs ; that is, springs on the higher and the lower ground.

Our needs temporal and eternal.—The God of nature and
the God of grace are one. Nature accordingly is a parable
of grace, and God's dealings with His children in the outward
world teaches us truths of the unseen spiritual and eternal
world. (1) *Achsah's need represents our far more urgent wants.*
Our heart by nature is dry and hard. There are no springs
of love and holiness. It is dried up by selfishness, and parched
by the world's withering atmosphere. In this state it can
bear no fruit unto God its Lord, and is fit only for the everlasting burnings. (2) *The consciousness of such a need should
drive us, like Achsah, to tell our sad case to Him who alone can
supply all our wants, our Father in Jesus.* Instead of com-
plaining *of* her father, she complained *to* him, so should we ;
and that in the right *time,* the present—and in the right *place,*
wherever we can meet Him, which is, wherever we pray—and
in the right *way,* which is prayer in the name of Christ,
through whom we are His adopted children. Our Father
knows all our needs before we ask Him, but He delights to
hear His children's voice, telling Him all in filial confidence
(Song Sol. ii. 14). His word to us is (Isa. xlix. 11), "Ask me
of things to come concerning my sons, and concerning the work
of my hands command ye me" (compare Matt. vii. 11). As
Achsah dismounted to fall at her father's feet, so must we come
down from our self-sufficiency (see Ps. x. 4 ; Gen. xvii. 3 ; 2
Cor. x. 5 ; Jer. xiii. 7), to fall low before our God. Then, His
encouraging question is, "What wilt thou ?" the same that
Jesus spake to the blind men at Jericho (Matt xx. 32), and
to the sons of Zebedee (Mark x. 36). He promises not merely
a half-kingdom, like Ahasuerus (Esth. v. 6), but the whole
kingdom, and that the kingdom of heaven (Rev. iii. 21). But

c

it may be objected, our will is disinclined toward God and
the heavenly kingdom. For this too there is a gracious and
adequate remedy. God worketh in us both to will and to do
(Phil. ii. 13); and God promises to His Son, "Thy people shall
be willing in the day of Thy power" (Ps. cx. 3). To doubt
God's power would be to deny His Godhead; for the essential
idea of His Godhead is that He is "able to do exceeding
abundantly above all that we ask or think." To doubt God's
willingness is to call in question His Godhead in another
respect; for "God is love." Believing both His power and
His love, we may assuredly believe, when we pray, that
whatsoever things we desire, we shall receive (Mark xi. 24).
(3) *We need the upper and the nether springs.* All that is
good for us here below, and the fulness of joy and pleasures
for evermore above. Earthly men hew themselves out
"broken cisterns, that can hold no water" (Jer. ii. 13). But
the believer goes to "the Fountain of living waters," and cries,
"With Thee, O Lord, is the fountain of life—Thou shalt make
me to drink of the river of Thy pleasures" (Ps. xxxvi. 8, 9;
compare John iv. 10). God begins by giving the upper and
heavenly blessings, and promises, if we make them our first
desire, He will add with them the lower (Matt. vi. 33). So
He dealt with Solomon (1 Kings iii. 11–13). So will He deal
with us, if we will but trust Him (Isa. xxxviii. 16, 17, 21).
"He will give grace here and glory hereafter, and will with-
hold no good thing from him that walketh uprightly" (Ps.
lxxxiv. 11). So that we shall experience that "godliness is
profitable unto all things, having promise of the life that now
is, and of that which is to come" (1 Tim. iv. 8).

II. THE PUNISHMENT OF INDECISION.

II.—1. *Judah's failure in the end; its cause and effect.*—As
Caleb is an illustration of the reward of decision, so the several
tribes are instances of the fatal effect of indecision in the work
of the Lord. Even Judah, after all its triumphs, "could not
drive out the inhabitants of the valley, because they had
chariots of iron" (ver. 19). But why not? Was not Jehovah
with Judah? and his "chariots are thousands of angels," before

whom earthly chariots are but fuel for the flame (Ps. lxviii. 17, xlvi. 9). Jehovah had not excepted 'the valley,' when He promised, "Behold, I have delivered the land into Judah's hand" (ver. 2). But Judah's faith yielded to fears, because of difficulties, when one bold blow, in dependence on Jehovah, would have destroyed the foe, and given lasting possession of the land. God is the God of the valley, as well as of the mountains. But unbelief hinders the working of God. It drew forth the marvelling of the Son of God, so that "He could do no mighty work in Capernaum (Mark vi. 5, 6). The men of Judah ran well for a time, but half-heartedness hindered further progress (Gal. v. 7). Nay more, the same cause led to their quickly losing again even some of the cities which they had conquered, as Gaza, Askelon, and Ekron. Furthermore, as men are more prone to follow the evil than the good, Judah's past courage was lost sight of, and the example of unbelief and indecision in the end, set by the leading tribe, was followed to its fatal issue by the rest.

2. *The lesson to us.*—Hence learn (1) *the unreasonableness of unbelief* because of adversaries, when the Lord is for us and with us (Rom. viii. 31–39). (2) *The danger of resting on past triumphs of faith,* and our sole safety in enduring to the end (Matt. xxiv. 13; Rev. ii. 10; 1 Cor. ix. 24–27). (3) *The evil influence upon others* which a halting and undecided professor of religion exercises (Rom. xii. 1, 2; 1 Kings xviii. 21; 2 Cor. iii. 2, 3).

3. *The growing degeneracy of the other tribes, following the chief tribe.*—Judah had for a time set an example of decision, by utterly destroying Hormah. That city was long ago devoted to destruction, but now at last was finally destroyed (see Eccl. viii. 11--13). Even the Kenites, a non-Israelite people, had showed their feeling that Jehovah was with Judah, by coming up from their nomad encampment at the city of palm-trees, and dwelling among the people of God; accordingly they received a present and an abiding reward; (see references at ver. 16). But Judah's failure in not destroying the inhabitants of the Philistine cities, both laid up in store for Israel a lasting scourge (and that by the hands of

the very people whom Judah had disobediently spared), and also influenced other less courageous tribes to make fatal compromises with the heathen around.

Thus (1) *Benjamin* did not drive out the Jebusites from Jerusalem, but connived at their dwelling with themselves. It is true, *the house of Joseph* (2) evinced at first becoming energy in smiting Bethel, and sparing only the man, with his family, who showed them the entrance, and in not allowing even him, when he preferred the ways of the Hittites, to settle among the people of God.   But otherwise the house of Joseph (Ephraim and Manasseh) showed no whole-hearted zeal for the cause of God : thus *Ephraim* lost the undisputed possession of Gezer by suffering the Canaanites to dwell among them.   (3) *Manasseh*, pusillanimously and without a struggle, acquiesced in the occupation of many leading cities and their dependencies by their original inhabitants, in the plain of Jezreel.   The resolute determination of the Canaanites was more than a match for the languid will of Manasseh.   So it will ever be, when professing believers shrink from the good fight of faith, and will not endure hardship, as good soldiers of Christ (2 Tim. ii. 2, 13 ; 1 Tim. vi. 12).   The world will not yield an inch to the man who is not resolute and courageous for God : nay, it will push him back, step by step, from the ground which he had gained : for one compromise entails a second, and that a third, and so on, as Manasseh lost town after town. Attempt in faith great things for God, and then you may confidently expect great things from God.   But if, forgetful of the honour of God whom you represent, you compromise religious principle, condoning the world's enmity to God in consideration of the earthly gain to the church, wherewith the world compounds for obedience, as the house of Joseph and *Zebulun* and *Naphtali*, when Israel became strong, contented themselves with levying tribute from the Canaanites, your graces will languish, your lusts will revive, and the prince of this world will regain his hold.   The only safe principle for the believer is that laid down in Holy Writ (2 Cor. vi. 14–18), "Be ye not unequally yoked together with unbelievers : for what fellowship hath righteousness with unrighteousness, and what communion hath light with darkness ?—And what agreement hath the temple of God with idols ? for ye are the temple of the living God—Wherefore come out from among them, and be ye separate, saith the Lord, and touch not the unclean thing, and I will be a Father unto you, and ye shall be my sons and daughters, saith the Lord God Almighty."

4. *Asher's degradation was still more humiliating.*—For the Asherites lived only by sufferance, among the Canaanites ; so completely had the latter gained the upper hand : and the reason given is very significant—" for they did not drive them out." Remember, Christian, in thy conflict, not to conquer thy spiritual foes is to be conquered by them. They will push the first advantage thou givest them over thee, until step by step thou art brought down from being their master, to become their dependent vassal.

5. But *the lowest point was reached by Dan.*—The Amorites would not even suffer the Danites to dwell among them, but forced them into the mountains out of almost all their inheritance, including even some cities in the mountains (ver. 35), so that they were forced to seek for room in the far away north at Laish (ch. xviii.). Take care, professor, lest through half-heartedness thou utterly lose the heavenly inheritance (Rev. ii. 5, iii. 15, 16).

III. 1. *Jehovah's threat before He punishes.*—(1) *The angel of Jehovah by coming up 'from Gilgal' reminds Israel of His covenant by circumcision there.* The same voice speaks to every backslider, " Remember from whence thou art fallen, and repent, and do the first works " (Rev. ii. 5). (2) *He reminds the assembled people of His past favours :* " I made you to go up out of Egypt, and brought you into the land which I sware unto your fathers." The Lord has wrought so glorious a salvation for us in fulfilment of His promise, that all should be constrained by love and gratitude to serve Him wholly. (3) *He reminds them also of His commands ;* for privilege and duty go together. But they had disobeyed, and leagued with the idolatrous people of the land. (4) So now *He appeals to themselves,* " Why have ye done this ? " If they had answered truly, they would have confessed it was through distrust of the word of Him who had given them such countless proofs of His love, His power, and His faithfulness to His word. A lion is in the way always, to the spiritual coward (Prov. xxvi. 13; contrast xxviii. 1). Covetousness too suggested that gain might be made by sparing the Canaanites, even at the cost of offending God. Compare Saul's sad case (1 Sam. xv. 3, 9, 15, 21–23). But what real gain can the professor promise himself in sparing his lusts, at the expense of his undying soul? (Job xxvii. 8; Matt. xvi. 26). The Israelites were speechless. So will the sinner be at last who wraps himself up in formalism, whilst dealing tenderly with, instead of crucifying, the flesh (Gal. v. 24; Matt. xxii. 12). God deigns to appeal to the transgressor's own conscience. What reasonable account canst thou give of thy perversity? None can be given (Rom. vi. 21). (5) *The punishment therefore shall follow corresponding to the sin. Yea, the sin itself shall be the punishment* (Prov. i. 31; Jer. ii. 19, vi. 19). The Canaanites spared by Israel, in disobedience to God, shall be the punishers of that disobedience. *You* would not drive them out, therefore "*I* will not drive them out before you" (Rom. i. 28). The professors who love the world shall be given up to the world. The pleasures, the ambitions, the gains of the world become 'thorns' whereby they "pierce themselves through with many sorrows" (1 Tim. vi. 10). Moreover, these lusts of the flesh unmortified become a 'snare,' entangling the soul to its destruction (2 Thess. ii. 10–12).

2. *The effect produced by this threat.*—(1) *The people lifted up their voice, and wept.* The place of meeting, Shechem, became the place of weeping, Bochim. How sin mars all joy! Yet the tears of those who mourn sincerely for sin are the preludes to joy (Matt. v. 4). Matthew Henry truly says, "It is a wonder sinners can ever read their Bibles with dry eyes." The Spirit of God must wound before He heals, but there is no other way to heavenly joy (Isa. lxi. 3; John xvi. 9). Indecision is no light sin, but betrays that double-mindedness which God abhors (Matt. vi. 22–24). (2) *They sacrificed there unto the Lord.* Tears cannot wash away sin; for the tears themselves need cleansing. "Without shedding of blood, there

is no remission" (Heb. ix. 22). Humiliation is necessary, but not sufficient. God has given the blood to make atonement for the soul, but not the blood of typical sacrifice. "The blood of Jesus Christ" alone "cleanseth from all sin." Weeping here, if it lead us to that atoning blood, will save us from weeping, wailing, and gnashing of teeth for ever. Oh, that each church assembly were a Bochim to prepare sinners, through penitence and faith, for the blessed home, where God will wipe away all tears from our eyes! (Rev. xxi. 4). Oh, that all would lay to heart the lesson here taught of the fearful consequences, not merely of commissions of sin, but of *omissions* of duty, such as proved so fatal to Israel! Oh, that all may be led to feel the irrationality of disregard to God, and backslidings from His ways, and to know the immutability of God's law that, when the church forsakes the Lord for the world, the world with whom she has sinned, shall be the instrument of her punishment!

GOD'S EPIPHANIES AND MAN'S APOSTASIES ; MERCY REJOICING AGAINST JUDGMENT.

JUDGES II. 6–III. 11.—(6) *And when Joshua had let the people go, the children of Israel went every man into his inheritance to possess the land* [repeated from Josh. xviv. 28–31, in order to form a link between the books of Joshua and Judges, and especially to bring into sharp contrast the age that had just passed, and the age in Israel's history which was now commencing]. (7) *And the people served the* LORD *all the days of Joshua, and all the days of the elders* [the chiefs of the nation] *that outlived Joshua, who had seen all the great works of the* LORD [in enabling Joshua to conquer the Canaanites], *that He did for Israel* [Joshua's influence for good survived himself (Prov. x. 7). But mainly the remembrance of Jehovah's mighty acts in behalf of Israel acted for good, and kept in the right way the eyewitnesses of those acts, still living. This is a resumption of the words in Josh. xxiv. 31; Ps. cxi. 4, cxlv. 4–7]. (8) *And Joshua the son of Nun, the servant of the Lord* [JEHOVAH,

the title of Moses previously (Deut. xxxiv. 5). In the later books
" the servant of *God* " is substituted (Dan. ix. 11; Neh. x. 29;
Rev. xv. 3). David is called "the servant of JEHOVAH" in the
title of Ps. xviii. So ministers, and all Christians, in the New
Testament (James i. 1; 2 Tim. ii. 24; John xii. 26); combined
with friendship and sonship (John xv. 15), and glory (Rev. xxii.
3, xxi. 7; Rom. viii. 15–17, 19, 21, 23). Service is inseparable
from sonship, as in the case of Christ Himself (Phil. ii. 7–11,
15)] *died, (being) an hundred and ten years old* [like his ancestor
Joseph (Gen. l. 26). Supposing that Joshua, like Caleb, was
80 at entering Canaan, 30 years would be the period of his
leadership—7 in active warfare, and 23 in retirement at Timnath-
heres. That 7 was the number of years of Joshua's campaigning, appears from the fact that Caleb was 85 when he claimed
Hebron (Josh. xiv. 10). The mission of the spies was in the
summer of the second year after the exodus (Numb. xiii. 20, xiv.
30). The whole period from the exodus to the crossing of
Jordan was 40. So that Caleb must have been 38 at the
exodus, and 78 at the Jordan; so that 7 out of his 85 must
remain for the time of Joshua's campaigns. Joshua is called
"a young man" just after the exodus (xxxiii. 11), in conson-
ance with the supposition that he was about Caleb's age then,
38 or 40 (hardly 45, as Josephus implies, *Ant.*, v. 1, 29): thus
he would be about 80–87 when campaigning: 87–110 at
Timnath-heres; his last address to Israel being "a long time
after that the Lord had given rest unto Israel from all their
enemies round about" (Josh. xxiii. 1)]. (9) *And they buried
him in the border of his inheritance in Timnath-heres* [*i.e.*,
portion of the sun, with allusion to Joshua's miracle when the
sun stood: the consonants being transposed from Timnath Serah,
"portion of abundance." Jerome calls our admiration to his
disinterestedness in that the distributor of possessions chose for
himself a mountainous portion. Not till all had been first
served did he get his portion (Josh. xix. 49). The Samaritans
and Jews alike identify Joshua's burial-place with *Kefr Haris*,
east of which is *Neby Kifl*, *i.e.*, "prophet of the division by
lot:" and close by is *Neby Culda*, corrupted perhaps from
Caleb. It is nine miles south of *Nablus*, or Shechem], *in the*

Mount of Ephraim, on the north side of the hill Gaash. (10) *And also all that generation* [most of those were grown up at the time of the conquest of Canaan] *were gathered unto their fathers* [so Gen. xxv. 8, "gathered to his people;" which cannot mean that Abraham was buried where his fathers had been buried, for he was far away from their land. It must denote *the unseen world of departed spirits,* to which his soul was gathered : compare Gen. xxxvii. 35, "I will go down into Sheol (not the *grave,* because he did not believe his son to be there, but to have been torn by the beasts) unto my son." This proves that the Old Testament believers looked to a future state of being] ; *and there arose another generation after them, which knew not the* LORD [by experimental knowledge (Hos. ii. 20, vi. 3)], *nor yet the works which he had done for Israel* [compare in contrast ver. 7]. (11) *And the children of Israel did evil in the sight of the* LORD [a phrase used seven times in Judges, to describe the seven apostasies of Israel to idolatry, which is the chief 'evil,' followed by the seven servitudes under (1) Chushan Rishathaim, (2) Eglon, (3) Jabin, (4) Midian, (5) Abimelech, (6) Ammon, (7) the Philistines. The opposite phrase is to " do right in the eyes of the Lord " (1 Kings xv. 5, 11)], *and served Baalim* [here begins the account, of the events "after the death of Joshua " (ch. i. 1), which were about to be narrated there, but were deferred till now, in order to narrate first the events immediately preceding, namely, the want of whole-heartedness on the part of the tribes even before Joshua's death, that want being an evil germ which developed itself more fully and fatally after Joshua's death, in the period of the Judges, now about to be described. The Angel at Bochim had already reproved Israel's half-heartedness in the Lord's cause in their leaguing with the Canaanites, and not throwing down their altars (ver. 2). The angel foretold (ver. 3), " their gods shall be a snare unto you :" so now it came to pass, the Israelites' sin became their punishment, by their being given up to serve Baalim, *i.e., Baals,* the plural expressing his various aspects and images, as different localities represented him. " The grammar of the devil, the author of idolatry, first taught men to decline God *plurally,* ' Ye shall be as *gods'* " (Damianus). Baal means *lord* or *owner;* whereas Adon, Adonai, means *lord* or *master.* The sun-god, worshipped on high places, by the Phœnicians and Canaanites as the source of life, generation, and reproduction. The name appears in Hanni-*bal*, Azdru-*bal*, Eth-*baal*]. (12) *And they forsook the* LORD [JEHOVAH] *God of their fathers, which brought them out of the land of Egypt* [see ver. 1 : base ingratitude !], *and followed other gods, of the gods of the people that (were) round about them, and bowed themselves unto them, and provoked the* LORD [JEHOVAH] *to anger.* (13) *And they forsook the* LORD ["JEHOVAH the fountain of living waters," for cisterns of their own hewing out, " broken cisterns, that can hold no water " (Jer. ii. 12, 13)], *and served Baal and Ashtaroth* [the plural of the name Ashtoreth, the Sidonian Astarte, the moon goddess, the female or passive principle of nature (1 Kings xi. 5). *Asheroth* in ch. iii. 7, as the Hebrew of " the groves," ought to be translated]. (14) *And the anger of the* LORD *was hot against Israel* [Deut. xxxii. 21, 22], *and He delivered them into the hands of spoilers* [the same Hebrew as 2 Kings xvii. 20] *that spoiled them, and he sold them* [Deut. xxxii. 30, *i.e.,* Ps. xliv. 12 ; Isa. l. 1. *He gave them helplessly* ; renounced His right in them, and gave them as slaves sold] *into the hands of their enemies round about, so that they could not any longer stand before their enemies* [Lev. xxvi. 37 ; Josh. vii. 11, 12]. (15) *Whithersoever they went out, the hand of the* LORD *was against them for evil, as the* LORD [JEHOVAH] *had said* [Lev. xxvi. 17 ; Deut. xxviii. 25], *and as the* LORD *had sworn unto them* [Deut. xxxii. 40–42, but they would believe neither His word, nor His oath, as if His threats were meant only to frighten them, until judgment overtook them]; *and they were greatly distressed* [straitened]. *Nevertheless* [verses 16–23 are an epitome of the whole book] *the* LORD *raised up judges* [the first introduction of the name from which the book is called. From ver. 14 to 23 a summary is given of the whole book, as illustrating God's holiness in the punishment of the trangressors, and on the other hand His grace seeking to win them to penitence, by saving interpositions, notwithstanding their perversity ; and His faithfulness to His covenant with His Church in all ages], *which delivered them out of the hand of those that spoiled them.* (17) *And yet they would not hearken* [*even*] *unto their judges* [so as not to relapse into apostasy which the judge could only suppress for the time (compare ver. 18, 19)], *but they went a whoring* [in spiritual adultery against Jehovah their heavenly Husband (Exod. xxxiv. 15 ; Isa. liv. 5)] *after other gods, and bowed themselves unto them* : *they turned quickly out of the way* [Exod. xxxii. 8] *which their fathers walked in* [in the days of Joshua, ver. 7], *obeying the commandments of the* LORD [for grace is not hereditary. Regenerate fathers often have degenerate sons] ; (*but*) *they did not so.* (18) *And when the* LORD *raised them up judges, then the Lord was with the judge* [Josh. i. 5], *and delivered them out of the hand of their enemies all the days of the judge : for it repented the* LORD [Rather "Jehovah *was moved with compassion*" (יִנָּחֶם, Ps. cvi. 34–45), where the thoughts and words rest upon this passage (compare cvi. 40 with ch. ii. 14 ; cvi. 45 with ch. ii. 20 ; cvi. 39, with ch. ii. 17 ; cvi. 41 with ch. ii. 14 ; cvi. 44 with ch. ii. 15 ; cvi. 45 with ch. ii. 18 ; cvi. 39 with ch. ii. 19 ; cvi. 25 with ch. ii. 20). The change was in them, not in Jehovah. Suffering humbled them, and God gave grace to the humble] *because of their groanings by reason of them that oppressed them, and vexed them.* (19) *And it came to pass, when the judge was dead,* (*that*) *they returned, and corrupted* (*themselves*) *more than their fathers* [had done under the preceding judge], *in following other gods to serve them, and to bow down unto them : they ceased not* [Hebrew, *they did not let fall* anything, *i.e.*, they diminished nought] *from their own doings, nor from their stubborn* [*hard*, the same Hebrew as is translated (stiff-necked (Exod. xxxii. 9, xxxiii. 3 ; compare Prov. xiii. 15, a different Hebrew word] *way* [Isa. ix. 13 ; Jer. v. 3. Chastisement unheeded brings down sorer punishment, and at last destruction. The tendency of evil is to grow worse in each generation, and so to incur accumulated punishment (Matt. xii. 43–45, xxiii. 32 ; Prov. xxix. 1)]. (20) *And the anger of the* LORD *was hot against Israel ; and He said, Because that this people* [*Goi*, the term for the *Gentiles*, because Israel had made herself *heathenish :* ' this ' too expresses denunciation (Isa. vi. 9, 10, where however *am*, the term for the elect people, is used)] *hath transgressed my covenant which I commanded their fathers, and have not hearkened unto my voice.* (21) *I also will not henceforth drive out any from before them of the nations which Joshua left when he died* [what the Lord had threatened already before Joshua's death, as the consequence of the people's unfaithfulness in leaguing with the heathen, and not throwing down their altars, but even harbouring secretly "strange gods among them" (ch. ii. 2, 3 ; Josh. xxiv. 15, 19, 20 ; also xxiii. 12, 13, 23). He now confirms absolutely, viz., that He will not drive out the nations from before Israel. He adds 'any:' "I will not henceforth drive out any from before them of the nations which Joshua left." God's breach of covenant was a righteous one, because His continuing its privileges was to depend on their faithfulness to it (Exod. xxxiv. 14-17 ; Numb. xiv. 34, margin). Ver. 20 follows in historical connection ver. 13 ; and ch. iii. 7, 8, resumes the same connection]. (22) *That through them I may prove Israel* [the nations not exterminated would be a 'snare,' tempting and entrapping them into sin, to their ruin (Josh. xxiii. 12, 13 ; Judg. ii. 3); on the other hand, if they stood the test, which would not try them so severely, should they prove faithful, they would enjoy the favour of God (Deut. viii. 2, 3). The very chastisement would then be a blessing, by proving their faith], *whether they will keep the way of the Lord to walk therein, as their fathers* [in Joshua's days] *did keep (it), or not.* (23) *Therefore the* LORD *left those nations, without driving them out hastily* [this limits the threat in ver. 21. He threatens, that he may not have to punish, when men by repentance disarm His anger. So long as Israel continued in apostasy, Jehovah would "not drive out any of the nations from before them ;" but whenever Israel repented, and so long as the Israelites continued faithful, Jehovah would let the originally promised extermination of the Canaanites to proceed again. Had Israel not fallen away, Jehovah would have exterminated the foe much sooner ; the hornet being "sent among them until they that were left, and hid themselves from Israel, should be destroyed:" not however instantaneously, or in one year, for Israel's good required an extirpation "by little and little, lest the land should become desolate, and the beast

of the field should multiply " (Exod. xxiii. 28–30 ; Deut. vii. 20,
22). Thus all the various promises and threats of Jehovah
appear in mutual harmony] ; *neither delivered He them into
the hand of Joshua* [the unfaithfulness had begun before
Joshua's death, and therefore the proving of Israel, by leaving
the nations in part as yet unsubdued when he died, was
needed. When Israel upon testing proved to be "reprobate
silver" (Jer. vi. 30), those nations became not merely trials,
but scourges].

CHAPTER III.

(1) *Now these (are) the nations which the Lord left* [the same Hebrew as in ch. ii. 23] *to prove Israel by them* [ch. ii. 22], (even) *as many of Israel as had not known all the wars of Canaan* [by their own experience, viz., the generation that came to manhood after the termination of Joshua's successful wars against the Canaanites in dependence on Jehovah (ch. ii. 10 ; Josh. xxiii. 1 ; compare Numb. xxi. 14), "the wars of the Lord"]. (2) *Only that the generations of the children of Israel might know to teach them war* [that Jehovah might teach them war, or as Speaker's Commentary translates, " Only that He might know the generations of Israel in teaching them war ; compare ver. 4] *at the least such as before knew nothing thereof* [what Israel needed to know experimentally, by Jehovah's teaching, was not ' war ' in general, but that the only successful mode of warfare on Canaan was that of Joshua, viz., with faithfulness to the covenant, and trust in Jehovah alone. Israel's failure once, through Achan's sin, had taught Joshua's army this lesson, by bitter experience (Josh. vii.). Necessity drives to prayer. Israel's distress through the remaining Canaanites would teach how only war can be successfully waged against the foe. Thereby Jehovah would ' prove ' Israel, whether they would keep His commandments ; for, to keep these, would be to ' know ' by Jehovah's teaching how to war (ch. ii. 22, iii. 4 ; Ps. xviii. 32–34)]. (3) *(Namely), five lords* [*sarnee*, literally *hinges*, or *axles*, metaphorically] *of the Philistines* [five was the political number], *and all the Canaanites, and the Sidonians, and the Hivites that dwelt in Mount Lebanon, from Mount Baal-hermon* [Baal-gad under Hermon

(Josh. xi. 3, 17)], *unto the entering in of Hamath* [apparently this enumeration is condensed from Josh. xiii. 2–6. " The entering in of Hamath" is the entrance to Canaan from the north between Lebanon and Anti-Lebanon, the fertile valley of Cœle-Syria. Possessed by Solomon (1 Kings viii. 65), and about to belong to Israel when restored, viz., to Dan (Ezek. xlvii. 16, xlviii. 1). The Philistines on the south-west, and the Sidonians, Hivites, and Canaanites in the north, having been left, by their inroads disabled Israel from exterminating all the other Canaanites from the towns in the centre of the land (ch. i. 19–36)]. (4) *And they were to prove Israel by them, to know* [as in 2 Chron. xxxii. 31, "God left Hezekiah to try him that He might know all that was in his heart." Rest too often produces rust. If there were no foe to try us, we should forget the secret of the good warfare (Ps. lix. 11). God knows all things to come by His foreknowledge, but after the event He "knows" it by evidence discernible by men (compare Gen. xxii. 12). He proves us, not that He may know, but to make us know] *whether they would hearken unto the commandments of the* LORD, *which He commanded their fathers by the hand of Moses.* (5) *And the children of Israel dwelt among the Canaanites, Hittites, and Amorites, and Perizzites, and Hivites, and Jebusites* [compare ch. i. 32, note. Israel, so far from exterminating the Canaanites, was glad to be allowed to dwell among them—a miserable declension for their high calling! In Josh. xxiv. 11; Deut. vii. 1, the Girgashites are added; *seven* nations in all, the number denoting *perfection* or totality. *Ten* nations are enumerated in Gen. xv. 19–21, *ten* being the number denoting the universality of the world kingdom. The Girgashites are enumerated in the *general* list as having been originally arrayed against Israel. But that they early withdrew from the conflict appears probable from the expression, "The Lord *cast out* the Girgashites"—" He will *drive out* the Girgashites " (Josh. iii. 10). Procopius, Belisarius' secretary, mentions an inscription on a monument in Tigitina (Tangiers): "We are exiles from before the face of Joshua the robber." Rabbi Samuel ben Nachman says, Joshua sent three propositions to the Canaanites—"Let those who chose fly; let those who choose

peace, make a treaty; let those who choose war, take arms."
So the Girgashites, fearing God, fled to Africa. The Gibeonites
made a league of submission. The thirty-one kings fought and
fell. This statement harmonises with the fact that Joshua in
no detailed account represents the Girgashites as *combatants.*
Only in a summary (Josh. xxiv. 11) are they named as fighting
along with the rest, probably only at the very first]. (6) *And
they took their daughters to be their wives, and gave their
daughters to their sons, and served their gods* [by not obeying
God in exterminating the Canaanites, the Israelites dwelling
among them exposed themselves to a temptation which they
had not the faith to resist. Intermarriages with the ungodly
put one in a disadvantage in fighting with the prince of this
world, and have ever led to apostasy (Gen. vi. 2–5; 2 Cor. vi.
14–18; 2 Kings viii.16–18; 2 Chron. xviii. 1,xix. 2; 1 Kings xvi.
31–33, xxi. 25, 26). The Canaanites had been left in judicial
retribution by God to prove Israel, and Israel could not stand
the self-imposed test]. (7) *And the children of Israel did evil
in the sight of the* LORD, *and forgat* [compare Deut. xxxii. 18;
1 Sam. xii. 9; but above ch. ii. 12, "they forsook"] the LORD
their God, and served Baalim and the groves [rather, "And *the
Asheroth, i.e., Ashtaroth,* akin to our English *Star,* and Greek
Aster. The *star-queen,* or moon-goddess, or goddess of the
heavenly hosts, in their influence upon earthly life. The term
for the wooden idols of the goddess was transferred to herself,
Asherah, and in the plural *Asheroth* (Exod. xxxiv. 13 ; Deut. vii.
5, xii. 3, xvi. 21). The *sacred tree* in Assyrian monuments
corresponds]. (8) *Therefore the anger of the Lord was hot
against Israel* [what was stated in general terms, Israel's sin,
and God's anger thereat (ch. ii. 11, 13, 20), is now detailed
more fully in its definite consequence, Israel's first subjugation],
and He sold them [compare ch. ii. 14, like captives sold as
helpless slaves] *into the hand of Chushan-Rishathaim king of
Mesopotamia* [*Aram-naharaim, i.e.,* Syria of the two rivers.
His name meant *the Ethiopian of double wickednesses.* The
primitive Babylonian race had a Cushite or Hamitic element,
as the vocabulary found in the oldest sites, Ur or Umqueir,
proves (compare Gen. x. 8–11; Hab. iii. 7). About 402 B.C. he

reigned about Haran in Syria, the region between the Euphrates and the Khabour (margin for Mesopotania, *Aram-Naharaim,* "Syria *of the two rivers* "), held by the Nairi; as cuneiform inscriptions of a date two centuries later prove. He probably established a temporary rule over several Mesopotamian tribes, which ended with the rise of Assyria to empire. Earlier still (Gen. xiv.) Chedor-laomer of Elam, and Amraphel of Shinar, had similarly invaded Palestine]. *And the children of Israel served Chushan-rishathaim eight years.* (9) *And when the children of Israel cried unto the* LORD, *the* LORD *raised up a deliverer* [Hebrew, SAVIOUR, type of Jesus, the Judge of Israel, Mic. v. 1] *to the children of Israel, who delivered them, (even) Othniel the son of Kenaz, Caleb's younger brother* [and son-in-law (ch. i. 13; Josh. xv. 16–19). This act of Othniel shows we must not understand that *all* who had seen Joshua's wars were dead (ch. ii. 7, 10)]. (10) *And the Spirit of the* LORD [*of Jehovah;* indicating His operation upon God's chosen instruments for effecting His purposes of grace according to His covenant. "The Spirit *of God* " is the expression denoting generally His supernatural power] *came upon him* [the Spirit endued him with supernatural wisdom, counsel, and might (Isa. xi. 2), type of Christ, to whom " God gives the Spirit not by measure " (John iii. 34). In ch. vi. 34, the expression is " clothed him"], *and he judged Israel, and went out to war* [the judge's functions were not only to save them from foreign oppressors, but to save them from the idolatry and apostasy which brought the chastisement upon them. The very notion of ' judging' Israel implied his *righting* them in relation to Jehovah, as well as to the foe] ; *and the* LORD *delivered Chushan-rishathaim king of Mesopotamia into his hand ; and his hand prevailed against Chushan-rishathaim.* (11) *And the land had rest forty years ; and Othniel the son of Kenaz died.*

I. *Israel's apostasy, punishment, and deliverance under the Judges in answer to prayer, illustrating God's righteousness, faithfulness, and grace.*

1. *Israel's adherence to the covenant under Joshua and the surviving elders who had seen Jehovah's mighty acts.*—The influence of one godly man, especially when he is in a leading

D

position, is most potent for good. Joshua was one who not only exhorted to godliness, but put in practice his own exhortation. Many preach abstinence from covetousness and selfishness, and yet live for self again, as if gain constituted their godliness, instead of godliness being great gain (1 Tim. vi. 5, 6). But Joshua not only would not bow down to palpable idols, but kept his heart from " covetousness, which is idolatry " in the sight of God (Col. iii. 5). He served all others before he served himself ; and then was content with the mountainous territory of Timnath-Heres as his inheritance. So must the Christian be willing to make himself the servant of all, in order to gain the more, and must even forego his temporal rights at times, lest he should hinder the gospel of Christ (1 Cor. ix. 12, 19). The effect of his disinterested piety, and his last exhortations to faithfulness, was, the people served Jehovah during all the days of Joshua. Nay more, even after his removal to his Lord, the remembrance of his godly consistency, and of the great works which the Lord had done by him, influenced the elders who had been eye-witnesses of those works to lead the people in the right way, and to keep down the corruptions which had already begun even before Joshua's death.

So the primitive Christians served the Lord with gladness and singleness of heart in the age immediately succeeding the ascension of our Lord (Acts ii. 42–47). But even in the days of the apostles there were germs of evil, which were only kept in check by their vigilant care (1 Cor. xi. 19 ; Rev. ii. 6, 14, 15, 20). But after their decease, and the removal of the apostolic fathers who outlived them, and who had been eye-witnesses of the miracles wrought by them, in the power of Jesus, the antitypical Joshua, the evil which, though latent, had been discerned by the apostles, broke out as they had foretold (Acts xx. 29, 30): " I know this that, after my departing, shall grievous wolves enter in among you, not sparing the flock ; also of your own selves shall men arise, speaking perverse things to draw away disciples after them "—" There shall be false teachers among you, who privily shall bring in damnable heresies, even denying the Lord that bought them ; and many shall follow their pernicious ways, and through covetousness shall they with feigned words make merchandise of you " (2 Pet. ii. 1–3). It was so with the generation that succeeded that of Joshua; they had not seen, and therefore they believed not. How many there are who in spiritual concerns will believe no eyes but their own (John xx. 29). May ours rather be the blessedness of those who " have not seen and yet have believed ! "

Israel's lapse into idolatry.—There is given at the outset a general summary of the main features of the book of Judges (ch. ii. 11, iii. 7). The series of events recur throughout in the same spiritual order. The professing people of God apostatise; God's righteousness binds Him to punish them : their distresses constrain them to cry to Him whom they had forsaken in their prosperity : His gracious compassion is moved by their groanings, therefore He raises up a judge to deliver them : then after the judgment is past, and the judge deceased, they relapsed and corrupted themselves again, " according to the true proverb, the dog is turned to his own vomit again ; and the sow that was washed, to her wallowing in the mire " (2 Pet. ii. 22).

Successive steps in their fall.—One sin leads on to another. Evil is a path sloping downward. The first step in Israel's declension was failure to exterminate the Canaanites, in accordance with God's command. This entailed the compromise of living among them, and maintaining intercourse with them. Then followed intermarriages (ch. iii. 6), that prolific source of degeneracy in all ages. Their not throwing down the altars of the Canaanites soon issued in their bowing down to the gods worshipped at those altars. The motto of Joshua, " the servant of Jehovah," was, " as for me and my house, we will serve Jehovah " (Josh. xxiv. 15) ; but the degenerate people of the next generation " served Baalim and Asheroth."

Cause of the evil.—The origin of their apostasy was, " they knew not the Lord." If men realised the truth, that whatever evil is done, is done " in the sight of the Lord " (ver. 11), whose " eyes are everywhere beholding the evil and the good," they would not dare to sin. If too they remembered all that

they owe to Him, in the past and in the present, they could
not but love Him; and knowing His infinite love, they would
shrink back with horror from the thought of forsaking Him for
any earthly idol. Well might God say of such unnatural and
suicidal wickedness, " Be astonished, O ye heavens at this, and
be horribly afraid. For my people have committed two evils;
they have forsaken Me the fountain of living waters, and
hewed them out cisterns, broken cisterns that can hold no
water " (Jer. ii. 12, 13).

Their forsaking the Lord consisted not in an open denial of
Jehovah, and opposition to His worship, but in the vain
attempt to combine the outward tabernacle service of the true
God with the sensuous nature-worship of the heathen. This
latter was more congenial to the corrupt heart, than the
spiritual religion of Him who is of purer eyes than to behold
iniquity. Conscience was on the side of Jehovah; inclination
preferred the gross worship of Baal. They persuaded themselves, under the plea of liberality, that it would be intolerance
and bigotry not to admit that the worship of the neighbouring
heathen had good in it, just as these recognised the gods of
other nations. So they compromised the matter by a verbal
and ceremonial recognition of Jehovah, whilst they gave their
hearts to the idols. But God warns us, " Go ye, serve ye every
one his idols: if ye will not hearken unto me, but pollute ye
My holy name no more with your gifts and with your idols "
(Ezek. xx. 38). We must make our choice between the Lord
and worldly idols, for we cannot serve both (1 John ii. 15;
Matt. vi. 24). The steps downward are sure. First the
Israelites " did not destroy the nations, concerning whom the
Lord commanded them: but were mingled among the heathen
and [as the necessary consequence] learned their works. And
they served their idols; which were a snare unto them [their
sin finally became their terrible punishment]. Yea, they
sacrificed their sons and their daughters unto devils, and shed
innocent blood, even the blood of their sons and of their
daughters " (Ps. cvi. 34–38).

Still there is the same scene enacted. Professing Christians
are tempted to compromise principle, in order to please the

world. Our high calling is to be in the world, not of the
world. It is not our being in the world that ruins us, but
our suffering the world to be in us : just as ships sink, not by
being in the water, but by the water getting into them.
Christ "gave Himself for us, that He might redeem us from
all iniquity, and purify unto Himself a peculiar people"
(Tit. ii. 14). Our privilege is to be witnesses for Christ, "the
epistle of Christ known and read of all men;" "shining as
lights in the world, the sons of God in the midst of a crooked
and perverse nation;" "the salt of the earth," seasoning it so
as to keep it from utter corruption (Acts i. 8; 2 Cor. iii. 2, 3;
Phil. ii. 15; Matt. v. 13, 14). But if professors be as salt that
hath lost its savour, through forsaking the Lord for the
fashions of the world, and its idols of gain, pleasure, and
ambition, they are not only worthless spiritually, but a positive
injury to the cause of God on earth.

*God's righteous indignation at, and His retributive punishment
of, their apostasy.*—God loved the people of His choice, yet is
jealous for His own holiness. His anger, though 'hot,' is not
passion, but judicial righteousness, which will by no means
clear the guilty. He marks His retributive justice by making
the tempters, to whom Israel yielded, to become Israel's
tormentors. The instruments of their sin became the instruments of their punishment. First, when Israel's zeal for the
Lord cooled, and they evaded, rather than fulfilled, God's
commandment to extirpate the idolatrous inhabitants of the
land, Jehovah would not drive out the enemy before them any
more, the penalty thus exactly corresponding to the offence.
Their career of conquest came to a stand; they barely kept
their own; a compromise took place—the Canaanites dwelling
among the Israelites in some places, and the Israelites by
sufferance dwelling among the Canaanites in others. Next,
when Israel sank still lower, and actually bowed to the idols
which had not been able to save the Canaanites, Jehovah sold
them into the hands of their enemies, the heathen, even as
the Israelites had sold themselves to be slaves to heathenish
corruptions (compare ver. 14 with 2 Kings xvii. 17; Isa. l. 1;
Rom. vii. 14, 25). Had they been faithful to God, He would

have been faithful to His promise: "There shall no man be able to stand before thee" (Deut. vii. 24). But as they had forsaken Jehovah, He was faithful to His threats: "They could not any longer stand before their enemies; for whithersoever they went out, the hand of Jehovah was against them for evil, as Jehovah had said" (Lev. xxvi. 17).

Let us learn from this, that the threats of God against backsliders and unfaithful professors are not empty words. Those who knowing God yet compromise with the world, shall be punished by the world and with the world. God means all that He saith. The transgressor's sin will find him out: "The backslider in heart shall be filled with his own ways" (Prov. xiv. 14). "With the froward God will show Himself froward" (Ps. xviii. 26). And as not one thing hath ever failed of all the good things which the Lord our God hath promised to His faithful people, so shall He bring upon the unfaithful all the evil which He has threatened (Josh. xxiii. 14, 15).

Jehovah's compassion because of Israel's distress, and His consequent interposition.—(1) Though Israel's sore distress was the righteous and necessary consequence of the people's sin, and was the fulfilment of Jehovah's word, and though He might have justly left them to reap as they had sown, yet their groanings, by reason of them that oppressed them, moved His compassion. It was not their repentance of sin, but His repentance because of their cry in distress, that brought Him to their help. So it was not our foreseen penitence, but God's grace, which moved Him to pity lost man, and to devise the means for man's salvation (2 Sam. xiv. 14 ; Isa. lix. 16, lxiii. 5, 9). (2) His mode of delivering them was by raising up judges or saviours from among themselves. So when God interposed to save men, "He took not on Him the nature of angels," but that of man, even "the seed of Abraham" (Heb. ii. 16). As man has fallen, so by the Man who is also God our Saviour, and our Judge, salvation for man is secured. As Jehovah was with the Judges whom He raised up, and by him delivered the Israelites out of the hand of their enemies (ver. 18); so the Father was ever with the Son (Acts x. 38, end), whom He raised up as "an horn of salvation in the house of His servant David, that we being delivered out of the hand of our enemies, might serve Him without fear" (Luke i. 69, 74).

Israel's relapse to corruption after the death of each judge.—It is a painful and humiliating picture of the corruption of our common nature. Holy writ is a continued history of God's epiphanies and man's apostasies. Well may God exclaim (Hos. vi. 4), "O Ephraim, what shall I do unto thee? O Judah, what shall I do unto thee? for your goodness is as a morning cloud, and as the early dew it goeth away!" The chastisements, and the gracious interpositions of God, seemed alike to fail in reforming this perverse people. Yet whilst we condemn them, is there nothing similar among ourselves? How often God hath stricken worldly professors of Christianity, yet with all our superior privileges we have not grieved. How often has the designed lesson of correction by sickness, losses, and trials been lost; how often the people refuse to return to Him that smiteth them, and will not seek the Lord of hosts? Israel's judges, after having fulfilled their saving mission, died. But our Saviour "ever liveth, able to save them to the uttermost who come unto God by Him" (Heb. vii. 25). The backsliding Christian forsakes for the idols of self and the world not a dead Deliverer, but the living Saviour, who is also our coming Judge. Each fresh interposition of Divine love leaves the sinner, if not renewed to holiness, more corrupt and hardened than ever. Then at last there remains to such only "a certain fearful looking for of judgment and fiery indignation, which shall devour the adversaries" (Heb. x. 27).

Jehovah's consequent resolution to stay Israel's victories, and to leave the Canaanites, in order to prove Israel.—Israel's transgression was, sparing the Canaanites, in neglect of God's command; Israel's punishment was, to be oppressed by the Canaanites whom God had doomed, but Israel spared. God doth "of our pleasant vices make instruments to scourge us" (Shakspere, *Lear*). The offending people were beaten with their own rod: "Because that this people hath transgressed my covenant, I also will not henceforth drive out any from before them of the nations which Joshua left, when he died." *Our* Joshua, though through death He destroyed him that had the power of death, has not yet put all things under Him and His people. A tempting world remains outside, and the corrupt old nature within each professing Christian. Our duty and our happiness consist in obeying our Lord's commands, by " mortifying our members which are upon the earth "— " crucifying the flesh, with the affections and lusts," and " being not conformed to this world, but being transformed by the renewing of our mind " (Rom. xii. 2 ; Gal. v. 24 ; Col. iii. 5). But if we give quarter to these, and even make provision for them, instead of these being our servants ministering to our pleasure, as we had hoped, they shall become our masters and cruel oppressors. God in righteous retribution chooses men's own delusions (Isa. lxvi. 4), and gives them over to a reprobate mind" (Rom. i. 28). Their own backslidings reprove them, and too late they will discover that it is an evil thing and bitter that they have forsaken the Lord their God (Jer. ii. 19). The spiritual paramours, after whom they have gone a whoring (ver. 17), become the executioners of God's just vengeance upon them (Ezek. xxiii. 9, 10, 20–30).

Yet the Lord still tried the Israelites by means of the spared Canaanites, whether they would profit by the chastisement. The Lord can overrule trial to good, if it lead men to search and try their ways, and to turn again to the Lord. The presence of the Canaanites need not have corrupted and seduced them, if only they had not yielded to, but resisted temptation, in the strength of the Lord. They had, no doubt, by their disobedience increased the severity of the temptation, and weakened their own power of resisting it. But God would have been the same Mighty One in their behalf, if they had sought Him, as He promises to be to us Christians : " There hath no temptation taken you, but such as is common to man : but God is faithful, who will not suffer you to be tempted above that ye are able ; but will, with the temptation, also make a way to escape that ye may be able to bear it " (1 Cor. x. 13)

The Lord left Canaanites for another wise and gracious purpose, namely, that Israel might know the true art of war.

There remained in united bodies the Sidonians and Hivites in the north, and the five great cities of Philistia in the south-west, besides scattered Canaanites in various regions throughout the land, among whom the degenerate Israelites were content to dwell, like tenants at will. God designed that even those enemies might do the Israelites good, if only Israel should prove amenable to spiritual instruction. A soldier can never be trained except by the discipline of campaigning. Now the existing generation of Israel knew not as yet the wars of Canaan. The secret of the art of war, as Joshua and his generation understood it, lay in faithfulness to Jehovah; holy courage in doing all the law, turning not from it to the right hand or to the left, was Joshua's mode of "making his way prosperous and having good success," according as God had promised, (Josh. i. 6–9). Disobedience and compromise disqualify utterly for fighting in the wars of the Lord. So in our spiritual conflict, the old nature, the flesh, is left in the hearts even of believers, in order that we may learn experimentally how to "war the good warfare," and "endure hardness as good soldiers of Jesus Christ," keeping on "the whole armour of God" (1 Tim. vi. 12, i. 18; 2 Tim. ii. 3; Eph. vi. 11). Even "heresies must be among us, that they which are approved may be made manifest" (1 Cor. xi. 19).

The Israelites, when proved thus, utterly failed.—They sank lower and lower, from bad to worse. They willingly dwelt among the heathen. Then they took their daughters for wives, and gave their daughters in marriage to idolaters. The result of such unequal marriages was, the bad corrupted the good, instead of the good winning over the bad. Lastly, they broke out into open evil in the sight of the Lord. And the reason of all this sad declension and apostasy is stated: "They forgat the Lord their God" (compare Deut. xxxii. 18; Isa. xvii. 10). What monstrous ingratitude that we should forget Him who never forgets us! Least of all should His elect church forget Him who saith, "Can a woman forget her sucking child, that she should not have compassion on the son of her womb? yea, they may forget, yet will I not forget thee" (Isa. xlix. 15). The true church can no more forget Him, than the bride could forget her wedding attire (Jer. ii. 32). But they who forget God shall be forgotten by Him, when the righteous shall be in everlasting remembrance (Hos. iv. 6 ; Ps. ix. 17).

Chronology of Judges.—The first period in the times of the Judges embraces 206 years. During it, three heathen powers successively oppressed Israel—Chushan Rishathaim of Mesopotania, Eglon of Moab, and Jabin of Hazar.

1. Oppression by Chushan Rishathaim, . .	(ch. iii. 8),	8 years
The rest after the deliverance by Othniel, .	(ch. iii. 11),	40 ,,
2. Oppression by Eglon, ...	(ch. iii. 14),	18 ,,
Rest after deliverance by Ehud (during which Shamgar smote the Philistines), . .	(ch. iii. 30, 31),	80 ,,
3. Oppression by Jabin, ...	(ch. iv. 3),	20 ,,
Rest after deliverance by Deborah and Barak,	(ch. v. 31),	40 ,,
4. Oppression by Midian, ...	(ch. vi. 1),	7 ,,
Rest after deliverance by Gideon, . .	(ch. viii. 28),	40 .,
Reign of Abimelech, ...	(ch. ix. 22),	3 ,,
Tola judge, ...	(ch. x. 2),	23 ,,
Zair judge, ...	(ch. x. 3),	22 ,,
		301 years

So Jephthah (ch. xi. 26) says, "Israel dwelt in Heshbon and Aroer *three hundred years.*"

5. Oppression by Ammon, ...	(ch. x. 8),	18 ,,
Jephthah judged after delivering Israel, .	(ch. xii. 7),	6 ,,
Ibzan, ...	(ch. xii. 9),	7 ,,
Elon, ...	(ch. xii. 11),	10 ,,
Abdon, ...	(ch. xii. 14),	8 ,,
6. Oppression by the Philistines, including the 20 years of Samson's judgeship (ch. xv. 20, xvi. 31), ...	(ch. xiii. 1),	40 ,,
		390 years

To this is to be added the period before the rising up of judges, during which in the absence of a regularly constituted authority (the sacred writer of Judges uses the term 'King,' as he was living under kingly government in Israel) : "Every man did that which was right in his own eyes" (ch. xvii. 6, xxi. 25). So Acts xiii. 20, "*About* four hundred and fifty years" in all: so Josephus, *Antiq.*, viii. 3, 1. It was just before the Judges' time that the flagrant idolatry of Micah and the Danites, and the fearful wickedness of Gibeah and its punishment by Israel under the high priesthood of Phinehas, the immediate successor of Eleazer the high priest under

Joshua, took place, as recorded in the closing chapters which form an appendix to the whole book.

Occasion of the raising up of the first judge.—The history of the raising up of Othniel as a deliverer is a miniature of the whole book. (1) *Israel's sin brought on the people God's judgments.* He is not a God all mercy, and who cannot be angry. Who knoweth the power of His anger (Ps. xc. 11). He sold them who by their iniquities had sold themselves. They had sold themselves as slaves to worldly and fleshly lusts (1 Kings xxi. 20, 25 ; Isa. l. 1, lii. 3 ; Rom. vi. 16, vii. 14, vi. 16 ; John viii. 34). So they must be slaves also outwardly and bodily, as they were inwardly and spiritually—and that, to a Cushite of the Hamitic race which had been doomed to be " a servant of servants," because of undutifulness (Gen. ix. 25). As the Israelites had broken through the hedge of their separation, they laid themselves bare to the heathen, and stripped themselves of the fence of God's protection. Their first oppression came from the region of Babylon, as their captivity ages after was in Babylon. (2) *Distress drove them to prayer* in trouble ; they called on Him whom in prosperity they had slighted (compare Isa. xxvi. 16). The world's enmity often is made a benefit to God's people : its friendship generally is fatal to them (James iv. 4 ; Exod. i. 2, ii. 23–25). Deep sorrow made them to cry aloud to God, whom formerly they had forsaken for idols. How many in eternity will bless the loving-correction of God in time ! Even now many a tried believer can say, " It is good for me that I have been afflicted," that I might learn Thy statutes " (Ps. cxix. 71). It is far better to suffer for a time, if suffering rouse the sinner from his spiritual apathy, than to escape suffering now, and suffer for ever hereafter. (3) *Israel's cry in distress brought Jehovah to their relief.*— He might justly have left them to the consequences of their own treachery towards Him. Their cry was called forth by pain, more than by penitence (Hos. vii. 14). Yet His Fatherly compassion yearned over His wayward children, now that they were in affliction. So He raised up a Saviour to be their deliverer. Though need drives us in the first instance to God, as the mighty famine in the far-off land was what induced the

prodigal to arise and go to his father; yet He does not reject
our prayers, but delivers us from wrath, and draws us to
Himself by His Son, our Saviour.   (5) *The saviour so raised
up, Othniel.*—It was the same bold warrior who in the days of
Joshua had won the hand of the daughter of his lion-hearted
brother Caleb by smiting Kirjath-Sepher. He then was young,
but now is old. But age cannot disqualify for service him whom
God calls to it : " For they that wait upon the Lord shall renew
their strength " (Isa. xl. 31 ; compare xlvi. 4 ; Ps. xcii. 14).
He was of the old stock that knew experimentally the secret
of war with Canaan, namely, faith in Jehovah.   (5) *His preparation for the work by God :* " The Spirit of Jehovah came
upon him."   The Holy Spirit is the Giver of life, light, and
love.   No man can know and serve God, except by the
inward teaching of the blessed Spirit (1 Cor. ii. 10, 11,
xii. 3).   But a special gift of the Holy Ghost is needed by
the minister who would rightly guide the flock of the Lord.
The sevenfold fulness of the Spirit rested on Messiah : "The
Spirit of wisdom and understanding, the Spirit of counsel and
might, the Spirit of knowledge and of the fear of the Lord,"
and the Spirit that made him " of quick understanding in the
fear of the Lord," so that He judged " not after the sight of
His eyes" (Isa. xi. 2, 3).   He gives a measure of this Spirit
to His servants.   (6) *Othniel's mode of procedure :* " He judged
Israel " first ; then he " went out to war."   He who would
fight successfully with foes abroad, must first overcome the
worst foe, sin, at home (compare 1 Sam. vii. 3–14).   The
Lord must be owned as our Lawgiver and our Judge, if we
would have Him to save us (Isa. xxxiii. 22).   (7) *The
issue.*   The Lord delivered Chushan-rishathaim into Othniel's
hand.   So " the land had rest forty years," the same period
as that of Israel's wandering in the wilderness.   Do we desire
rest in spirit during our earthly pilgrimage ?   Then let us
commit ourselves to Him whom " God hath exalted with His
right hand to be a Prince and a Saviour " (Acts v. 31).   He
will '*give*' us 'rest' on our first coming to Him ; He will enable
us to "*find* rest unto our souls," in taking His easy yoke and
light burden upon us, and learning of the meek and lowly

Lamb of God all our earthly days. He will at last bring us
home to the eternal "rest which remaineth for the people of
God" (Heb. iv. 9), "where the wicked cease from troubling,
and where the weary be at rest" (Job iii. 17; Matt. xi.
28–30).

EGLON AND EHUD, SHAMGAR AND THE PHILISTINES.

(12) *And the children of Israel did evil* [a characteristic phrase
throughout this book (ch. ii. 11, iii. 7, 12, iv. 1, vi. 1, xiii.
1), marking identity of authorship] *again* [Heb. "they *added to
do evil* "] *in the sight of the Lord; and the Lord strengthened
Eglon the king of Moab against* [so as to conquer and oppress]
Israel, because they had done evil in the sight of the Lord [1 Sam.
xii. 9]. (13) *And he gathered unto him the children of Ammon
and Amalek* [the foe of Israel from the first, and therefore
doomed by God to final destruction (Exod. xvii. 8–16; Numb.
xxiv. 20; Deut. xxv. 17–19; 1 Sam. xv. 2–33). What a
humiliation to Israel to be under such an unrelenting foe (ch. vi.
3–6, x. 7, 11, 12). Ammon and Amalek similarly joined against
Judah under Jehoshaphat (2 Chron. xx. 1; Ps. lxxxiii. 7)], *and
went and smote Israel, and possessed the city of palm-trees* [Jericho,
destroyed by Joshua sixty years before, but partially rebuilt
afterwards. As no Israelite dared to fortify it through fear of
Joshua's curse, it was easily taken by Moab, and made a base
for subjugating Israel (ch. i. 16). Josephus states that Eglon
built here a palace (Josh. vi. 26). The curse on it caused the
name 'Jericho' to give place to "the city of palm-trees"].
(14) *So the children of Israel served* [compare Gen. xiv. 4,
'served' *as vassals*. The period of the Judges is divided
between "the times of *servitude*" and "the times of *rest*"]
Eglon the king of Moab eighteen years [the same length of time
as Israel's oppression by Ammon lasted (ch. x. 8)]. (15) *But
when the children of Israel cried unto the Lord, the Lord raised
them up a deliverer* [so ver. 9, ch. ii. 16, 18; Neh. ix. 27], *Ehud
the son of Gera, a* [Heb. *the*] Benjamite [these names recur in
the tribe of Benjamin (1 Cor. vii. 10, viii. 3, 6; 2 Sam. xvi. 5,
xix. 16)], *a man left-handed* [Hebrew, *shut as to his right hand*,
viz., owing to want of use from childhood. It is a coincidence

indicating the veracity of the narrative, that the 700 *Benjamite* slingers were similarly left-handed as the *Benjamite* Ehud (compare 1 Chron. xii. 2)]; *and by him the children of Israel sent a present unto Eglon the king of Moab* [viz., *tribute*, as 'present' means in 2 Sam. viii. 2, 6; 1 Kings iv. 21; "they brought *presents*, and served Solomon" (Ps. lxxii. 10). Ehud must have held a high place among the Israelites; for they employed him as their tribute-bearer to the Moabite king, and assigned him a numerous retinue as his escort (ver. 18). (16) *But Ehud made him a dagger* ["*made* him," for, as under the Philistines (1 Sam. xiii. 19), so now under Moab, the making of iron weapons publicly was forbidden] *which had two edges* [typifying "the sword of the Spirit, the word of God" (Ps. cxlix. 6; Rev. i. 16, ii. 12; Heb. iv. 12] *of a cubit length; and he did gird it under his raiment upon his right thigh* [compare the Antitype (Ps. xlv. 3). Its presence on Ehud's right thigh would never be suspected, the left being the sword side; at the same time it would be convenient on his right thigh to his left hand, which was the hand that he used. He may have been one of the 600 Benjamites who escaped to the rock Rimmon, only that the date of that event must have been soon after Joshua's death, whereas the oppression of Eglon closed *more than sixty-six years* after Joshua (see my remarks on ch. ii. 6, iii. 11, the close), (ch. xx. 47)]. (17) *And he brought the present unto Eglon king of Moab; and Eglon (was) a very fat man* [probably living in luxury, and the pleasures of the appetite. Sudden destruction often comes upon such in the midst of their self-indulgence (Luke xxi. 34–36); so Belshazzar (Dan. v.; Rom. xiii. 12, 13; 1 Thess. v. 6–8; Ezek. xvi. 49]. (18) *And when he had made an end to offer the present* [and had returned some distance from Jericho homewards (ver. 19)], *he sent away the people* [the Hebrew implies *a considerable number* (Deut. xxxii. 30). The Lord saves *not* by a multitude (1 Sam. xiv. 6; 2 Chron. xiv. 11; Judg. vii. 4, 7). Ehud by being alone, was the more free to act; and if he failed, he alone would suffer, without imperilling the rest] *that bare the present*. (19) *But he himself turned again from the quarries* [*Pesilim :* so the Chaldee and Syriac versions and most Jewish

commentaries explain it. But Jerome and the Septuagint take
the usual meaning of the Hebrew, " *the graven images.*" The
Moabites probably set up these images as a token of their
supremacy, and to put the conquered Israelite territory under
the tutelage of their gods, at the place of Israel's first encampment five miles west of Jordan after their passage of that river
(Josh. iv. 3, 19, 20): here by circumcision the Israelites *rolled
off* the reproach of Egypt, whence the place was called Gilgal
(ver. 2, marg. 9). How humiliating that the reproach of the
heathen should be rolled back on them here! The sight of
these images set up to vex and to tempt Israel fired Ehud's
zeal against Eglon] *that (were) by Gilgal* [on the north side of
Wady Kelt, one mile and a third from *Eriha*, the modern Jericho,
stood Gilgal. Toward the east is a tamarisk, the traditional
site of Jericho ; 150 yards south-east of the tree is a pool built
of uncemented pebbles. South-east of this are twelve small
mounds, *Tel ayla't Jiljulieh*, ten feet in diameter and three
or four high, possibly remains of Israel's first encampment. So
Josephus (*Antiq.*, v. 1, 4, 11) states that Gilgal lay between
Jericho and the Jordan, one and a half miles east of Jericho,
and five and a half west of Jordan. But " the graven images "
('quarries') by Gilgal lay on Ehud's way from Jericho to
Mount Ephraim ; whereas the Gilgal of Josh. iv. 19 lay in
the opposite direction towards Jordan ; therefore the Gilgal
here may be Geliloth, west of Jericho, on the border of Judah
and Benjamin : unless Ehud fled the opposite way to elude
pursuit], *and said* [Ehud said the words *to the attendants,* for
he did not 'come' before the king till ver. 20 ; Ehud *bade
say* to the King], *I have a secret errand unto thee, O king, who
said, Keep silence* [Let there be quiet, *i.e.,* Let me be left alone].
And all that stood by him went out from him. (20) *And Ehud
came unto him; and he was sitting in a summer parlour, which
he had for himself alone* [rather " was *sitting alone* in an *upper
chamber of cooling* which he had ;" generally such chambers
were upon the flat roofs, open to the currents of air]. *And
Ehud said, I have a message from God unto thee* [Ehud was commissioned by God to save Israel ; but the *mode* of saving them,
assassination by a lie and treachery, was of his own devising.

Alloy is mixed with obedience even of men employed by God. Death was the message Ehud meant. Eglon understood him in a different sense]. *And he* [the king] *arose out of* (his) *seat* [from reverence toward the expected message from God (Numb. xxiii. 18 ; 1 Kings ii. 19). Ehud, in addressing a heathen king, used not the covenant name ' Jehovah,' Israel's God, but *Elohim*, the general name for the God of the universe]. (21) *And Ehud put forth his left hand* [his moving his left hand toward the hilt of the dagger on his right thigh did not excite Eglon's suspicion, such as moving his right hand would have created], *and took the dagger from his right thigh, and thrust it into his belly.* (22) *And the haft also went in after the blade; and the fat closed upon the blade, so that he could not draw the dagger out of his belly; and the dirt came out* [rather, " it (the dagger) came out at *the part between the legs," parsedonah*, from an Arabic root, " to part the legs "]. (23) *Then Ehud went forth through the porch, and shut the doors of the parlour upon him* [Eglon], *and locked them* [and took away the key which he had found inside, and with which he locked the door from outside when he went out]. (24) *When he* [Ehud] *was gone out, his* [Eglon's] *servants came, and when they saw that, behold, the doors of the parlour* (were) *locked, they said, Surely he covereth his feet* [for sleep, or else for performing the necessities of nature (see margin here, 1 Sam. xxiv. 3)], *in his summer chamber.* (25) *And they tarried till they were ashamed* [of their long tarrying (2 Kings ii. 17, viii. 11)], *and, behold, he opened not the doors of the parlour; therefore they took a key* [a second key, besides the one taken by Ehud. A piece of wood with pegs, corresponding to small holes in a wooden bolt within ; when put through the door-hole, the key drew the bolt (Song Sol. v. 4). The key could lock from without or within. The chief officer over the king's house held the palace key, as his badge of office (Isa. xxii. 15, 20–22 ; Rev. iii. 7)], *and opened* (them) ; *and behold, their lord* (was) *fallen down dead on the earth.* (26) *And Ehud escaped while they tarried, and passed beyond the quarries* [note ver. 19], *and escaped unto Seirath* [meaning *the hairy*, a continuation of the rugged, bushy hills which stretched to Judah's northern territory from Mount Ephraim (Josh. xv.

10), where "Mount Seir" is, not Edom, but a north boundary of Judah, now Mihsir, probably the same as Seirath (xvii. 15, 18)]. (27) *And it came to pass, when he was come, that he blew a trumpet* [compare ch. vi. 34; 1 Sam. xiii. 3] *in the mountain of Ephraim* [the *mountainous region* belonging to that tribe; often made the rallying place of the nation (ch. iv. 5, x. 1)], *and the children of Israel went down with him from the mount* [into the plain of Jericho], *and he before them* [as their leader to victory, of which Eglon's death was the earnest]. (28) *And he said unto them* [under the inspiration of God, as (ch. vii. 15)], *Follow after me* [not 'go,' but 'follow me'. If we would have others fight the good fight, we must lead the way]; *for the Lord hath delivered your enemies the Moabites into your hand. And they went down after him, and took the fords of Jordan* [near Jericho (Josh. ii. 7)] *towards Moab, and suffered not a man to pass over. (29) And they slew of Moab at that time* [i.e., in the course of the campaign] *about ten thousand men* [the whole force of Moabites in the Holy Land for keeping down the Israelites] *all lusty* [literally *fat;* their rich pastures fed fat kine; hence arose the plenty which bred self-indulgence and pride (Isa. xvi. 6; compare ver. 17, "very fat"; Deut. xxxii. 13–15)], *and all men of valour; and there escaped not a man. (30) So Moab was subdued that day under the hand of Israel. And the land* [chiefly Benjamin and Ephraim] *had rest fourscore years. (31) And after him was Shamgar* [compare ch. v. 6] *the son of Anath, which slew of the Philistines six hundred men with an ox-goad* [the Syrians and the people of Palestine to this day use such an instrument of wood, eight feet long and six inches in circumference at the thick end, which had an iron scraper for removing dirt from the plough; the thin end has an iron point wherewith to spur the oxen ploughing]; *and he also delivered Israel* [probably after the fourscore years' rest secured by Ehud's judgeship (ver. 30), and in the early part of Jabin's twenty years' oppression (ch. iv.). Whilst Jabin was oppressing northern Israel, the Philistines ravaged southern Israel and Judah. Anath seems to be akin to Anah (Gen. xxxvi. 2, 14, 20, 25), and so an Edomite name. The Philistines brought Judah so low by inroads, that they probably had no

E

better weapons than agricultural instruments (ch. v. 8), as in later days (ch. xv. 15, 16; 1 Sam. xiii. 19, 22, xvii. 40, 50; compare Homer, *Iliad* vi. 134, 135). Notwithstanding Shamgar's prowess, "the highways were unoccupied, and the travellers walked through by-ways," as there was no security (ch. v. 6). So this deliverance by him from the Philistines had only a temporary effect until Deborah arose].

THE MESSAGES OF GOD.

1. *Israel's apostasy, chastisement by Eglon, penitent cry, and deliverance by Ehud.*—(1) *Israel's relapse into sin.* What a sad significance there is in that little word 'again'! Israel, the chosen people of God, whose high calling was to be a "kingdom of priests and an holy nation" (Exod. xix. 6), "did evil," and this "in the sight of Jehovah," as if defying Him to His face; and, what was an awful aggravation, "Israel did evil *again*." After all that they had suffered by sin, and after so recent and so gracious a deliverance vouchsafed by God, they fell into apostasy again! "Neither ministry nor miracle, nor misery nor mercy, could mollify their hard hearts" (Trapp). The same history is being continually repeated. We marvel at their proneness to fall: yet how often does the professing church, and do we ourselves decline from our first love and our first works! Then when the Lord has in faithfulness chastised us, and afterwards restored us, in answer to penitent prayer, too frequently we have forgotten the lesson which chastisement was designed to teach us, and have relapsed into old sins again (compare 2 Pet. i. 9, ii. 20, 22). When the Israelites had escaped from their old oppression, they became less vigilant in shunning their old sin. In trouble they visited Jehovah, and poured out a prayer when His chastening was upon them (Isa. xxvi. 16). But "ease still recants vows made in pain as recreant and void." When the pain was gone, their penitence went with it, and they did evil again.

(2) *Their consequent punishment.*—God's message had been one of love to Israel. But as they would not hear, He must now send a sterner message—a message of punishment. God has many voices wherewith He speaks to man (Job xxxiii. 14).

God is at no loss for rods wherewith to chastise backsliders. The punishment increases in severity upon their increased rebellion. God will not cease to punish till men cease to rebel. Chushan Rishathaim, their former scourge, was from distant Mesopotamia. Now Jehovah strengthens their next neighbour, the king of Moab, to be the executioner of His vengeance on them. Eglon could have had no power against them, but that their apostasy constrained the Lord to put a sword in the hand of their enemy. Formerly Balak had no power to curse Israel, even though he had enlisted the prophet Balaam against them, so long as Israel was faithful to the covenant (Mic. vi. 5). But now another king of Moab, though a heathen, is made "the rod of Jehovah's anger" (Isa. x. 5), to smite the people. How sad it is when the God of Israel, who delights to "give strength and power unto His people" (Ps. lxviii. 35), is bound by His justice to strengthen their adversary against them! Let us learn to hate the sin of unfaithfulness, and to revere the holiness of God who will not spare even His own chosen people, when they backslide from Him (Rom. xi. 21, 22). It must have been most mortifying to Israel to see Jericho, the very city which had been delivered into their hands by a miracle, now made a Moabite stronghold to guard the passes of Jordan, and to keep Israel down in lasting subjection. Now too their old enemies Ammon and Amalek joined against them; for when the professing people of God seem depressed, their adversaries flock together to crush them (Ps. lxxxiii. 5–8). The Israelites would not serve their Lord with their corn, wine, and oil which He had given them; so now they must serve the oppressor, and pay him tribute of all (Hos. ii. 5–10; Deut. xxviii. 47, 48). Their former less severe servitude had failed permanently to amend them; therefore now they must suffer a worse one:—that servitude was for eight years, this is for eighteen. So if we will not be reformed by God by less chastisements, but will walk contrary unto Him, then will He also walk contrary unto us, and will punish us yet more for our sins (Lev. xxvi. 23, 24).

(3) *Israel's cry in distress, and the Lord's interposition.*—Not even Israel's past renewed provocations could take away the

power of prayer, when they turned from sin to the Lord. A new deliverer is raised up in answer to renewed prayer. When God means to deliver His people, He first stirs them up to pray for deliverance (compare Isa. xxx. 18, lxv. 24). Ehud was left-handed, and yet a man of Benjamin—a name which means *son of the right hand.* God uses weak things to confound the mighty ; and can "make strong for Himself" even the left-handed, so as to be "the man of His right hand" (Ps. lxxx. 17). Thus all must see that it was not Israel's arm that saved them ; but God's right hand and God's holy arm (Ps. xl. 3, xcviii. 1). So it is especially in the great salvation which Jesus has wrought for us. Like Ehud's tribal forefather, He was Benoni, "son of my sorrow" (Gen. xxxv. 18, marg.) ; "a man of sorrows" (Isa. liii. 3) ; before He became Benjamin, "son of the right hand," exalted by the right hand of the Father to be a Prince and Saviour (Acts v. 31 ; Ps. cx. 1).

(4) *The manner of deliverance.*—Israel presented tribute to king Eglon by Ehud. The Hebrew word for 'present' (*Minchah*) here is the same as elsewhere is used of the thank-offering presented to Jehovah by pious worshippers according to the Law. They had neglected to render to God the tribute due to the loving God ; so now, in retributive judgment, they must render to a heathen oppressor the offerings which through their sin had become his due. But now they are penitently returning to Him who smote them. So God will cast the rod of His anger into the fire (Isa. x. 5–7). The heathen oppressor meant not to execute God's purposes, but to further his own schemes. For these which he did mean, he shall be given to destruction, after that God has used him to chastise His people (compare 1 Kings xvi. 7, close). The sinner's motive, not the issue, is the test of the quality of his action. He shall not the less be condemned for his malice against the people of God, though by it he unconsciously carried out God's purpose respecting them (Ps. lxxvi. 10 ; Mic. iv. 12 ; Prov. xvi. 4). Ehud took a plan which, unless he was specially directed to it by God, was unjustifiable. We must distinguish between Ehud's faith and Ehud's error. No expression of

Scripture is used commanding or approving of the means which he took to obtain his end. Treacherous assassination is not a work emanating from the Spirit of God. Ehud's courage, patriotism, and faith were accepted of God, but not what was defective in his action : this needed cleansing with the blood of atonement. The end does not justify the means; and the condemnation of those is just who say, "Let us do evil, that good may come" (Rom. iii. 8). But God blots out the sin which alloys even the acts of faith of His children. The act was permitted, though not ordered, by God. God employed Ehud to be Israel's deliverer : and overruled his wrong act to carry out the divine purpose against Eglon. He may employ what instruments He pleases to carry out His decrees, whether the agency of nature, as the sea or the lightning, or that of man. Israel was commanded to extirpate the Canaanites, just as an angel was commissioned to slay all the first-born of Egypt in one night, and on another 185,000 Assyrians. Bishop Butler observes, there are some precepts in Scripture given to particular persons which would be immoral and vicious, were it not for such precepts ; but those are of such a kind that the precept changes the whole nature of the case and of the action. None of these precepts are contrary to immutable morality. If it were commanded to cultivate the principles, and act from principles of treachery, ingratitude, cruelty, the command would not alter the nature of the case or of the action in any of these instances. In Ehud's instance, neither the principle nor the particular act was commanded by God. It is not said of Ehud, as it was of Othniel, that "the Spirit of Jehovah came upon him." Nor does Ehud appear among the examples of faith in Heb. xi.

(5) *God's special message to Eglon.*—His name means a *calf ;* and his fatness indicated self-indulgence and pampering of the appetite. His god was his belly, and through his belly came his death blow (Phil. iii. 19). He had lived in pleasure on the earth and been wanton ; and like a fatted calf, he had unconsciously been nourishing himself for the slaughter (James v. 5). So the summer room, which was the scene of his luxury, became the place of his execution. The graven images

which he had set up as the security for his hold over subject Israel, was the starting point from which the slayer came to destroy him. Ehud addressed him, "I have a message from God to thee." Ehud probably had no commission from God save the general one of being called to be Israel's deliverer. Nevertheless, the act which Ehud was about to perpetrate, whatever criminality there was on Ehud's part, was in fact a solemn and awful message from God, summoning the soul of Eglon into His presence. God addresses man by the judgments of His hand, as well as by the judgments of His mouth (Isa. xxvi. 9; Mic. vi. 9). "The Lord's voice crieth, Hear ye the rod, and who hath appointed it." When God's messenger of death summons the sinner, "Thy soul is required of thee," king and peasant, rich and poor alike, must obey (Luke xii. 20). Eglon arose out of his seat to receive God's message. The reverence of this heathen king reproves the irreverence and indifference to God's solemn appeals manifested on the part of many professing Christians. When he received the fatal blow, " the fat closed upon the blade." How often pampering the appetite only prepares men for the slaughter, so that "they are inclosed in their own fat" (Ps. xvii. 10). What message but one of wrath could a proud oppressor of the Lord's people like Eglon expect? "What peace" could Joram look for so long as he followed the sins of his mother Jezebel? (2 Kings ix. 22).

(6) *Jehovah's message of deliverance to Israel.*—When the heathen king was fallen, Eglon escaped by the good providence of God. Then with the loud trumpet call he summoned Israel: "Follow after me, for Jehovah hath delivered your enemies into your hand." What Jehovah had already done, was an earnest of what He would yet do for Israel (Isa. xxvi.). It was a jubilee trumpet proclaiming liberty, joy, and peace to those who long had heard only the trumpet-blasts of the oppressor. Ehud invited them to follow him, only because the Lord was with him (Ps. cxxvii. 1). Jehovah's presence was the pledge of victory over all their enemies. Ehud uses the covenant-name, Jehovah, in addressing the people of the covenant. He had used only the general name 'God' in

addressing Eglon. "The name of Jehovah is a strong tower" to His people (Prov. xviii. 10). So using the means, and trusting in Jehovah for the issue, Ehud succeeded. Having secured the fords of Jordan, and so cut off communications between the Moabite garrison in Israel and their countrymen in Moab beyond Jordan, he made what had been their paradise to became their prison. When they and their king had promised themselves 'peace,' then sudden destruction came upon them, so that none of them escaped (1 Thess. v. 3). The choicest of Moab's men fell at a stroke: and the word was fulfilled, "For the oppression of the poor and the sighing of the needy, now will I arise, saith Jehovah" (Ps. xii. 5). Thus the land obtained a rest of four score years.

2. *Special application of the spiritual lesson*—(1) *The consequences of backsliding.* All the evil which men do, is "in the sight of the Lord." It is an aggravation of the sin which professing Christians do, that it is against Him who, as they confess, seeth all things. It makes the offence still worse, if it be a falling 'again' into the sin from which one has been delivered for a time. The righteous God then increases the penalty upon the increased transgression (Jer. ii. 19). Jehovah formerly strengthened His people with might by His spirit to overcome the world (1 John v. 4, 5); but now that they have forsaken Him for the world, He 'strengthens' the world to become their master, so that they may know by bitter experience what a heavy yoke the world's service is, as compared with His (2 Chron. xii. 8). Then in sad retrospect of past privileges, now forfeited through unfaithfulness, the backslider is led by the grace of God to think on his ways—

> "What peaceful hours I once enjoyed,
> How sweet their memory still !
> But they have left an aching void
> The world can never fill."

(2) *The Lord's return in mercy to them who return to Him in penitent prayer.*—When He has mercy in store for His people, He first moves them to prayer. Chastisement is over-ruled to their good, because it moves them to "acknowledge their offence, and seek His face : "Come, and let us return unto

the Lord: for He hath torn, and He will heal us; He hath smitten, and He will bind us up" (Hos. v. 15, vi. 1). And God hears our cry, because it is His Providence and His Spirit which have moved us to utter it. As sin 'again' brings chastisement again, so prayer again brings deliverance again.

(3) *Way of deliverance:* "God's thoughts are not our thoughts, neither are our ways His ways" (Isa. lv. 8). He chooses often the left-handed to be the men of His right hand. Out of weakness they are made strong (Heb. xi. 34; 1 Cor. i. 27–29; 2 Cor. xii. 9, 10; Ps. viii. 2). Above all· this is so in our salvation from man's cruel adversary, the prince of the powers of the air. The Ancient of days became an infant of days. He who laid the foundations of the earth and shut up the sea with doors, and made thick darkness a swaddling band for it (Job xxxviii. 6, 9), became Himself "the babe wrapped in swaddling-clothes, lying in a manger" (Luke ii. 12). By suffering death He overcame him that had the power of death, that is, the devil, and delivered us who through fear of death were all our lifetime subject to bondage (Heb. ii. 14). The weapon too with which He overcame Satan in the temptation, and with which He shall finally and for ever slay him and his host, is typified by Ehud's two-edged dagger: "The word of God is living, and powerful, and sharper than any two-edged sword" (Heb. iv. 12). It is "the sword of the Spirit" with which we too must conquer the wicked one (Eph. vi. 17). It is only when we have the word of God abiding in us, that we can overcome the wicked one (1 John ii. 14). The perfect victory is reserved till the time of His coming again, when He shall summon together His saints, Follow after me (Rev. xix. 13–15, 21), and then shall slay the wicked with the sharp sword which proceedeth out of his mouth, and shall consign their prince to the lake of fire (Rev. xx. 10; Isa. xi. 4).

(4) *Messages of God.*—Our heavenly Father is continually speaking to us by various agencies: "God speaketh once, yea twice, yet man perceiveth it not" (Job xxxiii. 14). He speaks alike to the oppressors and to the oppressed,—to the former in wrath, because of their malice against His people whom He permitted them to chastise, in furtherance of His own purposes,

not theirs (Isa. x. 5–18); to the latter, in consolation, when chastisement has had its designed effect in humbling them and drawing them to Himself (Isa. xl. 1, 2, lxi. 3–7). Every providential visitation which suddenly carries men into eternity is a message from God to the careless and impenitent: "Think ye that they were sinners above all men? I tell you, Nay; but, except ye repent, ye shall all likewise perish" (Luke xiii. 2–5). God's judgments upon backsliders have a voice of warning to all: "The backslider in heart shall be filled with his own ways" (Prov. xiv. 14). On the other hand, God's past mercy to those who have turned from their erring ways, is an encouraging message to those who desire restoration: "Return, ye backsliding children, and I will heal your backslidings" (Jer. iii. 22). And when the Holy Ghost awakens in any heart the cry for deliverance, all things shall conspire to ensure the believer's final victory over the oppressor, Satan, through the might of Jesus (Rom. viii. 31–37). All our joys and all our sorrows are messages from God to us; but we need the Holy Spirit to enable us rightly to interpret them. It is in His word especially that God speaks directly to His fallen children. The message of Ehud to Eglon was a message of death, but the Word is a message of life and peace. The ministers of the gospel have the ministry of reconciliation committed to them, that God was in Christ reconciling the world unto Himself, not imputing to them their trespasses (2 Cor. v. 19, 20); so their message to sinners already dead in sin, and under condemnation of eternal death, is, "Now then we are ambassadors for Christ, as though God did beseech you by us, we pray you in Christ's stead, be ye reconciled to God."

(5) *How God's messages should be received by whomsoever or howsoever delivered.*—Eglon, though a king, rose reverentially before Ehud, a vassal, on hearing that the latter bore a message from God to him. Will not this heathen in the day of judgment comdemn many professing Christians, who treat with indifference and often irreverence the word of God preached to them? Not merely opposition to the word, but neglect of it, will bring condemnation on the hearers (Heb. ii. 3). We ought to listen in the spirit of Samuel, saying, "Speak, Lord, for Thy

servant heareth" (1 Sam. iii. 9). Not as critics sitting in judgment upon the word, but submitting to its judgment "with all readiness of mind," like the Bereans (Acts xvii. 11); not as those who seek entertainment, like Herod (Luke xxiii. 8; Mark vi. 20); but as the Psalmist (lxxxv. 8), desiring to "hear what God the Lord will speak;" in the spirit of Cornelius and his company when about to hear Peter, "Now therefore are we all here present before God, to hear all things that are commanded thee of God" (Acts x. 33). The Spirit of God alone can dispose us to "receive the word, not as the word of men, but (as it is in truth) the word of God, which effectually worketh in them that believe" (1 Thess. ii. 13). Let us pray earnestly for the gift of the Holy Spirit.

(6) *The duty of continual preparedness for the Lord's message summoning us hence.*—The message of death finds most men as little expecting it, as did Eglon, or the rich fool (Luke xii. 20). So at the Lord's second coming; it is when they shall be saying, "Peace and safety, that sudden destruction shall come upon them, and they shall not escape" (1 Thess. v. 3). God needs not the dagger of a sudden assailant, like Ehud, to call us away hence. He has thousands of ways of sending the message of death: "Set thine house in order; for thou shalt die, not live" (Isa. xxxviii. 1). Our wisdom therefore is to be always ready. But He would have the believer rather to be looking for the blessed hope, and the glorious appearing of the great God and our Saviour, If death shall come first, preparedness for the Lord's coming again is the best preparation for our soul's dismissal in peace to go to be with Him. So whenever He shall come, whether He find us waking or sleeping (1 Thess. v. 10), He will find us watching (Luke xii. 37–40).

(7) *The final rest.*—The land had rest eighty years after the deliverance wrought through Ehud. It was a long season of rest, but what is it compared with the eternal rest which remaineth for the people of God in the heavenly Canaan? The rest of Israel was sooner or later sure to be interrupted; for "man is born unto trouble, as the sparks fly upward" (Job v. 7). But the rest which awaits the saints knows no interruption. They "rest from their labours" (Rev. xiv. 13), but not

from service of praise and blessed ministry (Rev. iv. 8, vii. 15, xxii. 3). Meantime they have to serve their own generation by the will of God (Acts xiii. 36). They serve now amidst abounding adversaries and manifold temptations (*see* 2 Cor. vi. 4–10); but God perfects strength out of their weakness. He can make a ploughman, as Shamgar with his ox-goad, and fishermen, as the apostles, to achieve great exploits for the deliverance of His church from the Philistine-like enemy. As Camillus and Curius went from the plough to save Rome from the Gauls; so the faithful minister, ordained and unordained alike, is called from, and in his secular vocation, to war a good warfare. He may have no special power or weapons of his own for the good fight, but in the strength of the Lord, and with the whole armour of God, he can and will prevail : for "God hath chosen the weak things of the world to confound the things which are mighty" (1 Cor. i. 27). Then how glorious will be the final triumph, when after having gotten the victory of faith we shall sing the song of Moses the servant of God, and the song of the Lamb. Be this blessed hope our encouragement now ; and may the sure promise cheer us in our present conflict : "Be thou faithful unto death, and I will give thee a crown of life" (Rev. ii. 10, xv. 3).

CHAPTER IV.

ISRAEL'S DELIVERANCE BY DEBORAH AND BARAK.

(1) *And the children of Israel again did evil* [see note ch. iii. 12], *in the sight of the Lord* [JEHOVAH], *when Ehud was dead* [implying that Ehud whilst living restrained them from idolatry (illustrating ch. ii. 18, 19). The judge's office, therefore, was not only to deliver them from the oppressor, but also to keep them from that apostasy which was sure, in God's retributive righteousness, to bring them again under the rod]. (2) *And the Lord* [JEHOVAH] *sold them* [even as they *sold themselves* to work evil in the sight of the Lord (1 Kings xxi. 20 ; note ch. ii. 14)] *into the hand of Jabin king of Canaan, that reigned in Hazor* [Jabin, meaning "the discerning," was a hereditary title of the Canaanite dynasty, as 'Pharaoh' in Egypt, and Abimelech among the Philistines of Gerar, and Hadad in Syria and Edom.   Joshua had conquered a Jabin more than a century earlier, and destroyed his capital Hazor with fire, lest there should be so strong a fortress in his rear.   But the Canaanites had rebuilt it, when suffered by Israel to remain, contrary to Jehovah's command : and the dynasty of Jabin, during Israel's oppression by Moab and the Philistines, regained the throne, and from Hazor, as the centre of government, oppressed Israel.   Hazor was situated north of the waters of Merom, now Lake Huleh, in Naphtali : "head of all those kingdoms," *i.e.*, chief city of Northern Palestine (Josh. xi. 1, 10, 11, xii. 19, xix. 36).   Now Tel Khuraibeh (*Robinson*), rather Tel-Hara, an ancient fortress, with wall, ruins, and pottery : see *Quart. Statem. Palest. Explor.*] ; *the captain of whose host* (was) *Sisera* [long remembered as a name

of terror and of triumph (1 Sam. xii. 9 ; Ps. lxxxiii. 9). Yet
from him descended the great Rabbi Akiba (*Bartolocci*, iv.
272), standard-bearer to Barcoceba in the Jewish war of independence. His name occurs among the Nethinim, or servants of
the temple, who returned from Babylon with Zerubbabel
(Ezra ii. 53 ; and in Neh. vii. 54, 55, associated with *Harsha*,
apparently connected with Harosheth], *which dwelt in
Harosheth of the Gentiles* [so called from the mixed races that
inhabited it : in "Galilee of the nations" (Isa. ix. 1). The
name means *workmanship, carving*. Donaldson conjectured
(*Prœlect. Philolog.*), that this being a timber district, rich in cedars
and firs, Jabin employed the Israelites in hewing wood at
Harosheth for transport to Zidon, and that these wood-cutters
armed with axes formed the soldiers of Barak's army. Harosheth
was west of the Lake Merom, from which the Jordan issues in
one stream. But Lieut. Conder places Haroshéth at *Harathiyeh*,
a tel or mound north of Kishon, which separates it from Mount
Carmel, and in the south-east corner of the plain of Akka].
(3) *And the children of Israel cried unto the* LORD [Jehovah
(see ch. iii. 9)] ; *for he had nine hundred chariots of iron*
[ch. i. 19 ; Josh. xvii. 16]; *and twenty years he mightly*
[tyrannically, 'sharply,' as the same word is translated in
ch. viii. 1 ; בְּחָזְקָה] *oppressed* [לָחַץ the same word as in Exod.
iii. 9], *the children of Israel*. (4) *And Deborah, a prophetess*
[Heb. '*a woman, a prophetess :*' a female in authority was so
rare a thing, that the reason is subjoined—she was a *prophetess*
(see verses 6, 9, 14, ch. v.), like Miriam (Exod. xv. 20) ; Huldah
(2 Kings xxii. 14)], *the wife of Lapidoth, she judged* [Heb.
judging, implying that she *permanently* judged : not merely
delivering them from the foe, but judging in civil causes],
Israel at that time [Deborah means a 'bee,' a personal, or an
official name, applied to poets, seers, and priestesses. The
symbol of a monarch in Egypt—a honey bee to her friends,
and a stinging bee to the enemy]. (5) *And she dwelt* [rather
sat in judgment (see Ps. ix. 4 ; Judg. v. 10)] *under the palm-
tree of Deborah, between Ramah* [now *Er-Ram in Benjamin*] *and
Bethel* [now *Beitin*, Josh. vii. 2] *in Mount Ephraim, and the
children of Israel came up to her for judgment* [the place of

justice was regarded as on a spiritual elevation, to which the
people 'came *up*' (Deut. xvii. 8). The supreme judge had
to decide such questions as the lower courts could not decide.
The 'Deborah-palm,' instead of the ordinary place of justice, the gate (Ruth iv. 1, 2), was suitable to the unsettled
times in which she judged; see note xx. 33]. (6) *And she
sent* [implying her authority] *and called Barak* [meaning
'lightning:' like the Boanerges of the New Testament (Mark
ii. 17), the Prince *Barca* (compare Matt. xxviii. 3; see
note vers. 8, 9)], *the son of Abinoam out of Kedesh-Naphtali*
[Josh. xix. 37, xii. 22: a Levitical city of refuge assigned
to the Gershonite Levites (xx. 7). Now *Kades*, on a high
ridge jutting out from the hills at the western edge of the
lake Huleh, the marshy basin through which Jordan passes
into the sea of Merom, from which Kades lies north-west
four miles distant], *and said unto him, Hath not the* LORD
[JEHOVAH] *God of Israel commanded* [James v. 10: Deborah,
'the prophetess,' speaks in the name of 'Jehovah of Israel,'
who was now about to interpose for His people against their
oppressor, as formerly in Egypt], (*saying*), *Go and draw*
[מְשֹׁךְ, *proceed in a long-drawn train* (xx. 27; Exod. xii. 21);
the captain and warriors drawing after him] *toward Mount
Tabor* [rising from the plain of Esdraelon or Jezreel, where
Sisera's chariots would be gathered. The mountain being on
the border of Zebulun, and near Issachar, would be a
convenient centre to which the Israelites could muster from
the north and south. Moreover, from it as from a vantage
ground, they could rush down upon the Canaanites, now Jebel
et Tur, a large flat-topped limestone mountain, with truncated
cone, north-east of the plain of Jezreel, standing alone. On
its top are the remains of ancient fortifications. The top is
an oblong almost a mile in circumference], *and take with thee
ten thousand men of the children of Naphtali, and of the children
of Zebulun* [*i.e.*, gather them first, then proceed to Mount
Tabor, and from that height descend upon the enemy encamped in the valley of Kishon. *Kishon* means *bent like a
bow :* a *torrent* (*nachal*) perennial for eight miles; fed from
sources along the whole plain of Jezreel. Now *Nah'r Mukatha*,

flowing north-west beneath the height Harothiyeh (Harosheth) into the bay of Acca and the Mediterranean. It is called 'that ancient river,' or torrent of the olden time, as being the scene of former battles (v. 21). The upper Kishon swells into a muddy torrent in the sudden rain storms of winter]. *And I will draw* [the same Hebrew as that for 'draw' in ver. 6. The people "willingly offered themselves" (ver. 3), being 'drawn' by Barak who belonged to Naphtali, a tribe prophetically famed for ability to "give goodly words" (Gen. xlix. 21). But God it was who really *drew* them. So spiritually (Song Sol. i. 4; John vi. 44, xii. 32)] *unto thee, to the river* [*Nachal,* 'a torrent,'] *Kishon, Sisera, the captain of Jabin's army, with his chariots, and his multitude* [God by His secret providence drew Sisera to the very spot about to be fatal to him. Sisera and his forces thought they were fulfilling their own counsel; "but they knew not the thought of the Lord, neither understood they His counsel"; for He was "gathering them as the sheaves into the floor," that "the daughter of Zion" might "arise and thresh" (Mic. iv. 12, 13): type of His gathering Antichrist and his forces to their place of doom (Rev. xvi. 14, 16, xix. 19, 20; Ps. lxxxiii. 9, 10). God draws His people to their salvation (ver. 6; Josh. vi. 44): the ungodly to their destruction (1 Kings xxii. 19–23). Barak's 'ten thousand' were but a little band against Sisera's 'multitude.' But their fewness magnified the power of God (2 Chron. xiv. 11; Judg. vii. 2, 7); *and I will deliver him into thine hand.* (8) *And Barak said unto her, If thou wilt go with me, then I will go; but if thou wilt not go with me, (then) I will not go* [his faith was sincere, but weak, like the strength of a child that cannot stand alone. He leant upon a *woman* (Deborah) for the confirmation of his faith; therefore, though he should conquer, yet the glory of completing the victory by slaying the leader of the enemy should be not his, but that of a *woman* (Jael) (ver. 9, 17, &c.). God's command and promise ought to have been enough for him (ver. 6, 7). He is ranked between Gideon and Samson in the list of examples of faith in Heb. xi. 32–34]. (9) *And she said, I will surely go with thee: notwithstanding the journey* [Heb. 'the way.' The

weaker vessel had the stronger faith. So sure is she of
success because of God's promise, that she calls the perilous
war which he was undertaking simply ' a way ' or ' journey ']
that thou takest shall not be for thine honour [God using
the weakness of a woman to inflict the decisive blow (1
Cor. i. 26–31)], *for the* LORD [Jehovah] *shall sell Sisera* [even
as before He sold Israel into Sisera's hand (ver. 2) *into the hand
of a woman* [Barak would think Deborah to be meant. The
event alone unfolded the prophecy]. *And Deborah arose, and
went with Barak to Kedesh* [not that in Naphtali, which is
distant 30 miles of most difficult country from Mount Tabor,
but at *Kadis*, along the sea of Galilee, within easy reach of
Mount Tabor, which was only 16 miles distant, and was the
scene of the battle. The sources of the Kishon are at *El
Mujahiyeh*, ' the springhead', 3 miles west of the foot of Mount
Tabor]. (10) *And Barak called Zebulun and Naphtali to Kedesh;
and he went up* [to Mount Tabor, ver. 12] *with ten thousand
men at his feet* [*i.e.*, following him, so margin Exod. xi. 8 ;
1 Kings xx. 10] ; *and Deborah went up with him.* (11) *Now
Heber the Kenite, (which was) of the children of Hobab* [rather
place the clause thus, " had severed himself from the Kenites,
(which were) of the children of Hobab "], *the father-in-law*
[rather " brother-in-law," as חֹתֵן, *chotheen*, means often. Reuel or
Raguel was Hobab's father, and Moses' father-in-law (Exod. ii.
18). Jethro, as being the elder brother, succeeded Reuel in the
hereditary priesthood. He left the Israelites to go to his home
in Midian, before they reached Sinai (Exod. xviii. 27). But
Hobab, at Moses' entreaty (Numb. x. 29–32), accompanied them,
and settled in Canaan (Judg. i. 16). Being the *younger*, he was
not, like Jethro, bound to his tribe by the duties devolving on
an eldest son. As Jethro helped Moses in counsel, so Hobab,
like an experienced Arab chief, was quick-eyed in discerning
the best places for encampment, water, and pasture. Hobab's
family by joining Israel escaped the doom of Amalek (1 Sam.
xv. 6)] *of Moses, had severed himself* [*permanently;* for the
Hebrew participle, *niphrad*, implies *continuous action*, instead of
the perfect. Like Ruth i. 16; 2 Cor. vi. 17] *from the Kenites,
and pitched his tent unto the plain* [rather ' the oak ' or ' tere-

binth' tree: אֵלוֹן] *of Zaanaim* (Josh. xix. 33). Zaanaim is
identical with Bitzaanaim, probably the modern *Bessum*, in
a broad plain between Mount Tabor and Kedesh or *Kadis*,
near *Adami* (*Dameh*) and Nekeb (*Nakib*), which are associated
with Zaanannim in Josh. xix. 33. The Kenite Heber's migration from Southern Judah, whither he had previously come
from Jericho (i. 16 ; 1 Chron. ii. 54, 55), took place a short
while before, probably owing to the pressure of the Philistines
on Judah (iii. 31, v. 6, 24). This is introduced here with a
view to the sequel ver. 17–22] *which* (*is*) *by Kedesh* [see note
ver. 10]. (12) *And they showed Sisera that Barak the son of*
Abinoam was gone up to Mount Tabor. (13) *And Sisera*
gathered together all his chariots, (even) nine hundred chariots of
iron, and all the people that (were) with him, from Harosheth of
the Gentiles unto the river of Kishon [*i.e.*, from west to east of
the plain of Jezreel ; unto the sources of the Kishon, at the
modern *El Mujahiyeh*, the 'springhead,' where there is an
extensive chain of pools and springs, 3 miles west of the foot
of Mount Tabor, the scene of the battle (*Palest. Explor. Quart.*
Statem., Jan. 1877, page 14, and Oct., page 191)]. (14) *And*
Deborah said unto Barak, Up ; for this (is) the day in which the
LORD [JEHOVAH] *hath delivered Sisera into thine hand : is not*
the LORD [JEHOVAH] *gone out before thee ?* [Isa. lii. 12; Mic. ii.
13]. *So Barak went down from Mount Tabor, and ten thousand*
men after him [rushing from the high ground down upon the
Canaanites posted southward at the foot of the conical mountain
on which Endor is situated. So Napoleon acted in his battle
of Tabor]. (15) *And the* LORD [JEHOVAH] *discomfited* [Exod. xiv.
24 : וַיָּהָם : the same Hebrew 'troubled'; applied to *God's con-*
founding the foe with a crash by miraculous interposition through
the phenomena of nature (Ps. cxliv. 6 ; 2 Sam. xxii. 15 ; Judg.
v. 20, implies that God arrayed the powers of nature against
Sisera)] *Sisera, and all (his) chariots, and all (his) host, with the*
edge of the sword before Barak [Ps. xcviii. 1, Jehovah's interposition left the foe a prey to Israel's sword] ; *so that Sisera*
lighted down off (his) chariot, and fled away on his feet [like a
common soldier. His chariot, which had been his help (Ps.
lxix. 22), became a hindrance, when God was against him].

F

(16) *But Barak pursued after the chariots, and after the host, unto Harosheth of the Gentiles; and all the host of Sisera fell upon the edge of the sword*: (*and*) *there was not a man* [Hebrew *unto one*] *left.* (17) *Howbeit Sisera fled away on his feet to the tent of Jael the wife of Heber the Kenite* [he fled to the *women's* tent which was separate from, and more secure than, the men's tent (see Gen. xviii. 6, 10, xxiv. 67). The Kenites retained their primitive tent life (Jer. xxxv. 6–10). If we identify Kedesh with *Kadis* (note ver. 10, 11) and Zaanaim with *Bessum*, the whole of Sisera's flight, instead of 30 miles over mountains 4000 feet high to Kedesh Naphtali (!), is but 5 or 6 miles from the battle-field in the opposite direction to the course whither his army was pursued towards Harosheth, a distance quite possible to him, though fatigued with the battle]: *for* (*there was*) *peace between Jabin the king of Hazor and the house of Heber the Kenite* [*i.e.,* with that clan of the Kenites. Their separation from their countrymen to join themselves to Israel was rewarded by their being exempted by God from the chastisement by Jabin with which God visited Israel for idolatry]. (18) *And Jael went out to meet Sisera* [having heard of the victory, and looking out for fresh tidings. On seeing Sisera, she forms her plan on the spur of the moment; she will complete the triumph over the foe of God's people. Her guile and treachery were the alloy in her faith. So the lie of Rahab so far marred her faith (Josh. ii. 4–6, 8–15); God's "children will not lie" (Isa. lxiii. 8; Zeph. iii. 13). The good end will not justify bad means], *and said unto him, Turn in, my lord, turn in to me* [the phrase of hospitality; turn in from the road (Gen. xix. 2, 3)]; *fear not. And when he had turned in unto her into the tent, she covered him with a mantle* [rug or counterpane, that he might sleep after his fatigue]. (19) *And he said unto her, Give me, I pray thee, a little water to drink; for I am thirsty. And she opened a bottle of milk* [ver. 25, giving him what was better than his request], *and gave him drink, and covered him.* (20) *Again he said unto her, Stand in the door of the tent, and it shall be, when any man doth come and inquire of thee, and say, Is there any man here?* *that thou shalt say, No* [the duplicity which he designed her to practise towards others she practised

on himself (Isa. xxxiii. 1)]. (21) *Then Jael Heber's wife, took a nail of the tent* [a tent plug], *and took an hammer in her hand, and went softly unto him, and smote the nail into his temples, and fastened it into the ground (for he was fast asleep and weary)* [which accounts for Sisera's not hearing Jael's approach, and for his non-resistance to the blow which killed him. Her burning sympathy with the oppressed, and her faith in Israel's God, whose worship she had espoused in opposition to the idols of Canaan, and her bold execution of her dangerous undertaking, deserve all praise, though, as in Ehud's case, there was the alloy of treachery and assassination (ch. iii. 20–30), Hence she and Ehud are not enumerated among the examples of faith in the list, Heb. xi.]; *so he died* [see Ezek. xxxii. 23]. (23) *And behold, as Barak pursued Sisera, Jael came out to meet him, and said unto him, Come, and I will show thee the man whom thou seekest. And when he came into her (tent), behold, Sisera lay dead, and the nail (was) in his temples.* [Barak thus, as Deborah had foretold (ver. 9), was too late to win the crowning honour of the victory by slaying Sisera : a woman had forestalled him.] (23) *So God* [ELOHIM here, the God who rules the world at large; but JEHOVAH, in covenant with His people, is found elsewhere, in chs. iv., v.] *subdued on that day Jabin the king of Canaan before the children of Israel* [Ps. lxviii. 35, xliv. 3, cxv. 1]. (24) *And the hand of the children of Israel prospered* [Hebrew, *went going on and being hard* (see marg. Gen. xxvi. 13 ; 2 Sam. v. 10). Barak's victory gave the first impulse to a series of efforts, eventuating in the utter overthrow of the Canaanite kingdom of Jabin, and the complete independence of Israel, so that the Canaanites no more recovered their power over Israel], *and prevailed against Jabin the king of Canaan, until they had destroyed Jabin king of Canaan*

CHAPTER V.

SONG OF DEBORAH AND BARAK.

(1) *Then sang Deborah and Barak the son of Abinoam on that day* [it is well to praise *at once*, whilst the heart is full of gratitude for the deliverance vouchsafed. Delay dulls heartiness. Eaten bread is soon forgotten (2 Chron. xx. 26; Isa. xxxviii. 9–22; Luke i. 64–79)], *saying* ['sang' is singular and feminine; therefore the song was the composition of *Deborah alone*, who was at once prophetess and poetess: so David (2 Sam. xxiii. 1, 2. Vers. 3, 7, 12, prove that she was the sole composer. Barak, probably, with a chorus of men, took up the second verse, and sung it as an antiphone, summing up as it does the substance of the song. So Miriam with the chorus of women took up as an antiphone the first verse of Moses' ode of thanksgiving at the Red Sea (Exod. xv. 1, 20, 21). The song falls into *three sections*, each section containing *three strophes*. The first and second sections begin with a call to praise God (ver. 2, 12); the third (ver. 22–31) closes with a prayer embodying the prophetical anticipation (grounded on the victory over Jabin) of the destruction of all the foes of Jehovah, and of the triumph of them that love Him (ver. 31)].
(2) *Praise ye the* LORD [JEHOVAH] *for the avenging of Israel* [so Montanus, Junius, Tremellius, Munster and Castalio, and Belg. versions. Literally, "for avenging the avenges of Israel" (Ps. xviii. 47). But Gesenius takes it from an Arabic root, as the Cod. Alex. of the Septuagint, and as the parallelism of the clauses favours, "for the leading of the *leaders* (the princes) in Israel," answering to "for the *people* willingly offering themselves," also ver. 9, corresponds; so also in Deut.

xxxii. 42. Keil less probably translates " for the fact that the
strong showed themselves *strong* " (פְּרָעוֹת), *the hairy ones, i.e.,* ' the
strong '], *when* [*rather for the fact that*] *the people* (ver. 18)
willingly offered themselves. [In the time of the Judges, when
as yet there was no king to raise a levy, the mustering of an
army depended on the example set by the leaders of the
nation, and the voluntary rising of the people. This willingness is the gift of God (ch. iv. 10 ; 1 Chron. xxix. 5, 9 ; Ps. cx.
3 ; 2 Chron. xvii. 16 ; 2 Cor. viii. 5 ; Phil. ii. 13)]. (3) *Hear, O
ye kings* [God's dealings with Israel, the representative nation,
are designed to be a lesson to all nations and their princes
(Ps. ii. 2, 10–12)], *give ear, O ye princes : I (even) I will sing
unto the* LORD [JEHOVAH] ; *I will sing (praise)* [*Zimmeer*, " chant
a psalm to an instrumental accompaniment"] *to the* LORD
[JEHOVAH] *God of Israel.* (4) LORD [JEHOVAH], *when Thou
wentest out of Seir, when thou marchest out of the field of Edom*
[the prophetess makes Jehovah's original manifestation of
Himself as Israel's God at Sinai (Exod. xix.), where He gave the
Law as the seal of His covenant with them as His peculiar
people, the starting point of her thanksgiving (Deut. xxxiii. 2).
To Israel advancing from the west, Jehovah's glory appeared
flashing from Sinai, and from Seir and Edom to the eastward
of Sinai. That primary and chief manifestation was the basis
for all subsequent manifestations of His grace to Israel ; such
as now the victory vouchsafed over Sisera (Deut. iv. 33)], *the
earth trembled, and the heavens dropped, the clouds also dropped
water* [Exod. xix. 16, 18 ; Ps. lxviii. 8, 9 : " Thou didst send a
plentiful *rain*," not expressly mentioned in the history, but
implied in the ' cloud ' there noticed (Hab. iii. 3–6)]. (5) *The
mountains melted from before the* LORD [JEHOVAH], *(even) that
Sinai* [the prophetess graphically pointing to it as if before her
eyes] *from before the* LORD [JEHOVAH] *God of Israel.* (6) *In the
days of Shamgar the son of Anath* [see ch. iii. 31], *in the days
of Jael, the highways were unoccupied, and the travellers* [those who
were obliged to travel. Literally (*holkee nethiboth*) " those who
went (usually) on beaten paths "] *walked through byways* [*crooked
ways.* Deborah shows that, highly as Jehovah had exalted Israel,
apostasy brought the nation low, until she arose. Although

Shamgar had for a time delivered Israel from the Philistines in the south (iii. 31), and though Jael, who afterwards slew Sisera, was then alive (and possibly had helped Shamgar against the Philistines, before her husband Heber's migration from the south of Judah to Zaanaim in the north), Israel was brought so low that none durst venture on the public roads through fear of the enemy].   (7) (*The inhabitants of*) *the villages ceased* [*perazon;* Speaker's Commentary after Gesenius translates ' princes ' (or magistrates); Septuagint, δυνάσται ; Jerome, ' warriors.' But it would be untrue to say the magistrates ceased at the very time when (ver. 6) Shamgar and Jael were judges in Israel. The Rabbins rightly explain the words, *the inhabitants of the open flat country with unwalled villages,* in contradistinction to the walled towns (Deut. iii. 5 ; 1 Sam. vi. 18 ; Ezra xxxviii. 11 ; Zech. ii. 4 ; Hab. iii. 14)], *they ceased in Israel, until that I Deborah arose, that I arose a mother* [one ruling with maternal care (2 Sam. xx. 19). So 'father ' (Isa. xxii. 21)] *in Israel.* (8) *They chose new gods* [the cause of all the misery of Israel, apostasy : idolatry is almost as old as the fall, yet it is a *novelty.* The Ancient of days was everlasting before it (Deut. xxxii. 17).   " The serpent's grammar first taught men to decline God plurally, ' Ye shall be as gods ' " (Trapp)]; *then* (*was*) *war in the gates* [the enemy, in execution of God's wrath (Deut. xxxii. 19–22), pressed up to the very ' gates ' of Israel's towns.   The gates, the usual scene of the administration of justice, became the scene of war]: *was there a shield or spear seen among forty thousand in Israel* ? [So under the Philistine oppression (1 Sam. xiii. 19–22 ; note Judg. iii. 31): just as Porsena the Etrurian king forbade the vanquished Romans to use iron, except in agriculture (Pliny xxxiv. 14)].   (9) *My heart* (*is*) [*drawn*] *towards the governors of Israel that* [or else, repeat " My heart is (also) toward those that " (Maurer)] *offered themselves willingly among the people.* [See note ver. 2.]   *Bless ye the* LORD [JEHOVAH].   (10) *Speak* [שִׂיחוּ, *Reflect,* viz., on Jehovah's deliverance of Israel.   Not only ' bless ' Him with the *mouth* (ver. 9), but ' meditate ' with the *heart* (margin ; compare Rom. x. 9, 10).   But Maurer translates " sing;" our English version translates the same Hebrew in Pss. cv. 2, cxlv. 5,

'speak'], *ye that ride on white asses, ye that sit in judgment*
[the colour meant is *white-spotted ;* 'asses with white spots'
were highly prized; for there are no asses white all over.
Riders on white-spotted asses (x. 4, xii. 14) were *the better
classes,* who are further described as those " that sit on *carpets,*"
or " *coverings,*" or else " saddle clothes:" מִדִּין, from מַד with the
archaic plural ending, such as are put upon asses (Matt. xxi. 7).
The Hebrew pointing opposes the English Version 'judgment'],
and walk by the way [*the humbler classes* that walk on foot, in
contradistinction to the former, the upper classes. Ye too have
reason to meditate, or speak in praise of Jehovah, for having
made the public ways free from the enemy (ver. 6)]. (11) (*They
that are delivered) from the noise of archers in the place of
drawing water* [some explain, *away from* (as in Numb. xv. 24)
the tumult of hostile archers who assailed any Israelites that
repaired to the places of drawing water. After praising
Jehovah for rendering their *public roads* passable, the prophetess
adds, that they have also now access to their *places of drawing water,* without fear of the *hostile archers,* who formerly
infested them, in order to rob and carry them away as captives
(Exod. ii. 17–19 ; Gen. xxvi. 18–21 ; Jer. iv. 29). A great
blessing in a country which suffers from want of water.
Deborah being herself from Benjamin, naturally makes 'archers'
to represent warriors in general, as being the kind of warfare
for which the tribe was famed (1 Chron. xii. 2). Piscator
translates מִן best, *on account of* the noise, &c., *i.e., on account of
deliverance from* the noise, &c.], *there shall they rehearse* [relate
in thanksgiving] *the righteous acts* [acts of *saving* His people, in
righteous faithfulness to His covenant (1 Sam. xii. 7 ; Mic. vi.
5). God's salvation is always in the way of *righteousness,*
not merely mercy (Isa. xlvi. 13)] *of the* LORD [JEHOVAH],
(*even) the righteous acts (toward the inhabitants) of His villages
in Israel* [see note ver. 7. The Israelites, now that Sisera
was overthrown, could leave their hiding places in the
heights and the walled towns, and return to the villages and
open plains] ; *then shall the people of the* LORD [JEHOVAH]
go down to the gates [viz., of their cities, for the peaceful
pursuits of commerce and for justice, the gates being the

usual place for both : now that there was no longer "war in the gates" (ver. 8)]. (12) *Awake, awake* [the tone in the Hebrew is on the last syllable of both, *'uri', 'uri'*, to express the rapid outburst of praise to Jehovah], *Deborah ; awake, awake; utter a song* [she stirs up her own spirit in suitable song to describe the conflict, and stirs up Barak to lead away the captives; giving all the glory to Jehovah]; *arise, Barak, and lead thy captivity · captive* [lead away captive, as the fruit of thy victory, men, sheep, and cattle (margin, Amos iv. 10; marg., 2 Chron. xxi. 17)], *thou son of Abinoam.* (13) *Then he made him that remaineth* [the small remnant left in Israel] *have dominion over the nobles* [the haughty oppressors] *among the people: the* LORD [JEHOVAH] *made me have dominion over the mighty.* [So the Masoretic pointing requires the translation to be יְרַד, coming from רָדָה, ' rule.' Only a remnant of Israel joined in the conflict—" ten thousand " (ch. iv. 10)—a mere handful, to oppose ' the nobles ' and ' the mighty ' of Sisera's vast army; but Jehovah was for the remnant, so they gained " dominion over the mighty." Rather point it יָרַד, perfect : in the same sense as יָרְדוּ (ver. 14). " Then *came down* (from their refuges in the heights to the battle plain of Jezreel) what remained (the remnant) of nobles of the people (Israel);" Jehovah (ch. iv. 6, 14) came down to me (Deborah, ver. 7, *i.e., to my joy*) among the mighty (Jehovah came down among the heroes of Israel against the foe)]. (14) *Out of Ephraim (was there) a root of them against Amalek* [rather " out of Ephraim (there came down to the battle those) whose root (literally, ' a root of those') was (*i.e.*, who had settled and taken root, Isa. xxvii. 6) *in* Amalek," viz., in the " mount of the Amalekites," as it was called from its original occupants : for though the Edomite Amalekites dwelt in the region between Egypt and Palestine and the Sinaitic peninsula, the earlier Amalekites sprang from Ham, according to Arab writers, and spread from the Persian gulf westward, so that traces of them occur in central as well as southern Pales-tine (Gen. xiv. 7 ; Judg. iii. 13, xii. 15)]; *after* [*i.e.*, following] *thee* [Ephraim came] *Benjamin, among thy* [Ephraim's] *people* [Benjamin lived farther south, and so would come *behind* Ephraim in marching to the battle plain of Jezreel : at the same time it is implied, that Benjamin was *subordinate* in importance to the more powerful tribe Ephraim, and came on with Ephraim's ' people ']; *out of Machir* [*i.e.*, from *western* Manasseh, ' Machir,' Manasseh's only son, poetically standing for the tribe, and here only the *western cis-Jordanic* portion of it (Gen. l. 23 ; Numb. xxvi. 29, &c., xxvii. 1). Gilead (Judg. v. 17) stands for eastern Manasseh] *came down governors* [ver. 9, Commanders in war], *and out of Zebulun they that handle* [*Mashak*, ' draw,' as in ch. iv. 6] *the pen of the writer* [rather " marchers (in long *drawn* train), with (בּ) the staff (*shebet*) of the musterer-general" (סֹפֵר, the writer or numberer who levied the troops—2 Kings xxv. 19, " The principal scribe of the host"— 2 Chron. xxvi. 11): so in general, *the military leader*]. (15) *And the princes of* [in בּ] *Issachar (were) with Deborah ; even Issachar, and also Barak* [so the old versions rightly read *Saree*, instead of *Sarai*, ' my princes ': for Deborah did not belong to Issachar, and she would hardly speak of herself at first in the *first* person ' my,' then in the *third* person " with Deborah ;" *with the forces of Zebulun and Naphtali*, answering to ' Issachar ']: *he was sent on foot* [*i.e.*, was *impelled* by warlike enthusiasm to *rush down on foot ;* literally, as in Job xviii. 8, *was driven through his feet*] *into the valley* [of Jezreel]. *For the divisions* [rather " *at* the *brooks* of Reuben ; " as in Job xx. 17, Reuben being famed for his pastures, must have possessed many *brooks*, בִּפְלַגּוֹת] *(there were) great thoughts* [resolutions] *of heart* [but no practical result ensued]. (16) *Why abodest thou among the sheepfolds* [מִשְׁפְּתָיִם, the enclosures made of hurdles, in which during the summer the flocks are kept by night. The great number is used because the folds of this sort were divided into *two* parts for the different kinds of flock. Found also in Gen. xlix. 14, English Version, " two burdens," where, as here, an indolent agricultural people is pictured, preferring endurance of oppression to a war of independence. Very differently Reuben acted at Moses' call ; instead of 'sitting' among their 'sheepfolds,' they accompanied their brethren to war (Numb. xxxii. 6–33)], *to hear the bleatings of the flocks* [*Sheriquoth :* rather *pipings* of the shepherds whilst guarding their flocks : instead of obeying the summons of the trumpet's shrill war-blast]. *For* [לְ *in connec-*

tion with: not ב as in ver. 15, *at*] *the divisions* [rather *brooks*] *of Reuben* (*there were*) *great searchings of heart* [one letter alone is altered from ver. 16 : *Hique*ʀ*ee* instead of *hique*ǫ*ee :* mag- nanimous *resolutions* ending in empty *deliberations,* and those deliberations proving to be such *searchings* of Reuben's heart, as showed him wanting in the hour of trial and of Israel's need (Dan. v. 27; so Luke ii. 35; 1 Cor. xi. 19)]. (17) *Gilead* [*i.e.,* the tribes of Gad and the eastern half Manasseh. For the western half Manasseh joined in the war; ver. 14, 'Machir'] *abode beyond Jordan* [eastward; taking no part in the war]: *and why did Dan remain in ships ?* [Joppa the sea- port was in the territory of Dan (Josh. xix. 46, marg.) Pro- bably the Danites traded with the Phœnicians. Selfish love of commercial gain kept Dan from making any sacrifice for the nation's independence, " dressing up their own cabins, when the whole ship was in danger" (Trapp)]. *Asher continued* [*sat* still] *on the sea-shore* [Hebrew, " the *haven of the sea,*" as in Gen. xlix. 13, *i.e.,* the Mediterranean (Josh. xix. 28, 29)], *and abode in his breaches* [*i.e.,* the creeks and river mouths by which his coast was *broken*]. (18) *Zebulun and Naphtali* (*were*) *a people* (*that*) *jeoparded* ['despised.' Compare as to the Christian warfare, Paul's contempt of life, and all things for Christ (Acts xx. 24; Phil. iii. 8; Rev. ii. 10] *their lives unto the death in the high places of the field* [*i.e.,* on Mount Tabor]. (19) *The kings came* (*and*) *fought* [the triumphal ode makes a sudden transition to describe the foe's advance]; *then fought the kings of Canaan* [allied with Jabin, and arrayed in battle under Sisera's command. So the elder Jabin had other Canaanite kings allied to him (Josh. xi. 1, 2, 5)] *in Taanach by* [*over* על] *the waters of Megiddo* [the battle was not fought at Taanach or Megiddo, but near Mount Tabor (ch. iv. 6, 7), " Drew toward Mount Tabor—to the river Kishon " (Josephus, *Ant.,* v. 5, 3). The sources of the Kishon are at *El Mujahiyeh,* " the spring- head," a chain of pools three miles west of Mount Tabor. Had the battle been at Taanach, he would have had to leave the stronghold of Mount Tabor, and traverse fifteen miles over a boggy plain to attack the Canaanites posted strongly on the low hills of Taanach. The words " in Taanach " must either be a district name for *all* the plain of which Taanach was the capital, or translate it "in sandy soil," which is the soil found near Tabor. Megiddo (from the root *jeded*, "to cut down;" meaning *the grazing place*, 'cut down' by sheep) answers to the ruin *Mejedd'a* in the Jordan valley, near Bethshean, *i.e., Beisan;* and the valley of Megiddon is that which leads down from Jezreel to Bethshean; and the "waters of Megiddo" answer to the strong stream *Nahr Jalud*, supplied from large springs round *Mejedd'a* (*Palestine Explor. Quart. Statem.*, Oct. 1877, pp. 190–192; Jan. 1877, pp. 18–20)]; *they took no gain of money* [not even a *piece of silver*: בֶּצַע, a piece *broken* off. The kings went into battle, expecting rich booty after slaying the Israelites, but they did not get as much as a single piece of silver (compare ver. 30)]. (20) *They* [the stars] *fought from heaven* [the reason why the kings utterly failed: Jehovah from heaven fought against them: (note iv. 14, 15; Ps. xviii. 40, lxviii. 35)]; *the stars in* [Heb. 'from'] *their courses* [*i.e.*, from on high] *fought against Sisera.* [Josephus (*Ant.*, v. 5, 4) says that a tempest with violent rain and hailstorm beat in the faces of the Canaanites just as the battle began. The overflow of the Kishon (ver. 21) confirms this. So in Josh. x. 10, 11, the heavenly bodies exercise an influence on the atmosphere as to tempests, rain, hail, and lightning. If the battle began before day, whilst "the stars" were still visible, the allusion would be the more appropriate, or probably it was the time of the autumn storms, when *meteoric falling stars* flashed upon the defeated host as they fled away by night]. (21) *The river of Kishon swept them away* [Ps. lxxxiii. 9, 10], *that ancient river* [*nachal quedumim*, "the torrent of olden time," famed of old as the scene of valorous deeds and battles. Ewald less probably translates "the torrent of *battles*"], *the river Kishon. O my soul, thou hast trodden down strength* [Deborah apostrophises herself exultingly, as the remembrance of the down-treading of the foe by the Israelite army which she led, and with which she identifies herself, rises to her mind's eye. So, in ver. 12, 13. Keil translates, not so well, "Go on, my soul, in strength," still celebrating the victory (ver. 22–31)]. (22) *Then were the horse-hoofs broken by the means of the prancings, the prancings of their mighty ones* [the repetition implies the *incessant continuance of the headlong course of the warriors.* Anciently horses were not shod ; hence their hoofs were ' broken ']. (23) *Curse ye ·Meroz* [if Meroz be *Merasas* or *Murussus,* a ruin four miles north-west of Beisan on the southern slopes of the hills which continue 'little Hermon,' the men of Meroz commanded the pass, and could have prevented the escape of any of Sisera's host in that quarter. *Raumer* identifies Meroz with *Kefr Musr,* south of Tabor. I prefer the former, from the contrast to Jael's conduct. The angel of Jehovah (Josh. v. 14, 15), by the mouth of Deborah, curses Meroz for *omission of service,* where there was afforded a grand opportunity, faint-heartedness and neutrality, where there can be no neutrality (Matt. xii. 30, xxv. 30), as, on the contrary, He blesses Jael for her zeal in behalf of Israel, and faith in intercepting the foe, though her act was sullied by the alloy of treachery. So surely did the curse work, that Meroz is only known now as the city cursed for indifference], *said the angel of the* LORD [JEHOVAH], *curse ye bitterly* [' with cursing '] *the inhabitants thereof ; because they came not to the help of the* LORD [JEHOVAH, *i.e.,* to join in His battle. Those more remote are *blamed.* Meroz, close by, whose opportunity of service was greater, is bitterly *cursed*], *to the help of the* LORD [JEHOVAH] *against* [or *among*] *the mighty.* (24) *Blessed among women shall Jael the wife of Heber the Kenite be; blessed shall she be above* [Heb. *min,* ' apart from,' ' in comparison with '] *women in the tent* [though a Kenite, and a woman, she showed a zeal for Israel which was lacking in the people of Meroz, though Israelites and men : see iv. 11, 17–22. The women's fitting place was " the tent " (Prov. vii. 11 ; Tit. ii. 5), as men's place was the battle field. In the tent Jael, by her patriotic act for her adopted nation, wrought a deliverance which the men of Meroz declined to attempt in the field]. (25) *He asked water, (and) she gave (him) milk : she brought forth butter* [rather '·curdled milk ' (Speaker's Comm.), or else ' cream ' (Keil)] *in a lordly dish* [Heb. ' dish of lords,' *i.e.,* one reserved for noble guests. Wooden platters are commonly used by the Arabs. Copper dishes are reserved for chiefs. The Bedawin have a delicious preparation of curdled milk called *leben,* which they

offer to guests as a delicacy, especially refreshing to one
who is weary; it has a strange *soporific* effect. Jael probably had this effect in view when she offered it to Sisera].
(26) *She put her* [left] *hand to the nail* [tent plug], *and
her right hand to the workman's hammer* [or mallet]; *and
with the hammer she smote* (Heb. 'hammered') *Sisera; she
smote off his head, when she had pierced and stricken* [rather,
"she *smote* his head (not *smote it off:* see ver. iv. 21), and
struck and pierced"] *through his temples.* [He who sought
to crush Israel with 900 iron chariots, was himself crushed
with one iron nail.] (27) *At* [between] *her feet he bowed, he
fell, he lay down; at* [between] *her feet he bowed, he fell; where
he bowed, there he fell down dead.* [The boldness of her act is
expressed in the accumulation of words in the last half of ver.
26 and in ver. 27, the fact that he who so long had been the
terror of Israel fell at a single blow.] (28) *The mother of
Sisera* [the poetess transports us from Sisera's death-chamber
to Sisera's palace far away. What a contrast! Here his mother,
looking from an upper chamber, would be impatiently awaiting
his return with foreboding fears] *looked out of a window, and
cried* [in anxiety] *through the lattice, Why is his chariot (so)
long in coming? why tarry the wheels of his chariots?* (29)
Her wise ladies ['the wisest of her princesses.' Irony. How
the reality showed the folly of their 'wisdom' (1 Cor. i. 19;
Isa. xxix. 14)] *answered her, yea, she returned answer to herself*
[*i.e.,* she tried to allay her own anxiety by the hopes expressed
in ver. 30. Rather the Hebrew is, "but she [אַף הִיא] was
turning back her words to herself;" favouring Keil's explanation : But she would not be quieted by the bright anticipations
of her ladies. She kept repeating to herself her own anxious
question, "Why is his chariot so long in coming?" Then after
this parenthesis, follow the words of her ladies]. (30) *Have
they not sped?* [Heb. 'found' booty. They doubt not Sisera
has been detained by the division of the large booty. Bitter
mocking of the poetess! Sisera himself was all the while
lying a mangled corpse!] *have they (not) divided the prey*
[spoil]; *to every man* [Heb. " to the head of each hero"] *a damsel*
[Heb. '*a womb.*' How debased must these princesses have

become, to speak thus of the dishonour of their sex !] (*or*) *two?
to Sisera a prey* [spoil] *of divers colours* [diverse-coloured cloths],
a prey [spoil] *of divers colours of needlework, of divers colours of
needle-work on both sides* [or the Hebrew dual may mean two
such pieces of divers-coloured needle-work. Sisera's princesses
unintentionally bear testimony to the industry of Israel's
daughters (Rom. xii. 11; Prov. xxxi. 22)] (*meet*) *for the necks of
(them that take) the spoil?* [Hebrew for the necks of the spoil,
i.e., of those to whom the spoil is due, as Sisera and such brave
heroes. So we find, in Job xxxii. 7, ' days ' used for " *men of
days*": ' sin ' for " *a man of* sin " (Prov. xiii. 6). Otherwise
translate " for necks *as* spoil," viz., for the necks of Sisera's
favourites, as his wife, his mother, and his princesses, who
when mentioning spoil would not forget themselves. This I
suggest as preferable to the conjecture of Ewald to read שֵׁגָל,
' the royal spouse,' for שָׁלָל, ' spoil,' on the ground that the
latter has been *thrice* written before, and that the ל thrice used
implied three distinct classes (" *to* every man—to Sisera—for
the neck of the royal spouse ") among whom the booty was to
be divided. My suggestion distinguishes three classes, and
preserves the Hebrew plural 'necks,' which Ewald must explain
singular, ' neck ']. (31) *So let all Thine enemies perish, O* LORD
[JEHOVAH, Ps. lxviii. 1–3; 1 Sam. ii. 10]; *but* (*let*) *them that
love Him* (*be*) *as the sun, when he goeth forth in his might* [Mal.
iv. 2; Dan. xii. 3; Matt. xiii. 43]. *And the land had rest
forty years.*

THE BONDAGE, THE ANSWER TO PRAYER, THE CONFLICT AND VICTORY, THE THANKSGIVING.

1. *The bondage.*—(1) *Its origin.* We have here in typical
miniature the history of redemption. Man's sin is the cause
of man's misery. His misery moves God to mercy. But
when mercy has removed the scourge which sin had entailed,
the sinner revolts ' again ' (Isa. i. 5; Hos. xi. 7). The source
of Israel's distress was " They chose new gods " (ch. v. 8). If
they had been enjoying God, they would have desired none else.

The source of the worldliness of many professors is, they do not
make full proof (Rom. xii. 2) of what God in Christ is to His
people. Idols bring with them chastisements. God overrules
chastisement to be the means of driving His people to prayer.
The way of transgressors is hard ; and the backslider, reproved
by his own backslidings, at last knows to his cost, and
sees that it is an evil thing and bitter, that he has forsaken Jehovah his God (Jer. ii. 19). The cry of carnal men
is merely that of pain by reason of the multitude of oppressors,
but the Israel of God calleth upon God our Maker, whose
prerogative it is to " give songs in the night " (Job xxxv. 9, 10).

(2) *Its severity.*—The servitude of the Israelites under Jabin
was of longer duration than either of the former servitudes, and
it was the more galling, as being within their own borders.
Jehovah, who had ' redeemed ' them (Deut. vii. 8), ' sold ' them
now into the hands of the heathen. The retribution was just ;
they had sold themselves to heathenish ways, so now He sold
them to the heathen oppressor. So always, when the professing church and its individual members yield themselves up to
worldly ways, the Lord righteously gives them over to the world
to distress and harass, that they may learn by experience the
contrast between His happy service and the degrading yoke of
the prince of this world (see 2 Chron. xii. 8 ; John viii. 34 ;
Rom. vi. 16 ; 2 Pet. ii. 19). The Israelites were afraid to
show themselves on their own public roads, and at the places
of drawing water (v. 6, 11). How many Christians so-called
are, through fear of the world, ashamed to avow their convic-
tions in public, or even to resort to prayer meetings or other
religious assemblies, where they might draw the water of life !
(Mark viii. 38 ; John iii. 2, xix. 38.) The carnal influences
around them as effectually disarm them of the shield of faith,
and the sword of the Spirit, as Israel was stripped of shield
and spear among its thousands (v. 8), lest they should rise
against the oppressor. Hence they are an easy prey to the
fiery darts of the wicked one. The place of spiritual privileges
(v. 11) is one of special danger. Worldly thoughts there
intrude, and Satan will tempt us, amidst the services of the
closet and of the sanctuary, to wander in thought after earthly

idols of pleasure, gain, and ambition. This is the way to be uncomfortable in our religion. The Laodicean professor, who aims at being as like the men of this age as possible, and seeks to combine the service of God and Mammon, misses both worlds. He cannot enjoy thoroughly this world, nor has he any real delight in the heavenly world. Such a one lacks all spiritual power, for worldly policy is incompatible with spiritual power. If Jehovah were to leave such a time-server to himself, he must be lost. But the objects of His grace are in due time chastised of the Lord, that they may not be condemned with the world (1 Cor. xi. 32). Their 'peace' is taken from them, in order that they may return to the only rest for the soul (Ps. cxvi. 6, 7; Matt. xi. 29–31). They are put in mental bondage through fear of death (Heb. ii. 15; Prov. xxviii. 1; Ps. liii. 5), that calling upon God in trouble, and being delivered, they may no longer be in terror of God (Gen. iii. 8, 10), but see His face with joy, and know Him in Christ Jesus as their Deliverer and their Life (Job xxxiii. 23–28).

2. *The answer to prayer.*—To the eye of man there seemed no hope for Israel, few in number of soldiery and without arms, whereas their oppressors were an armed multitude, supplied with 900 war chariots of iron, and supported by royal allies (iv. 3, 7, v. 19). Such was man's state, helplessly bound under the power of the strong man armed, who kept his palace in peace (Luke xi. 21), and unable to resist the principalities, powers, and world rulers of this present darkness (Eph. vi. 12—in the Sinaitic, Vatican, and Alexandrine MSS.). But Jehovah looked when there was none to help, and saw that there was no man, and wondered that there was no intercessor: therefore His own arm brought salvation (Isa. lix. 16, lxiii. 5). The means used were so inadequate in themselves to the deliverance of Israel, that none could doubt it was wholly of God, in answer to His people's cry. Deborah, a woman, summoned Barak, who had some faith, yet a faith so feeble that it could not stand alone. He commanded but ten thousand men. But one power they had, which was more than a match for all their foes. It was the same as that which saves man: "Is not Jehovah gone out before thee?" (iv. 14). The Lord Jesus

the Breaker is come up before, and has broken through the gate
of death, the penalty of our sin which He paid, and has passed
before us, as our Head, ensuring our eternal salvation (Mic. ii.
13 ; Hos. xiii. 14). Barak's case may encourage weak believers.
God can make even them more than conquerors through
Christ. ˙Only let them not lean on a human arm, but cry to
Jehovah Jesus, not to any fellow-man : " If Thou wilt go with
me, then I will go " (iv. 8).

3. *The conflict and victory.*—*The instruments of obtaining
the triumph over Israel's oppressors* were—(1) *the people* who
" willingly offered themselves " (ver. 2). So, in our redemption,
God forces no man. Each of us can bar the door of his heart
against the Lord Jesus, who knocks begging admittance (Rev.
ii. 20). But the Lord Himself alone can open the door, as He
opened the heart of Lydia (Acts xvi. 14), and will open it if
we pray (Ps. cxix. 18). His people shall be willing in the day
of His power (Ps. cx. 3). The same power which drew Sisera
into Kishon to his destruction, drew Barak and his ten thousand
men into Mount Tabor to their deliverance (iv. 6, 7). So it is
only by the gracious influences of the Holy Spirit that the
Father draws the sinner to his Saviour, leading him to pray,
" Draw me, and we will run after Thee," and drawing him in
answer to the prayer (John vi. 44, 65 ; Song Sol. i. 4).
Moreover, after having been so drawn, we need to yield ourselves wholly up to the gracious Spirit, in order to fight effectually the good fight of faith (Rom. vi. 13, 19). This was the
secret of Nehemiah's success (iii. 20, iv. 6): "The people earnestly
repaired," for they " had a mind to work." Compare the case
of Hezekiah (2 Chron. xxxi. 21, and Col. iii. 23 ; Gal. iv. 18).

(2) *The governors of Israel* also were the foremost that
offered themselves willingly among the people (v. 9). Their
example influenced the rest. Deborah induced Barak ; and
Barak in turn induced the men of Zebulun and Naphtali ; and
these again influenced the great tribe of Ephraim, also Benjamin,
western Manasseh, and the princes of Issachar (v. 14, 15).
Thus good is self-propagating. None can say, I am too
insignificant to render help in the battle of the Lord ; for God
chooses the weak things of the world to confound the things

G

which are mighty (1 Cor. i. 27). It is so especially in the deliverance wrought by our Redeemer. He, the antitypical Barak, was " made of a woman," in order that He might bruise the serpent's head for us (Gen. iii. 15 ; Gal. iv. 4, 5). Having ascended up on high, Jesus " led captivity captive " (Judg. v. 12 ; Ps. lxviii. 18 ; Eph. iv. 18). Sin and the curse, Satan and Death, are the captives which he led in triumphal procession to their ultimate destruction (Rev. xx. 10, 14 ; Col. ii. 15 ; 2 Pet. ii. 4. Religious and patriotic enthusiasm impelled Barak to rush down on foot (v. 15) at all risks, into the valley where the enemy awaited him in their chariots. Zeal for the will of the Father and for our deliverance impelled the Captain of our salvation to volunteer to descend from heaven to this lower world, and in the greatest humiliation to encounter and overcome our great adversary (Heb. x. 5–10). His true followers share in some degree His zeal (Acts v. 41 ; Phil. ii. 17). So, being willing now to spend and be spent in His service, " jeoparding their lives in the high places of the field," like Zebulun and Naphtali (ver. 18, Acts xv. 26), they shall share His coming triumph.

(3) *The powers of nature* fought, at God's bidding, for Israel against the foe (iv. 15, v. 20, 21). So in the final triumph of Christ Jesus and His saints over Antichrist and the powers of darkness, " the sun shall be darkened, and the moon shall not give her light, and the stars shall fall from heaven, and the powers of the heavens shall be shaken " (Matt. xxiv. 29).

4. *The thanksgiving.*—(1) *Those who shall join in it.* Deborah and Barak sang their ode of triumph on the day of the victory. Not a day should be lost in rendering to God the glory due for His grace. All the willing commanders and soldiers and people of Israel joined in it. We Christians have to sing of an infinitely greater deliverance than that of Israel from Jabin. Every soul that has known it experimentally will sing, " The Lord has brought me up out of an horrible pit, out of the miry clay, and set my feet upon a rock, and established my goings. And he hath put a new song in my mouth, even praise unto our God " (Ps. xl. 1–3 ; so Isa. xii. 1–3). That song shall be ever ' new,' sung by the redeemed

to the Lamb, to whom they shall ascribe all the glory of their salvation (Rev. v. 9, 10, vii. 9, 10).

Jael received a blessing, answering typically to that bestowed on the Virgin mother of the blessed Jesus (v. 24; Luke i. 28). The approval of her faith in the God of Israel, who was the mainspring of her action, does not imply approval of the treachery, by which the true character of her act was obscured. Yet, in spite of the grievous mixture of dross, true faith is always precious, because, as it grows, it has power to overcome the corruptions which alloy it. In the grand day of perfected redemption, there will be no alloy : the church triumphant will then have accomplished, through her Head, the bruising of Satan under her feet, of which Jael's act was the type (Rom. xvi. 20; Gen. iii. 15; Rev. xx. 10, 14). Compare the blessing for doing good to the Lord's people, as Jael was blessed for opposing God's enemies (Matt. xxv. 34).

(2) *Those shut out from it. First*, there are *the open enemies of Israel and of Israel's God.*—The allied kings of Canaan, with their iron chariots, and vast multitudes, and long-continued success in crushing Israel, thought that "nothing would be restrained from them which they imagined to do." In awful contrast to the wife of Heber, the mother of Sisera and her princesses were exulting, with revolting indelicacy, over her son's supposed acquisition of Israelite women to satisfy the brutal lusts of himself and his soldiery. But the Lord looked down from heaven in His displeasure, and in a very brief space swept away every vestige of their hosts, and laid low the haughty oppressor, who bowed down dead at the feet of a woman ! Such shall be the doom of the kings and their hosts leagued together under the last Antichrist. When "they shall take counsel against the Lord and His anointed, the Lord shall have them in derision ; then shall He speak unto them in His wrath, and vex them in His sore displeasure " (Ps. ii. 4, 5 ; Rev. xvi. 14, 16, xvii. 12–14, xix. 11–21).

Secondly, there are those *waverers*, like Reuben, whose character Jacob depicted, " Unstable as water, thou shalt not excel " (Gen. xlix. 3). On hearing of Barak's noble enterprise for the deliverance of Israel, the men of Reuben had great thoughts and magnanimous resolutions, but they never embodied them in action; just as their forefather had *resolved* to rescue Joseph from the unnatural brethren, but from vacillation and indecision lost the opportunity for acting (xxxvii. 21, 22, 29, 30). They oscillated between heeding the trumpet call of duty which summoned them beyond Jordan, and heading the pipings of the shepherds which would detain them where they were at their ease. Their deliberations were such "searchings of the heart" as proved them to be wanting in the time of testing. Let us beware of such "conferrings with flesh and blood" when the call of Jesus is plain. Indecision is fatal to the soul (Gal. i. 16; Luke ix. 57–62, xiv. 33; 1 Kings xviii. 21).

Thirdly, there are *those, like Gilead, who remain as they are, without even a thought of duty and the call of the Lord* (v. 17). Those like Reuben are conscious of what they ought to do, but do it not. Others do not even give the subject a serious thought. Dan remained in ships. Commerce superseded all other claims, even to the disregard of his nation's independence. Self is the idol of all such. Gain is their god. Peace at any price, even with the sacrifice of truth, and the cause of God, is their motto. Asher sat still by his sea-coast ports, though momentous issues were involved in the struggle. None can share the triumph of Jesus who through love of their ease have shrunk from the good fight. It is only on condition that we suffer with Christ we shall reign with Him. Not to be decidedly for Him is to be against Him (2 Tim. ii. 12; Matt. xii. 30).

Lastly comes the case of *those who, like Meroz, have the best opportunities and the greatest abilities for serving the good cause, and yet "come not to the help of Jehovah against the mighty"* (v. 23). On them shall descend the bitterest curse. For "unto whomsoever much is given, of him shall be much required" (Luke xii. 47, 48; Matt. xxv. 41–43; 1 Cor. xvi. 22).

Here we all have cause for much searchings of heart. Let us see that we be not among those who, through instability, self-seeking, or neglect of precious opportunities, shall be shut out in the day of the Lord's coming glory with His saints. Let us see that, like Zebulun and Naphtali, we be ready to

jeopardise our lives unto the death in the high places of the
field (v. 18). Let us see that we be of one mind with God
concerning His enemies (v. 31; Ps. lxxxiii. 9, cxxxix. 21,
22 ; 2 Chron. xix. 2). Whilst we pray for our own. enemies,
we must pray against *God's* enemies, and long for the time
when He shall put them all under His feet. Then as, when
first we believed, the mountains of our sin "melted before
Jehovah," the Sun of righteousness (ver. 5), and the terrors of
Sinai gave place to the sweet gospel of Jesus, so at His coming
again all evil shall flee from before Him, and "the righteous
shall shine forth as the sun in the kingdom of our Father"
(ver. 31) for ever.

CHAPTER VI.

ISRAEL'S OPPRESSION BY MIDIAN : CALL OF GIDEON AS DELIVERER :
PRELIMINARY PURIFICATION FROM IDOLATRY.

JUDGES VI. 1–32.—(1) *And the children of Israel did evil in
the sight of the* LORD [JEHOVAH (ch. ii. 11, note iii. 7, iv. 1)] ;
and the Lord [JEHOVAH, without whom Midian would have
been powerless against Israel] *delivered them into the hand of
Midian* [named from Abraham's son by Keturah (Gen.
xxv. 2). The old Egyptian *Madi*, with a plural ending. The
race extended from the desert north of Arabia along the east
of Palestine. They joined Moab in desiring Balaam to curse
Israel, and then in tempting Israel at Shittim to whoredom
and idolatry with Baal Peor. By the Lord's command, Israel
smote those next Moab utterly and their five kings, with
Balaam their wicked counsellor, and burnt their cities
(Numb. xxv. 17, 18, xxxi. 2–17). But after the lapse of
200 years they recovered strength ; and, owing to their con-
sanguinity, they were able to corrupt Israel more readily than
the accursed Canaanites could. As a nomadic people, they
abounded in cattle, beeves, sheep, and asses ; also countless
camels, now in the time of the Judges (vii. 12), though the
former only (Numb. xxxi. 28), not also the latter, appear in
Moses' time. They probably occupied some of Sihon's ' cities '
and " goodly castles " (xxxi. 10), which they did not build, and
of which probably some remains are still existing in the ruins in
the *Lejah*] *seven years* [the number marking Divine completeness.
Though not so long as other oppressions, it was more severe.
Each successive year of the same brought Israel lower and
lower, until all other helps failing, Israel cried to Jehovah].

(2) *And the hand of Midian prevailed against Israel* [by their numbers (ver. 5, ch. iii. 10, end)]: *and because of the Midianites the children of Israel made them the dens* [rather *ravines*, מִנְהָרוֹת, from נָהַר, 'torrents,' hollow them out] *which (are) in the mountains, and caves, and* [*mountainous*] *strongholds* [the article marks that *the* ravines and caves were still well known as Israel's hiding places; some were natural caves in the limestone, others formed or adapted by digging for the purpose of concealment of treasures, supplies, and stores. Plunder, rather than extermination, was the object of the Midianites, even the grain grown in the uplands of Manasseh had to be hidden from them]. (3) *And (so) it was, when Israel had sown* [hoping to reap], *that the Midianites came up* [in harvest time], *and the Amalekites* [ch. iii. 13, note], *and the children of the east* [Job i. 3. A general name for the nomad and predatory tribes living east of Palestine and in the desert; called 'Ishmaelites' in viii. 24, inasmuch as being connected with Arabia. The Midianites too are so called (Gen. xxxvii. 27, 28); both springing from the one forefather Abraham, and resembling one another in mode· of life], *even they came up against them.* (4) *And they encamped against them, and destroyed the increase of the earth, till thou come unto Gaza* [crossing the Jordan near Bethshean, now *Beisan*, and passing westward to the plain˙of Jezreel, their headquarters even to the present day, and spreading thence till they reached the south-western sea-coast of Gaza]; *and left no sustenance for Israel* [by successive invasions each year], *neither* [*and* neither] *sheep, nor ox, nor ass.* (5) *For they came up with their cattle and their tents, and they came as grasshoppers* [locusts] *for multitude* [and for all-consuming voracity]; *both they and their camels were without number* [they brought with them all the equipments of Bedouin life, even to the camel, the animal of the desert; so that the whole country was for the time being in their hands]; *and they entered into the land to destroy* [devastate] *it.* (6) *And Israel was greatly impoverished* [*yiddal*, from *dalal*, 'weakened'] *because of the Midianites; and the children of Israel cried unto the* LORD [JEHOVAH: the effect of affliction (iii. 9, 15, iv. 3; Ps. lxxxviii. 34-38, cvii. 6; Isa.

xxvi. 16 ; Hos. v. 15, vi. 1)]. (7) *And it came to pass, when
the children of Israel cried unto the* LORD [JEHOVAH] *because of
the Midianites,* (8) *That the* LORD [JEHOVAH] *sent a prophet*
[Heb. *a man, a prophet;* not an angel (Heb. ii. 16). Unnamed,
as in 1 Kings xiii. 1. Many have a name with God who are
unknown to the world (2 Cor. vi. 9 ; conversely Rev. iii. 1 ;
Luke xvi. 19, 20)] *unto the children of Israel, which said unto
them* [before giving relief in answer to their cry in distress,
Jehovah sends the prophet to show them that their apostasy,
notwithstanding God's great benefits, is the cause of the
chastisement, in order that, being thus led to repentance, they
may be in a suitable state of mind to profit by the deliverance.
So Gideon sets Israel right with God (ver. 24, 25), by casting
down Baal's altar, and building Jehovah's, as the necessary
preliminary to Israel's deliverance], *Thus saith the* LORD
[JEHOVAH] *God of Israel, I brought you up from Egypt, and
brought you forth out of the house of bondage* [he presumes the
people to be familiar with Exod. xx. 2, proving that the
Pentateuch was then extant]; (9) *and I delivered you out of the
hand of the Egyptians* [Exod. xviii. 9], *and out of the hand of
all that oppressed you, and drave them out from before you, and
gave you their land.* (10) *And I said unto you, I* (am) *the*
LORD [JEHOVAH] *your God ; fear not the gods of the Amorites*
[1 Kings xxi. 26 ; 2 Kings xxi. 11], *in whose land ye dwell*
[2 Kings xvii. 35, 30 ; Jer. x. 2. The Amorites were, as the
Hebrew name means, 'high-landers,' in contrast to the
Canaanites, the 'low-landers.' They sprang from Canaan
(Gen. x. 15, 16). Being as mountaineers the most powerful of
the occupants of Canaan, the other Canaanites are sometimes
as here called by their name (Gen. xv. 16 ; Josh. xxiv. 15, 18)] :
but ye have not obeyed my voice. (11) *And there came an*
[rather, as Heb. *the*] *angel of the* LORD [JEHOVAH, note ch. ii. 1],
and sat under an [rather '*the*'] *oak* [terebinth : *the well-
known* terebinth : compare ver. 24] *which* (was) *in Ophrah
that* (pertained) *unto Joash the Abiezrite* [as distinguished from
Ophrah in Benjamin (Josh. xviii. 23). In Manasseh not far
from Shechem (ix. 1, 5). Gideon's place of birth, residence, and
burial (vi. 11, 24, viii. 32). The seat of his idolatrous ephod

(viii. 27). Epher, with Abiezer or Jeezer of Manasseh, probably formed it (1 Chron. v. 24, vii. 17, 18; Numb. xxvi. 30; Josh. xvii. 2). Joash, head of the Abiezrites, was lord of the town, now *Erfai*]: *and his son Gideon* [meaning the '*hewer*,' a name given him as a warrior (Isa. x. 33) and the hewer down of Baal. Joash's youngest son, fifth of Israel's judges] *threshed* [rather "was knocking out" with a stick, חָבַט] *wheat by* [בְּ rather '*in*'] *the wine-press* [usually they threshed on an area of hard earth, a 'threshing floor' in the open field, with threshing carriages armed with teeth, or else oxen which trod out the grain. Only the very poor knocked out the grain of their gleanings with a stick (Ruth ii. 17). That Gideon was obliged to knock out his little grain in the wine-press, a pit sunk in the ground or hewn in the rock, implies the soreness of the Midianite oppression], *to hide* (it) *from* ["to cause it to flee," margin: personification, as men fled, so they had to make their grain flee, *i.e.*, remove it with all possible speed "from the face of" (Heb.)] *the Midianites.* (12) *And the angel of the* LORD [JEHOVAH] *appeared unto him* [former judges Othniel, Ehud, Barak, had been moved by the Spirit of God; but to Gideon alone Jehovah appeared in person to intimate that the God who had made theophanies to the patriarchs (ver. 13; Gen. xii. 1, 7, xxviii. 13, 14; Exod. iii. 2–8) was the same Jehovah, ready to save their posterity, if only Israel will return to the covenant], *and said unto him, The* LORD [JEHOVAH] *is with thee, thou mighty man of valour* [this promise of JEHOVAH'S presence with Gideon is the guarantee that, through the might of Jehovah thereby conferred, Gideon would prove a "mighty man of valour" (Exod. iii. 12; Josh. i. 5; Luke i. 28). Jehovah's calling him "mighty man of valour" made him so, by the inherent energy of the Divine word (Rom. iv. 17)]. (13) *And Gideon said unto Him, Oh my Lord* [not LORD; for Gideon does not recognise Him as JEHOVAH: he uses only the ordinary form of respectful salutation, 'Master,' 'Sir;' *Adoni*], *if the* LORD [JEHOVAH] *be with us, why then is all this befallen us* [calling to mind Deut. xxxi. 17: "Are not these evils come upon us, because our God is not among us?" The stranger's word seemed a mockery in the face of the actual facts surrounding him, Gideon's own occupation at the time being a sad illustration of the depth of the existing oppression]. *And where (be) all his miracles which our fathers told us of, saying, Did not the* LORD [JEHOVAH] *bring us up from Egypt* [ver. 8]? *but now the* LORD [JEHOVAH] *hath forsaken us* [the answer to the people of God when reasoning thus in affliction is given by Him (Isa. xl. 27, 28, xlix. 14, 15)], *and delivered us into the hands of the Midianites.* (14) *And the* LORD [JEHOVAH] *looked upon him* [Heb. "turned toward," "had respect to" (Ps. xxv. 16): *Yippen el*], *and said, Go in this thy might* [given now by my call, and gracious regard. The strength of conscious weakness out of which Jehovah perfects strength (Isa. xl. 29–31 ; 2 Cor. xii. 9, 10 ; Heb. xi. 34). Herein "the Angel of JEHOVAH" manifested Himself as JEHOVAH, and so appropriately assumes here His name (compare Acts vii. 38 with Exod. xix. 20)], *and thou shalt save Israel from the hand of the Midianites*: *have not I* [a phrase giving strong assurance (ch. iv. 14)] *sent thee?* [Exod. iii. 10, 12, 14; Josh. xx. 21.] (15) *And he said unto him, Oh my Lord* [rather, as it is no longer *Adoni*, as in ver. 13, but *Adonai*, 'Lord :' so also in ver. 22. Gideon recognises now that the speaker is not mere man, but the '*Lord*'], *wherewith shall I save Israel?* [Gideon no longer questions the possibility of Israel's deliverance, but expresses his sense of weakness personally, and in respect to his family. So Moses, Exod. iii. 11, iv. 10] ; *behold, my family* ['thousand,' Numb. i. 16] (*is*) *poor* [the humblest] *in Manasseh, and I* (*am*) *the least in my father's house.* (16) *And the* LORD [JEHOVAH] *said unto him, Surely I will be with thee* [Exod. iii. 12 ; Josh. i. 5 ; the secret of power (Zech. iv. 6 ; 2 Cor. iv. 7)], *and thou shalt smite the Midianites as one man* [at one blow; as easily and completely as if slaying one man (Numb. xiv. 15)]. (17) *And he said unto Him, If now I have found grace in Thy sight, then show me a sign* ['*oth*, a miracle, to assure me it is not a phantasm, but] *that* [(שׁ for אֲשֶׁר, colloquially) it is] *Thou* [JEHOVAH who] *talkest with me.* (18) *Depart not hence, I pray thee, until I come unto thee, and bring forth my present* [*Minchah*, "sacrificial gift" to God, consisting of the food usually set before an honoured guest : not strictly a *sacrifice.* From *manach,* "to give," not in its usual sense, atoning for sin, but an *eucharistic gift* to God as King (Lev. ii. 1–6), the unbloody 'meat offering :' but, in Gen. iv. 3–5, 'sacrifice' generally], *and set* (*it*) *before thee. And he said, I will tarry until thou come again.* (19) *And Gideon went in, and made ready a kid* [*of the goats* (Gen. xviii. 7, 8)] ; *and unleavened cakes* [as being quickly baked, and best suited for an offering to God (Gen. xix. 3 ; Lev. ii. 11)] *of an ephah* [containing 3 *seahs* or 'measures :' the quantity ordinarily used at one baking (1 Sam. i. 24 ; Matt. xiii. 33). An omer was the daily portion of manna for one person (Exod. xvi. 16). An ephah contained 10 omers] *of flour ; the flesh he put in a basket, and he put the broth in a pot, and brought* (*it*) *out unto him under the oak* [terebinth tree], *and presented* (*it*). (20) *And the angel of God* [it is JEHOVAH in ver. 11, 12, 21, 22–26 ; but here ELOHIM ; marking that ELOHIM and JEHOVAH are ONE] *said, Take the flesh and the unleavened cakes, and lay* (*them*) *upon this rock* [close by as an altar ; unhewn, as the Law required (Exod. xx. 24–26], *and pour out the broth* [a libation ; a drink offering (Gen. xxxv. 14)]. *And he did so.* (21) *Then the angel of the Lord* [JEHOVAH] *put forth the end of the staff* [the accompaniment of a *traveller* (Gen. xxxii. 10 ; Exod. xii. 11] *that* (*was*) *in his hand, and touched the flesh and the unleavened cakes ; and there rose up fire out of the rock* [thus the 'sign' sought for was granted (ver. 17)], *and consumed the flesh and the unleavened cakes* [(Lev. ix. 24.) Gideon probably hoped that the angel of Jehovah, by tarrying under the oak till he should return, and then eating of the offering presented, would at once attest the reality of the vision, and His goodwill to the offerer (Gen. xviii. 3–8; compare Luke xxiv. 37–43). But instead, he consumes the offering with fire, and then suddenly disappears]. (22) *And when Gideon perceived that He was an angel of the* LORD [JEHOVAH], *Gideon said, Alas, O Lord God* [*Adonai* JEHOVIH, the last vowel being assimilated to Adonai*i*]! *for because I have seen an* [or the] *angel of the* LORD [JEHOVAH] *face to face* [Gideon feared he should die in consequence (Gen. xxxii. 30 ; Exod. xxxiii. 20)]. (23) *And the Lord* [JEHOVAH] *said unto him, Peace* (*be*) *unto thee* [John xx. 21, 26] *; fear not: thou shalt* *not die.* (24) *Then Gideon built an altar there unto the* LORD [JEHOVAH], *and called it Jehovah-shalom* [" Jehovah (is) peace." So Abraham named a place *Jehovah-jireh* (Gen. xxii. 14) ; and Moses named an altar *Jehovah-nissi* (Exod. xvii. 15). Gideon's altar was not for sacrifice, but as a memorial of Jehovah manifesting Himself there as ' Peace ' to Israel, through Gideon (see Jer. xxix. 11); the pledge that He would deliver His people from Midian by Gideon]: *unto this day it* (*is*) *yet in Ophrah of the Abiezrite* [*i.e.*, unto the time of the writer of Judges]. (25) *And it came to pass the same night* [following the day vision (ver. 12): no time is to be lost in carrying out a good undertaking], *that the* LORD [JEHOVAH] *said unto him* [in a vision (vii. 9)], *Take thy father's young bullock* [rather *ox-bullock,* for it was seven years old : פַר usually *a bullock for sacrifice.* So in the Hebrew (Hos. xiv. 3): " So will we render as *bullocks* our lips," *i.e.,* our praises as our *sacrifice.* The repetition " that thy father hath " with " the altar of Baal," as here " thy father's " with ' bullock,' implies that the bullock had been destined for sacrifice to Baal], *even* [not ' and,' as margin : for there was but *one* bullock : if there had been two, God would have directed Gideon what to do with each, but God directs him only as to the one (ver. 26–28)] *the second bullock of seven years old* [*the second in age* among Joash's bullocks : its age significantly alluded to the *seven* years of Midianite oppression, sent by God for Israel's apostasy, for which the seven-year old bullock is to be the typical atonement, now that Israel penitently turns to Jehovah. Before that Gideon, Israel's representative, can be employed to set Israel free, he must first cleanse his father's house of Baal-idolatry, and consecrate himself wholly unto Jehovah by a burnt-offering (see note ver. 26). So Jacob removed all idols from his household, as the first preliminary to being at peace with God, and so being allowed to be at peace with the surrounding hostile Canaanites (Gen. xxxv. 2–5], *and throw down the altar of Baal that thy father hath, and cut down the grove that* (*is*) *by it* [rather " *the Asherah* that is *upon* it," a wooden pillar, the Canaanite symbol of the moon-goddess, the star queen representing nature's passive powers, as Baal the sun-god represented its active powers (Deut.

xvi. 21, Heb.): "Thou shalt not plant for thee any tree as an
Asherah." The idol was the stem of a tree, stripped of its
boughs, set upright in the ground, and carved with emblems
(note iii. 7). The verbs used, 'make,' 'set up,' 'build,' are
inapplicable to a 'grove' (1 Kings xiv. 15, 23; 2 Kings xvii.
10; 2 Chron. xxxiii. 19]. (26) *And build an altar unto the*
LORD [JEHOVAH] *thy God upon the top of this rock* [rather
'stronghold' (distinct from the 'rock' at the wine-press, ver.
20, but see note ver. 28), the *fortress* of Ophrah, the most con-
spicuous spot; probably near the altar of Baal (ver. 28), which
was usually put on a high place (ix. 46). Baal's altar must
fall before building acceptably the altar to Jehovah: the two
worships cannot be combined (1 Kings xviii. 21; Ezek. xx. 39)]
in the ordered place [*Be-ma'arakah* rather means "with the pre-
parations," viz., those required for sacrifice; consisting in taking
the wood of the Asherah-pillar, just "cut down," as the wood
for the burnt-offering to Jehovah; *'Arak* is used for "laying the
wood in order" for sacrifice (Gen. xxii. 9; 1 Kings xviii. 33),
and "setting" the shew-bread on the table (Lev. xxiv. 6)], *and*
take the second bullock, and offer a burnt-sacrifice [literally, "make
to ascend a holocaust;" its name *'Olah* implies that the *whole*
ascended in the smoke and flame toward heaven, symbolising
unreserved *ardent self-consecration* to Jehovah (Rom. xii. 1).
Gideon was no priest, and the place not the legal one for
sacrifice. But God's will legalises what otherwise would have
been illegal. So Elijah (1 Kings xviii. 36)] *with the wood of*
the grove [rather ' the Asherah-pillar '] *which thou shalt cut down*
[what had been consecrated to idolatry, is turned to the service
of Jehovah (Luke xi. 22; Rom. vi. 19)]. (27) *Then Gideon*
took ten [the recognised legal number constituting a church, and
required for performing public sacred duties (Montanus)] *men*
of his servants, and did as the LORD [JEHOVAH] *had said unto*
him: and (so) it was, because he feared his father's household
[rather 'house,' the Abiezrite *clan* (Numb. i. 2, iii. 15)], *and the*
men of the city [probably a remnant of the Canaanites, as
distinguished from the Abiezrite clan of his father. The men
of the city accordingly were the foremost zealots for Baal (ver.
28, 29). Such a Canaanite remnant was in Shechem (ix. 28,

note)], *that he could not do (it) by day, that he did (it) by night.*
(28) *And when the men of the city arose early in the morning,
behold, the altar of Baal was cast down, and the grove* [rather
" the Asherah-pillar "] *was cut down that (was) by* [on] *it, and the
second bullock was offered upon the altar (that was) built* [viz., to
Jehovah, the wood of the Asherah (ver. 26) having been used
for the burnt-offering, and traces of it being still visible.
Therefore the altar of Jehovah must have been built near that
of Baal, just cast down.   Piscator identifies " this rock " (ver.
20), with " this rock," or rather 'stronghold' (ver. 26).   If so,
the wine-press must have been near the 'rock-fortress ;' and the
sacrificial altar built to Jehovah on its 'top' will be at the
same locality as the appearance of the angel of Jehovah and
the offering and memorial altar of Gideon to Jehovah on the
rock adjoining to the wine-press in the first instance (so 2 Sam.
xxiv. 25, compared with 2 Chron. iii. 1): the sacrificial altar
will, in this view, be on the top, the memorial altar 'Jehovah-
Shalom' (ver. 24) lower down on the rock].   (29) *And they
said one to another, Who hath done this thing ? And when they
inquired and asked, they* [the people questioned] *said, Gideon
the son of Joash hath done this thing.*   (30) *Then the men of the
city said unto Joash, Bring out* [for execution (Gen. xxxviii. 24)]
*thy son, that he may die ; because he hath cast down the altar of
Baal, and because he hath cut down the grove that (was) by it*
[rather " the Asherah-pillar that was upon it"].   (31) *And
Joash said unto all that stood against him* [or " before (עַל) him," as
chief magistrate of Ophrah.   Questions of offence against
religion were tried *before* the judge (Job xxxi. 28)], *Will ye
plead for Baal ? will ye save him ?* [the 'ye' is emphatical.
What need *you* trouble yourself to plead for and save him ? If
he be a god, he can take care of himself].   *He that will plead
for him, let him be put to death whilst (it is yet) morning*
[rather " let him be put to death (by Baal ; you may leave it
to Baal to put him to death) before it is morning :" lit. " *until*
the morning," *i.e.,* wait until the morning, leaving the sacri-
legious one to Baal to slay by that time]; *if he (be) a god, let
him plead for himself* [*i.e.,* avenge his own wrong upon the
perpetrator], *because (one) hath cast down his altar.*   (32)

Therefore on that day he called him Jerubbaal [or impersonally "*He was called* (by the people) Jerubbaal," *i.e.,* the one with whom Baal should plead. The Jews in ridicule of idolatry changed Baal into *Bosheth* (shame), or *Besheth,* and used Jerubbesheth for Jerubbaal (2 Sam. xi. 21). Compare Eshbaal, Ishbosheth (1 Chron. ix. 39 ; 2 Sam. ii. 8)], *saying, Let Baal plead against him, because he hath thrown down his altar.*

GIDEON AND THE FLEECE.

JUDGES VI. 33–40. (33) *Then all the Midianites, and the Amalekites* [akin to the Edomites, being descended from Amalek, the grandson of Esau (Gen. xxxvi. 12 ; see note ver. 3, above). Balaam under the Spirit said of them (Numb. xxiv. 20, Heb.) : "Beginning of the heathen (was) Amalek, and its end shall be even to the perishing." In age, power, and celebrity this Bedouin tribe was certainly not "the first of the nations," but, as the margin says, "the first of the nations that warred against Israel" (Ezek. xvii. 8). It was the first that opened the conflict of heathendom against the kingdom of God. The heinousness of their sin at the outset lay in this, when Israel at Rephidim had no water to drink, and God miraculously supplied it from the smitten rock, the Amalekites tried to deprive God's people of a chief necessary of life, just supplied by miracle, thus fighting not so much with them as with God. Instigated by the same hatred of Israel, as the covenant people of God, they joined with the Canaanites in discomfiting Israel at Hormah (Numb. xiv. 43–45). Next they were in league with Eglon against Israel. And now they, in league with Midian, the oppressor of the people of God], *and the children of the east* [see note ver. 3], *were gathered together, and went over* [crossing the Jordan from the east to its western side, after having followed the course of the Jabbok up to the place of its entering the Jordan], *and pitched in the valley of Jezreel* [known in later times as the great plain of Esdraelon, extending across central Palestine from the Jordan to the Mediterranean, and separating Mount Carmel and the Samaritan hills from those of Galilee. Its wonderful richness and its exposed position have tempted the invader from the earliest times. Jezreel, the city in Issachar, was the royal residence of Ahab, now *Zerin.* The plain has been the great battle field of Palestine in ancient, as in modern times]. (34) *But the Spirit of the* LORD [JEHOVAH: as the English version always marks by the capitals, whereas it marks, in contradistinction, *Adonai* by small letters, Lord] *came upon* [לְבְשֶׁה, 'clothed,' as margin rightly has it, invested him like a coat of mail, encompassing him with invincible might (compare 1 Chron. xii. 18, margin; 2 Chron. xxiv. 20; Luke xxiv. 49); " endued with power from on high ": literally, " *arrayed in power,*" &c. : ἐνδύσησθε; compare Isa. lxi. 10; Eph. vi. 11] *Gideon, and he blew a trumpet* [to summon the people against the enemy]; *and Abiezer* [*i.e.,* the Abiezrite clan, to which belonged Joash and his son Gideon, living in Ophrah, which was on a hill facing from the south the plain of Jezreel. Originally in Gilead, but latterly in the portion of Manasseh west of the Jordan (Numb. xxvi. 30; Josh. xvii. 2)] *was gathered* [Hebrew, the Abiezrite clan *let itself be summoned*] *after him.* (35) *And he sent messengers throughout all Manasseh, who also was gathered after him* [*i.e.,* the Manassites *west* of Jordan: the tribes on the *east* of the Jordan took no part in the war]; *and he sent messengers unto Asher, and unto Zebulun, and unto Naphtali* [the tribes in the north], *and they came up* [עָלָה, rather they *advanced:* the Asherites and Naphtalites could not 'come up' from their mountains, but could only go down to the plain of Jezreel] *to meet them* [*i.e.,* to meet *the Manassites,* who were coming from the south: all converging towards the plain of Jezreel, the battle field in Issachar, to act together in concert under Gideon against the enemy]. (36) *And Gideon said unto God, If Thou wilt save* [Heb. *If Thou art saving*] *Israel by mine hand, as Thou hast said,* (37) *Behold, I will put* (Heb. *I putting, I am laying*] *a fleece of wool* [Heb. *the shorn of the wool,* the mass of wool just cut, and still adhering together as one mass] *in the floor* [the open space, exposed to the winds, which was used for winnowing chaff from grain]; (*and*) *if the dew be on the fleece only, and* (*it be*) *dry upon all the earth* (*beside*), *then shall I know that Thou wilt save Israel by mine hand, as Thou hast said.* (38) *And it was so : for he rose up early in the morrow, and thrust* [pressed] *the fleece together, and wringed* [squeezed] *the dew out of the fleece, a bowl-full of water.* (39) *And Gideon said unto God, Let not Thine anger be hot against me, and I will speak but this once : let me prove, I pray Thee, but this once with the fleece ; let it now be dry only upon the fleece, and upon all the ground let there be dew.* (40) *And God did so that night : for it was dry upon the fleece only, and there was dew on all the ground.*

SECOND STAGE IN THE TIMES OF THE JUDGES, FROM GIDEON
TO JAIR, 95 YEARS.

1. *Occasion of the call of Gideon : Israel's apostasy to the heathen world punished by the heathen Midianites.*—Just before the occurrence of the facts narrated in this passage, Gideon had received his call from God. The angel of Jehovah, that is, Jehovah the uncreated Word, in visible form, anticipatory of the incarnation, appeared to him under a terebinth in Ophrah, a town belonging to Joash, his father. Former Judges—Othniel, Ehud, and Barak—had been moved by the Spirit of God to their work of delivering Israel from the oppressor ; but to Gideon alone a theophany was vouchsafed in order to intimate that the God who had visibly manifested himself to the patriarchs, was the same Jehovah, ready to save their descendants, if only they would penitently return to the covenant. It was the time of Israel's sore trouble. In earlier ages Midian with Moab, after having vainly sought to curse Israel by the mouth of Balaam, had too well succeeded in bringing a plague on the elect people, by tempting them to whoredom with their women : and had then, in consequence, been smitten severely by Israel, according to God's command (Numb. xxv. 17, 18, xxxi. 1–16). But now after 200 years, in renewed strength, with the Amalekites and other marauding children of the east, they were employed as God's instrument for chastising His people for their apostasy. For it is a principle of God's retributive justice, everywhere illustrated throughout the sacred history, that when His people forsake their spiritual Husband (Isa. liv. 5) and Lord, to join themselves to the world, the same world which was the instrument of their sin becomes the

H

instrument of their punishment. The Midianite hordes, like swarming locusts, consumed all their produce, except the little which they contrived to hide in caves and holes (Judg. vi. 2, 4, 5, 6, 11). "The hand of Midian was strong (so the Hebrew) against Israel, and, because of the Midianites, the children of Israel made them the dens [else ravines] which are in the mountains, and caves, and strongholds." The word 'made' implies that, besides using the natural caves as places of refuge, just as they were, they adapted them, by enlargement and otherwise, to their purpose. These places the Israelites used not so much to shelter themselves in, as to conceal their possessions and grain from the enemy. For, like genuine Bedouins, the Midianites were more intent on plunder, than on exterminating the people themselves; "they destroyed the increase of the earth, till thou come unto Gaza (spreading from the plain of Jezreel to which they came from beyond Jordan towards the east, to the extreme south-west of the land), and left no sustenance for Israel, neither sheep, nor ox, nor ass;" "both they and their camels were without number, and they entered into the land to destroy it."

2. *Affliction the instrument of correction: consequent prayer and profit by the word.*—God permitted His people to be brought so low, in order that affliction might drive them to prayer, and that thus their extremity might become His opportunity. Such was the result in the gracious ways of His Providence. But before helping them, the Lord sent a prophet to reprove them by reminding them of His having originally delivered them out of Egypt, and then driven the Canaanites out from before them, and given them the land, with the injunction that they should not serve the gods of the Amorites, which injunction, notwithstanding all His goodness, they had disobeyed (ver. 7–10).

3. *Divine epiphany to Gideon. Idols must be cast down before Jehovah.*—Next God called Gideon by two revelations. In the first, by a visible manifestation of the Angel of Jehovah, He summoned him, in the strength of Jehovah, to deliver Israel from the oppressor Midian. Next, in a dream of the night, Jehovah commanded him to throw down his father's altar to Baal, and to

offer to Jehovah his God, as a burnt-offering, his father's bullock
of seven years old; as God had given Israel into the hands of
Midian for seven years on account of apostasy, so the offering
of the 'second' in age of Joash's bullocks, namely, the bullock
of seven years old, was to be the typical means of wiping away
their sin, and so of removing its penalty. Baal's altar must be
destroyed, before Jehovah will have an altar erected to Him.
We cannot serve our heart-idols and Jehovah at the same time.
Compare 1 Kings xviii. 21; Ezek. xx. 39: "Go ye, serve ye
every one his idols, and hereafter also, if ye will not hearken
unto me : but pollute ye my holy name no more with your
gifts, and with your idols." Gideon was ordered also to cut
down "the grove" by Baal's altar. The reference is to the
Asherah, a Canaanite idol representing the goddess of nature—
not a statue, but a wooden pillar. Baal and Asherah were the
two chief deities of the Canaanites. Gideon was to build
Jehovah's altar on the top of the rock, and with preparation
[בְּמַעֲרָכָה, marg., " *in an orderly manner* "] to use the wood of the
Asherah which he had hewed down, as the wood for the burnt-
offering (Gen. xxii. 6, 9; Deut. xvi. 21).

4. *Boldness for God brings its own reward.*—As in the
first manifestation Jehovah acknowledged Gideon, so in this
second one He required Gideon to acknowledge Jehovah.
Gideon accordingly, with ten men of his servants, overthrew
Baal's altar, and cut down the Asherah-pillar by it in the night;
for he durst not do it by day, through fear of his father's household, and the men of the city. But God does not reject the
first sincere efforts of His children to do His will, though
attended with timidity (John iii. 2, xix. 38). Gideon did not,
by secrecy, effect his purpose of escaping detection. The men
of the city, zealous for their idol, upon inquiry early in the
morning as to the sacrilege committed in the night, discovered
the perpetrator, and required that Joash should give up his son
to death for it. But Joash replied, "Will ye plead for Baal?
he that will plead for him [by putting the destroyer of Baal's
altar to death] shall be put to death himself; let us wait till
the morning [*i.e.*, till *to-morrow*, to give him time to avenge the
insult which he has received, not as English version, "Shall be

put to death whilst it is yet morning "]; if he be a god, let him plead for himself." Hence Gideon received the name Jerubbaal, "Let Baal fight," *i.e.*, vindicate his own cause on the destroyer of his altar.

5. *The Spirit of God qualifies the weakest for work, and guarantees success.*—Then followed the gathering together of the enemy to the plain of Jezreel. And the Spirit of Jehovah clothed Gideon as with a coat of mail. At his trumpet call his own clan, recognising the champion and deliverer of Israel in him who, as an iconoclast, braved Baal's revenge with impunity, was the first to rally around him. The neighbouring tribes, Manasseh, Zebulun, and Naphtali, next obeyed his summons by heralds. But still there were remnants of doubt and fear in Gideon, though he was very different in respect to faith from what he was when the Angel of Jehovah first appeared to him. At that first revelation Gideon was knocking out with a stick (like poor gleaners, Ruth ii. 17) wheat in (not ' by ') the wine-press sunk in the rock, to make it safe from the Midianites, as he durst not venture to thresh in the floor or hardened area in the open field. He was at the time probably pondering in sadness on the calamities of Israel, and wondering whether Jehovah, to whom he along with his people had cried (ver. 7), would come as in the days of old (ver. 13) to their help. Whilst he was thus engaged in sighing prayerful 'meditation' (Ps. v. 7), the Lord answered (Isa. lxv. 24). The angel of Jehovah appeared, and said unto him, "Jehovah is with thee, thou mighty man of valour." This Divine word imparted to Gideon the qualifications needed for the coming struggle. The very call of God guarantees the requisite strength. But gloom and doubt still clouded Gideon's faith. So he answered, "O my Lord, if Jehovah be with us, why then is all this befallen us"? Evidently he had in mind the words of Jehovah by Moses (Deut. xxxi. 17), foretelling the fatal issue of Israel's apostasy : "They will say in that day, Are not these evils come upon us, because *our God is not among us ?*" God *was* not among them, whilst they were in impenitence, but now that they have cried unto Jehovah, He turns to them. So Jehovah, who is identified here with the angel of Jehovah,

looked upon Gideon, and said, "Go in this thy might"—the might which thou now hast by my gift. Gideon's own sense of powerlessness fitted him as a vessel to receive the Divine strength: Jehovah's might thus became his might (Isa. xl. 29–31). Jehovah's mission guaranteed his success against Midian: "Thou shalt save Israel from the hand of the Midianites; have not I sent thee?" These words removed his despair of the possibility of deliverance. Consciousness of the insignificance of his family and of his own personal weakness was now his remaining cause of fear: "Wherewith shall I save Israel?" The Lord meets this difficulty, as in the case of Moses (Exod. iii. 11, 12), with the reply, "Surely *I* will be with thee, and thou shalt smite the Midianites as one man "—*i.e.*, as with a single blow (Numb. xiv. 15). Still Gideon craved a sign to assure his faith. The angel of Jehovah granted his wish by touching with the end of the staff in his hand the flesh of a kid, and the unleavened cakes, which Gideon offered to God as his sacrificial gift (*Minchah*); and so causing fire to rise out of the rock, and consume his offering. The acceptance of the offering intimated that Jehovah would again receive Israel's prayers, upon their forsaking the idols of Canaan and returning to Him. The altar, which Gideon named Jehovah-Shalom, *i.e.*, "Jehovah is peace," because of the Divine words of comfort to him amidst his fears, "Peace be unto thee," was an additional assurance that the Lord now entertained thoughts of peace to Israel, and would deliver His people from their oppressors, as He promised, by the hands of Gideon (Jer. xxix. 11).

6. *Weak faith craves a sign, and Jehovah vouchsafes it: the dew on the fleece.*—But before setting out on his perilous enterprise with the assembled army, Gideon desired a further sign from God to assure him of success. His prayer for a sign did not betoken want of faith, but weakness of faith. The flesh strove against the willing spirit, and so created misgivings and fears. From all that he had seen and heard, Gideon must have believed that Jehovah both could and would keep His word, and deliver Israel by him whom He had so miraculously called. But his faith was not above liability to temptation and conflict; and the severity of that conflict became the most intense, when

the promised deliverance by such seemingly inadequate strength on his part was on the eve of its accomplishment. "Wherefore Gideon with his faith sought for a sign from God against the more vehement struggle of the flesh, in order that his faith might be the more confirmed, and might resist the opposing flesh with the greater force; and this petition for a sign was combined with prayer for the strengthening of his faith" (Seb. Schmidt).

The sign which Gideon asked, and which the Lord vouchsafed, was one especially significant. The sign was admirably calculated both to confirm his faith, and at the same time to assure the children of God in all ages that He will keep His promise of making perfect His strength in their weakness (2 Cor. xii. 9). Dew in Palestine falls in the early summer, and again most abundantly in the autumn. At these seasons no rain falls, but the dew descending gently, yet copiously, supplies the absence of showers from heaven. Thus the dew was in the Holy Land a leading source of its former fertility. Thus, when Isaac was bestowing the richest blessing on Jacob, he said, "God give thee of the dew of heaven, and the fatness of the earth, and plenty of corn and wine" (Gen. xxvii. 28). So too Moses, in foretelling the blessedness of Joseph, said, "Blessed of the Lord be his land for the precious things of heaven and for the dew" (Deut. xxxiii. 13). Thus dew naturally became the image of spiritual influences. As the withdrawal of the dew brought barrenness, so the withdrawal of God's grace is attended with spiritual deadness and drought. On the other hand, as the dew diffusing itself with gentle, silent, benignant influence produced verdure and fruitfulness, so the presence of God's grace brings with it peace, life, and fruitfulness. The fleece taken from the shorn sheep was a suggestive image to Gideon of Israel in the nation's depression by the Gentiles: for Israel was the Lord's people, and "the sheep of His pasture." Yet the woolly fleece, when saturated with dew from above, whilst the ground all around is parched, vividly symbolised the people of the Lord, like Naphtali (Deut. xxxiii. 23), "satisfied with favour, and full with the blessing of Jehovah."

The type may be viewed in a threefold relation :—1. Its

relation to Gideon and his enterprise; 2. Its relation to
Israel, past, present, and future; 3. Its relation to the church
of Christ and its professing members.

1. *The dew in relation to Gideon's enterprise.*—To Gideon
in his fears, the filling of the fleece with dew from heaven,
whilst the earth around was dry, intimated that, whereas
Israel was heretofore, through apostasy, as dry spiritually
as the heathen around (compare the "dry places," Matt. xii.
43), Jehovah was now about to fill Gideon and His nation with
His reviving grace: Israel is now to be endued with the
strength from on high, even as Gideon their champion has been
already "clothed" with "the Spirit of Jehovah," whilst the
heathen oppressors remain dry and powerless spiritually. The
reversing of the sign at Gideon's request, and the dryness of
the fleece, whilst the dew rested on the earth around, assured
him that Jehovah could and would manifest his power even
amidst the weakness and helplessness of His people, in the
face of the nations which were flourishing all around. It is of
such as Gideon that the Epistle to the Hebrews (xi. 32–34)
testifies, that they "out of weakness were made strong." As
Milton says of the martyrs," they shook the powers of darkness with the irresistible power of weakness."

The sign was a fit prelude to what followed. The timid
were first thinned out of Gideon's army, leaving, out of 32,000
men who set out with him, only ten thousand. Even these
latter were "too many" for the Lord's purpose (Judg. vii. 2–4);
as the Lord said, "Lest Israel vaunt themselves against me,
saying, Mine own hand hath saved me." So, in order to insure
the ascription of the victory to God alone, the army was
reduced to 300, by retaining those alone whose unwearying
energy was shown by their drinking at the fountain Harod
("the spring of trembling," now *Ain Jahlood*) what water they
could lift with their hands, not delaying to kneel and drink: a
type of Messiah's zeal (Ps. cx. 7): "He shall drink of the
brook in the way, therefore shall He lift up the head." Then
followed Gideon's reconnoitring expedition, with Phurah his
servant, into the Midianite host. There he heard the Midianite's
dream of a 'barley-cake' overturning the 'tent.' The 'barley-

cake,' being the food of the poor, symbolised Israel in the
nation's present distress; the 'tent' symbolised the nomad
life of Midian, a life of freedom and power (see Judg. vi. 5).
The poor and weak one should overturn the rich and mighty.
So it came to pass.   Gideon divided his little band of 300 into
three attacking columns; and in " the beginning of the middle
watch," *i.e.*, at midnight, at his command, and following his
example, they all stood without moving, round about the
Midianite camp, blew the trumpets, and brake the pitchers in
their left hands which covered the torches, so that these
suddenly flashed upon the foe.   They needed not to fight, but
simply to stand and behold the salvation of the Lord : compare
Exod. xiv. 13.   At their startling battle-shout, " The sword of
Jehovah and of Gideon," a panic arose among the Midianites,
as they imagined that each trumpet holder had a *company* at
his back (as indeed he had, though unseen: Gen. xxxii. 2; Song
Sol. vi. 13); and the Lord set every man's sword against his
fellow, so that a great slaughter took place, and the remnant
fled in hot haste to the Jordan.   The final issue of this victory,
and of the two succeeding victories—one at Jordan, and the last
one at Karkor—was that out of 120,000 Midianites only 15,000
survived.   Israel in the strength of Jehovah lighted upon the
foe, " as the dew falleth on the ground " (2 Sam. xvii. 12), so
that not one was left in the Holy Land.

2. *The dew in relation to Israel, past, present, and future.*—The
type has a deeply interesting relation to Israel, the elect nation,
(1) First, *in the past.* The fleece filled with dew, whilst the ground
around was utterly dry, answers to Israel filled with heavenly
blessings from the Lord, whilst the Gentile world was a moral
wilderness, dry and unwatered by the dews of His grace.   It
was not because of Israel's merits, but because of God's
gratuitous choice, that the nation was singled out to be the
paradise of Jehovah, cut off from the spiritual waste; just as
the dew is not of man's procuring, but of God's bestowing.
Had Abraham, the forefather of the nation, been left to himself,
he would have continued an idolater, like all his neighbours in
Ur of the Chaldees, a city dedicated to moon-worship; see
Josh. xxiv. 2, 3.   But the Lord chose Abraham before that

Abraham chose the Lord, and made a covenant of grace with him and his seed. There was much imperfection in him, and Isaac, and Jacob. Both the former denied their own wives through fear of man; Jacob deceived his own father, and obtained the blessing by a lie; Jacob's sons, excepting Joseph and perhaps Benjamin, were far worse. Yet God remembered His own covenant of grace, and preserved Israel in Egypt as a separate people unto Himself in the land of Goshen, like a fleece full of heavenly dew in the midst of a dry and parched land. Then with a mighty hand and outstretched arm, Jehovah led them safely out of Egypt, and through the wilderness of forty years' wanderings, and established them in the goodly land of promise. There, notwithstanding frequent provocations and backslidings, Israel abode, by the blessing of the Lord, an oasis in the desert. The tribes were knit together in one godly fellowship; and meeting at the great religious feasts of the nation in Jerusalem, in proportion as they fulfilled their high calling of God, they realised the beautiful ideal of the inspired Psalmist (cxxxiii. 1, 3): " Behold, how good and how pleasant it is for brethren to dwell together in unity ! As the dew of Hermon, and as the dew that descended upon the mountains of Zion ; for there the Lord commanded the blessing, even life for evermore." Locally, Hermon in the distant east, was so far from Zion in the west, that the dew of the former could not literally descend upon the latter. But " the dew of Hermon," means *a lovely dew.* Brotherly unity resembles such a dew which descended upon Zion, where this unity was so beautifully exemplified in the best days of the nation. Jehovah commanded His blessing upon the holy brotherhood assembled there; for Zion was then the representative seat of the kingdom of God upon earth. The world outside the kingdom of grace, being in its natural corruption, had no such blessing. But Israel had it, and with it the dew of ever fresh youth and undying vitality " for evermore."

(2) *The dew representing the present state of Israel.*—The place remaining dry, whilst all the ground around was saturated with the refreshing dew, represents Israel in a state forming a sad contrast to the former image and what it represents. Israel

has now for ages been spiritually dry, without any of the dews of heavenly blessing which descend from Jehovah, the God of the covenant. And what makes her case the sadder, is, she is singular in her state. For the gospel of the grace of God in Christ Jesus is making many a spiritual desert throughout the Gentile world to become a garden of the Lord, blooming with the life-giving dews of the Spirit poured down from on high. *Individual* Jews here and there are receiving the grace of God, and finding life and peace in Jesus. There is even now in Israel "a remnant according to the election of grace"; for the gathering out of whom, our prayers and self-sacrificing efforts are much required (Rom. xi. 5). But, *as a people*, the Jews still stand in strange isolation, scattered among all nations, yet, contrary to what is usual under such circumstances, amalgamating with none. In spite of themselves, they are the standing witnesses of the truth of Christianity, and by their own very state attest powerfully the fulfilment of Old Testament prophecy. If you desire a graphic picture of their present anomalous state, answering to the dry fleece in the midst of ground on every side saturated with the refreshing dew, read the third chapter of Hosea, the fourth and fifth verses, a picture so true to the life in every particular, that you might fancy it drawn in our present age, not a prophecy delivered some 2500 years ago : "The children of Israel shall abide many days without a king, and without a prince, and without a sacrifice, and without an image, and without an ephod, and without teraphim." The ten tribes lost their king and polity seven centuries before Christ. Judah, though at the Babylonian captivity losing her independent ' king,' had after the return from Babylon "a prince," until she rejected and crucified the Messiah. Then, through that, the crowning sin of her apostasy, she too lost her national polity. Every effort to restore it has been frustrated. A seemingly miraculous interposition defeated the apostate Julian's attempt to rebuild the temple at Jerusalem for the Jews. She ' abides ' in solitary isolation, as a separated wife ; as Jehovah foretold, "Thou shalt abide for me" (Hos. iii. 3). The people who formerly doated on idols abhor utterly any ' image.' They whose nationality and religion centre in priesthood and sacrifice, tenaciously cling to their law, though debarred from offering any 'sacrifice,' since the site of the temple, the only place where sacrifice could lawfully be offered, has been and is in the hands of their enemies for 1800 years. No one save the Spirit of God, by whom the prophets spake, could have foreseen such a state of things, so exceedingly improbable, anomalous, and contrary to all that man could have anticipated.

(3) *The dew representing the future of Israel.*—The relation of the type to the future of Israel. As the fleece was full of dew at first, and all the earth dry ; and next, the fleece was dry, and all the earth wet; so the blessed time is coming, when the fleece shall be again full of dew, and all the earth, through its instrumentality, shall be filled with the dew of the Lord. The prophet Micah (v. 7) prophesies, " The remnant of Jacob shall be in the midst of many people, as *a dew* from the Lord, as the showers upon the grass, that tarrieth not for man, nor waiteth for the sons of men." A remnant though Israel be, like the small dew, yet upon her restoration she shall exercise a world-wide influence in quickening the nations heretofore spiritually dead. The ' dew ' shall become multiplied into the ' showers,' with their countless millions of drops refreshing the thirsting earth. This shall be at the manifestation of " the King who cometh in the name of the Lord," to reign in Zion and over the whole earth (Luke xix. 38). " They shall call Jerusalem the throne of Jehovah ; and all the nations shall be gathered unto it : neither shall they walk any more after the imagination of their evil heart " (Jer. iii. 17). " He shall come down like rain upon the mown grass, as showers that water the earth "—" He shall have dominion also from sea to sea, and from the river unto the ends of the earth " (Ps. lxxii. 6, 8). The Jews are the most cosmopolitan of all peoples, and this characteristic will doubtless be overruled to the fulfilment of God's purposes of grace to them in the latter days, and through them to the whole world ; for " if the fall of them be the riches of the world, and the diminishing of them the riches of the Gentiles, how much more their fulness "? and " if the casting away of them be the reconciling of the world, what shall the receiving of them be, but life from the dead "? (Rom. xi. 12, 15).

(3) *The dew in relation to the church of Christ and its professing members.*—Lastly, the type has a profitable lesson to teach us, in its relation to the Christian church and its professing members. (1) The fleece represents not only Israel, but Israel's antitype, Jesus, and, secondarily, His people who are one with Him. Originally He had from everlasting the fulness of the Godhead; for "it pleased the Father that in Him should all fulness dwell" (Col. i. 19); as the Psalmist sings (Hebrew Ps. cx. 3), "Out of the womb of the morning heaven Thou hast Thy youth-dew;" yet the Son of God "emptied Himself" (Phil. ii. 7, ἐκένωσεν). The fleece reminds us of Him who "openeth not his mouth, as a sheep before her shearers is dumb" (Isa. liii. 7). He was the 'root' full of sap and vigour from above, yet springing "out of a dry ground," when He sojourned on earth. The fleece was full, but the ground around had no dew from heaven. Then at His crucifixion, the church might say, "Our bones are dried, and our hope is lost" (Ezek. xxxvii. 11): just as the fleece was dried, whilst the earth around was saturated with dew. But at His resurrection, not only did He live again, but becomes the Lord of life to us. Full of grace and truth Himself, He fulfils His word to us: "I will be as the dew unto Israel" (Hos. xiv. 5). And at His coming again, His church shall realise His promise: "Thy dead men shall live, together with my dead body they shall arise. Awake and sing, ye that dwell in dust; for thy dew is as the dew of the herbs, and the earth shall cast out the dead" (Isa. xxvi. 19). Thus the fleece shall be hereafter full of dew, and the regenerated earth be "filled with the knowledge of the glory of the Lord as the waters cover the sea" (Habak. ii. 14).

Meantime the effect of Christ's presence as a dew in the soul is, "He shall grow as the lily, and cast forth his roots as Lebanon" (Hos. xiv. 5). Does any feel it is not so with him? Then do as Israel and Gideon did—cry unto the Lord. Prayer will fill the fleece with the heavenly dew. How the dew sparkles! How it beautifies all that it touches! How quietly, how silently the dewdrops, hanging with their brilliant sparkle upon myriads of grass blades, do their good work! The hotter the day, the greater the dew : so the greater your need, the more will be the grace given you, in answer to your believing cry. You will be like the full fleece, amidst the parched and empty world. But ever remember that grace, like the dew, comes wholly from God ; and as the Lord Jesus has the fulness of the Spirit, so out of His fulness must we all receive and grace for grace (John i. 16, iii. 34). Moreover, there is great danger of losing the dew. The Lord complains of many professors who had promised well : " Your goodness, as the early dew, goeth away " (Hos. vi. 4). The glare and heat absorb the dew. Therefore shun the world and its temptations. If you would retain the dew of grace, keep in the shade. Go wherever the dew falls. Neglect no private or public means of grace. Secure the morning and evening dew in the closet.

(2) The dry fleece amidst the dew-covered ground is a symbol of the sad state of many a one, who remains spiritually dead and lifeless, whilst dews of heavenly blessing are descending on every side. Tidings reach the church of spiritual revivals in all directions, through the outpouring of God's Holy Spirit. Why should any remain barren, and fit only for the burning, when he might have, for the asking, grace given that he may become a tree of righteousness, the planting of the Lord, to bloom in the heavenly paradise ? You may be surrounded, like the dry fleece, with the dews of heaven descending through spiritual ordinances, as Bible readings, sermons, and sacraments, and yet all the while remain unblessed in soul yourselves. Put in your claim for a share in God's promise of the Holy Spirit,

> " Lord, I hear of showers of blessing
> Thou art scattering full and free,
> Showers the thirsty land refreshing—
> Let some droppings fall on me,
> Even me !

> " Pass me not, O gracious Father,
> Sinful though my heart may be ;
> Thou might'st leave me, yet the rather
> Let Thy mercy light on me,
> Even me !

" Pass me not, O gracious Saviour
Let me love and cling to Thee ;
I am longing for Thy favour,
Whilst Thou'rt calling, O call me,
Even me !

" Pass me not, O mighty Spirit,
Thou canst make the blind to see,
Witnesses of Jesus' merit—
Speak the word of power to me,
Even me !"

Then, full of grace yourself, you will diffuse the blessed dew to others. God uses weak instruments, like Gideon and his 300 men, to confound the mighty. Only, like him, be " *clothed with* the Spirit of Jehovah." Put ye on the Lord Jesus Christ. Appropriate the thanksgiving : "I will greatly rejoice in the Lord, my soul shall be joyful in my God ; for He hath clothed me with the garments of salvation, He hath covered me with the robes of righteousness" (Isa. lxi. 10). So shall you be the honoured instrument of turning many to righteousness, and of wearing a crown of righteousness, which shall shine hereafter, not as the evanescent though brilliant dewdrop, but as the stars for ever and ever.

CHAPTER VII.

GIDEON'S VICTORY OVER MIDIAN : JEHOVAH'S STRENGTH MADE PERFECT IN WEAKNESS.

(1) *Then Jerubbaal, who (is) Gideon* [see Gen. xxxii. 28 ; Rev. iii. 12], *and all the people that (were) with him, rose up early* [so far from becoming slack, his faith is quickened by God's promise], *and pitched beside* [rather '*above*,' עַל, for the people came *down* to the water (ver. 4, 5). Beside the fountain would have been too exposed a position for Gideon's little band] *the well of Harod* [now *Ain Jalud*, עֵין, here Gideon plays upon the name (ver. 3): "Whosoever is *afraid* (*hared*), let him return." It is a fine spring at the foot of Mount Gilboa, issuing from a cavern, and forming a pool with rushy banks and a pebbly bottom, 100 yards long. Translate '*spring*' for '*well*.' *Beer* is a *well;* but *Ain*, a *spring*]; *so that the host of the Midianites were on the north side of them, by the hill of Moreh* [now *Jebel ed Duhy,* 'little Hermon ;' on the northern side of the valley of Jezreel, and of the height, probably Mount Gilboa, where Gideon's 300 were posted (see 1 Sam. xxix. 1). The interval between Moreh, or *Jebel ed Duhy,* and Ain Jalud is two or three miles, affording ample space for the hosts of Midian and Amalek], *in the valley.* (2) *And the* LORD [JEHOVAH] *said unto Gideon, The people that (are) with thee (are) too many for me to give the Midianites into their hands, lest Israel vaunt themselves* [1 Cor. i. 29] *against me, saying, Mine own hand hath saved me* [Deut. viii. 17. Israel's 32,000 (ver. 3) seem few as compared with Midian's 135,000 (ch. viii. 10. In man's judgment, they needed increase, not diminution. But God would show that He can save by them that have no power

(2 Chron. xiv. 11), so that the glory may be all His own].
(3) *Now therefore go to, proclaim in the ears of the people, saying, Whosoever (is) fearful and afraid* [note, ver. 1], *let him return and depart early* [so Rabbi Levi: *Yitzpor*, akin to *tzaphirah*
'morning' (Ezek. vii. 10). But *Gesenius* and Keil, from an Arabic
root, *to go in a circle*, "let him slink away" in winding by-paths]
from mount Gilead [Deut. xx. 8. As Gideon's army was
stationed west of the Jordan, and was gathered out of the same
quarter, the mountain range of Gilead east of the Jordan
cannot be here meant. It is probably a familiar designation
of the *Manassites* (representatives of Gideon's whole army),
derived from the original settlement of their half tribe east of
the Jordan, though in the present war the *western* Manassites
alone of the tribe took part (vi. 35). 'Gilboa,' whereon
Gideon was encamped, is the conjecture of Clericus, but no
MS. or old version warrants it. Lieut. Conder, (*Tent Life,
Palest.*, ii. 69) thinks the Mount Gilead here is part of the Gilboa
chain above the river *Jalud* (see note 'Harod' above). Gilead
is perhaps a name akin to Jalud]. *And there returned of the
people twenty and two thousand; and there remained ten thousand*
[less than a third. The nearness of the all-devastating foe
made them 'fearful']. (4) *And the* LORD [JEHOVAH] *said unto
Gideon, The people (are) yet (too) many; bring them down unto
the water* [of the well Harod], *and I will try* [צָרַף, meaning
literally to *purify* precious metals of their dross: so Isa. i. 25;
Zech. xiii. 9; compare Jer. xv. 19] *them for thee there; and it
shall be (that) of whom I say unto thee, This shall go with thee,
the same shall go with thee; and of whomsoever I say unto thee,
This shall not go with thee, the same shall not go.* (5) *So he
brought down the people unto the water; and the* LORD [JEHOVAH]
said unto Gideon, Every one that lappeth [licketh up] *of the water
with his tongue* [after having taken the water from the brook
with the hollow of his hand], *as a dog lappeth, him shalt thou
set by himself; likewise every one that boweth down upon his knees
to drink* [the former men were the energetic warriors who did
not, like the latter, self-indulgently kneel down to drink
freely in the ordinary way, but, remembering the battle before
them, took only such moderate refreshment as would strengthen

them for it with the least possible delay, and never, even for a time being off their guard or laying aside their armour; type of Messiah's zeal (Ps. cx. 7)]. (6) *And the number of them that lapped, (putting) their hand to their mouth, were three hundred men; but all the rest of the people bowed down upon their knees to drink water.* [Though the test was a good one for finding out the bravest men, it was one which Gideon would never have practised so as to diminish his army, already so much reduced, in the face of 135,000 enemies (viii. 10), unless Jehovah Himself had ordered it. The Divine command to Gideon to purge out from his small army all but 300, tested his faith in God's promise, and his obedience. When the victory followed, it could be ascribed to Jehovah alone, who made such a little band successful against such a vast host]. (7) *And the* LORD [JEHOVAH] *said unto Gideon, By the three hundred men that lapped will I save you, and deliver the Midianites into thine hand* [God's promise rewarded Gideon's past obedience, and encouraged him to a further act of obedience required, namely, that he should send away the 9700 to their homes]; *and let all the (other) people go every man unto his place.* (8) *So the people* [the 300] *took victuals in their hand, and their trumpets* [rather, as the Septuagint and the Chaldee versions, "They (the 300) took the victuals *of the people* that had been sent away and their own war trumpets "]; *and he sent all (the rest of) Israel every man unto his tent, and retained those three hundred men* [furnished from the dismissed men with a pitcher filled with victuals and a war trumpet apiece]: *and the host of Midian was beneath him in the valley* [of Jezreel (vi. 33, vii. 1)]. (9) *And it came to pass the same night that the* LORD [JEHOVAH] *said unto him, Arise, get thee down unto the host* [' *into* ' the foe's ' *camp,*' to smite it]; *for I have delivered it into thine hand* [in my sure purpose (iv. 14)]. (10) *But if thou fear to go down, go thou with Phurah thy servant down to* [אֶל, *to,* not as in the former clause בְּ, *into* the midst of it, to smite it, but to ' the outside' of it, to reconnoitre] *the host* [' encampment,' *Mahaneh*]: (11) *And thou shalt hear what they say; and afterward shall thine hands be strengthened to go down* [*into* בְּ] *the host* [' encampment ']. *Then went he down with Phurah his servant unto* [*to* אֶל] *the outside of the armed men* [*Chamushim*, from *chamash*, 'sharp,' 'active' in battle (Gesenius); or else 'quinquefied,' from *chameesh*, 'five,' 'marshalled' as an army in the 'five' parts—the centre, two wings, front and rear guard (marg., Exod. xiii. 18). *Five* was a sacred number among the Egyptians (Gen. xlvii. 2; Isa. xix. 18). The Hebrews may have adopted it in civil concerns from them. The Midianite armed men, "arrayed in divisions," are thus distinguished from the general mass, consisting of camp followers, wives, children, cattle, and camels, probably *in the rear* (ch. vi. 5); (*that*) *were in the host* ['encampment']. (12) *And the Midianites and the Amalekites, and all the children of the east, lay along the valley like grasshoppers* ['locusts'] *for multitude; and their camels* (*were*) *without number, as the sands by the sea-side for multitude* [Josh. xi. 4]. (13) *And when Gideon was come, behold,* (*there was*) *a man that told a dream unto his fellow, and said* [the Dibon Moabite stone shows how similar the Moabite language was to Hebrew, hence Gideon understood the Midianite, whose language was akin to the Moabite], *Behold, I dreamed a dream, and, lo, a cake* [*a round cake* (Gesenius)] *of barley-bread* [the food of the poor, and so the symbol of the poor Israelite *cultivator*, in the nation's present humiliation] *tumbled* [in Gen. iii. 24, *mithapeek* is used of the sword "turning itself"] *into the host* [the camp] *of Midian, and came unto a* [rather *the*] *tent* [that of the captain of the host. "The tent" represented the nomad life of Midian, averse from the labour of cultivating the soil, and loving the freedom of tent life], *and smote it, that it fell, and overturned it* [upside down], *that the tent lay along* [in ruins]. (14) *And his fellow answered and said, This* (*is*) *nothing else save the sword of Gideon* [the barley-cake *turning* or *brandishing* itself suggested the interpretation that it meant a sword (note on 'tumbled,' ver. 13)] *the son of Joash, a man of Israel;* (*for*) *into his hand hath God delivered Midian, and all the host* ['the camp,' the very words of God in ver. 9; and therefore repeated by Gideon to his men (ver. 15). The coincidence between the Midianite's interpretation of his fellow's dream and God's promise to Gideon himself, and the Providence which caused the interpretation to be given just at that moment, and also the panic which the interpretation implied as existing among the Midianites, combined to assure of victory the Israelite leader]. (15) *And it was (so), when Gideon heard the telling of the dream, and the interpretation thereof, that he worshipped* [God, with joyful thanksgiving for the pledge of assurance vouchsafed], *and returned into the host* [camp] *of Israel, and said, Arise; for the* LORD [JEHOVAH] *hath delivered into your hand the host* [camp] *of Midian.* (16) *And he divided the three hundred men (into)* [so 1 Sam. xi. 11; 2 Sam. xviii. 2] *three companies* [so as to assail the camp from three different quarters (ver. 18, 21); Gideon heading one, the other two under their respective leaders imitating him], *and he put a trumpet in every man's hand, with empty pitchers, and lamps* [rather 'firebrands,' as in ch. xv. 4, 5], *within the pitchers* [to hide the flame till the decisive moment]. (17) *And he said unto them, Look on me, and do likewise; and, behold, when I come to the outside of the camp, it shall be (that), as I do, so shall ye do.* (18) *When I blow with a trumpet, I and all that (are) with me, then blow ye the trumpets also on every side of all the camp, and say, (The sword)* [supplied from ver. 20] *of the* LORD [JEHOVAH], *and of Gideon.* (19) *So Gideon, and the hundred men that (were) with him, came unto the outside of the camp* [concealed in their advance by the folds of the rolling ground] *in the beginning of the middle watch; and they had but newly set the watch* [the Israelites originally divided the night into three watches,—the first from sunset to 10 P.M. (Lam. ii. 19); the middle from 10 P.M. to 2 A.M. (here); and the morning from 2 A.M. to sunrise (Exod. xiv. 24; 1 Sam. xi. 11). In Roman times the Jews had four watches (Matt. xiv. 25; Mark xiii. 35). The first sentries of the Midianites had been relieved, and the second posted; so that the host, calculating on a long rest till the morning watch, had given themselves up to sleep, when Gideon's band from three different quarters startled them (1 Thess. v. 3)]; *and they blew the trumpets, and brake the pitchers that (were) in their hands.* (20) *And the three companies blew the trumpets, and brake the pitchers, and held the lamps* ['fire-brands'] *in their left hands, and the trumpets in their right* hands to blow (*withal*) ; and they cried, *The sword of the* LORD [JEHOVAH], *and of Gideon* [borrowing this watchword from the Midianite's dream (ver. 14), from which Gideon knew his name was a terror to the foe]. (21) *And they stood every man in his place round about the camp ; and all the host ran* [hither and thither, not knowing what was the matter], *and cried* [in alarm], *and fled* [supposing that an army was behind the fire-brand-bearers, and that these were lighting the way for the hosts behind them. Their own *camp* was in darkness : the sudden flashing of the lights and blowing of trumpets confused them, so that they mistook friend for foe, and fleers for pursuers. By standing still, each trumpeter seemed to be leaving a passage for the armed men to advance into the Midianite camp. (See the remarks on ch. vi. ; also 1 Sam. xiv. 20 ; 2 Chron. xx. 23). Suspicion of treachery would arise in the mixed host of Midianites, Amalekites, and Arabs. The Chethib or Hebrew text read " *caused to flee,*" *yanisu,* for the Queri or margin reading *yanusu,* ' fled ;' *i.e.,* they carried away their goods to a place of safety (as in ch. vi. 11, margin ; Exod. ix. 20). The Chethib is probably the original reading, and the Queri an emendation, to escape the difficulty of the sense]. (22) *And the three hundred blew the trumpets, and the* LORD [JEHOVAH] *set every man's sword against his fellow* [suspecting treachery], *even throughout all the host ; and the host fled to Bethshittah* [' house of the Acacia,' now *Shatta*] *in Zererath* [probably Zeredath near Succoth, in the plain of the Jordan, 2 Chron. iv. 17], (*and*) *to the border of Abel-Mcholah* [" field of the dance," now *Wady Maleh,* north of the Jordan valley ; Elisha's birth-place south of Bethshean (Scythopolis), Zartanah (1 Kings iv. 12, xix. 16) ; belonging to the half tribe of Manasseh living west of the Jordan. Their course was directly down the main road to Jordan], *unto Tabbath* [further south in the Jordan valley]. (23) *And the men of Israel gathered themselves together out of Naphtali, and out of Asher, and out of all Manasseh* [viz., the men of these tribes who had been sent away before the battle, and who were now on their way home. When the news of Midian's defeat reached them, they speedily assembled again to join Gideon in pursuing the foe. Zebulun (vi. 35), though not mentioned, is probably understood as included in ' Naphtali,' the tribe with which it was so closely connected (ver. 18)], *and pursued after the Midianites.* (24) *And Gideon sent messengers throughout all mount* [the hill country of] *Ephraim, saying, Come down against the Midianites, and take before them* [for the Midianites could only move slowly with their herds and flocks] *the waters unto Beth-barah* [meaning "house of the passage." Probably the same as Bethabara (John i. 28). The modern *'Abarah* is one of the main fords of Jordan, just above where the Jalud river, flowing down the valley of Jezrael and by Beisan (Bethshean), debouches into Jordan. Christian tradition made the fords of Jericho the scene of John's baptism. But how then could Christ in one day have travelled eighty miles to Cana (Kefr Kenna)? (John ii. 1.) But if *'Abarah* was the scene, then He would have but twenty-two miles to travel in going to Cana. Moreover, the other reading of oldest MSS. ' Bethany,' akin to *Batanœa, Bashan,* accords; for the *'Abarah* ford is near the hills of Bashan, whereas the Jericho fords are far away. The ' waters,' as distinguished from the ' Jordan,' were the streams and large pools which the Midianites had to cross before reaching it, viz., Wady *Maleh, Fyadh, Jamel, Tubâs,* &c., which flow down from the east of the hilly region of Ephraim to Beth-barah and the Jordan] *and Jordan. Then all the men of Ephraim* [who heretofore had taken no part in the war of deliverance, Gideon not having presumed to summon that haughty tribe (Josh. xvii. 14–18; Judg. viii. 1–3)] *gathered themselves together, and took the waters unto Beth-barah and Jordan.* (25) *And they took two princes of the Midianites, Oreb and Zeeb; and they slew Oreb upon the rock Oreb, and Zeeb they slew at the wine-press of Zeeb.* [We should not have known, if we had the book of Judges alone, the greatness of the slaughter of Midianites; but it comes out with all the particularity of truth in incidental notices in other Scriptures: Isa. x. 26, ix. 4; Ps. lxxxiii. 9–11. East of Jordan, probably now *'Ash el Ghorab, i.e.,* " raven's nest," a sharp conical rock. *Tuwayl el Diab,* " Wolf's den," a wady and mound, answers to the wine-press of Zeeb, *i.e.,* ' the wolf,' two miles north-west of

'Ash el Ghorab], *and pursued Midian, and brought the heads of Oreb and Zeeb to Gideon on the other side of Jordan* [Gideon having cleared the Bethshean valley of Midianites, crossed at the southern end of Succoth, and continued the pursuit along the eastern bank. The Ephraimites intercepted Oreb and Zeeb, who followed the western bank southwards, intending to cross at Jericho. The men of Ephraim sent the heads of Oreb and Zeeb to Gideon on the other side of Jordan].

CHAPTER VIII.

GIDEON'S VICTORY OVER SELF PRELIMINARY TO HIS COMPLETE
    CONQUESTS OF MIDIAN, AND CHASTISEMENT OF CHURLISH
    SCOFFERS.

(1) *And the men of Ephraim said unto him* [when they
brought the heads of Oreb and Zeeb to him on the east side
of Jordan (vii. 25). Their pride and jealousy were excited,
because he had undertaken and succeeded in such a great war,
without their co-operation, as they considered their tribe the
leading one (see ch. xii. 1). "The envy of Ephraim" was
proverbial (Isa. xi. 13). Pride is the parent of envy. Jacob's
preferring Ephraim before Manasseh was made a plea for
pride; but true greatness is in humility (Gen. xlviii. 14, 17–19)]
Why hast thou served us thus ["what is this thing thou hast
done unto us"?], *that thou calledst us not when thou wentest to
fight with the Midianites? And they did chide with him
sharply.* (2) *And he said unto them, What have I done now in
comparison of you?* [illustrating Prov. xv. 1, xvi. 32, xix. 11.
The present victory over his own spirit exceeded his past
victory over Midian, and prepared for the final triumph. As
by pride cometh contention, so by humility and meekness
cometh peace (Matt. v. 5). Contrast Jephthah (Judg. xii.
1–6), and the deadly end of strife to the originators of the
quarrel (Prov. xvii. 14, xiii. 10)]. *(Is) not* [even] *the gleaning
of the grapes of Ephraim better than the* [whole] *vintage of
Abiezer?* [Ephraim's 'gleaning' means their victory over the
retiring Midianites; that it was a crushing defeat, appears
from Isa. x. 26. Gideon salves over their wounded pride by
implying, they had effected more in the brief time since they
joined him, than he had in the whole campaign. "The

vintage of Abiezer" means the Abiezrite Gideon's victory
with his 300. He ascribes the victory not to himself, but to
the whole clan of Abiezer. Ephraim had slain the two
Midianite princes, which he had failed to do]. (3) *God hath
delivered into your hands the princes of Midian, Oreb and
Zeeb ; and what was I able to do in comparison of you?
Then their anger* [Heb. *ruach,* 'spirit' (Prov. xxxv. 28 ; Eccl.
vii. 9] *was abated toward him, when he had said that.* (4) *And
Gideon came to Jordan* [the history goes back to narrate Gideon's
movements after the battle on the west of Jordan, and his
crossing it eastward (vii. 25, end) in the meantime. After
having sent messengers to beg Ephraim to intercept the main
body of the fleeing Midianites before they could cross the river,
he and his 300 men, though faint, pursued to the east side of
Jordan Zebah and Zalmunna, the kings of Midian, and their
15,000 men who had succeeded in crossing, before he could
overtake them], (*and*) *passed over, he and the three hundred men
that* (*were*) *with him, faint, yet pursuing* (*them*) [contrast 1 Sam.
xxx. 10]. (5) *And he said unto the men of Succoth* [evidently
east of the Jordan, for Gideon came to it, after having crossed
Jordan, going south and east ; see Josh. xiii. 27. The course
of the Jabbok (*Zerka*) is the only convenient route by which
the caravans of commerce and the hordes of Midian could pass
from the east and south to the west of Jordan ; and is therefore
termed (ver. 11), " the way of them that dwelt in tents." Now
in the great plain, north of the Jabbok, one mile north of the
stream and three miles from where it leaves the hills, there is a
Tel named *Der'ala,* answering to the name by which Succoth
was known in the time of the Talmud, 'Ter'alah.' Broken
pottery abounds on it. To the east is a ford of the Jabbok
named *Mashra'a Canaan, i.e.,* " Canaan's Crossing." Gideon
having crossed the Jordan by one of the fords near Bethshean,
hurried down the Jordan valley as far as to Succoth, and
halted there to refresh his wearied men. But the men of
Succoth, as living on the great route between Canaan and the
east, feared the vengeance of Midian, and therefore refused
supplies to Gideon, preferring to be neutral till they should
see the issue of Israel's struggle with Midian. Succoth was

on the direct route between the Jabbok and Shechem (now Nablus) by way of the Damia ford: so the order of places enumerated in the 60th Psalm is "Shechem, the valley of Succoth (on the route to Gilead), Gilead." Here Jacob found pasture abundant along the Jabbok stream for his flocks and herds, and therefore "built an house" at Succoth, "and made booths for his cattle" (Gen. xxxiii. 17, margin)], *Give, I pray you, loaves of bread unto the people that follow me* [Gideon is more concerned for his men than for himself]; *for they (be) faint, and I am pursuing after Zebah and Zalmunna, kings of Midian* [Oreb and Zeeb were only *military chief captains* (שַׂר, *Saree,* applied to Sisera (iv. 2), or 'princes:' Zebah and Zalmunna were the (מַלְכֵי, *Malkee*) 'kings.' After the men of Succoth had failed to join their brethren in the national struggle of independence, the least they could do was to help Gideon's fainting little band with bread: they had not the common humanity to do so (compare Deut. xxiii. 3, 4)]. (6) *And the princes of Succoth said, (Are) the hands* [Heb. 'the palm,' 'the hollow of the hand,' *Kaph,* the *grasp*] *of Zebah and Zalmunna now in thine hand, that we should give bread unto thine army?* [Compare Nabal's churlishness (1 Sam. xxv. 8–11). Contrast Barzillai's conduct and reward (2 Sam. xvii. 27–29, xix. 33–40). Fear of Midian's vengeance, pusillanimous regard for self alone, and contempt of the smallness of Gideon's force (300 pursuing 15,000), whereby they betrayed their unbelief towards God, actuated the men of Succoth. Their seemingly prudent policy proved to be most imprudent. The venture of faith is the true wisdom, and in the end furthers one's best interest. They added insolence to unkindness]. (7) *And Gideon said, Therefore when the* LORD [JEHOVAH] *hath delivered Zebah and Zalmunna into mine hand, then I will tear* [Heb. 'thresh' (so Amos i. 3; compare 2 Sam. xii. 31; Isa. xli. 15)] *your flesh with the thorns of the wilderness, and with briers* [they had identified themselves with the ungodly, who are symbolised by "briers and thorns," therefore with 'briers' and "thorns of the wilderness" (*i.e., strong thorns,* for the wilderness is their natural soil, Isa. v. 6), they must be chastised (2 Sam. xxiii. 6, 7; Isa. xxvii. 4)]. (8) *And he went up thence to Penuel* [which was *higher up* towards the mountains than Succoth, which lay more in the valley and on the north of the Jabbok. Penuel was a frontier 'tower' or fortress, built in the earliest times to repel invaders from the east who always came along the course of the Jabbok. Jeroboam, among his first acts on becoming king, "went out" and rebuilt it: otherwise hordes might have by this route advanced to the Damia ford of the Jordan, and swept up the *Wady Fari'a*, and attacked Shechem his capital (1 Kings xii. 25). Four miles above "Canaan's Crossing," following the course of the stream, in a line with the valley which run from east to west, from its lowest level rise two conical hills, 250 feet high, called "Hills of Gold," from their yellow sandstone, one on one side of the stream, and the other on the other side. The ruins on the western hill are more numerous. On the eastern hill, halfway up the side, is a platform several hundred feet long, and supported by a strong wall. This was probably the foundation of the fortress. The great unhewn stones mark the age long prior to Roman times. That this was the Penuel tower seems likely, as no other ruins occur along this great Jabbok thoroughfare up to Kalat Zerka, 50 miles from the mouth of the river. The name given by Jacob *Peni-el*, "the face of God," from his having seen God as man there, answered to the physical conformation of the place, which would always fix on it the name], *and spake unto them likewise; and the men of Penuel answered him as the men of Succoth had answered (him).* (9) *And he spake also unto the men of Penuel, saying, When I come again in peace, I will break down this tower* [on which you rely as sure to save you from the penalty of your insolence]. (10) *Now Zebah and Zalmunna (were) in* [the] *Karkor* [from a root 'to dig,' *soft level ground:* akin to Kerak, "an even floor," within less than a day's march from Succoth (ver. 13, 14), near Nobah and Jogbehah (ver. 11). The Hebrew article implies it was a *well known region:* perhaps the rich plain *En-Nukrah* in the Hauran], *and their hosts with them, about fifteen thousand (men), all that were left of all the hosts of the children of the east* [after their slaughter by Gideon, and their second slaughter by Ephraim at the rock Oreb]: *for there fell an hundred and twenty thousand men that drew sword.* (11) *And Gideon went up by the way of them that dwelt in tents* [*i.e.*, by their usual route in passing into and from Canaan] *on the east of Nobah* [formerly Kenath (Numb. xxxii. 42), now *Nowakis*] *and Jogbehah* [a city fortified by Gad (Numb. xxxii. 35), *Jebeiha* now, a ruin seven miles to the north-east of Es-Salt], *and smote the host; for the host was secure* [Gideon took a circuit past the most easterly frontier city of Gad, so as to fall on them from the east, a quarter whence they apprehended no danger, especially *at night*, and least of all from such an handful of men as 300, and those wearied with fighting and pursuing (1 Thess. v. 3)]. (12) *And when Zebah and Zalmunna fled, he pursued after them, and took the two kings of Midian, Zebah and Zalmunna, and discomfited* ['terrified'] *all the host* [taken by surprise, and therefore panic-struck, by the attack at night: ver. 13 proves it was a *night* attack. Had it been by day, the Midianites would have seen his small numbers. They never feared a night attack again by a foe which had been engaged with them on the previous night. (13) *And Gideon the son of Joash returned from battle before the sun* (*was up*) [the English version wrongly puts in italics *was up*, as if these words were not in the Hebrew: the literal translation is, " from in connection with the going of the sun" (compare Gen. xix. 15, " when the morning arose "). The use of the same Hebrew, *Heres, for the sun*, in xiv. 18, sustains this meaning here, in opposition to the Septuagint, Peshito, and Arabic, which translate " from the ascent of Heres " or Heheres, a place now unknown in front of Succoth. Gideon attacked Succoth at so early an hour as to take them by surprise]. (14) *And caught a young man of the men of Succoth, and inquired of him ; and he described unto* [rather " wrote down for "] *him the* [names of the] *princes of Succoth, and the elders thereof,* (*even*) *threescore and seventeen men* [enabling Gideon to know whom to punish, viz., the guilty rulers, and whom to spare, viz., the innocent people]. (15) *And he came unto the men* [*i.e.*, the elders] *of Succoth, and said, Behold Zebah and Zalmunna, with whom ye did upbraid me, saying,* (*Are*) *the hands of Zebah and Zalmunna now in thine hand, that we should give bread unto thy men* (*that are*) *weary ?* (16) *And he took the elders of the city, and thorns of the wilderness, and briers, and with them he taught* [יֹּדַע, *caused them to know* to their cost. Rightly read by English version : for commonly Scripture, in referring to the same fact, varies the word, in order to bring out a fresh truth (compare Ps. lvi. 13 with cxvi. 8). The reading יָדֹש, 'thresh,' from ver. 7, seemingly adopted by the Septuagint and Vulgate version, and approved by Speaker's Commentary, is just what a copyist would insert to harmonise ver. 16 with ver. 9 (compare Prov. x. 13, xix. 29, xxvi. 3). Dame Experience keeps a dear school, but fools will learn in none other] *the men of Succoth.* (17) *And he beat down the tower of Penuel* [compare ix. 46, 47], *and slew the men of the city* [the representative men, the elders, as in the case of Succoth (ver. 5, 6, 8, 9). These had possession of the tower, and so could domineer over the people. As judge of Israel, Gideon punished them]. (18) *Then said he unto Zebah and Zalmunna, What manner of men (were they) whom ye slew at Tabor ?* [whither Gideon's brethren had fled, to hide in the dens of the mountains from before the Midianites (vi. 2), but were caught and slain]. *And they answered, As thou (art), so (were) they ; each one resembled* [" like the form of "] *the children of a king.* (19) *And he said, They (were) my brethren, (even) the sons of my mother* [a closer relationship than brothers only by the same father (Gen. xliii. 29 ; Ps. lxix. 8)] : *(as) the* LORD [JEHOVAH] *liveth, if ye had saved them alive, I would not slay you* [the Midianite kings had not slain them in open battle, but murdered them in cold blood. They therefore must pay with their blood the innocent blood they shed (Gen. ix. 5 ; 1 Sam. xv. 32, 33)]. (20) *And he said unto Jether his first-born, Up, (and) slay them* [Gideon devolves on his son his own duty of avenging his brethren's blood (2 Sam. iii. 30) on the Midianite kings, in order to add to death the disgrace of their falling by a boy's hand; also in order to give his son a share in the honour of slaying the foes of God. So Christ shall honour His saints (Ps. cxlix. 6–9 ; Rev. xix. 13–15)] : *but the youth drew not his sword ; for he feared, because he (was) yet a youth.* (21) *Then Zebah and Zalmunna said, Rise thou, and fall upon us ; for as the man (is, so is) his strength* [full strength to kill speedily belongs to men of full age, not to boys]. *And Gideon arose, and slew Zebah and Zalmunna, and took away the ornaments* ['little moons' or crescent-shaped ornaments of silver or gold, worn as amulets round the neck (ver. 26 ; Isa. iii. 18). The custom prevailed among the Arabs as late as Mahomet's time] *that were on their camels' necks.*

THE DEFEAT OF MIDIAN A TYPE OF THE OVERTHROW OF SATAN'S KINGDOM.

1. We observe *the men chosen to conquer in the wars of the* LORD.—The 32,000 Israelites thought themselves too few, and therefore were 'fearful;' Jehovah thought them too many. So in the gospel warfare, it was when the disciples were few and weak, that the Lord wrought mighty results by them (Acts iv. 13–31). Deborah blamed those who "came not to the help of Jehovah;" yet here He sends away those who come. For God would show that He can make the weakest mighty, through God, to the pulling down of Satan's strongholds (2 Cor. x. 4, 5). The believer who would conquer, must be stripped of every creaturely confidence. There is a continual tendency in the natural heart to "vaunt itself against Jehovah, saying, Mine own hand hath saved me" (compare Habuk. i. 16). Yet the same heart is as easily cast down unto unbelieving terror, like the fearful Israelites who shrank from battle. "So bladder-like is the soul, that, filled with the wind of vain-glory, it grows great, and swells in pride ; but if pricked with the least pin of grief or fear, shrivelleth to nothing" (Trapp). He who seeks either glory or salvation in the Christian warfare, must glory in the Lord alone (see 1 Cor. i. 26–31). He who will not give God the honour of the victory, is shut out from the honour of His service. At the same time, He will not be served by those who in fear shrink from the good fight : "The fearful and unbelieving shall have their part in the lake that burneth with fire and brimstone" (Rev. xxi. 8). He seeketh as His soldiers those who take earthly refreshments as necessaries by the way, like the three hundred, but do not rest in them. The process of judgment and testing is even now going on, whereby "the precious are taken forth from the vile" (Jer. xv.

19 ; John ix. 39, xii. 47, 48). Those alone who in the strength
of the Holy Spirit are " zealously affected always in the good "
cause (Gal. iv. 18), and who can master themselves, shall master
the prince of this world (1 Cor. ix. 25–27 ; 2 Tim. ii. 3–6 ;
Tit. ii. 12). Many are called, but few chosen. If those called
prove unworthy, the Lord will raise up other instruments.
Hence we can understand why at times He allows the
supporters of His church to be so diminished ; it is that He
may be exalted in His own strength (Ps. xxi. 13).

2. *The weapons of their warfare.*—The accoutrements of
Gideon's band were as strange, and as little likely to ensure
success, as the band itself was in numbers seemingly powerless
to meet the numerous foe.   (1) Each man took no more *victuals*
than he could carry *in his hand,* thus living literally from hand
to mouth.   So the Christian must live each day content with
God's provision for the day, as to both soul and body.   The
manna of to-day will not suffice for to-morrow.   He must wait
on God afresh to-morrow for the things of the morrow (see
Matt. vi. 11, 34 ; Deut. xxxiii. 25 ; 1 Kings viii. 59, margin.
(2) Each man bore a *trumpet* in his right hand.   So each
soldier of Christ carries the gospel trumpet.   The minister
especially must lift up his voice as a trumpet (Isa. lviii. 1).
As the walls of Jericho fell by the trumpet blast, so Satan's
kingdom must fall by the preaching of the everlasting gospel
(Rev. xi. 15).   (3) Each man bore in his left hand *an earthen
pitcher,* with a torch light hidden within.   So we Christians
have " the light of the glorious gospel of Christ, who is the
image of God," whilst we are still in a fragile body (see 2
Cor. iv. 4–18).   The pearl of great price is often hidden in an
unsightly oyster shell.   The breaking of the vessel, so far from
quenching the light, only brings it to view—flashing destruction
to the foe, salvation to the Israel of God.   So it is often when
the believer's body is breaking up, that the light from the
spirit within shines the brightest.   The light beamed forth
from Stephen's face just when he was about to be crushed by
the stones hurled by his persecutors.   The gospel *trumpet*
sounds at the same time that the *light* shines forth.   That
preacher's words are as thunder, whose life is as the lightning.

" Look on me, and as I do, so shall ye do," is the word of
command to us from the Captain of our salvation, the antitype
to Gideon (John xiii. 15 ; Heb. xii. 2). " Looking unto Jesus,"
and doing as He did, we shall find Him " the Finisher," as He
is " the Author of our faith."

3. *The complete victory which crowns their conflict.*—(1) *It
is a victory gained by the Lord for man, and through man.* The
sword which smote Midian was the sword *of Jehovah ;* without
Jehovah in the forefront, Gideon's name would have been but
a worthless cipher, without the figure which alone could give
it value. So man can do nothing severed from Christ ; yet
Christ will have man, when made willing in the day of His
power, to be His instrument ; therefore it is added, " the sword
of Gideon." God first worketh in His people to will and to
do : then they must in His strength work out that which He
has wrought in them (Phil. ii. 12, 13). (2) *It is a victory of
faith through hearing the word of God.* The Midianites themselves betrayed their sense of inability to withstand the God
who was with Gideon ; so the powers of darkness cower before
Jesus (Matt. viii. 29). The rock of worldly men's confidence is
not as our Rock, even our enemies themselves being judges
(Deut. xxxii. 31 ; Jer. xl. 3). Gideon went down as his own
spy, to hear for himself : so faith comes by hearing (Rom.
x. 17). (3) *It is a victory in which saint combines with saint.*
Phurah accompanied him, for two are better than one : and the
Lord Jesus sent out the seventy two by two. Phurah was but
a servant, yet his name will be immortal, when mighty kings
and conquerors shall be forgotten, because he was associated
with Gideon. So the Lord will give unto those now associated
with Him in the heavenly warfare an everlasting name (Isa.
lvi. 5). (4) *It is a victory with the sword of the Spirit, the word
of God.* The sword of Gideon hung idle at his side. It was
the shout, " The sword of the Lord and of Gideon," that won
the victory. So the sword which routs Satan's hosts, is the
sharp two-edged sword which goeth *out of the mouth* of Him
who is the Word of God (Rev. xix. 13, 15, 21 ; Isa. xi. 4 ; 2
Thess. ii. 8 ; Heb. iv. 12). The barley-cake, rolling down from
above, overturned Midian's tents. So He who fed five

thousand with five barley loaves, makes the preaching of the cross, which is to them that perish foolishness, to be unto us which are saved, the power of God (1 Cor. i. 18). The Israelites needed but to stand still in their places, and to see the salvation of the Lord. Jehovah did all for them. One of them chased a thousand : and whithersoever their enemies fled from death, they ran into it. So it shall be in the great day of the Lord. At the blast of the archangel's trumpet (of which the trumpets of Gideon's 300 were the type), the ungodly shall hide themselves in the rocks of the mountains from the wrath of the Lamb (Isa. ii. 21; Rev. vi. 15–17). As Oreb had formerly forced Israel to hide in the rocks, so was he slain at the rock Oreb (vi. 2); and as Gideon was formerly forced to hide his corn by the wine-press (vi. 11) from the Midianites, so their prince Zeeb was slain by the Israelites at the wine-press of Zeeb. The places of their shelter became the places of their slaughter. They were punished in kind, the instrument of their sin being made the instrument of their punishment. So it shall be in the final award. "The Lord of hosts shall stir up a scourge for "Antichrist, " according to the slaughter of Midian at the rock of Oreb " by Ephraim (Isa. x. 26). The transgressor's own wickedness shall reprove him ; his sin shall find him out ; and he shall too late see, to his eternal self-reproach and remorse, that it was an evil thing and bitter that he forsook the Lord (Jer. ii. 18 ; Isa. iii. 9 ; Prov. i. 31 ; Rev. xxii. 11.

FINAL TRIUMPH OF THE MEEK : CHASTISEMENT OF MOCKERS :
RETRIBUTIVE BLOOD-SHEDDING OF THE BLOOD-SHEDDERS.

1. The meek and lowly King of glory hath said, " Blessed are the meek, for they shall inherit the earth " (Matt. v. 5). To conquer self in the strength of Jehovah, and "not to be overcome of evil, but to overcome evil with good," is a grand first victory, and prepares us for greater victories. One of Satan's favourite devices is to sow discord among those who are brethren in the common war against the powers of evil. Ephraim strives against Manasseh (Isa. ix. 21); and Gideon, "Why hast thou

served us thus?" None are louder in finding fault than those who are most in fault. Passionate invective betrays a bad cause. "Reason runs low when chiding flies high" (M. Henry). Instead of chiding, Ephraim ought to have been congratulating Gideon, and thanking God, for his success in the common conflict. Unless Gideon had immediately quenched the spark of strife, it would have burst forth into a deadly flame (compare ch. xii.). For "a brother offended is harder to be won than a strong city" (Prov. xviii. 19). Then the fruit of the victory, just won over the foe, would have been lost through the mutual strifes of the conquerors. If we Christians have the cause of our Lord more at heart than the honour of self, we will "esteem others better than ourselves" (Phil. ii. 3), "in honour preferring one another" (Rom. xii. 10). Yet whilst ready to humble ourselves in order to honour our brethren, we will be, like Gideon (ver. 3), jealous for the honour of the Lord, and will never let regard for others prevent our giving all the glory to Him. So in the great vintage to come, every man shall have his praise of God, according to his efforts against the enemy, whether he have been but a gleaner, or a gatherer of many clusters for the great Master (1 Cor. iv. 5; Rev. xiv. 18–20).

2. *Chastisement of mockers.*—As Gideon knew when to yield, so he knew when to be stern. So the soldier of Christ, whilst he will readily yield to the brethren fighting in the same holy cause, will faithfully denounce the terrors of the Lord to false brethren and unbelieving mockers. Gideon and his brave three hundred men were worn and weary, yet following on in their course, with what little strength they had, relying on Jehovah—"faint, and yet pursuing." Herein they typify the Christian warrior—"troubled on every side, yet not distressed; cast down, but not destroyed" (2 Cor. iv. 7–10, vi. 9, 10). "The excellency of the power of God" to sustain has most scope for exercise in our weakness, if only we "run with patience the race set before us, looking unto Jesus" (Heb. xii. 1, 2; 1 Cor. ix. 24–27).

Gideon in pursuing the foe came to Succoth. Here, if anywhere, he might have calculated on receiving refreshments for his weary band. He had every right to demand from the

K

citizens, as being Israelites, military succours. But he limited his request to their supplying the first necessary of life, "loaves of bread." Common humanity ought to have made them willing, yea glad, to satisfy the hunger of fainting fellow-men. The tie of religious and national brotherhood was a still stronger claim. But selfishness, cowardly fear of Midian, and disbelief in God's faithfulness to his promise of victory to Gideon, steeled their heart: they proved themselves traitors to the Israel of God; and they added insult to their unfeeling refusal. According to their unbelief, it happened unto them. The scourge of the tongue wherewith they insulted Gideon (Job v. 21), brought upon them "the overflowing scourge" (Isa. xxviii. 18). Instead of the sweet brier, wherewith God chastens His children, they were made to feel the tearing brier of vengeance (Ps. lxxxix. 32, xciv. 12, 13). So it shall be in the day of retribution. The Lord Jesus will say to those on the left hand, "Depart, ye cursed, into everlasting fire," the fit place for scratching briers and thorns; "for I was an hungered, and ye gave me no meat" (Matt. xxv. 41–45). He who is the meek and loving Lamb of God will show himself the avenging God of wrath to the scorners. The Arabian proverb says, "Take heed thy tongue cut not thy throat"; when the Lord shall come, "He shall convict all the ungodly of all their *hard speeches* which ungodly sinners have spoken against Him" (Jude 15). "Judgments are prepared for scorners, and stripes for the back of fools" (Prov. xix. 29). Especially in the last days shall there be 'scoffers,' saying, "Where is the promise of His coming?" and refusing to believe it, until they 'see' it (2 Pet. iii. 3, 4; Isa. v. 19, lxvi. 5; Jer. xvii. 15; Amos v. 18). Though the followers of Christ are now a "little flock," and the world seems far the stronger, yet faith enables us to overcome the world, and to act as knowing that ours is the winning side. Every ministration of love, every service of good to the brethren for our dear Lord's sake, shall be richly rewarded, as surely as the unprofitable servant shall be cast into outer darkness.

3. *Retributive blood-shedding of the blood-shedders.*—Zebah and Zalmunna had cruelly murdered Gideon's brethren in cold

blood, having followed them to their hiding place in Mount
Tabor. They thought, at the time, that they were perfectly
secure from all penal consequences. Sins long forgotten by
man, must be answered for to God. It is thus that always
Satan deludes men into sin, by promising them impunity,
saying, " Ye shall not surely die." The Midianite kings then
had hundreds of thousands on their side. But God speedily
reduced their thousands to hundreds. Still, having once
crossed the Jordan, and reached the wild region of "the way of
them that dwelt in tents," they thought themselves beyond the
reach of the avenger. But justice overtook them (see Amos
ix. 2, 3), just when the host was 'secure' (ch. xviii. 27).
As "judgment began " with the men of Succoth and Penuel,
who were of Israel, "the house of God;" so it next fell with
heaviest weight on the godless heathen enemy (1 Pet. iv. 17).
Zebah and Zalmunna paid with their own blood for the
innocent blood which they had shed long previously. So it
shall be in the coming end of this age : " When men shall say,
Peace and safety ; then sudden destruction cometh upon them,
and they shall not escape." The deeds of darkness, which
transgressors supposed would never come under the cognizance
of God, " because sentence against an evil work is not executed
speedily " (Eccles. viii. 11–13), shall then be brought to light.
And the prophecy of the angel shall be fulfilled : " They have
shed the blood of saints and prophets, and Thou hast given
them blood to drink " (Rev. xvi. 6). Let us learn, with patient
continuance in well-doing, to wait for that time of retribution
to the saint as well as to the sinner. Though the world know
nothing of our struggle with our spiritual foes, it is no less a
real and arduous life-long conflict : let us persevere, however
faint, yet pursuing. The hindrances from treacherous professors, Israelites in name but Midianites in heart, are especially
perilous. But all difficulties shall be surmounted at last ; and
the remembrance of the past conflict will enhance the bliss of
the heavenly home, where conflict shall be unknown, after that
we shall have been made " more than conquerors through Him
that loved us " (Rom. viii. 37).

GIDEON'S REFUSAL TO RULE BECAUSE OF LOYALTY TO GOD :
HIS DEVIATION FROM GOD'S LAW BEARS DEADLY FRUIT.

(22) *Then the men of Israel* [probably only of Manasseh,
Asher, Zebulun, and Naphtali (ch. vi. 35)] *said unto Gideon,
Rule thou over us, both thou and thy son, and thy son's son also*
[the name *Abimelech,* "father of a king" (ver. 31), which he gave
to his concubine's son, looks like as if he afterwards harboured
the thought of establishing an hereditary kingship, which at
first he rejected disinterestedly] : *for thou hast delivered us from
the hand of Midian.* (23) *And Gideon said unto them, I will
not rule over you, neither shall my son rule over you : the* LORD
[JEHOVAH] *shall rule over you* [not only modesty and humility
prompted his reply : but loyalty to the King of the Israelite
theocracy, Jehovah (1 Sam. viii. 7, xii. 12, 17; Numb. xxiii.
21). Moses indeed contemplated the contingency of their
desiring an earthly king, and laid down laws concerning him
(Deut. xvii. 14–20); but this, though permitted in condescension
to Israel's infirmity, was not the highest ideal; Israel's true
glory was to have Jehovah among and over them as King].
(24) *And Gideon said unto them, I would desire a request of you,
that ye would give me every man the ear-rings* [or *nose-rings,*
margin (Ezek. xvi. 12; Isa. iii. 21; Job xlii. 11; Gen. xxiv.
47)] *of his prey : (for they had golden ear-rings, because they
(were) Ishmaelites)* [the general name for the Arabian nomads,
including the Midianites (Gen. xxxvii. 25, 28). Gideon, though
he rejected the tempting offer of kingship, yielded to the
temptation of securing to himself the continuance of his *quasi-
priestly* office in relation to Jehovah and the people. He had
been honoured with the vision of the angel of Jehovah, calling
him to be judge and deliverer of Israel. His gift had been
accepted, as a well-pleasing sacrifice ; by Divine direction he
had built an altar to Jehovah, and sacrificed a bullock as a
burnt offering with the wood of the Asherah, after destroying
it and the altar of Baal (ch. vi.). By thus re-establishing the
worship of Jehovah, he had restored God's favour to Israel ;
and God had granted him several revelations]. (25) *And they
answered, We will willingly* [Heb., " *Giving we will* "] *give (them).*

And they spread a garment [*Simlah,* the upper garment, a large square piece of cloth], *and did cast therein every man the ear-rings of his prey.* (26) *And the weight of the golden earrings that he requested was a thousand and seven hundred shekels of gold* [the weight of Rebekah's nose-ring was half a shekel (Gen. xxiv. 22). If these Ishmaelite rings were of the same weight, then 1700 shekels would imply that 3400 wearers of rings were slain], *besides ornaments* [(ver. 21), note, *Saharonim; crescent-shaped,* worn on the necks of men, women, and camels], and *collars* [*Netiphoth,* 'ear-drops'], *and purple raiment that* (*was*) *on the kings of Midian, and besides the chains that* (*were*) *about their camels' necks* [*i.e.*, beside the spoils of the kings which Gideon had already appropriated (ver. 21). The Arabs at the present day ornament their camels' necks with a cloth or leather band, on which cowries are sewed in the form of a crescent. Moses mentions "gold, silver, brass, iron, tin, and lead" (Numb. xxxi. 22, 50–54) among the spoils which Israel took from Midian; also "jewels of gold, chains, bracelets, rings, ear-rings, and tablets." Capt. Burton has found abundant mines of these metals in Midian, and traces of mine-workings, Roman and pre-Roman. Madi is the old Egyptian name found in papyri: the plural is Madian. The northern mining district, the port of which is Makua, has not been much worked. The southern, with Wedj as its harbour, shows traces of ancient scientific labour. Even carelessly cupelled specimens yielded 15 to 20 per cent. of silver. In the southern district, gold mining takes the place of silver and copper. The Marreh or volcanic district is covered with ruins of mining works. In parts the snowy quartz hill had been so burrowed into that it has fallen in. Thus the accuracy of Scripture is verified in ascribing such abundance of the precious metals to a land now so desolate]. (27) *And Gideon made an ephod thereof* [*i.e.*, defrayed with the gold (1700 shekels) the cost of workmanship and of the twelve stones in the breastplate (*choshen*), and the two on the shoulders, and of the chains of gold twist for fastening the *choshen* upon the ephod, and of the material worked throughout with gold threads, and of the gold braid in which the precious stones were set, and of the

gold rings (Exod. xxviii. 6–30)], *and put [kept] it in his city,
(even) in Ophrah; and all Israel went thither a whoring after it*
[Gideon made no image, nor did he expose the holy coat for
worship. His error lay in his usurping the prerogative of the
Aaronic priesthood, by assuming the ephod, as a permanent
instrumentality (1 Sam. xiv. 3, xxiii. 6, 9, 10) for consulting
Jehovah by means of the Urim and Thummim. These were
either *lots,* or more probably stones with Jehovah's attributes,
' lights ' *(urim)* and ' perfections ' *(thummim)* engraven on them,
placed within the folds of the double *choshen* or breastplate.
By gazing at them the high priest, in his ephod, before
Jehovah, was absorbed in ecstatic contemplation, and enabled to
declare the Divine will. The altar (vi. 26) afforded Gideon a
divinely sanctioned place for worshipping Jehovah with sacrifice.
Thus he drew away the people from the one lawful sanctuary ;
and thereby undermined the theocratic oneness of Israel, and
paved the way for the nation's apostasy to Baal idolatry, which is
spiritual 'whoredom,' after his death. Gideon's pretext, whereby
he justified his act to himself and others, was probably the fact
that Jehovah had manifested Himself to him directly, as He had
not to any other ruler since Joshua], *which thing became a snare*
[*i.e.,* the cause of *destruction,* as a snare suddenly entrapping its
victim: not as the English implies, the means of *ensnaring into
idolatry* (Luke xxi. 35 ; Isa. viii. 14)] *unto Gideon and to his
house.* (28) *Thus was Midian subdued before the children of
Israel, so that they lifted up their heads no more. And the
country was in quietness* [(so v. 31) " the land had rest "] *forty
years in the days of Gideon* [so long as he lived]. (29) *And
Jerubbaal the son of Joash went* [as in Ezek. ii. 1, pictorially
representing the fact] *and dwelt in his own house* [the name
' Jerubbaal,' here resumed from ch. vii. 1, is used throughout
ch. ix. It brings into vivid contrast the repose which
succeeded the conflict. The Baal-conqueror, who overthrew
Midian, declined the crown, to retire into domestic privacy].
(30) *And Gideon had threescore and ten sons of his body
begotten; for he had many wives* [another blemish in his otherwise generally upright character (Deut. xvii. 17 ; 1 Kings xi.
1–3). (31) *And his concubine that was in Shechem* [a

Canaanite probably (ix. 28)], *she also bare him a son, whose name he called* [*Yasem*, 'set'] *Abimelech* [Gideon gave him this *surname* after he had grown up and manifested qualities which warranted the expectation he would prove a *kings-father—i.e.,* founder of a dynasty of kings; or else Gideon yielded to the ambitious views of the mother in naming the son so; for Abimelech is a native *Canaanite* name (Gen. xxvi. 1)]. (32) *And Gideon the son of Joash died in a good old age* [Gen. xxv. 8], *and was buried in the sepulchre of Joash his father, in Ophrah of the Abiezrites* [vi. 11; Job v. 26. The penal consequences of his declension did not ensue till the time of his sons. So in the case of Solomon and Ahab (1 Kings xi. 34, 35, xxi. 29)]. (33) *And it came to pass, as soon as Gideon was dead, that the children of Israel turned again, and went a whoring after Baalim* [from which Gideon had turned them (vi. 25–28), an instance of the general fact stated in ii. 19], *and made Baal-berith their god* [*i.e., lord of the covenant* (ix. 46); Baal in covenant with the people, and they with him. A sad defection from Jehovah in covenant with them (Gen. xv. 18, xvii. 2), Baal substituted for Jehovah! Shechem was the seat of this Baal worship (ix. 4). Gideon's concubinage was there (ver. 31). Whoredom paves the way for idolatry (1 Kings xi. 1–8; Hos. iv. 11, 12)]. (34) *And the children of Israel remembered not the Lord their God, who had delivered them out of the hands of all their enemies on every side:* (35) *neither showed they kindness to the house of Jerubbaal, (namely) Gideon* [the combination of names points to the debt of gratitude due to Gideon as the one who delivered them first from Baal-worship, then from its penal consequence, bondage to Midian], *according to all the goodness which he had showed unto Israel* [it was just retribution that as he had been latterly turning away from the law of God, so they should turn away from him and his seed].

CHAPTER IX.

ABIMELECH'S SUCCESSFUL USURPATION THROUGH MURDER AND
CONSPIRACY : JOTHAM'S PROPHECY VERIFIED : FRIENDSHIP
BASED ON SIN IS HOLLOW : THE SLAYER IS SLAIN.

(1) *And Abimelech the son of Jerubbaal went to Shechem, unto
his mother's brethren* [ch. viii. 31 : of the original *Canaanite*
population, which ought to have been exterminated according
to God's command. Gideon's neglect of this eventuated in
his concubinage with them entailing judgment upon his house
after his death], *and communed with them, and with all the
family of the house* [*i.e.*, the whole clan] *of his mother's father,
saying,* (2) *Speak, I pray you, in the ears of all the men* [Heb.
ba'alee, 'masters'; often found in the Phœnician dialect.
Applied to the men of Gibeah (ch. xx. 5); and the Canaanite
citizens of Jericho (Josh. xxiv. 11); and to the men of Keilah
(1 Sam. xxiii. 11, 12). The continual recurrence of this word
(ver. 2, 6, 7, 18, 20, 23, 24, 25, 26, 39, 46, 47, 51) can hardly
be accidental; it probably alludes to *the majority of them being
Canaanites* (see ver. 28), and connected with the Phœnician
Baal-worship of Canaan] *of Shechem, Whether (is) better for
you, either that all the sons of Jerubbaal, (which are) threescore
and ten persons* [the name employed, 'Jerubbaal,' or *destroyer
of Baal,* was one well calculated to prejudice against his
seventy sons the men of *Shechem,* who were *worshippers of Baal.*
The seventy sons had not aspired to kingship; but it suits
Abimelech's purpose to *assume* they did], *reign over you, or that
one* [only, *i.e.,* I Abimelech] *reign over you? remember also
that I (am) your bone and your flesh* [your kinsman (Gen. xxix.
14). Abimelech sets at nought his father's explicit wish, " my
son shall not rule over you " (viii. 23)]. (3) *And his mother's*

*brethren spake of him in the ears of all the men of Shechem all
these words; and their hearts inclined to follow Abimelech; for
they said, He (is) our brother.* (4) *And they gave him threescore
and ten (pieces) of silver* [*i.e.,* shekels] *out of the house Baal-
berith* [viii. 33. Temple treasures were often used for political
ends (1 Kings xv. 18). The seventy silver pieces or shekels
(Numb. vii. 13, 14) would allow one each for the murder
of Gideon's seventy sons: at so little did Abimelech value
the blood of his brethren. How awful that sacred money
should be employed for murder! But idolatry and unnatural
bloodshed go together], *wherewith Abimelech hired vain* [*reequ,*
'empty' of moral principle] *and light* [*pochazim,* literally
boiling up: so *wanton, desperate*] *persons, which followed him.*
(5) *And he went unto his father's house at Ophrah, and slew his
brethren, the sons of Jerubbaal, (being) threescore and ten* [note
ver. 18] *persons, upon one stone* [Abimelech formally executed
them, as though it were not an assassination, but a judicial
execution at one particular spot marked by a great stone. It
is not unlikely that, as the *threescore and ten* pieces of silver
were supplied him out of the house of Baal-berith, the *threescore and ten* persons slain, one for each piece, were intended
to be expiatory victims to Baal for the sacrilege done to him
by Jerubbaal their father. As Jerubbaal had sacrificed to
Jehovah upon the altar rock, using the sacred bullock and the
Asherah grove associated with Baal worship, to consume his
burnt-offering; so the Baal worshippers, who had been offended
at his act, but who durst not show their displeasure heretofore,
now that he is dead, wreak their vengeance on his sons at
Abimelech's instigation, and offer them all together upon an
altar-like stone (see ch. vi. 25–30; 1 Sam. vi. 14, 15]: *notwithstanding, yet Jotham, the youngest son of Jerubbaal, was left; for
he hid himself* [polygamy begets treachery and fratricide,
especially when ambition instigates men. A false religion
removes all moral restraints. Abimelech's bloody act at
Shechem was the precursor of the extermination of dynasty
after dynasty in the kingdom of the ten tribes which was
founded by Jeroboam at the same Shechem, and upheld by
idolatry (1 Kings xv. 27–29, xvi. 10, 11, 18; 2 Kings x. 7,

xv. 13–16, 25, 30]. (6) *And all the men of Shechem gathered together, and all the house* [the inhabitants, the men or masters (*baalee*) ver. 46] *of Millo* [the citadel of Shechem, distinct from but close to the town, called "the tower of Shechem" (ver. 46–49). The word means a rampart consisting of two walls, with the intervening space *filled* (from *malee*) with rubbish. The Millo in Jerusalem was a similar tower (2 Sam. v. 9 ; 1 Kings ix. 15, xi. 27 ; 2 Kings xii. 20], *and went and made* [the phrase "went and made" implies *going in a determined course* (Isa. lvii. 17)] *Abimelech king* [whereas God was the true King of the Israelite theocracy (1 Sam. viii. 7). The title 'king' was not offered to Gideon, but only that of 'ruler' (note viii. 22, 23). Even it he rejected. But the son snatches at the Canaanite title, being a true Canaanite in spirit] *by the plain* [rather *the terebinth tree*] *of the pillar* [rather *the memorial;* the two nouns together express "*by the memorial terebinth*." Gesenius takes it (as in Isa. xxix. 3), "by the terebinth (oak) of the *garrison*," מֻצָּב, *mutztzab.* The rendering 'memorial' (the thing set up) better brings out the significant fact that Abimelech's usurpation of royalty took place *on the spot where the memorial stone was set up by Joshua* (xxiv. 1, 25, 26), when he held the national assembly for renewing Israel's covenant with the true covenant-God, Jehovah : the oak was associated with Israel's forefathers— Abraham (Gen. xii. 6, where translate "*oak* of Moreh"), and Jacob (Gen. xxxv. 4). Hard by was the temple of the falsely-called *covenant-god*, Baal-berith (ver. 46)], *that was in Shechem.* (7) *And when they told (it) to Jotham, he went and stood in the top of mount Gerizim* [2500 feet above the Mediterranean, commanding one of the finest views in Palestine], *and lifted up his voice and cried* [comp. Prov. viii. 1, 3, ix. 3], *and said unto them* [De Saulcy argues that, as the top of Gerizim is 500 yards above *Nablous,* on the south of which it rises, the voice could not be heard, and that not *Nablous,* but the ruins *Louza* (*Luz*), on Gerizim, answer to ancient Shechem; he has identified there the foundations of Sanballat's temple. But the acoustic properties of the place are attested by Tristram. Jotham probably stood on the side of the summit towards the people, who, according to Josephus, were keeping a feast outside the city. Gerizim was the hill from which the blessings of the law were declared, as being the southern mount, and as the Hebrews associated life and light with the south. Ebal was the hill of the curses (Josh. viii. 30–35) on the north. Jotham, on the hill of *blessing*, utters the *cursing*, their sin turning the blessing into the curse (yet there is nothing of violent invective: he contents himself with witnessing for God the certain consequences of cruelty and ingratitude: see 1 Pet. iii. 9; 2 Tim. ii. 24, 25)], *Hearken unto me, ye men [' lords,' baale] of Shechem, that God may hearken unto you* [see Prov. xxviii. 9]. (8) *The trees went forth* [it might seem he ought rather to have said that 'the bramble' (Abimelech) went to the trees, than the trees to the bramble. But the Holy Spirit rightly directs the words to express that the Israelites were already burning with desire for a king: already they had applied to Gideon, begging him, his son, and his son's son (answering to the *three* trees, the olive, fig, and vine specified) to rule (viii. 22). Heb., "The trees *going went*," implying *eagerness in going*. This suicidal wish at last was conceded by God to their hurt, under Saul (1 Sam. viii. 4–20)] (*on a time*) *to anoint a king* [see 1 Sam. x. 1, oil representing the Holy Spirit's unction (Ps. ii. 6; Isa. xi. 1–3)] *over them; and they said unto the olive-tree, Reign thou over us.* (9) *But the olive-tree said unto them, Should I leave* [by your persuasion, *hechodalti*, an unique form 'cause to cease'] *my fatness, wherewith by me they honour God and man* [for oil was used in the sacred lamps, the whole burnt offerings, the peace offerings, the meat offerings, and the holy ointment (Lev. ii. 1–16; Exod. xxx. 24, 25, xxxv. 14); also for food, medicine, light, anointing the person, to mollify the skin, heal injuries, and strengthen muscles (Ps. civ. 15, cxli. 5; Isa. i. 6; Luke x. 34; 2 Chron. xxviii. 15; Mark vi. 13; James v. 14)], *and go to be promoted* [נוע, *to hover in agitation: to soar and float in the air;* for laborious and restless anxiety is the penalty of royalty; shall I tear myself from the soil in which I am firmly rooted *to soar in perpetual unrest*] *over the trees?* (10) *And the trees said to the fig-tree, Come thou, (and) reign over us. But the fig-tree said unto them, Should I forsake my sweetness, and my*

good fruit, and go to be promoted [to soar restlessly] *over the
trees ?* (12) *Then said the trees unto the vine, Come thou,*(and)
reign over us. (13) *And the vine said unto them, Should I leave
my wine, which cheereth God* [not that God drinks wine ; though
the God-man drank it, and shall drink it anew in the Father's
kingdom (Matt. xxvi. 29). But He accepted libations of wine
poured forth in His honour at sacrifices (Lev. xxiii. 13 ; Numb.
xv. 5, 7, 10] *and man* [Ps. civ. 15 ; Prov. xxxi. 6 ; Jer. xvi. 7],
and go to be promoted [to soar restlessly] *over the trees ?* (14)
Then said all ['all' is not in vers. 8, 10, 12 ; for *the bramble*
did not join the trees in offering the kingdom to the olive,
the fig, and the vine. But *all* the trees were unanimous in
offering it to the bramble : not one of them all wished it for
himself except the bramble] *the trees unto the bramble* [not our
trailing blackberry, but the *Paliurus rhamnus aculeatus,* a low
stunted tree, with drooping jagged branches and sharp thick
thorns, affording no shade : only scratching those who touch
it : fit emblem of the base-born, self-important, mischievous
Abimelech, who accepted the kingdom to the ruin of the
offerers ; whereas the noble Gideon and his sons declined it],
Come thou, (and) *reign over us.* (15) *And the bramble said unto
the trees, If in truth* [implying the bramble's delight at the
unexpected honour : he can scarcely believe it *true*] *ye anoint
me king over you,* (then) *come* (and) *put your trust in my shadow*
[What irony ! The shadow of a bramble, which if you were to
lie under, and move hand or foot, would scratch, not shade
you !] ; *and if not, let fire come out of the bramble, and devour
the cedars of Lebanon* [despicable as the bramble is, even it, if
set on fire, as its only end is burning, can burn up the stately
cedar (Exod. xxii. 5 ; Ps. lviii. 9 ; Heb. vi. 8). Jotham hints
that a worthless man soon betrays the tyrant-spirit ; he makes
the bramble betray this in his very first speech accepting the
kingdom, ' If all my commands are not instantly obeyed, and
you do not abjectly put yourselves under me, then let destruction from me come upon, not merely the commonalty, but the
noblest ']. (16) *Now therefore, if ye have done truly* [Heb., as in
ver. 15, 'in truth,' Jotham here begins the interpretation : and
appeals to the people's conscience to judge, whether or not the

bramble's view of 'truth' is right] *and sincerely, in that ye have made Abimelech king, and if ye have dealt well with Jerubbaal and his house, and have done unto him according to the deserving of his hands;* (17) (*for my father fought for you, and adventured* [Heb. *cast away*] *his life far, and delivered you out of the hand of Midian.* (18) *And ye are risen up against my father's house this day, and have slain his sons* [viz., by giving out of the house of Baal the money wherewith Abimelech hired men to help him in assassinating them], *threescore and ten* [the round number for the actual number sixty-nine: for Jotham escaped (ch. viii. 30, ix. 56)] *persons upon one stone, and have made Abimelech, the son of his maid-servant, king over the men of Shechem, because he (is) your brother)* [ver. 2, 3]. (19) *If ye then* [resuming the 'if,' ver. 16] *have dealt truly aud sincerely* [the same Heb. as in ver. 16] *with Jerubbaal and with his house this day, (then) rejoice ye in Abimelech, and let him also rejoice in you* [I wish both parties joy in one another]. (20) *But if not* [as is the fact, ver. 17, 18], *let fire come out from Abimelech* [as the bramble prayed, ver. 15], *and devour the men of Shechem, and the house of Millo; and let fire come out from the men of Shechem* [this is a new feature that was not in the fable, but is introduced by Jotham here first. Bad men are punished by the bad], *and from the house of Millo* [for the revolt of Thebez where Abimelech was killed (ver. 50–54), was connected with Shechem's revolt from Abimelech], *and devour Abimelech.* (21) *And Jotham ran away, and fled* [the accumulation of verbs marks *the haste and narrow escape* of Jotham after his faithful warning: so Elijah, 1 Kings xix. 3] *and went to Beer* [eight miles north of Eleutheropolis, on the road from Jerusalem to Gaza, in the plain (Jerome): now *El Bireh*, near the mouth of the *Wady es Surar*], *and dwelt there, for fear of Abimelech his brother.* (22) *When Abimelech had reigned three years over Israel* [Heb., governed, 'was prince over': *yasar*, from *Sur*; not 'reigned.' The Shechemites alone "made him king": the rest of Israel (probably only northern Israel, Ephraim and Manasseh) submitted to his usurped despotism as prince, of necessity, not of choice], (23) *Then God sent an evil spirit* [*a* demon, in judicial retribution (1 Sam.

xvi. 14–23, xviii. 10, xix. 9). 'God,' *Elohim,* as the God of
justice, sent it, not *Jehovah,* the covenant God of His people]
*between Abimelech and the men of Shechem ; and the men of
Shechem dealt treacherously with* [conspiring secretly against]
Abimelech [nothing is more unstable than popularity gained by
wickedness. The friendship of the wicked is a lie], (24) *That the
cruelty* [*chamas* "the wrong" or 'violence'] (*done*) *to the threescore and ten sons of Jerubbaal might come, and their blood be laid
upon Abimelech their brother* [who ought to have been their
defender : an awful aggravation of the crime (Gen. iv. 8, 9)],
which slew them ; and upon the men of Shechem, who aided him
[Heb., *strengthened his hands :* viz., by supplying the money to
hire murderers (ver. 4, 5] *in the killing of his brethren* [compare
1 Kings ii. 5, 32, 33 ; Matt. xxiii. 35]. (25) *And the men of
Shechem set liers in wait for him* [to waylay himself, if he
should come that way : at all events to get all they could from
passers-by, his officers and others] *in the top of the mountains*
[Ebal and Gerizim, between which Shechem lay], *and they
robbed all that came along that way by them* [thereby rendering
administration of law impossible, and bringing his government
into contempt : brigandage preparing the way for open rebellion] :
and it was told Abimelech. (26) *And Gaal the son of Ebed*
[probably a roving Shechemite captain of freebooters ; one of
the ancient stock of the Hivite Hamor (ver. 28), welcomed by
the Shechemites as a suitable leader of revolt. Ebed means " a
servant." As Abimelech by the mother's side, so Gaal by the
father's side, was son of a servant, and a Canaanite. Here was
bramble fighting with bramble !] *came with his brethren* [his clan
and followers], *and went over* [simply ' passed ' from where he
had been] *to Shechem : and the men* [Heb., *ba'ale,* ' lords '] *of
Shechem put their confidence in him* [heretofore there had been
secret plotting : Gaal develops it into open revolt at the idolatrous feast of Baal-berith]. (27) *And they went out into the
fields* [which till Gaal came they durst not do, through fear of
Abimelech, whose anger they had provoked (ver. 27)], *and
gathered their vineyards, and trode* (*the grapes*), *and made merry*
[*hillulim,* rather " they made *praise-offerings,*" *i.e.,* thank-offer-
ings accompanied with praise-songs. The offerings consisted of

the fruits which orchards and newly planted vineyards bore in
the fourth year : thereby the vineyard was sanctified to Jehovah
(margin, Lev. xix. 24), in Hebrew the same word as here,
' praise-offerings.' The Shechemites transferred them to Baal-
berith their idol !], *and went into the house of their god* [how
righteous the retribution, that as out of the house of Baal-
berith came the instrument of sin, so from it should come the
judgment on the sin (ver. 4, 5)], *and did eat and drink*
[drunkenness preparing men for all violence], *and cursed
Abimelech* [renouncing allegiance with reviling insults, in
violation of (Exod. xxii. 28 end: compare ver. 28 ; 2 Sam. xix.
21 ; Isa. viii. 21). Gaal saw now his opportunity of inciting
them to open rebellion, and of being made their leader]. (28)
And Gaal the son of Ebed said, Who (*is*) *Abimelech* [compare 1
Sam. xxv. 10], *and who* (*is*) *Shechem* [the ' who,' Heb., *mi*, must
refer to *persons*, not things. *Who* are the *Shechemites*, as
represented by Abimelech's " officer Zebul," that we should
serve them ? (The LXX. paraphrase " the son of Shechem," or
the view which takes ' Shechem ' for *Abimelech*, as an arbitrary
assumption. Gaal explains himself ; for " the son of Jerubbaal "
explains " Who is Abimelech?" " Zebul his officer " explains
" Who is Shechem ? " Gaal here does not speak of the Shechemites in general, with whose ancient line he rather would identify
himself, but of a petty section, the 'Shechem' whom Zebul repre-
sented] *that we should serve him?* (*Is*) *not* (*he*) *the son of Jerubbaal ?* [Gaal uses this name rather than ' Gideon,' to stigmatise
him as *overthrower* of the altar of *Baal* their god, for which act
the Shechemites themselves had tried to slay him (ch. vi.
30, 31)] ? *and Zebul his officer? Serve the men of Hamor the
father* [in paternal kindness as well as by natural generation]
of Shechem [Gen. xxxiii. 19, xxxiv. 2 ; Josh. xxiv. 32. Serve
the patricians of the city, who are sprung from the ancient stock
of Hamor, instead of serving the one man, Zebul, Abimelech's
officer, representing but a petty section of Shechem. Abimelech
was but half a Shechemite, viz., on his mother's side (ver. 18,
viii. 32) ; from her he took his Canaanite name (Gen. xxvi. 1).
But on his father's side he was an Israelite. Remnants of the
Hivites or Canaanites had survived the destruction by Israel,

and revived the worship of Baal. Possibly the term *Baale*, applied to "the men of Shechem," may hint the same fact (note ver. 7)] : *for why should we serve him?* (29) *And would to God this people were under my hand* [my rule ; the usual style of pretenders to rule (2 Sam. xv. 4)] ! *then would I remove Abimelech. And he said to Abimelech, Increase thine army, and come out* [he challenges Abimelech through Zebul, and defies him]. (30) *And when Zebul the ruler of the city heard the words of Gaal the son of Ebed, his anger was kindled.* (31) *And he sent messengers unto Abimelech privily* [the Septuagint and Chaldee support the English version of the Hebrew *Bethormah*, " with deceit," *i.e., dissembling his sentiments before Gaal*, the section of Shechemites who still adhered to Abimelech being too weak to oppose Gaal till Abimelech should come. But Kimchi translates " in Tormah," *i.e.,* Arumah, the name of the place where Abimelech resided (ver. 41)], *saying, Behold, Gaal the son of Ebed, and his brethren, be come to Shechem ; and, behold, they fortify* [*tzarim*, from *tzur :* rather " stir up," " excite "] *the city against thee.* (32) *Now therefore up by night, thou and the people that (is) with thee, and lie in wait in the field.* (33) *And it shall be, (that) in the morning, as soon as the sun is up, thou shalt rise early, and set upon* [Heb., *phashatta*, " spread out " thy troops against] *the city ; and, behold, (when)* [rather omit the *when*, which is not in the Hebrew] *he and the people that (is) with him come out* [*will have gone out*] *against thee* [*or towards thee (eeleka)*. The scheme was that when Gaal should have gone forth from Shechem to begin the campaign against Abimelech, or else simply to protect the people in the field (ver. 27, 42), without a suspicion that the latter was so near, and when he was coming ' towards ' Abimelech who lay in wait, Abimelech should get between Gaal and the city, and take it by surprise], *then mayest thou do to them as thou shalt find occasion* [Heb., " as thine hand shall find," *i.e., as the occasion shall require*]. (34) *And Abimelech rose up, and all the people that (were)* [*i.e.,* the troops that he had] *with him by night, and they laid wait against Shechem in four companies* [Heb., ' heads ']. (35) *And Gaal the son of Ebed went out, and stood in the entering of the gate of the city : and Abimelech rose up,*

and the people that were with him, from lying in wait [with the
intention of stealthily advancing into the city when Gaal should
have left it, but this intention failed in part, owing to Gaal
seeing Abimelech's men]. (36) *And when Gaal saw the people,
he said to Zebul* [who through fear had not heretofore dared to
oppose Gaal, but temporised], *Behold, there come people down
from the top of the mountains. And Zebul* [coming out to the
gate with Gaal] *said unto him* [to deceive him, and gain time for
Abimelech's four companies to effect a junction], *Thou seest the
shadow of the mountains (as if they were) men.* (37) *And Gaal
spake again, and said, See there come people down by the middle*
[Heb., *Navel, the elevated centre*] *of the land, and another company
come along by the plain of Meonenim* [rather "The *Wizard's
oak :*" the Hebrew is translated "Observers of times" in Deut.
xviii. 10, 14. Abimelech's idolatrous force possibly observed
omens here to augur as to the success of their expedition
(compare ver. 6 above and Gen. xxxv. 4), a distinct oak]. (38)
Then said Zebul unto him [throwing off the mask, when
Abimelech was near], *Where (is) now thy mouth, wherewith
thou saidst, Who (is) Abimelech, that we should serve him ? (Is)
not this the people that thou hast despised ?* [Satan tries to
persuade sinners, hell is but a 'shadow' (ver. 36) without a
substance : then taunts those whom he tempted (Matt. xxvii.
4). They shall then too late repent having said, "Who is the
Almighty that we should serve him" (Job xxi. 15 ; Exod. v. 2) ;
and having despised the people of God, when they see them
returning with Christ (Zech. xiv. 5 ; Rev. xix. 14)]. *Go out, I
pray now, and fight with them.* (39) *And Gaal went out before*
[*not at the head of,* for Gaal had only "the people with him"
of his own retinue (ver. 33), but "in the sight of"] *the men*
['masters,' 'owners,' *baale*] *of Shechem* [whose champion he
wished to prove himself (ver. 26, 29)], *and fought with
Abimelech.* (40) *And Abimelech chased him, and he fled before
him, and many were overthrown (and) wounded, (even) unto the
entering of the gate* [whither Abimelech chased him, but was
not able to force an entrance after him. Thus there were
inside two opposing factions, Zebul's and Gaal's, until the
former drove out the latter]. (41) *And Abimelech dwelt* [*yeesheb,*

L

rather 'remained,' with his army, literally 'sat down'] *at Arumah* [see note ver. 31] : *and Zebul thrust out Gaal and his brethren* [his retinue], *that they should not dwell in Shechem* [the faction opposed to Abimelech in Shechem was weakened by Gaal's defeat (ver. 40). So the party of Abimelech headed by Zebul gained accessions from the fickle multitude, and expelled Gaal]. (42) *And it came to pass on the morrow, that the people went out into the field* [not to war with Abimelech, but to their field labours after the vintage (ver. 27)] ; *and they* [Zebul and his party] *told Abimelech* [that now is his opportunity]. (43) *And he took the people* [*his own men:* he had thrown the Shechemites off their guard by retiring to Arumah, as if he meant no further operations against them, and was content with the expulsion of Gaal], *and divided them into three* [he probably joined *two* of the *four* companies (ver. 34) into which he had divided his men, as *one* company under himself] *companies, and laid wait in the field, and looked, and, behold, the people (were) come forth out of the city ; and he rose up against them* [from his ambush, when they had no apprehension of danger], *and smote them.* (44) *And Abimelech and the company* [Heb., "*the companies*" in one company or band, see note ver. 43] *that (was) with him, rushed forward* [*pashtu,* "spread themselves out"], *and stood* [took their station] *in the entering of the gate of the city* [his purpose now, as before (ver. 34), was that while his other divisions were smiting the Shechemites in the field, the company which he commanded in person should occupy the city gate. Gideon his father similarly had divided his men into three companies, and led one himself (vii. 16, 19). Abimelech's stratagem in the former instance was foiled by Gaal's caution (ver. 35). But now the people had gone out into the field, and Abimelech by occupying the ground before the gate with one company, was able to intercept their return after they were smitten by his two other companies] : *and the two (other) companies ran upon all (the people) that (were) in the fields, and slew them.* (45) *And Abimelech fought against the city all that day : and he took the city, and slew the people that (was) therein, and beat down the city, and sowed it* [the site] *with salt* [symbolising his detestation, and his dooming the ground,

not only never to be built upon (Mic. iii. 12), but to become
perpetually a *barren* salt waste (margin, Job xxxix. 6 ; Ps. cvii.
34 ; Jer. xvii. 6). He gave it over to the curse of Sodom and
Gomorrah (Deut. xxix. 23). Salt injures vegetation, and is
the symbol of *perpetuity*]. (46) *And when all the men* [*baale*,
' *masters* ' or inhabitants] *of the tower of Shechem* [the " house
of Millo " (ver. 6, note)] *heard* (*that*), *they entered into a hold*
[*tzeriach*, ' high place ' (1 Sam. xiii. 6] *of the house* [temple] *of
the god Berith* [the covenant-god Baal-berith, to seek safety
in the sanctuary. They, with the folly of idolaters, thought
their god would defend his temple and them. The place too
was strong, as temples often were, especially when used as
treasuries. Moreover, Abimelech, they hoped, would remember
the debt of gratitude he owed for the money he received out
of that very temple, and would spare them there, notwithstanding their having subsequently joined the Shechemites in revolt
(ver. 4)]. (48) *And Abimelech gat him up to Mount Zalmon*
[a hill near Shechem, identified by Dr Stanley with Ebal
(*Sin. and Pal.*, 236, note 4). The word means ' shady,' " Black
Forest " (Ps. lxviii. 14), where the sense is, the bright victory
after the gloomy conflict was like the glittering snow which
relieves the blackness of Salmon's forests], *he and all the people
that* (*were*) *with him ; and Abimelech took an ax* [Heb., " *the axes*,"
for himself and his men. A certain number of axes was part
of the army's equipment for such purposes] *in his hand, and
cut down a bough from the trees, and took it, and laid* (*it*) *on his
shoulder, and said unto the people that* (*were*) *with him, What ye
have seen me do, make haste,* (*and*) *do as I* (*have done*) [the son
imitates Gideon his father's language in giving directions to his
men (vi. 17, 18)]. (49) *And all the people likewise cut down
every man his bough, and followed Abimelech, and put* (*them*) *to
the hold* [which was probably of wood, at least in part], *and set
the hold on fire upon them; so that all the men of the tower of
Shechem died also* [besides the men of Shechem itself] *about a
thousand* [in all, including both] *men and women* [fulfilling to
the letter Jotham's curse (ver. 20)]. (50) *Then went Abimelech
to Thebez* [meaning ' *brightness*.' According to Eusebius, thirteen
Roman miles from Neapolis (Shechem), on the road to Scytho-

polis (Beisan or Bethshean); now *Tubas*, north of Shechem (Robinson, *Pal.*, iii. 156). Its inhabitants had no doubt joined in the revolt against Abimelech], *and encamped against Thebez, and took it.* (51) *But there was a strong tower within the city, and thither fled all the men and women, and* [*i.e.*, namely] *all they of the city, and shut* (*it*) *to them, and gat them up to the* [flat] *top of the tower.* (52) *And Abimelech came unto* [even up to] *the tower, and fought against it, and went hard unto* [approached even up to: Heb., *'ad*] *the door of the tower* [reckless of the certain danger of missiles hurled down from the crowded roof, so desirous was he, through thirst for revenge] *to burn it with fire.* (53) *And a certain woman cast a piece of millstone* [for *women's* office was to grind corn in the quern or hand *millstone* (Luke xvii. 35). Being movable, it would be carried up as essential for preparing food ; and it could be used as a missile. Gesenius rightly explains פֶּלַח רֶכֶב, not merely a fragment, but *the whole upper millstone,* with its *cut* lower side fitting to the upper side of the lower stone : literally, " the *rider-millstone,*" so called from its riding in and on the lower stone. *Pelach,* 'millstone,' is from *palach,* "to cut" (Deut. xxiv. 6). *Rechob* means a 'rider'] *upon Abimelech's head, and all to* [Old English for *altogether*] *brake* [not 'break'] *his skull.* (54) *Then he called hastily unto the young man his armour-bearer, and said unto him, Draw thy sword, and slay me* [compare Saul's death (1 Sam. xxxi. 4)], *that men say not of me, A woman slew him. And his young man thrust him through, and he died.* (55) *And when the men of Israel* [his army, as distinguished from the rebels] *saw that Abimelech was dead, they departed every man unto his place.* (56) *Thus God rendered the wickedness of Abimelech, which he did unto his father* [*upon his head*, as in ver. 57 (compare ver. 24)] *in slaying his seventy brethren.* (57) *And all the evil of the men of Shechem* [his accomplices in the murder] *did God render upon their heads: and upon them came the curse of Jotham the son of Jerubbaal.*

GOD'S RETRIBUTIVE RIGHTEOUSNESS ILLUSTRATED IN THE CON-
TRASTED ISSUES OF FAITHFULNESS AND APOSTASY EVEN
IN THIS WORLD.

1. *Gideon's unambitious spirit : loyalty to God, Israel's true
King : peaceful retirement in his own home, when he might have
been a king : his victory over the foe without, and his moderation
as a judge in administering internal affairs, secured to Israel
forty years' rest: his death in a good old age* (ch. ix. 22–35). (1)
Gideon's piety. The Israelites offered Gideon the rule over them.
Few men would have refused so tempting an offer. But Gideon
knew that he could not accept it without trenching upon God's
prerogative. Jehovah had appointed the Judges by the special
designation of His Spirit to rule by the grace of God, not by
the will of the multitude. Gideon wished still to rule only as
God's viceroy ; nor did he covet to entail upon his children an
usurped authority. Herein he showed his piety towards God,
modesty as regarded himself, and true patriotism towards his
fellow-countrymen. His great services to Israel in the deliverance from the oppressor might seem to warrant his elevation.
But the privilege of doing them good was in his eyes its own
best reward. And a good conscience towards God and man
afforded him far higher satisfaction than could be obtained by
the possession of a precarious and illegal sway.

In the spiritual application, our wisdom is to make request
to the Lord Jesus : " Rule Thou over us, for Thou hast delivered
us." He hath " saved us," at the cost of His own life-blood,
" from our enemies and from the hand of all that hate us."
And His very design was " that we, being delivered out of the
hand of our enemies, might serve Him without fear in holiness
and righteousness before Him all the days of our life " (Luke i.
71, 74, 75). " Servati sumus ut serviamus "—*saved* by God, that
we may *serve* God. He who is the Prophet, Priest, and Redeemer
of His people is the fittest One to whom we shall render our
heart's allegiance, and say, " The Lord is our Judge, the Lord is
our Lawgiver, the Lord is our King " (Isa. xxxii. 22). The
loyal servant of Jesus will shrink from accepting for himself
any of the honour which belongs to the Master alone. So

Paul (Acts xiv. 14, 15; 1 Cor. i. 13); so Peter (Acts x. 25, 26); so the angel (Rev. xix. 10). (Contrast Isa. x. 13, 15, xlii. 8; Habak. i. 16).

(2) *Gideon's modesty and wisdom.*—What he had sought in his service against Midian, was not his own aggrandisement, but Israel's welfare. The true minister of God should act on the principle, "I seek not yours, but you" (2 Cor. xii. 14, 15; 1 Cor. ix. 18, 23). Ambition and self-seeking mar the service of God, and injure the minister's own soul. The service itself is its own highest honour and best reward. The acquisition of power entails loss of ease. The increase of comforts bears no proportion to the increase of cares which greatness entails.

Gideon's *wisdom* too appears in his choosing to remain in the station to which the Providence of God had called him. Midian was now subdued through his agency, and the country was entering on a period of rest which lasted for forty years. The number was the same as that of Othniel's and of Barak's judgeships, and might remind Israel of their forty years of wandering in the wilderness, the penalty of apostasy, just as their present forty years of rest was the fruit of repentance. Restlessness can never bring happiness. The adage is true, " He who carves for himself often cuts his fingers; he who leaves God to carve for him, shall never have an empty plate." " Let every man wherein he is called, therein abide with God " (1 Cor. vii. 24). " Seekest thou great things for thyself, seek them not " (Jer. xlv. 5). How wise was the Shunammite woman's answer when offered greatness: " I dwell among mine own people " (2 Kings iv. 13). Had Gideon accepted greatness, it would have been at the cost of comfort and of conscience. As it was, having ministered for the Lord in public, he now humbly seeks to enjoy the Lord in private; not spoiled by successes and honours, he did not covet a palace, but, his duty having been done, he retired to his own house, whence he had come; like Cincinnatus, who was called from the plough to save his country, and when he had conquered the foe, returned to the plough again. Moreover, what he sought not for himself he sought not for his children—an hereditary crown; for ambition could never promote their real good. God blessed Gideon with a numerous family. And he was gathered to his fathers in peace, honoured and respected, in a good old age—an illustration of the promise, "Thou shalt come to thy grave in a full age, like as a shock of corn cometh in in his season" (Job v. 26). He had lived long enough to "serve his own generation by the will of God," and what more ought to be desired?

2. *Gideon's great error; its injurious effects in his lifetime, and still more fatal consequences afterwards.*—(1) *Gideon's sin, and its bad effects on himself and his family.* Scripture, unlike mere human biographies, tells faithfully the failings of its heroes. The record of the believer's blemishes is as edifying as that of his graces. Others are thereby warned not to trust in their own hearts, which are by nature desperately wicked, but in the grace of God, which alone can keep them from similar falls. "Watch and pray, that ye enter not into temptation." Gideon, though he declined the kingship, virtually assumed a kind of priesthood, by making an ephod, and with it consulting Jehovah to ascertain the Divine will. His pretext probably was that Jehovah had so specially revealed Himself to him, and commanded him to build an altar (vi. 26). But the ephod was an invention of his own; and it is the very condemnation declared against Israel—"They went a whoring with *their own inventions*" (Ps. cvi. 39). Good intentions are no excuse for self-willed inventions. "Will-worship," whatever "show of wisdom" it may have, is self-condemned; for it rests with God, not with man himself, to prescribe the mode of worship acceptable to the Holy One (Col. ii. 23). An oracle of Gideon's own contrivance, and made out of the golden amulets of idolaters, could never be pleasing to God, and was a bad return to make for the Divine favour in granting him victory. It "became a snare unto Gideon" himself, by lessening his zeal for the house of God in Shiloh. Still more so to his family. Besides his error in making an ephod, he committed another evil in multiplying wives; and worse even than this, in connecting himself with a concubine and a Canaanitess. She it was, probably, who moved him to call their son by the name of the Canaanite king, Abimelech,—a presage of the kingship which she coveted

for her son. Gideon showed the same partiality to the son of
the concubine that Abraham had shown to the son of the bond-
maid (Gen. xvii. 18), even to the degree of tacitly allowing the
hope of the kingdom which he had professedly rejected for his
sons as well as for himself. The Holy Ghost has from the
beginning taught us the sin, folly, and trouble to families
involved in violating the original law of Paradise, that one man
should be joined to one wife in holy unity (Matt. xix. 4–8).
His partial apostasy from the unity of the Divine worship, as
represented by the one only priesthood at Shiloh, was doubtless
closely related, as effect and cause, to his connection with a
concubine woman of the corrupt Canaanite stock, for idolatry
and adultery go hand in hand (Mal. ii. 14, 15 ; 1 Kings xi. 3,
4 ; Deut. xvii. 17). Shechem, the scene of his concubinage,
proved to be the seat of the Baal worship which ensued.

(2) *Gideon's sin had a deadly effect on the nation.*—One false
step of a good man leads multitudes astray. All Israel went
a whoring, in spiritual fornication (Ezek. xvi., xxiii.; Rev.
xvii.), after Gideon's ephod. Sin is a growing evil. It is as
the letting out of water through the small aperture of a dyke's
embankment.

> " Vice is a monster of such hideous mien,
>   That to be hated needs but to be seen;
>   But seen too oft, familiar with her face,
>   We first endure, then pity, then embrace."

Fond of change, political and religious, the Israelites had been
checked by Gideon as to the former, but indulged in the latter.
They had the excuse that so good a man had set up the ephod,
made out of the golden prey wrested from the enemy, as their
plea for rendering it reverence ; by slow but sure degrees, the
reverence grew into superstition, and their superstition into
idolatry ; and this ended in their ruin. No sooner was Gideon
dead than they turned again to their idols, from which, as well
as the consequent bondage, he had delivered them, and which
were speedily to prove their destruction. So the time is fast
coming to all who give their hearts to the ornaments which
feed the lust of the eye, and to the idols of the flesh, when
their sin shall prove their ruin for ever. False worship paved

the way for false gods. "They chose new gods" (v. 8)—Baalim
and Baal-berith, "the Lord of the covenant." Satan apes the
prerogative of Jehovah. But the covenant with hell only leads
the covenanters to hell; the covenant with Jehovah secures
everlasting peace (Isa. xxviii. 15–18). If Gideon could have
risen from the grave, and seen the consequence of his one grand
error, how he would have grieved! His fellow-countrymen
fell into base ingratitude towards God in the first instance:
"They remembered not Jehovah their God, who had delivered
them out of the hands of all their enemies." God's judgments
and mercies alike were forgotten. No wonder then that,
secondly, they showed no kindness to the house of their earthly
deliverer, Jerubbaal, the Baal-conqueror, notwithstanding all
his goodness to them. They who remember not their Heavenly
Father, are not likely to remember earthly benefactors. Apostates from God are sure to be unthankful to men.

3. *Israel's apostasy punished, not as heretofore by foreign
oppression, but by internal strife: the destroyers destroyed:
treachery meets treachery.*—(1) (ver. 1–6) *Abimelech's usurpation
based on fratricidal murder.* "Lust when it hath conceived,
bringeth forth sin; and sin, when it is finished, bringeth forth
death "—death to others first, and death to the sinner himself
at last (James i. 15). The mother of Abimelech kindled in
her base-born son the spark of ambition. The name which he
bore, with his father's sanction, and which suggested the notion
of kingship, fanned the flame.

> "The evil which men do lives after them.
> The good is oft interred with their bones."

Scarcely was his father buried out of sight than Abimelech
flies in the face of his father's will—"neither shall my son rule
over you." Without call from God or man, without natural
claim or hereditary right, he aspires to the kingdom. God
permitted it, because it was right that a wicked and apostate
nation should be punished by the wicked ruler of their own
appointment. Heretofore their punishment for apostasy had
been from foes outside; but now that they are weary of the
heavenly King of the theocracy, they must be scourged by the

whip that they prepared for themselves within. Israel, impatient of Jehovah's light yoke, must learn the bitterness of the yoke of the idolatrous king whom she has chosen. Thus the eternal principle of God's righteous *retribution in kind* is illustrated : " Thine own wickedness shall correct thee, and thy backslidings shall reprove thee : know therefore and see, that it is an evil thing and bitter, that thou hast forsaken the Lord thy God " (Jer. ii. 19 ; see Prov. i. 31).

The arts which Abimelech used to compass his end were, pretended concern for the public gain whilst seeking his own, depreciation of the good in order to exalt himself, false accusation, as if Gideon's seventy legitimate sons designed to exercise jointly the supreme power, flattering promises to his mother's family, that his advancement involved their advancement : " Whether is better for you, either that all the sons of Jerubbaal reign over you, or that one reign over you ? remember also that I am your bone and your flesh." Bad men measure others by themselves. They suspect or charge the good with the ambition of self-seeking which are their own characteristics. They cajole men of their own stamp by appealing to their passions and sordid interests. So having gained over his mother's clan, by them he won also all the men of Shechem, who said " he is our brother :" his kingship will advance our city to be the royal metropolis of the kingdom. Then they gave him money from the temple of Baal-berith ; and he who undertook to rule the Israel of Jehovah, became pensioner to an idol ! His authority, which ought to have overthrown the altars of Baal, as his father had done, rested on the bribes of idolaters. Therewith he hired assassins like himself. And Israel, the holy nation, which was bound to shed the blood of the blood-shedder, with one voice advanced the murderer of his seventy brethren to the throne.

Learn the hardening effect of ambition. It bursts the bonds of natural affection and of conscience. It will sacrifice the dearest and most sacred objects to gain its unhallowed end : like Abimelech who, in cold blood, slew his own brothers, all except Jotham. It will use the holy names of justice and religion to justify its violent deeds ; just as Abimelech pretended it was a judicial execution for conspiracy (whence it was perpetrated publicly, and at one time and on one stone): and the *seventy* pieces of silver were given in the name of religion, for the killing of the *seventy* sons of the Baal-conqueror, to propitiate the God for the sacrilege. Israel, whose fathers had so vigorously avenged the murder of the Levite's concubine, now not only does not avenge the murder of the sons of the nation's deliverer, but sets up a concubine's son, the murderer, on the throne (ch. xix. 20). On the very spot where Joshua erected the memorial of Israel's covenant with Jehovah, there degenerate Israel covenants with a Baal-berith and Baal's hireling king Abimelech.

Have we not here a type of man's awful sin in selling in the name of religion, and betraying for thirty pieces of silver, and then murdering, in the name of justice (John xix. 7), the innocent Saviour, the Prince of life and desiring a murderer to be granted them? (Acts iii. 14, 15.)

(2) *Jotham's fable presaging the mutual destruction of Shechem and Shechem's murderous king* (ver. 6–21). His witness against their sin. God has never left His cause without a witness in the worst times (1 Kings xix. 18). His Providence saved Jotham from the general massacre of his brethren, and then endued him with his Spirit, qualifying him to announce the eternal principles of God's righteousness on which prophecy rests. On the mountain of blessing, he declares the sure curse which must overtake the transgressor—a gloomy omen for a coronation day! The act of bloody fratricide might have forewarned Abimelech's Shechemite brethren, what kind of a "brother" he would be to them, when promoted to be their king. They had been the first to raise him up, and they must be the first to feel the weight of his sceptre (Ps. vii. 15, 16).

Jotham's preface is solemn, and calculated to arrest attention: "Hearken unto me, that God may hearken unto you." If we would have God hear us in prayer, we must hear whatever God the Lord speaks in monition: "He that turneth away his ear from hearing the law, even his prayer shall be abomination." Reproof is not pleasant to hear, but, if heeded, it saves from what will be infinitely more unpleasant in the end—the withdrawal of the grace of God for ever (see Prov. i. 24–31).

Jotham's fable is perhaps the oldest in existence (1209 B.C.). The *fable* represents man's relations to his fellow-men. The *parable* rises higher, for it represents the relations between man and God; it rests on the fact that man is made in the image of God, and that the world of nature reflects the spiritual realities of the unseen world. The *fable* rests on what man has in common with the lower creatures, and on the analogies traceable between him and them. The resemblances in the case of the *fable* are only fanciful (compare 2 Kings xiv. 9, the only other fable, strictly speaking, in Scripture); in the *parable* they are real analogies; hence the Divine Son of man uses the parable often, the fable never.

First, is shown *the error of the trees.*—They went in hot haste and ill-timed eagerness seeking out a king. But there was no occasion for them anointing a king over them; for are they not all "the trees of the Lord, which he hath planted" (Ps. civ. 16), and which, therefore, he will not fail to tend? So the Israelites only betrayed their ingratitude and unbelief in seeking a king when Jehovah was their King. Professing Christians in the middle ages, impatient of having only an invisible Head, whose manifestation we are to wait for, set up a temporal and visible head, the Bishop of Rome. Thus the visible church, instead of realising her high privilege in having the Lord Jesus by His Holy Spirit invisibly reigning in her, and coming up out of the wilderness as the Bride waiting for the visible coming of the Bridegroom and King, became the harlot riding on the visible world-power and assuming its gauds, and therefore doomed to be punished by that very world-power on whom she rested (Rev. xvii.). The same eternal principle of Divine righteousness shall be vindicated, and with the same retributive penalty in the case of all the Protestant churches, and in each professing Christian, if, instead of walking by faith in the unseen Saviour, and waiting for His speedy return in person, we insist on having objects of sense and sight as our guide and stay—if, instead of being pilgrims, we must have our kingship now (see 1 Cor. iv. 8; Hos. xiii. 11; 1 Sam. viii. 11–19; Isa. viii. 21, 22). Let us rather glory in this, that we are "trees of righteousness, the planting of the Lord that He may be glorified." And if in times past "other lords" beside Jehovah—lusts (Rom. vi. 16–18); and false prophets, Antichrist especially (Matt. xxiv. 11–24; 2 Thess. ii. 9; John v. 43)—have had dominion, let Israel's resolve henceforth be, "by Him only we will make mention of His name" (Isa. xxvi. 13).

Secondly, the wisdom of the good trees.—The trees to which the offer of the kingdom was made first were not the showy, but the *fruitful* ones—the olive, the fig, and the vine. So those worthiest to rule are those men who yield most fruit for the public good. But these are just the persons who, like Gideon, are least disposed to obtrude themselves, or even to accept office when thrust upon them; for they know that he who would rightly govern, must "go up and down" as a drudge to state cares. He must forego all personal interests, and sacrifice the sweets of leisure and retirement, for the good of the community; and worse still, must endanger his own fatness and spirituality, whilst set in high places. The olive represents the honours, the fig the sweetness, the vine the cheering power which a good man possesses in the sight of God and man. For man's true calling is to honour God and to benefit his fellow-men. Saul soon lost his humility and meekness under provocation, when raised to the throne. Of how many bad rulers who, before their accession, were amiable and good, might the description of Tacitus be given—"A good emperor, if only he never had become one"—*Bonus imperatur, nisi imperasset* (1 Sam. ix. 21, x. 22, 27, xi. 12, 13; contrast xiii., xv., xvi. 14, xviii. 9, xix. &c).

Thirdly, the folly, self-conceit, and mischievousness of the bramble.—The worthless and bad aspire to the exaltation from which the good in their wisdom shrink. Those least fit to lead are most ambitious to rule, and the populace are too often ready to court such as their leaders. The bramble, not deserving to be numbered among the trees, scratching all who touch it, first came in with the curse, and its end is burning (Gen. iii. 18; Heb. vi. 8). This is the just emblem of "folly set in great dignity," "when the vilest men are exalted" (Eccl. x. 6; Ps. xii. 8). Such place-seekers, without a scruple as to fitness, rush on to promotion, and, as if born to empire, swagger with

great swelling words of vanity. They promise great things to
those who will come and trust in their ' shadow ' (so Absalom,
2 Sam. xv. 4, 5). But " the silly sheep, flying to the bramble
for shelter, is sure to lose part of his fleece, if not of his flesh"
(Trapp). Then the threats of such upstarts are as arrogant as
their promises. Whilst they demand unlimited confidence,
woe be to him who dares to thwart their will! Such was
Abimelech. His reign began with an atrocious and wholesale
murder—the sure earnest of a history, mercifully brief, but
written throughout in characters of blood.

One alone is worthy of universal empire. All other men
have more or less abused the trust, reigning for self and
worldly aims, instead of wholly for God. Those have been the
best rulers who, when called of God to office, have not sought
their own gain and honour, but the glory of God and the
service of man, studying more to be good than great. Antichrist cometh in his own name, and will be received by those
who would not receive the true Christ (John v. 43). They
will know to their cost what a fatal choice they made, in preferring the flatterer and destroyer to their Saviour (Zech. xi.
16, 17; Dan. xi. 36–38, xii. 1 ; 2 Thess. ii. 3–12). But the
saints trust in Him who is " the Shadow of a great rock in a
weary land" (Isa. xxxii. 2); therefore they shall, in transfigured
bodies, share the kingdom with Him, when at His second
coming " He shall take to Himself His great power and reign,
and when the kingdoms of this world shall become the kingdoms of our Lord and of His Christ " (Rev. xi. 15, 17).

Fourthly, Jotham's application of the parable.—They had done
what they ought not, and they must bear what they would not.
The appeal is to their own consciences—man's " domestic
chaplains " (Trapp)—whose reproofs none can evade. If ye
have done truly towards Jehovah, whose kingship ye have
rejected, and gratefully towards my father who perilled his life
for you, then I wish you joy out of your king. But if, as
your consciences witness, the reverse be true, and my father's
merits to you have met the basest returns from you, then you
will prove a mutual curse the one to the other. Those who
do ill, can only fare ill. Nay more, those who help one another

in evil, shall be the instruments of one another's punishment.
The friendship that is based on sin is hollow, and ends in
bitterness. God employs the wicked to punish the wicked.
(3.) (ver. 22–57).—*Fulfilment of Jotham's prophecy: vindication of God's righteousness in the mutual punishment of the
accomplices in guilt.*—Abimelech reigned three years, and
seemed to have carried off the reward of wickedness with
impunity. But "if thou seest oppression and violent perverting
of judgment, marvel not, for He that is higher than the highest
regardeth; and there be higher than they" (Eccl. v. 8). The Lord
reigneth, and has given *three years* of probation to the transgressor,
but now there must be no longer delay of vengeance (see Isa.
xvi. 14; Luke xiii. 7). "The triumphing of the wicked is
short" (Job xx. 5). God has only to let loose men's bad
passions, that evil men may be the scourges of one another;
and then, "though hand join in hand, the wicked shall not be
unpunished" (Prov. xi. 21). The devil, the grand mischief-
maker, was permitted to sow jealousy between the confederates
in guilt, the Shechemites and the king of their own making.
The purpose of God was that thereby the blood of the innocent
might come not only on Abimelech, but on the Shechemites
who abetted him in the murder. For they had shed blood,
and Divine justice retributively will give them blood to drink
(Rev. xvi. 6). The Shechemites, with the characteristic fickle-
ness of the multitude, soon repented of their choice. It had
been better, if they had repented of their sin. But where
there is no conscience, we must not expect consistency.
Abimelech had taught them treachery towards his father, and
his father's sons; it was God's righteous retribution, that he
should be punished by their treachery to himself (Isa. xxxiii. 1).
"He that killeth with the sword, must be killed with the
sword " (Rev. xiii. 10).

*God's government of the world in righteousness traceable
throughout history.*—In the very temple from which they had
got the price of blood to make him king, they met to curse
and contrive his death. Gaal the Canaanite son of Ebed, whose
name means 'slave,' was the one in whom they now put confidence to deliver them from Abimelech the son of a Canaanite

concubine. It was bramble in conflict with bramble, potsherd striving with potsherd. If they were renouncing Baal, and their other sins, for Jehovah, there would have been hope for them. But Satan cannot cast out Satan; and Gaal, whom they now trusted, was no less turbulent and ambitious than Abimelech whom they discarded. It was but exchanging one bad demagogue for another. Untaught by bitter experience, and pleasing themselves with their fool's paradise, they were fast ripening for ruin. Gaal's swagger pleased them, whilst he poured contempt, not only on Abimelech and his officer Zebul, but on Abimelech's noble father, the Baal-conqueror: "Is not he the son of *Jerubbaal ?*" Gaal's words convicted him as an evil-speaker of dignities, the last one of all to be trusted. Gaal's vauntings were soon dissipated, when he was tested in action. Boasters are often forced to change their tone, and be dismayed before those whom they had scorned. The Shechemites and their city, when they were promising to themselves peace and safety, were overtaken with sudden destruction. Abimelech designed this destruction to be in vengeance for their rebellion against him; but God overruled it to be His avenging of the blood of Gideon's sons on them as the accomplices of Abimelech (Isa. x. 6, 7). Violent men mean to vindicate their own honour—God uses them to vindicate His. The true key of history, amidst much that is dark, sad, and mysterious, is this, God reigning in righteousness by His secret and veiled Providence, overruling men's crooked policy in spite of themselves to further God's purposes, and thereby giving an earnest of His coming judgment of the world in manifestly revealed equity.

The destroyer destroyed.—Abimelech has so far succeeded; but now comes his turn to be reckoned with. "When thou shalt cease to spoil, thou shalt be spoilt" (Isa. xxxiii. 1). A small city, Thebez, which he expected would be an easy prey to him after the capture of the greater city Shechem, proved his ruin. The town had been taken, and nothing seemed now restrained from him which he imagined to do. But death comes on the transgressor just at the time, and from the quarter, that he least expects it. God uses the weak things of the world to confound the mighty. In several particulars herein God manifested His retributive justice. Abimelech was slain with *one stone*, even as he had killed his brothers "upon one stone." The instrument of death fell on his *head*, and it was upon his head that the usurped crown had been set. It was a *woman* killed him, even as he had used the influence of a woman, his Canaanitish mother, and that of her clan, to effect his usurpation. *Vain glory* and ambition had been his idol all his life : and now he must die an inglorious death—slain by a woman ! Yet something worse remained. He tries to avert the stigma so degrading to a warrior, to be slain by a woman (compare Judg. iv. 9). His servant shall thrust him through. Fool that he was, he has only branded himself with the additional and more awful infamy of self-murder ! Jealous of his short-lived reputation, he was reckless of his immortal soul. The exultation at his accession was far exceeded by Israel's joy at his death. As was said of Boniface VIII.—he "came in like a fox, reigned like a lion, and died as a dog." How numerous are such vain fools, who rush into death of body and soul, anxious about what man may say of them, fearless of the Almighty Judge.

Righteous issue of this tragical history.—The Lord's justice was vindicated by the judgments He executed, and a warning was given to all ages that sin shall find out the sinner. Even in this world ingratitude, filial impiety (Exod. xx. 12), bloodshed and cruelty, though successful for a time, recoil upon the perpetrators (Eccles. viii. 11–13 ; Isa. iii. 10, 11). Wrong to a parent is a heinous sin, and brings a heavy punishment. God's endurance waits long, but suddenly cuts off in the end. The longer the penalty of sin is in coming, the heavier it is at last. Men's own wickedness becomes at the last their scourge. Bloodshed can never be a lasting cement, and alliances based on conspiracy for evil come to an end the moment that self-interest comes in the way (see 2 Sam. xiii. 3–5, 32, 33). Conspirators in evil are made their own mutual executioners of judgment. No tower of human strength can save. The Shechemites perish with their tower before Abimelech, then Abimelech perished before another tower. But " the name of

M

the Lord is a strong tower, the righteous runneth into it and
is safe" (Prov. xviii. 10). The peace of Israel was restored
after this awful episode of usurpation and civil conflict. And
the contrasted histories of Gideon and Abimelech, at once give
a foretaste of the coming universal judgment, and prove that
even now, "Verily there is a reward for the righteous: verily
He is a God that judgeth in the earth" (Ps. lviii. 11).

CHAPTER X.

TIMES OF PEACE UNDER TOLA AND JAIR : TIMES OF TROUBLE
THROUGH APOSTASY : DELIVERANCE UNDER JEPHTHAH.

(1) *And after Abimelech* [who though an usurper of kingship,
yet was son of Gideon, and *de facto,* though not *de jure,* judge]
there arose [at God's call], *to defend* [Heb., *Lehoshia,* " to save "
(Neh. ix. 27) " saviours who saved them "] *Israel* [from *internal
conspirators* like Abimelech, or *external foes* like Midian, and
above all from the *apostasy and idolatry* which had so often
provoked God to send such executioners of His wrath against
Israel. That Tola kept Israel from idols, appears from the
fact that, when he and Jair were dead, Israel relapsed into
idolatry], *Tola the son of Puah* [both bore names the same as the
original founders of families in Issachar (Gen. xlvi. 13 ; Numb.
xxvi. 23). Puah is written also Pua and Phuvah], *the son of
Dodo* [not " his uncle " as the Septuagint translate it ; but a
proper name (2 Sam. xxiii. 9 ; 1 Chron. xi. 12], *a man of
Issachar ; and he dwelt in Shamir in Mount Ephraim* [Tola
resided here, rather than in his own tribe Issachar, as being a
more convenient centre of government. Van de Velde identifies
it with the modern *Khirbet Sammer,* a ruin in the mountains
overlooking the Jordan valley, ten miles south-east of *Nablus*
or Shechem. Distinct from Shamir *of Judah* (Josh. xv. 48)].
(2) *And he judged Israel* [*i.e.,* the northern and eastern tribes ;
not the southern tribes, Judah, Benjamin, and Simeon, which
had no share in Gideon's victory, and had not come under
Abimelech's usurpation] *twenty and three years, and died, and was
buried in Shamir.* (3) *And after him arose Jair, a Gileadite*
[of course, not the same as Jair the Manassite, who in the time

of Moses gave the name Havoth-Jair to the towns of Bashan
which he had conquered (Numb. xxxii. 41). This name was
brought into use again by the sons of the judge Jair. ˊThe
earlier Jair took Argob or Trachonitis, the *Lejah*, and called
from his own name certain villages or groups of dwellings,
twenty-three in number originally, which afterwards the sons
of the judge Jair increased to thirty; they probably also fortified
and enlarged the towns. *Havoth* means 'dwelling-places,' from
Havah, "life," as the German *Leben*, 'life,' is a termination of
many names of towns; so Eisleben. The total number of such
villages of Jair in Argob was sixty, of which thirty-seven were
conquered by Nobah (a family of sons of Machir related to
Jair) and twenty-three by Jair (Josh. xiii. 30 ; 1 Kings iv. 13 ;
1 Chron. ii. 22, 23). As Nobah was of a subordinate branch of
the Jair family, Moses comprehends the whole sixty under Jair's
name, Havoth-Jair. Og's sixty fenced cities, Moses observes
as a marvellous monument of God's grace to Israel, are become
even "unto this day" (the day when he wrote) 'Havoth-Jair,'
the dwellings of Jair (Deut. iii. 14)], *and judged Israel twenty
and two years.* (4) *And he had thirty sons that rode on thirty
ass-colts* [a sign of high rank. The Oriental ass is a superior
animal : Israel had not yet imported horses. Moreover, the ass
was used in times of *peace ;* horses for *war* (see ch. v. 10, xii.
14 ; 1 Kings x. 28, i. 33 ; Zech. ix. 9], *and they had thirty* [see
note ver. 3] *cities* [עֲיָרִים, a varied form for עָרִים, used because of
its likeness to עֲיָרִים, *asses*], *which are called Havoth-Jair unto this
day, which (are) in the land of Gilead* [villages are cities to a
contented mind (Henry)]. (5) *And Jair died, and was buried
in Camon.* (6) *And* [after Jair's death ; for a good ruler
restrains the evil] *the children of Israel did evil again in the
sight of the* LORD [JEHOVAH (compare note, ch. ii. 11, iii. 7,
iv. 1, vi. 1), the often-recurring monotonous formula expressing
Israel's stupid obstinacy in so often going back to their old
bad way, in spite of its often experienced fatal consequences,
and daring to do so *in the face of Jehovah,* who had so often
punished them], *and served Baalim, and Ashtaroth* [see note,
ch. ii. 11, 13], *and the gods of Syria* [Heb., *Aram,* divided
into many tribes having their respective 'gods,' viz., Aram of

Zobah, of Beth Rehob, of Damascus, of Ishtob, of Maacha, and of Mesopotamia, and probably of Hamath (2 Sam. viii. 3, 5). These tribes were subsequently joined into one state. The Hebrew terms for one "using divination" (*Quoseem*), "a witch" (*mekasheeph*, Deut. xviii. 10), and "idolatrous priests" (*Kemarim*, 2 Kings xxiii. 5), are of Syriac derivation], *and the gods of Zidon* [Baal and Ashtoreth], *and the gods of Moab, and the gods of the children of Ammon* [Milcom or Molech and Chemosh of Moab], *and the gods of the Philistines* [Dagon or Derceto. *Seven* idols are mentioned here as served by Israel, just as *seven* heathen nations are mentioned (ver. 11, 12), out of whose hands Jehovah had delivered His people. Israel had repaid the sevenfold Divine deliverance with sevenfold idolatry. *Their fulness of iniquity* rivalled *His fulness of grace. Seven* is the number that seals God's works as *perfect*, as creation was completed by the seventh day], *and forsook the Lord, and served not Him* [Jehovah's worship cannot be combined with that of idols; so idolaters, beginning with the attempt at combination, soon give up even the semblance of worshipping Jehovah (Ezek. xx. 39). The prosperity of heathen nations around them, their great numbers, and the absence in Jehovah's worship of all gratifications to the carnal appetite, such as dancing, artistic performances, and scenes, all of which, even actual libertinism, were common in the worship of idols (Numb. xxv.) betwitched Israel]. (7) *And the anger of the* LORD [JEHOVAH] *was hot against Israel* [see ch. ii. 14], *and He sold them into the hands of the Philistines* [(Deut. xxxii. 30; Ps. xliv. 12; Isa. l. 1). Renounced His right in them, and gave them up as slaves, helplessly sold to their foes, even as the Israelites had sold themselves as slaves to heathenish corruptions (2 Kings xvii. 17; Rom. vii. 14, 15)], *and into the hands of the children of Ammon* [these, though put second, preceded the Philistines in oppressing Israel. The Ammonites are placed in this order, with a view to the following verse which proceeds to describe their vexing Israel. The Philistines in some degree had vexed Israel at the close of Moab's oppression, and the beginning of Jabin's (note, ch. iii. 31).

Their power gradually increased, so that from vexing *the south-western* parts of Israel in Shamgar's days, they now, towards the close of the Ammonite oppression, so mastered *all* Israel as. to prevent any smith's work throughout the land (note, ch. v. 8; 1 Sam. xiii. 19, 22)]. (8) *And that year they* [the Ammonites] *vexed* [the same Hebrew as Ex. xv. 6, ra'atz " dash in pieces "] *and oppressed* [Heb., 'crushed,' as in Deut. xxxviii. 33. *Rotzetzu*] *the children of Israel* [put the stop here, marking " that year " (viz., the year when, shortly after Jair's death, Israel apostatised, and God sold Israel into their hands) as the year of their " dashing in pieces and crushing Israel." Then is added in the next sentence the *duration* of the oppression], *eighteen years* [they crushed] *all the children of Israel that (were) on the other side Jordan, in the land of the Amorites, which (is) in Gilead* [the land of Sihon, king of the Amorites, and Og of Bashan (Numb. xxi. 21, &c.) ' Gilead ' here comprises all the land of the Amorites east of Jordan occupied by Israel (Josh. xxii. 9)]. (9) *Moreover the children of Ammon passed over Jordan to fight also against Judah, and against Benjamin, against the house of Ephraim* [not content with oppressing Israel east of the Jordan, the Ammonites, towards the close of the eighteen years of oppression, crossed over and invaded the Israelite southern and northern tribes west of Jordan, Judah, Benjamin, and Ephraim]; *so that Israel was sore distressed* [the same Hebrew word as ch. ii. 15, " in great straits "]. (10) *And the children of Israel cried* [*za'aqu*, the cry of pain seeking help (Hos. vii. 14); not yet real hatred of their sin] *unto the* LORD [JEHOVAH], *saying, We have sinned against Thee, both because* [namely, in that וְכִי describes their sin in detail] *we have forsaken our God* [dereliction of duty enjoined], *and also served Baalim* [Heb., " *the* Baals," viz., of the several surrounding nations, each having its own Baal. Positive commission of sin forbidden (Jer. ii. 12, 13)]. (11) *And the* LORD [JEHOVAH] *said unto the children of Israel, (Did) not (I deliver you)* [not in the Hebrew : God leaves Israel herself to supply the omission)] *from the Egyptians* [at the Exodus, i.–xiv.], *and from the Amorites* [Numb. xxi. 21–35, Sihon and Og], *from the children of Ammon* [under

Eglon of Moab (ch. iii. 13)], *and from the Philistines* [by Shamgar (ch. iii. 31; so in 1 Sam. xii. 9) "the Philistines" come between 'Sisera' and Moab]? (12) *The Zidonians also* [leagued with Jabin king of North Canaan, over which Zidon exercised a protectorate (ch. xviii. 7; 28], *and the Amalekites* [whose assaults on Israel began as early as at Horeb (Exod. xvii. 8–16), and were renewed in concert with Moab at Eglon's invasion (ch. iii. 13), and with the Midianites (ch. vi. 3)], *and the Maonites* [no mention before occurs of these as oppressors of Israel. Possibly they are the same as the Mehunim or Meunites of 2 Chron. xxvi. 7, the inhabitants of Maan (as 1 Chron. iv. 41, ought to be translated, instead of "the habitations"), a city near Petra, east of Wady Musa, in the mountainous region west of the Arabah. Then "the Maonites" may represent *the Midianites* in general, the name of an adjoining kindred tribe standing for the whole. Both the best MSS. of the Septuagint (Alexandrine and Vatican) read (Μαδίαμ) 'Midian.' But no *Hebrew* MS. *now extant* supports this reading. It is most unlikely that Israel's great oppressor, Midian, should have been unnoticed. Therefore, either the Septuagint preserves the true original reading; or, if we must read as *existing* MSS., "the Maonites" must represent *the Midianites] did oppress you; and ye cried to me, and I delivered you out of their hand.* (13) *Yet ye have forsaken me, and served other gods: wherefore I will deliver you no more* [*i.e.*, in your state of apostasy, wherein it is only the punishment, not the sin, which extorts from you your cry to ME. Israel must change—God cannot change. But if Israel will truly repent, God will also (Jer. xxvi. 13). "Yea, God will pardon such sin as no man would pardon (Jer. iii. 1), nor god either (Mic. vii. 18)" (Trapp)]. (14) *Go and cry unto the gods which ye have chosen; let them deliver you in the time of your tribulation* [ironical, as 1 Kings xviii. 27; fulfilling Moses' prophetical song (Deut. xxxii. 37, 38). God will laugh and mock at the calamity of the hardened transgressor (Prov. i. 26). Israel 'chose' new gods (ch. v. 8), which had not proved their godhead by any services, in preference to Jehovah, whose services Israel had so richly experienced. God's delay in hearing tested Israel's sincerity: so it turned out for their profit, for so they "accepted the punishment of their iniquity" (see vers. 15, 16; Lev. xxvi. 40, 41)]. (15) *And the children of Israel said unto the Lord, We have sinned: do Thou* [do not punish us by *foreigners*, but do THOU] *unto us whatsoever seemeth good unto Thee* [(2 Sam. xxiv. 14). True repentance meekly bears whatever chastisement God inflicts]; *deliver us only, we pray Thee, this day* [so Pharaoh (Exod. x. 17; Isa. xxvi. 16)]. (16) *And they put away the strange gods from among them* [(Josh. xxiv. 23; 1 Sam. vii. 3). Prayer and repentance show their sincerity by giving up all idols. This was the crowning point (Hos. xiv. 8; Prov. xxviii. 13; Job xxxiv. 31, 32], *and served the Lord* [JEHOVAH]: *and His soul was grieved* [*tiquetzar* 'shortened,' so vexed (ch. xvi. 16)] *for the misery of Israel* [He could no longer forbear the manifestation of His fatherly affection, or leave unnoticed the wrongs done to His people by the foe. So God, in Jer. xxxi. 20; Isa. lxiii. 9, 15, 16]. (17) *Then the children of Ammon were gathered together* [Heb., "caused themselves to be summoned together," only to be "broken in pieces" (Isa. viii. 9)], *and encamped in Gilead* [with the purpose of dispossessing Israel of all their territory east of Jordan as far as the river Jabbok (ch. xi. 13), probably also to invade Western Palestine beyond Jordan (x. 9)]: *and the children of Israel assembled together* [penitence and faith now gave them courage to do what they durst not before (Prov. xxviii. 1)], *and encamped in Mizpeh* [Hebrew, *Mizpah* usually with the article "*the* Mizpah" or *watch-towers*. Mizpeh (masculine) is the town; Mizpah (feminine) is the district (Josh. xi. 3, 8). Laban gave this name to Gilead, "the heap of witness," the memorial of his covenant with Jacob; for he said, "Jehovah *watch* between me and thee when we are absent one from another." Identical with Ramoth Gilead, now *Es-Salt* or Ramoth-Mizpeh, now mount *Jebel Osha* to the north-west (Josh. xiii. 26). Distinct from Mizpeh-Moab and Mizpeh-Benjamin]. (18) *And the people (and) princes* [rather "the people, namely, the princes," *i.e.*, the people as represented by the princes] *of Gilead said one to another, What man (is he) that will begin to fight against the children of Ammon? he shall be head over all the inhabitants of Gilead* [the Gileadites, as an independent people, elect their own head and commander-in-chief without consulting the tribes west of Jordan: he is called (in ch. xi. 6, 11) their 'captain' in war, as well as 'head' in civil relations].

CHAPTER XI.

(1) *Now Jephthah the Gileadite was a mighty man of valour,
and he (was) the son of* [*a woman*] *an harlot* [or concubine. In
1 Chron. vii. 14, Manasseh's concubine, who bare Machir father
of Gilead, is described as an 'Aramitess' or Syrian. Jephthah,
at his father's death, fled to the land of Tob, an Aramean
settlement (2 Sam. x. 6, margin); probably to the land of his
mother's kindred. Therefore she was probably a Syrian. The
vicinity of the Gileadite half tribe of Manasseh to Syria led to
marriages with Syrians, and to apostasy to "the gods of Syria"
(ch. x. 6)]; *and Gilead* [not the original founder of the clan, but
a descendant who bore the name of his famous ancestor] *begat
Jephthah.* (2) *And Gilead's wife bare him sons: and his wife's
sons grew up, and they thrust out Jephthah, and said unto him,
Thou shalt not inherit in our father's house* [just as Ishmael the
son of the concubine, and the sons of Keturah, were sent away
by Abraham, not to inherit with Isaac the son of the wife
(Gen. xxi. 10, xxv. 5, 6). Though not entitled to share his
father's inheritance, he was entitled to sustenance: therefore
Jephthah upbraids them (ver. 7)]; *for thou (art) the son
of a strange woman.* (3) *Then Jephthah fled from* [the face
of] *his brethren, and dwelt in the land of Tob* [north-east
of Peræa, bordering on Syria and Ammonitis (2 Sam. x.
6, 8). Ptolemy mentions a *Thauba* south-west of Zobah.
There is still a *Tell Dobbe* ruin south of the Lejah]: *and
there were gathered vain* [ch. ix. 4, unprincipled (1 Sam. xxii.
2)] *men to Jephthah, and went out with him* [on marauding
Bedouin-like expeditions. Probably he carried off booty from

the Ammonites chiefly—a just reprisal for their inroads on Israel (ch. x. 8, 9)]. (4) *And it came to pass in process of time* [Heb., "*after days,*" as in ch. xiv. 8, xv. 1 ; Josh. xxiii. 1, *i.e.,* a considerable time after Jephthah's expulsion in youth], *that the children of Ammon made war against Israel* [here the account of the war is resumed from ch. x. 17, preparatory to describing the victory under Jephthah]. (5) *And it was so, that, when the children of Ammon made war against Israel, the elders of Gilead went to fetch Jephthah out of the land of Tob.* (6) *And they said unto Jephthah, Come and be our captain* [*Quatzin,* in war here, as in Josh. x. 24. Elsewhere 'ruler' or 'prince' in general : akin to the Arabic *Kady* (Isa. i. 10, iii. 6, 7 ; Mic. iii. 1, 9)], *that we may fight with the children of Ammon.* (7) *And Jephthah said unto the elders of Gilead, Did not ye hate me, and expel me out of my father's house?* [the elders of Gilead who came to Jephthah probably included some of his brethren who had expelled him. His fellow tribesmen and the elders had at least supported his brothers in the expulsion, and privation of sustenance, which was an unjust action (note, ver. 2). Still, it was not just to charge them all with the wrong act of his brethren]. *And why are ye come unto me now when ye are in distress?* (8) *And the elders of Gilead said unto Jephthah, Therefore* [because thou wast formerly wronged, and we wish to make thee amends. Wisely they do not reason with a passionate and resentful man like Jephthah] *we turn again to thee now, that thou mayest go with us, and fight against the children of Ammon, and be our head over all the inhabitants of Gilead* [though as a *Mamzer* or illegitimate son (Deut. xxiii. 2), he was ordinarily disqualified from entering the congregation of the Lord, yet under special circumstances God gives an extraordinary call. God imposes positive precepts as ordinarily binding on us, but not as a necessity binding Himself. The elders were divinely guided to choose as leader him whoever should begin to fight against the Ammonites (ch. x. 18). Jephthah fulfilled this requirement, in having probably already made inroads on Ammon. The law as to the exclusion of bastards, being made for Israel's good, must give place to God's choice of Jephthah, now that Israel's

good required him as the leader (compare Matt. xii. 7)]. (9)
*And Jephthah said unto the elders of Gilead, If ye bring me
home again to fight against the children of Ammon, and the*
LORD [JEHOVAH] *deliver them before me* [as in Josh. x. 12; Deut.
ii. 31], *shall I be your head?* [or as Keil explains (without a
question which the impression in ver. 10, " according to thy
words," less suits ; for it presupposes an *affirmative* statement
on the part of Jephthah) " I will be your head ;" the ' *I* '
being emphatic as distinguished from ' *ye* ']. (10) *And the
elders of Gilead said unto Jephthah, The* LORD [JEHOVAH] *be
witness* [Heb., *hearing, i.e.,* Judge (Gen. xxxi. 48, 49)] *between
us, if we do not so according to thy words* [Jephthah betrays a
more self-seeking spirit than Gideon (ch. viii. 22, 23). But it
was the elders' own proposal that he should be head, and he
took office at the risk of losing his life in the fulfilment of
its responsibilities in the war. Therefore God, who is quick
to discern the good side of His servants' actions, commends
Jephthah as an example of ' faith ' (Heb. xi. 32, 33)]. (11)
*Then Jephthah went with the elders of Gilead, and the people
made him head and captain over them: and Jephthah uttered all
his words* [repeated the conditions and obligations under which
he accepted the headship] *before the* LORD [JEHOVAH (compare
Hezekiah, 2 Kings xix. 14)] *in Mizpeh* [*i.e.,* as in Jehovah's presence, the Witness of oaths and Punisher of their violation. Not
that the ark or altar was there, as the Speaker's Commentary
(ch. xx. 18, note) supposes, suggesting that whilst Shiloh was
the chief residence of the ark (Jer. vii. 12), yet the tabernacle,
being movable, was as occasion required moved to where the
judge and congregation were (1 Sam. i. 3, iv. 3, vii. 16). But
there is no mention of the ark here in the context. The high
priest with the ephod may have been summoned to Mizpeh
or Ramoth Gilead, as being a Levitical city (Josh. xxi. 34, 38),
but there is no clear proof that the words " before the Lord "
express more than that he solemnly confirmed his engagement
as before the omnipresent God of Israel. Jehovah was present especially when his people assembled (Deut. xxiii. 14)].
(12) *And Jephthah sent messengers unto the king of the children of Ammon, saying, What hast thou to do with me* [Heb.,

"What (is there) to me and thee ?" (Josh. xxii. 24 ; 2 Sam. xvi. 10 ; Matt. viii. 29). He would settle (Deut. xx. 10) the issue by appeal to right before resorting to force], *that thou art come against me* [Jephthah regards himself as representing Israel], *to fight in my land?* (13) *And the king of the children of Ammon answered unto the messengers of Jephthah, Because Israel took away my land, when they came up out of Egypt, from Arnon* [on the south, flowing into the Dead Sea] *even unto Jabbok* [on the north, flowing into Jordan], *and unto Jordan* [on the west : the eastern boundary was the wilderness (ver. 22)] ; *now therefore restore those (lands)* [viz., that of Moab, and that of Ammon (ver. 15)] *again peaceably.* (14) *And Jephthah sent messengers again unto the king of the children of Ammon,* (15) *And said unto him, Thus saith Jephthah, Israel took not away the land of Moab, nor the land of the children of Ammon* [the king of Ammon's claim had an appearance of justice : for one portion of the land occupied by Israel had belonged to Moab and Ammon formerly. But Israel had not wrested it from them, for God had forbidden Israel to attack Ammon, Moab, and Edom (Deut. ii. 5, 9, 19 ; 2 Chron. xx. 10). Part of it had been wrested from Moab by Sihon king of the Amorites (Numb. xxi. 26). Part also was wrested by him from Ammon, as is implied by the statement in Josh. xiii. 25, 26, that Gad received in addition to Gilead "half the land of the children of Ammon unto Aroer that is before Rabbah," *i.e.*, the land to the east of Gilead, on the western side of the Upper Jabbok, *Nahr Amman* (Deut. ii. 37, iii. 16). Israel, in taking Sihon's territory, took the portions already absorbed by Sihon from Ammon and Moab, but did not take in addition any of the land possessed by the latter in the time of Moses]. (16) *But when Israel came up from Egypt, and* [rather " *then* Israel "] *walked through the wilderness* [the same Hebrew (*halak*, walked,' &c.) expression as in Deut. i. 19, ii. 14 ; Josh. v. 6. "The wilderness of wanderings," or *El-Tih*, is meant (Deut. i. 19)] *unto the Red Sea* [the *Yam Suf*, Israel's last station before reaching Kedesh, was Ezion Gaber, on the gulf of Akaba, the eastern tongue of the Red Sea (Numb. xxxiii. 36, 37 ; 1 Kings ix. 26], *and came to Kadesh* [Kadesh-

Barnea. Fürst explains Barnea, "son of wandering," *i.e.*, Bedouin. The Speaker's Commentary explains it "country of convulsion" (compare Ps. xxix. 8); called also Meribah Kadesh. Rithmah (from *retem*, "a broom," the chief shrub of the desert), was near, and therefore is the name given instead of Kadesh, in Numb. xxxiii. 18 : here was Israel's encampment in their first march towards Canaan in the summer of the second year after the exodus. From this encampment (Numb. xii. 16, xiii. 20, 25), they sent the spies, waiting forty days for them. Moses and the tabernacle still "abode in Kadesh many days," whilst the people vainly tried to reverse God's sentence (Numb. xiv. 44; Deut. i. 34–46). Then Israel compassed Mount Seir, *i.e.*, wandered in the desert of Paran till all that generation died (ii. 1). The wilderness of Zin is the northern part of the Paran desert, and is also called "the wilderness of (*i.e.*, adjoining) Kadesh" (Numb. x. 12, xiii. 21, xxxiii. 30; Ps. xxix. 8). Thirty-eight years subsequently they reached the same locality, and encamped at Kadesh (Numb. xx. 1, 22, xxxiii. 36, 37), in the fortieth year after leaving Egypt, when just about to enter Canaan. Only a few incidents are recorded of the thirty-eight years of wandering, which comprise the seventeen stages (Numb. xxxiii. 19–36), between the first time and the second. At Kadesh, the Wady el Ghuweir affords access north-westwards through mountainous Edom : at Hor, their next stage after Edom, they were "in the edge of the land of Edom" (Numb. xxxiii. 37); and Moses describes Kadesh as a city "in the uttermost of Edom's border" (Numb. xx. 16). Here, accordingly, Moses sent to ask a passage "by the king's highway." Kadesh, *i.e.*, 'holy,' may be the name given from the long stay there of the *sanctuary* and priests. En-Mishpat, "fountain of judgment," another of its names (Gen. xiv. 7), corresponds, inasmuch as *judgment* and *sanctity* go together, and emanate from the one and the same Jehovah]. (17) *Then Israel sent messengers unto the king of Edom, saying, Let me, I pray thee, pass through thy land : but the king of Edom would not hearken (thereto). And in like manner they sent unto the king of Moab : but he would not (consent) : and Israel abode in Kadesh* ["many days" (Numb. xx. 1; Deut. i. 46). In

Deut. i. 19, ii. 14, the interval between the encampment at
Kadesh-Barnea and Israel's crossing the brook Zered, before
entering Canaan, is said to be thirty-eight years. So also in
Numb. xiii. 26, Kadesh is mentioned as the place where the
spies returned to *at the beginning of the thirty-eight years'
wandering.* Elsewhere (Numb. xxxiii. 36), Kadesh is mentioned as the place at which Israel arrived *at the end of the
thirty-eight years.* Therefore Kadesh must have been the point
from which they started, and to which they returned, the
thirty-eight years intervening. The seventeen stages named
in Numb. xxxiii. 19–36, are the headquarters of the scattered
people. The camp with the tabernacle, the priests, and the
chiefs, was the nucleus and rallying-point, whilst the congregation was dispersed in various directions during the thirty-eight
years. The embassy to the king of Moab is not mentioned in
the Pentateuch, as it did not directly affect Israel's further
advance. Otherwise Jephthah shows an accurate knowledge
of, and almost exact agreement with, Moses' inspired history in
Numbers and Deuteronomy, and confirms thereby the early
date of the Pentateuch, as opposed to modern objections]. (18)
Then they went [Heb., 'walked'] *along through the wilderness*
[to Mount Hor], *and compassed the land of Edom* [(Numb. xxi.
4, 10, 11). From Mount Hor they went down the Arabah to
the Red Sea: and so on to Obath and Ije-Abarim in the
wilderness before Moab. So they went round Edom and
Moab, and came on the east of Moab's boundary], *and the
land of Moab, and came by the east side of the land of Moab,
and pitched on the other side of Arnon* [*i.e.,* on the upper
course of the Arnon where it flows through the desert],
but came not within the border of Moab ; for Arnon (was) the
[eastern] *border of Moab* [(Numb. xxi. 13 ; Deut. ii. 1–9, 14, 19,
24). The branch of the Arnon (*Seil es Saideh*), flowing north-
west through the wilderness into the Dead Sea ; now *Wady
el Mojeb,* flowing through a rugged ravine]. (19) *And Israel
sent messengers unto Sihon king of the Amorites, the king of
Heshbon ; and Israel said unto him, Let us pass, we pray thee,
through thy land into my place* [from ver. 19 to 22, Jephthah
follows almost word for word Numb. xx. 17, xxi. 21–27 ;

Deut. ii. 26–30, where the words, " over Jordan—the land
which the Lord our God giveth us," answer to " my place "
here]. (20) *But Sihon trusted not Israel* [*i.e.*, the *promises of
Israel*, detailed in Numb. xxi. 22 ; Deut. ii. 27, 28 ; but
omitted for brevity by Jephthah, yet *hinted at* in his word
' trusted,' which presupposes *promises*] *to pass through his coast;
but* [not confining himself to refusing Israel's request for leave
to pass through his land] *Sihon gathered all his people together,
and pitched in Jahaz* [in the plain, now called the Belka, on
the extreme south of Sihon's land, but north of the Arnon.
The battle was probably fought on the hill-slope called still
Shihan : here is a network of cyclopean walls, from which,
Josephus says, the Amorites were dislodged by Israel's slings
and arrows, and fled two miles to the edge of the Arnon
gorge], *and fought against Israel.* (21) *And the* LORD [JEHOVAH]
God of Israel [so ver. 23 ; Deut. ii. 30, 33, " JEHOVAH thy God
—our God." In contrast to what Chemosh gave his worshippers (ver. 24)] *delivered Sihon and all his people into the hand
of Israel, and they smote them : so Israel possessed all the land of
the Amorites, the inhabitants of that country.* (22) *And they
possessed all the coasts of the Amorites from Arnon even unto
Jabbok* [now *Zerka.* It flows into Jordan midway between the
sea of Galilee and the Dead Sea, forty-five miles north of the
Arnon. Jabbok formed the Amorite border between Rabbah
and Gerasa : Israel did not pass this boundary into Ammon
eastward : but westward Israel took the Ammonite land
already absorbed by Sihon], *and from the wilderness even unto
Jordan.* (23) *So now the* LORD [JEHOVAH] *God of Israel*
[Deut. ii. 24] *hath dispossessed the Amorites from before His
people Israel, and shouldest thou possess it* [their possession, the
Amorite land]? (24) *Wilt not thou possess that which Chemosh
thy god* [Chemosh was the idol of Moab, the original owner of
the land before his dispossession by the Amorites (Numb. xxi
29): " Moab—people of Chemosh." Ammon's god was Molech;
but being akin to Moab, the Ammonites also worshipped
Chemosh. Depicted on coins with sword, lance, and two
torches at his side. A black star was his symbol ; and Dibon
was his chief seat of worship On the black stone of Dibon,

recently discovered, the Moabite king, Mesha, ascribes all his successes, in war against Israel, to Chemosh, or Ashtar-(Astarte)-Chemosh, to whom he offered, in sacrifice, all the warriors taken at Ataroth] *giveth thee to possess?* [Is it not the fact, that what Chemosh thy god (according to thy false creed) giveth thee to possess (Jer. x. 5), that thou possessest?] *So whomsoever the* LORD [JEHOVAH] *our God shall drive out from before us, them will we possess* [Ammon and Moab gained their territory by forcibly dispossessing the ancient inhabitants (Deut. ii. 10–21). Instead of attributing their success to Jehovah, they attributed it to Chemosh. What Chemosh, *on their own showing,* gave them, that they have. They have no reason, therefore, to complain if Israel retains, by right of conquest and of prescription, what Jehovah gave *them* by dispossessing the Amorites]. (25) *And now (art) thou anything better than Balak the son of Zippor king of Moab? did he ever strive against Israel, or did he ever fight against them?* [No. He bribed Balaam to curse Israel; but this he did in order to save from Israel *the territory yet remaining to him,* not to wrest from Israel the Moabite land, originally conquered by Sihon, then appropriated, with the rest of the Amorite land, by Israel (Numb. xxi. 26). If then Balak, king of Moab, did not claim back from the Israelites the Moabite land, which they had taken from the Amorites, what claim to it can the king of Ammon have now, especially after Israel's possession of it for 300 years? Ammon was with Moab in hiring Balaam (Deut. xxiii. 4). Moab was the more civilised and agricultural; Ammon the more fierce, Bedouin-like, and marauding half of Lot's descendants (contrast Isa. xv., xvi. ; Jer. xlviii., with 1 Sam. xi. 2 ; Amos i. 13 ; 2 Sam. x. 1–5, xii. 31). Moab and Ammon were excluded from the Lord's congregation, *i.e.,* from full Israelite citizenship, not from spiritual privileges if proselytes, for ten generations, because they joined in hiring Balaam : whereas Edom, who had not hired him, was only excluded to the third generation (Deut. xxiii. 2, 46 ; Neh. xiii. 2)]. (26) *While Israel dwelt* [quoted from Numb. xxi. 25, 31] *in Heshbon and her* [dependent] *towns, and in Aroer* [facing Rabbah of Ammon ; ' built,' *i.e.,* restored and enlarged by Gad (Numb.

N

xxxii. 34; Josh. xiii. 25): distinct from the Aroer of Reuben (Josh. xiii. 9, 10), which was one of "the cities that belong to Arnon"] *and her towns, and in all the cities that (be) along by the coasts* [sides : *i.e.*, along the course] *of Arnon, three hundred years? why therefore did ye not recover (them) within that time?* [If Ammon had any right to them, the claim ought to have been made in Moses' time, 300 years ago : it is too late now, otherwise no length of time could give a prescriptive title (see, on the 300 years, remarks on chs. ii. and iii. "Chronology of Judges")]. (27) *Wherefore I* [Israel represented by Jephthah] *have not sinned against thee, but thou doest me wrong to war against me : the* LORD [JEHOVAH] *the Judge be judge this day between the children of Israel and the children of Ammon* [Gen. xvi. 5, xxxi. 53]. (28) *Howbeit the king of the children of Ammon hearkened not unto the words of Jephthah which* [spoken by messengers whom] *he sent him.* (29) *Then the Spirit of the* LORD [JEHOVAH] *came upon Jephthah* [with supernatural influence upon his human spirit (ch. iii. 10). Thus the victory was to be, not by might, nor by power of man, but by Jehovah's Spirit (Zech. iv. 6). The Gileadites already had chosen him : God now, by imparting His Spirit, shows His appointment of Jephthah as judge to all Israel. The Spirit consecrated to the office of Judge, and also qualified for it. Type of the inauguration of Messiah, the grand antitype (Isa. lxi. 1; Luke iv. 18, 21; Matt. iii. 16], *and he passed over* [through] *Gilead* [the part of it between the Arnon and the Jabbok ; the land of Reuben and Gad] *and Manasseh* [*i.e.*, the land of the half tribe of Manasseh, comprising northern Gilead and Bashan], *and passed over* [the Jabbok, ON TO] *Mizpeh of Gilead* [he raised new forces in Gilead and Bashan, and then with them marched to Mizpeh to join the army he had left at his camp there (ch. x. 17)], *and* [with his combined forces] *from Mizpeh of Gilead he passed over (unto)* [to attack] *the children of Ammon.* (30) *And Jephthah vowed a vow unto the* LORD [JEHOVAH], *and said, If Thou shalt without fail deliver* [Heb., "If *giving thou shalt give*"] *the children of Ammon into mine hands,* (31) *Then it shall be, that whatsoever cometh forth* [Heb., "that which (or *whoever*) coming forth shall have come forth"] *of the doors of my house to meet me* [he must mean a *man* or *woman* : for a *beast* would not " come forth *of the doors of his house to meet him.*" It would have been a paltry vow to promise to sacrifice *the first beast* that should meet him] *when I return in peace from the children of Ammon, shall surely be the Lord's, and* [the Hebrew can mean ' OR ': an alternative : *or else.* But it is better to translate ' and,' the second clause which follows defining more precisely the first] *I will offer it up for a burnt-offering* [Jephthah shrank from defining the person to be offered ; this he leaves to God to order by His providence, no doubt hoping that his daughter (if indeed, in his ardent zeal for Israel against the oppressor, she entered his thoughts at the time) would not be demanded]. (32) *So Jephthah passed over unto the children of Ammon* [resumed from ver. 29, where he broke off to narrate his vow before the campaign] *to fight against them; and the* LORD [JEHOVAH] *delivered them into his hands.* (33) *And he smote them from Aroer* [an Israelite town (ver. 26) which the Ammonites had seized : so that Israel was fighting in self-defence, to expel the enemy from the land given by Jehovah to His people], *even till thou come to Minnith* [at the fourth milestone on the way from Heshbon to Rabbah of Ammon, according to Eusebius. Famous for wheat (Ezek. xxvii. 17)], *(even) twenty cities, and unto the plain of the vine-yards* [rather Abel Keramim : Abela, seven miles from Rabbath Ammon or Philadelphia, according to Eusebius and Jerome. Thus Jephthah's pursuit of the foe was first southwards to the neighbourhood of Heshbon, then northwards to the border of Bashan], *with a very great slaughter. Thus the children of Ammon were subdued before the children of Israel.* (34) *And Jephthah came to Mizpeh* [of Gilead, his home (ch. xi. 11)] *unto his house, and, behold, his daughter came out to meet him with timbrels and with dances* [as Miriam and all the women after her with timbrels and dances celebrated Moses' victory at the Red Sea (Exod. xv. 20 ; so 1 Sam. xviii. 6, 7)]; *and she (was his) only child : beside her* [Heb., masculine used for feminine, as the idea of *child* in general was in the writer's mind] *he had neither son nor daughter.* (35) *And it came to pass, when he saw her, that he rent his clothes, and said, Alas ! my daughter ! thou*

hast brought me very low [after having been raised so high by
the victory : compare the Antitype weeping in the very hour
of triumph (Luke xix. 38–41)], *and thou art one of them that
trouble me : for I have opened my mouth* [in a vow] *unto the*
LORD [JEHOVAH], *and I cannot go back* [Ps. lxvi. 13, 14 ; Numb.
xxx. 2 ; Deut. xxiii. 21–23]. (36) *And she said unto him, My
father, (if) thou hast opened thy mouth unto the* LORD [JEHOVAH],
do to me according to that which hath proceeded out of thy mouth
[compare Isaac's submission to his father (Gen. xxii. 7, 9);
filial obedience, piety, and patriotism appear in her reply]; *for-
asmuch as the* LORD [JEHOVAH] *hath taken vengeance for thee of
thine enemies, (even) of the children of Ammon.* (37) *And she
said unto her father, Let this thing be done for me : let me alone
two months, that I may go up and down* [Heb., "go and go
down": *i.e.,* go down from the Mizpeh height of her home to
the valley and then *go up*] *upon the mountains, and bewail my
virginity, I and my fellows* [to become a wife and mother
was the great desire of Israelite women. To be unwedded and
childless was deemed a great calamity and reproach (compare
Isa. iv. 1 ; 1 Sam. i. 6 ; Luke i. 25 ; Gen. xxx. 23). The seed
of the woman, according to the protevangelical promise (Gen.
iii. 15), was to crush the serpent's head : hence arose the
yearning desire of maternity]. (38) *And he said, Go. And he
sent her away (for) two months : and she went with her companions, and bewailed her virginity upon the mountains.* (39)
*And it came to pass, at the end of two months, that she returned
unto her father, who did with her (according) to his vow which
he had vowed : and she knew no man* [see remarks below]. *And
it was a custom* [ordinance] *in Israel,* (40) (*That*) *the daughters
of Israel went yearly* [from year to year (Exod. xiii. 10)] *to
lament* [rather 'to celebrate' in praises, *tinnah*] *the daughter of
Jephthah the Gileadite four days in a year.*

CHAPTER XII.

(1) *And the men of Ephraim gathered themselves together* [were called together, or gathered by summons], *and went* [Heb., "passed over," viz., the Jordan] *northward,* [crossing at the ford near Succoth. Or else for 'northward,' translate " to Zaphon," mentioned with Succoth in Josh. xiii. 27], *and said unto Jephthah, Wherefore passedst thou over* [the same word as in ch. xi. 29] *to fight against the children of Ammon, and didst not call us to go with thee ? we will burn thine house upon thee* [over thine head (compare ch. xiv. 15, xv. 6)] *with fire.* (2) *And Jephthah said, I and my people were at great strife* [Heb., " *A man of strife* have I been, I and my people " (so Isa. xli. 11, margin). We were engaged in such desperate strife, as ought to have enlisted your help, as brethren] *with the children of Ammon ; and when I called you* [distinct Hebrew from 'call' in ver. 1 : *Ez'aqu,* " I implored you." Either he or they told an untruth ; probably they : as proud and angry people are reckless of what they say], *ye delivered me not out of their hands* [the call to Ephraim is not detailed before. Jephthah speaks not merely in his own person, but in the person of *his people,* who appealed for help virtually, when encamped in Mizpeh (ch. x. 17, 18). Jephthah went over Gilead and Manasseh, gathering forces, which also was a virtual appeal to all patriotic Israelites (xi. 29). The *Gileadites* may have expressly invited Ephraim, and been refused, just because Jephthah had been appointed without consulting Ephraim]. (3) *And when I saw that ye delivered* [Heb., " thou deliveredst "] (*me*) *not, I put my life in my hands* [Heb., *palm* (1 Sam. xix. 5, xxviii. 21 ;

Job xiii. 14), put my life in extreme risk], *and passed over against the children of Ammon, and the* LORD [JEHOVAH] *delivered them into my hand* [which ye made no effort to do (ver. 3 ; compare Ps. cxviii. 8, 9)]: *wherefore then are ye come up unto me this day, to fight against me ?* (4) *Then Jephthah gathered together all the men of Gilead, and fought with Ephraim* [contrast Gideon's gentleness under Ephraim's provocation, and the result (ch. viii. 1–3 ; Prov. xv. 1). Their grievous words stirred up anger] ; *and the men of Gilead smote Ephraim, because they* [the Ephraimites] *said, Ye Gileadites (are) fugitives of Ephraim, among* [Heb., *in the midst of*] *the Ephraimites, (and) among* [in the midst of] *the Manassites* [because the Ephraimites had taunted the Gileadites with being fugitive runaways (so 1 Sam. xxv. 10) from *Ephraim* (which the Ephraimites in their arrogance identified with *Israel*), in the midst of Ephraim and of Manasseh (*i.e.,* dwelling in the midst of those two noble tribes which sprung from Joseph's two sons, but *unworthy to bear the name of either*). The Ephraimites do not deign to notice Reuben or Gad. In ver. 5, the same phrase "fugitives of Ephraim" (Engl. version, 'those Ephraimites which were escaped') is used of the *Ephraimites* in the ordinary sense, and not of the Gileadites in the contemptuous sense. Their sneer was aimed at Jephthah, who had been a *fugitive* of the half tribe of Manasseh, cast out of his father's house, and his followers with him (xi. 3). Those who had called others 'fugitives,' proved to be the 'fugitives' themselves. Their words proved prophetical of their own doom (Ps. lxiv. 8)—a fire that burned themselves (James iii. 6): they were paid in their own coin, with realities answering to their contemptuous words]. (5) *And the Gileadites* [after defeating the Ephraimites in battle] *took the passages of Jordan before the Ephraimites* [*i.e., facing* them : to cut off their retreat (see ch. iii. 28, vii. 24)]: *and it was (so), that when those Ephraimites which were escaped said, Let me go over ; that the men of Gilead said unto him, (Art) thou an Ephraimite ? If he said, Nay ;* (6) *Then said they unto him, Say now Shibboleth* [*a stream.* The Ephraimites commonly left out the aspirate by defective pronunciation. "Ask leave to cross the Shibboleth"] ; *and he said Sibboleth : for he could not frame* [Heb., "He was not preparing," viz., his heart (the omission is so supplied in 2 Chron. xii. 14, xxx. 19). He took no heed] *to pronounce (it) right. Then they took him, and slew him at the passages of Jordan : and there fell at that time of the Ephraimites forty and two thousand* [probably the whole number of invaders, part slain in battle, and part at the fords of Jordan (so ch. iv. 16). Those who begin strife, generally suffer in the end (Prov. xvii. 14, xxvi. 17)]. (7) *And Jephthah judged Israel six years; then died Jephthah the Gileadite, and was buried in (one of) the cities of Gilead* [the sacred historian does not define *which* city, but says indefinitely (*Hebrew*) "in the cities" (so in Gen. xiii. 12, xix. 29 ; Neh. vi. 2, Hebrew. But the Septuagint "*his* city" (י for '), viz., Mizpah : for the burial places of other judges are given (viii. 32, x. 2, 5).

PEACE THE FRUIT OF RIGHTEOUSNESS : TROUBLE THROUGH SIN : DELIVERANCE UPON PENITENCE.

1. *Tola's rule* (ch. x. 1, 2).——Tola under God restored Israel to the faithfulness toward the Divine covenant from which the nation had fallen under Abimelech. Peace followed in the train of righteousness. Such times, though affording the fewest events to record, are the best to live in. Tola was a man of Issachar, whose tribesmen under David "had understanding of the times to know what Israel ought to do" (1 Chron. xii. 32). Such Tola proved himself, during his long and happy government of twenty-three years. His name means a ' worm.' A type of Him who said at His first coming, "I am a worm, and no man" (Ps. xxii. 6) : and who, just because He was ' lowly,' shall come again to have " dominion to the ends of the earth," and to " speak peace to the nations " (Zech. ix. 9, 10). So His people also, because feeble in themselves as a ' worm,' but helped by Jehovah their Redeemer, shall "thresh the mountains" (Isa. xli. 13– 15) : for it is the ' meek ' who " shall inherit the earth."

2. *Jair's rule* (ver. 3–5).——Jair's name means 'splendid,' yet no splendid act of his, according to men's estimate, is

recorded. But his just and peaceable rule of twenty-two years
has in it more splendour before God, than if he had waded to
empire through seas of blood, and reared stately edifices at the
cost of millions. He and his thirty sons, who rode on ass-colts
as subordinate judges on circuit (ch. v. 10, xii. 14), typify the
King who "cometh riding upon a colt, the foal of an ass"
(Zech. ix. 9), and about to "reign in righteousness," and His
transfigured saints, who as "princes shall rule in judgment"
(Isa. xxxii. 2 ; 1 Cor. vi. 2).

3. *Third period of the times of the Judges under Jephthah and
Samson* (ver. 6–xvi.).—As the *first period* of the times of the
Judges ends with Deborah and Barak, embracing 206 years, from
the commencement of the oppression by Chushan Rishathaim ;
so the *second period* ends with Jair, comprising 95 years : the
two periods combined give a total of 301, answering to the
"three hundred years" in xi. 26. Thus the *third period* begins
with Jephthah and lasts 89 years, ending with the forty years'
oppression by the Philistines (xiii. 1–xvi. 31). The whole
extends to 390 years. In this third period, after a gracious
rest given by Jehovah to Israel for the long period of forty-
five years, the nation lapsed into apostasy again, and were
therefore now given up to the oppression of two heathen
nations at one time, Ammon and the Philistines. Thus the
section (ch. x.) 6–18 is the introduction to the two histories,
—that of Jephthah (xi. 1–xii. 7), the deliverer from the
Ammonite oppression of eighteen years ; and that of Samson
(xiii.–xvi.), who 'began' to deliver Israel (xiii. 5) from the
Philistine oppression, but who left this deliverance to be
completed (not until the oppression had lasted forty years) by
Samuel, after he had converted the people to Jehovah their
God.

4. *Israel's double sin, and its double punishment* (ver. 6–9).—
Israel's sin was one enough to make the "heavens astonished
and horribly afraid:" "My people have committed two evils ;
they have forsaken ME, the fountain of living waters, and
hewed them out cisterns, broken cisterns, that can hold no
water" (Jer. ii. 12, 13). Notwithstanding the lengthened rest
so graciously given by Jehovah during the judgeships of Tola

and Jair, Israel (1) forsook the Lord, and (2) served the senseless idols of the surrounding heathen. Seeking to ingratiate
themselves with the world, at the cost of losing the favour
of God, they lost the favour of both in the end. Nay more,
the very heathen, whom they sought to conciliate by irreligious
compromise, were made the executioners of God's wrath by
His righteous retribution. It ever is so; wherein one sins,
therein is he punished. Formalists begin with trying to
combine worldliness with the service of God. Soon they sink
down to the abandonment of God, and the service of the god
of this world. Then the world itself turns on the apostate
from God (Rev. xvii. 16). Too late he finds to his cost the
truth of God's threat, "Thine own wickedness shall correct
thee, and thy backslidings shall reprove thee: know therefore,
and see, that it is an evil thing and bitter, that thou hast forsaken Jehovah thy God" (Jer. ii. 19).

5. *Israel's repentance* (ver. 10–16).—God saith, "I will go
and return to my place, till they acknowledge their offence, and
seek My face; in their affliction they will seek me early. Come,
and let us return to the Lord: for He hath torn, and He will
heal us" (Hos. v. 15, vi. 1). Pain wrung from Israel the cry,
"We have sinned." As yet it was the cry of the suffering flesh,
not of the penitent heart. God, therefore, for the time rejects
it. Deep conviction of sin must be wrought by the delay in
answering, before grace is bestowed. For this end the sinner
must be made to feel—(1) God's great favours in the past;
(2) his own base ingratitude and relapse; (3) the utter in-
sufficiency of earthly idols to satisfy, help, or save; and (4)
above all, the misery and ruin of one's state, when God
threatens "I will deliver you no more" (ver. 11–14). True
penitents pray on, and wait still upon Jehovah, even though
He hide His face (Isa. viii. 17). Next they put away the evil
of their doings: "The best repentance is a new life" (Luther).
We must repent *from* sin as well as *for* sin. "What have I
to do any more with idols?" (Hos. xiv. 8). They then repeat
their confession of sin, and surrender themselves to God,
acknowledging His sovereign right to do unto them whatsoever
seemed good unto Him. They pray for deliverance this once,

as those who confess they have no claim on it, and who resolve not to backslide again. So now that they are new men, God stands in a new relation to them, namely, that of the gracious Father, who grieves for their affliction, and who will deliver them from the oppressor, whom their penitence has disarmed of his power against them. His threat, "I will deliver you no more," could no longer hold good, unless God were to change His unchangeably righteous character. The change is in them, not in Him. Heretofore sin had disunited Israel, but now the service of the one Jehovah gives the bond of union; and when the Ammonites assembled, the Israelites too assembled—those to their ruin, but Israel to their salvation. So it shall be in the last great day of our dispensation; the Antichristian hosts shall be gathered together for perdition, the saints for their triumph and eternal glory (Rev. xvi. 14, xvii. 13, 17, xix. 19; compare Ps. l. 5; Matt. xxiv. 31; 2 Thess. ii. 1).

6. *Jephthah's appointment as Head and Deliverer* (ver. 17, 18, xi. 1–11).—The Israelites by idolatries had made themselves children of whoredoms and aliens from God's covenant; the son of a concubine, and an outcast, is therefore (in order to humble them in remembrance of their sin) to be their deliverer. God knows how to make adversities qualify His instruments for fulfilling His purposes. He chooses things which are despised to confound the mighty (1 Cor. ii. 27, 28). If Jephthah had not been forced by his hard treatment at the hand of his brethren to use his abilities, they would have lain dormant for want of scope for exercise. Hard campaigning forms the soldier and commander. An army without such a one is a mob without unity, a body without a head. But Jehovah is the true Head. Therefore Jephthah, when appointed, "uttered all his words before Jehovah." So must we, if we would conquer in the good warfare (see Exod. xxxiii. 15).

7. *Jephthah's appeal to right, and then to force, against Ammon* (xii. 12–33).—Arms should not be resorted to until all other lawful means of settlement have failed. Though Jephthah was a mighty man of valour, he preferred persuasion, on the ground of right, to the sword; and only had recourse to war when all that is dearer than life itself must otherwise

have been sacrificed. Then he waited not for their attack in his land, but attacked them in their own. The invaders were invaded, the spoilers spoiled. So in our good fight of faith, the healthiest Christianity is that which stands not on the defensive, but assumes the aggressive. We must make inroads on Satan's kingdom, and win for him souls from the kingdom of our dear Lord, if our own faith and love are not to become cold and stagnant (John iv. 29).

8. *Jephthah's vow* (ver. 30, 31, 34–36).—Though not positively unlawful, the vow betrayed remainders of doubt and weakness of faith. Though the Spirit had come on him, whose presence might have sufficed to assure him of victory without bargain on his part, he suffered the flesh to suggest the thought, that by promising some great sacrifice to God, he could ensure it. Our vows ought to be, not in order to purchase God's favour, but to testify our gratitude. It is wise also to avoid such vows as may afterwards prove an entanglement to conscience (Eccl. v. 2–6; Prov. xx. 25; Deut. xxxiii. 22). When we vow, the promise ought to be fulfilled (Acts v. 1–4; Ps. xv. 4, lxvi. 14, lxxvi. 11; Numb. xxx. 2, 3). But there are exceptional promises, such as that of Herod, involving the life or welfare of our neighbour, which would involve less sin by their breach than by their fulfilment (Mark vi. 23–27). Here we ought to recede from our vow, and seek pardon for having rashly made it. There are, however, vows which need never cause regret, if made in faith, and the fulfilment of which will entail not lamentations, but everlasting joy—the baptismal vows of parents in behalf of children, and the vows of the latter when arrived at the age of maturity. Nay, they will be strong inducements to the performance of the duties so promised in confirmation, and at the supper of the Lord. "Thy vows are upon me" (Ps. lvi. 12). "I have opened my mouth to the Lord, and I cannot go back."

9. *Its mode of fulfilment* (ver. 37–40).—It is clear that Jephthah contemplated a human burnt-offering; for it is human beings, not brutes, that 'come forth' from a general's 'doors,' to meet him and congratulate him on a victory. But a literal human sacrifice was forbidden as an abomination

before Jehovah (Lev. xviii. 21, xx. 2–5). Human beings, belonging of right to Jehovah, were to be redeemed (Exod. xiii. 13, xxxiv. 20; Numb. xviii. 15). Persons devoted under a ban (*cherem*) were slain, not as a sacrifice or burnt-offering, which was a voluntary act, but in fulfilment of the command of God, who required their righteous execution (Numb. xxi. 2, 3; Deut. xiii. 12–18; 1 Sam. xv. 33), therefore these could not be redeemed (Lev. xxvii. 28). Jephthah's vow of burnt-offering was not of this kind, but was a voluntary gift. He made it not hastily in the heat of battle, but before setting out. His other acts were deliberate. He did not unsheath the sword until his reasonable appeals to right had been rejected by Ammon. If he gathered a band of freebooters, it is no more than godly David did. Jephthah looked to Jehovah as the only Giver of victory, and uttered all his words before Him ere setting out. His intimate knowledge of the Pentateuch appears in his message to Ammon; he must therefore have known from it that a literal human sacrifice is against the spirit of the worship of Jehovah. The plea of ignorance cannot be alleged to palliate such an heinous crime. Nor would the " Spirit of Jehovah" have come upon him had he been a Moloch-worshipper (compare 2 Kings iii. 27). Lastly, though believers are not exempt from infirmities, he would never have been set before us as an example of ' faith ' for our imitation, had he been guilty of the gross and abominable heathenism of immolating his innocent daughter (Heb. xi. 32). But all the requirements of the case are fulfilled, if we suppose *he devoted his only daughter to life-long virginity as a spiritual burnt-offering consecrated to Jehovah.* What she, " a bud not allowed to unfold itself " (P. Cassel), and her companions mourned, was her ' virginity,' not her being about to be put to death. The words " upon the mountains " confirm this view. It would be utterly unnatural that, if she were so soon to die, she his only child should spend two months of her respite far away from her loving father's home. Her bewailing her virginity *upon the mountains* is just what modesty would suggest. Their solitude and silence suited lamentations of disappointed hopes, which could not be uttered with propriety in the busy haunts of men.

The final words, " and she knew no man," would be superfluous, if her sacrificial death were meant, for already it was stated she was a virgin. But the reason of their insertion is clear, when we understand them as explaining the previous clause, " did with her according to his vow." The sacred historian hereby implies approval of the act, which he would never have bestowed on a literal human sacrifice ; contrast his disapproval of a much lighter transgression (viii. 27). If Jephthah's daughter had been literally immolated, it would have been an antitheocratic abomination, to be classed with Lot's incest, and not to be recorded in Holy Writ, except for genealogical considerations which have no place here. Nor would Scripture notice the yearly celebration of the offering of Jephthah's daughter, if that offering had been one so abhorrent to the law. What the daughters of Israel went yearly to 'praise' was her willingness to sacrifice for life her natural aspirations as the conqueror's daughter, from motives of filial obedience, patriotic devotion, and self-renouncing piety. Literal burnt-offerings could only be offered at the lawful altar, or before the ark of the tabernacle, and by the Levitical priests. These would never have consented to such an unlawful act. And if Jephthah himself offered it upon an altar of his own, the inspired historian would not have termed it a fulfilment of the vow of a burnt-offering to Jehovah, since it would not have been this, but a sacrifice to the bloody idol Moloch. Jephthah's spiritual offering of his daughter is somewhat like, notwithstanding differences, Abraham's offering of his son Isaac in will, but not in deed. God had a right to dispose of Isaac's life; but Jephthah had none over his daughter's life, without the command of God. Had God commanded him to sacrifice her, which He did not, He would doubtless have interposed to prevent it, as in Isaac's case. Her consecration has its analogue in the women who ministered in the tabernacle, renouncing the world, and dedicating their lives to Jehovah (Exod. xxxviii. 8 ; 1 Sam. ii. 22). The Hebrew (*'olah*) for burnt-offering means a 'going up' on the altar, a *whole* offering, as distinguished from sacrifice of which only a part was offered—a complete surrender to Jehovah. The lesson for us is the living sacrifice which the sense of God's mercies in Christ require (Rom. xii. 1, 2).

10. *Jephthah's chastisement of Ephraim's pride* (xii. 1–6).— "Only by pride cometh contention," and "who can stand before envy?" (Prov. xiii. 10, xxvii. 4). The Ephraimites had already shown their proud spirit towards Gideon after his success against Midian, and only the meekness of that noble hero averted a deadly strife (ch. viii. 1–3). But quarrelsome men at last find their match. The envious man frets at another's success, and becomes his own tormentor. Then a brother, once offended by senseless jealousy, is harder to be won than a strong city (Prov. xviii. 19). The tongue of the Ephraimites kindled the flame (James iii. 6): "Wherefore didst thou not call us to go with thee?" Retributively, their tongue, in its inability to pronounce aright, betrayed them, and was the occasion of their slaughter. They taunted Jephthah and the Gileadites with being 'fugitives,' and soon they became 'fugitives' themselves, at the mercy of those whom they had reviled. Taunts lightly fly, but not lightly wound. When men fasten names of reproach on others because of birth or country, as is so often done, God makes the reviler's own tongue to fall upon themselves (Ps. lxiv. 8). Those who were so proud of the name of 'Ephraimites,' were soon brought to be afraid to own their country. They who had threatened to burn Jephthah's house were cut off for ever from their own. The stone of reproach which they had rolled upon others rebounded upon themselves. Surely "pride goeth before destruction, and an haughty spirit before a fall" (Prov. xvi. 18). Jephthah's judgeship was but for six years: for his wrath was cruel, however justly incurred by Ephraim: without an heir to perpetuate his name, he passed away (Ps. lv. 23). Thus the righteousness of God appears continually in His retributive judgments even in this present world, proving that He is the Moral Governor, notwithstanding that Satan be for a time prince of this world through man's sin.

11. *Jephthah type of the Lord Jesus.*—It was when the 'soul' of Jehovah was "grieved for the misery of Israel" (x. 16), that He raised up a deliverer. So it was because the Father pitied

us in our lost state, He raised up the Mighty One to be our
Saviour (Isa. lxiii. 5, 9). Jephthah was son of a concubine,
and therefore cast out by his brethren. So Jesus, sprung from
Thamar and Rahab (Matt. i. 3, 5), was rejected by His own
brethren and nation (John i. 2, vii. 5; Isa. liii. 3). Compare
other types, Joseph and Moses (Acts vii. 9, 35). But as in
Jephthah's case, so in that of the Lord Jesus : " The stone which
the builders refused is become the head of the corner" (Ps.
cxviii. 22). Jephthah gathered a band of vain men to him.
Publicans and sinners flocked round Jesus, and unto Him hereafter shall the full gathering of the people be (Gen. xlix. 10).
It is not until we are in distress of soul, insolvents unable to
pay our debt to God's law, that we gather unto Him now.
Jephthah forgave his brethren's and the Gileadites' unkindness
to him, and at their call in time of need came to their rescue.
It is when we were without strength, Christ died for the
ungodly (Rom. v. 6). "If the Lord deliver the Ammonites
before me, shall I be your head?" was Jephthah's question.
So Christ will be our Saviour only on condition that we accept
Him as our Lord and our King (1 Cor. xii. 3). Instead of
feeling " we will not have this man to reign over us " (Luke
xix. 14), our hearts must say to the Saviour, " O Lord our God,
other lords beside Thee have had dominion over us, but by Thee
only will we make mention of Thy name " (Isa. xxvi. 13; Rom.
vi. 16–18). As Jephthah was called by men (xi. 11, 29) and
anointed by the Spirit of Jehovah; so Jesus (Matt. iii. 13–17;
Heb. v. 4, 5). The anointing of Christ and of His church is one
and the same,—of Him without measure, of us according to the
measure of His gift (Eph. iv. 4, 7; John iii. 34; 1 Cor. xii. 11).
Jephthah's " uttering all his words before Jehovah," before the
conflict, has its counterpart in Jesus' sublime communion with
the Father on the eve of His redeeming work on Calvary (John
xvii.). Jephthah contested the question with Ammon on the
ground of right, and not of mere might. So Jesus rests His undertaking to redeem man, not merely on His Almighty power, but on
the ground of justice, as "the Lord OUR righteousness." He claims
man's acceptance before God, not merely as a matter of sovereign
grace and love, which it is, but as a matter of right, seeing that

He, as the Son of man our Head, has fulfilled all the obedience
required by God's law, and all its demands against us for our
disobedience, by His spotless life and sin-atoning death ; so that
He " thoroughly pleads our cause " as our strong Redeemer, that
He may give rest to His people, and disquiet the adversary
(Jer. 1. 34, xxiii. 6). As Jephthah pleaded against Ammon
prior possession, so Jesus pleads that the Lord's people are
His from everlasting ages, before Satan's usurpation (Eph. i. 4 ;
Rev. xiii. 8 ; Tit. i. 2). Israel had won the land by conquest
according to the donation of God. So the redeemed are the
Father's gift to the Son, who wrests them by conquest from the
strong man armed (John vi. 37, xvii. 6, 9, 11, 12, 24 ; Luke xi.
22). Jephthah involuntarily gave up his only daughter, an
innocent virgin, to ensure deliverance to his people: God of His
own infinite grace spared not His only begotten Son, but
delivered Him up ; and the Son gave up His own spotlessly
pure soul freely for us all. Even after Jephthah's victory the
Ephraimites mocked and persecuted him. And after Jesus'
conquest of Satan, in His resurrection and glorious ascension,
His countrymen still reviled His name and country, as the
Galilean, and persecuted Him in the person of His followers,
whom they called " the Nazarenes " (John vii. 41, 52, i. 46 ;
Acts ii. 7, iv. 1–10, ix. 1–4, xxiv. 5). The day of reckoning
fast approaches, as in the case of the Ephraimites, when for every
idle word men must give account, and by their words shall be
justified or else condemned. A man may now assume the guise
of a Christian ; but if Christ be not in his heart, the Shibboleth
of his mouth is sure to detect him, as Peter's Galilean speech
betrayed him (Matt. xii. 34–37, xxvi. 73 ; James iii. 10–13).
Certainly at the Lord's coming no lying pretence of being what
men are not will avail to save them from wrath. Those who
are on the Lord's side alone shall enjoy eternal rest and glory
with Him.

BRIEF SEASONS OF REST : PHILISTINE OPPRESSION : DIVINE
ANNOUNCEMENT OF SAMSON'S BIRTH.

JUDGES XII. 8–XIII.—(8) *And after him Ibzan of Bethlehem*
[not Bethlehem of Judah or Ephratah ; or else it would have
been so expressed (xvii. 7, 9 ; Ruth i. 2; Mic. v. 1); but
Bethlehem of Zebulun (Josh. xix. 10, 15). So Elon was a
Zebulonite (ver. 11). The men of Zebulun had already proved
their patriotic bravery (iv. 10, v. 18). The three Judges
succeeding Jephthah ruled the tribes east of Jordan, and
the northern tribes west of Jordan] *judged Israel.* (9) *And
he had thirty sons, and thirty daughters, (whom) he sent abroad*
[gave in marriage to husbands abroad], *and took in* [their
stead] *thirty daughters from abroad for his sons* [what a
contrast to Jephthah, whose only child, a daughter, was
doomed to perpetual virginity !]. *And he judged Israel seven
years.* (10) *Then died Ibzan, and was buried at Bethlehem.*
(11) *And after him Elon, a Zebulonite, judged Israel; and he
judged Israel ten years.* (12) *And Elon the Zebulonite died,
and was buried in Aijalon* [called from Elon, its founder or
owner. Answering to the ruins *Jalun*, four hours east of
Akka], *in the country of Zebulun.* (13) *And after him Abdon
the son of Hillel* [probably the same as Bedan (1 Sam. xii. 11) :
the Phœnicians often omit the initial A (ע)], *a Pirathonite* [see
1 Chron. xxviii. 14], *judged Israel.* (14) *And he had forty sons
and thirty nephews* [rather in modern English, *grandsons ;* as
' nephew ' means, in Spenser and Shakspere, and other old
English writers], *that rode on threescore and ten ass-colts* [imply-
ing their dignity (ch. v. 10, x. 4 ; see notes and remarks] ; *and he
judged Israel eight years.* (15) *And Abdon the son of Hillel the
Pirathonite died, and was buried in Pirathon* [now *Fer'ata*, six
miles west of Shechem (*Nablous*). Or *Fer'aun (Palest. Explor.
Quart. Stat.)*], *in the land of Ephraim, in the mount of the
Amalekites* [who had an early settlement in the neighbouring
highlands, subsequently occupied by Ephraim (see ch. iii. 13,
v. 14, vi. 3)].

O

CHAPTER XIII.

(1) *And the children of Israel did evil again in the sight of the* LORD [JEHOVAH. See on this formula for apostasy (ch. ii. 11, iii. 7, 12, iv. 1, vi. 1, x. 6)]; *and the* LORD [JEHOVAH] *delivered them into the hand of the Philistines forty years* [double the number of years of the oppression under Jabin. The Philistines had already harassed Israel (iii. 31): see remarks on the *third period of the times of the Judges under Jephthah and Samson* (3), (chs. x., xi., xii.). Here at xiii. begins the second of the two histories (*Jephthah and Samson*), to which the section (ch. x. 6–18) is the common introduction. The Philistines were harassing Israel at the time of the announcement of Samson's birth (ver. 5); therefore the "forty years" (ver. 1) begin just before his birth. He judged Israel for twenty years (ch. xvi. 31), which begin from his first exploits (xiii. 25). The forty years comprise all Samson's life, and extend beyond his death. His judgeship must have begun some considerable time before he was twenty years old : he was probably a mere youth when his espousing a Philistine woman was the occasion of his attacking them. The end of the forty years was after Samson's death, under Samuel (1 Sam. vi. 1, vii. 2–13), "twenty years" after the transfer of the ark to Kirjath-Jearim, which was just after its restoration by the Philistines, who had kept it seven months from the time of its capture at Eli's death. Therefore Eli was for a time Samson's contemporary ; and Eli's death and the capture of the ark must have been some time after Samson first appeared as judge and deliverer]. (2) *And there was a certain man of Zorah* [originally of Judah, in the Shephelah, or low rolling hills between the

mountains and plains (Josh. xv. 33 ; 'valley,' Hebr., *Shephelah*):
subsequently assigned to Dan (Josh. xix. 41) as a suitable
border fortress : now *Sur'ah*, just below the brow of a sharp
conical tell at the shoulder of the ranges which form the north
side of the Wady Ghurab. Manoah possibly commanded the
military post at "the camp of Dan" (*i.e.*, the encampment of
the Danite emigrants (xviii. 8, 11, 12) between Zorah and
Eshtaol (xiii. 25): a check on the Philistines, who were in
force three miles off at Timnath (xiv. 1–4, xv. 6). Samson's
birthplace and the family burial-place was between Zorah and
Eshtaol (xvi. 31). The charge to Samson not to drink wine,
or eat what came of the vine, was the severer test of faith,
because Zorah and the neighbourhood were famed for their
choice vines (ch. xv. 5, xvi. 4 ; Gen. xlix. 11, Hebrew], *of the
family of the Danites* ['family' is used for 'tribe'; for all the
Danites form one family, the Shuhamites (Numb. xxvi. 42,
43). In Samson Jacob's prophecy was to be fulfilled, "Dan
shall judge his people" (Gen. xlix. 16)], *whose name (was)
Manoah ; and his wife (was) barren, and bare not.* (3) *And the
angel of the* LORD [JEHOVAH] *appeared unto the woman, and said
unto her, Behold now, thou (art) barren, and bearest not* [God
first awakens the sense of need, and then He promises to
supply it (Matt. xx. 32). Or, probably, at this time she was
feeling sadly her childless state ; God sends comfort just when
His people feel their trouble most. So at the births of Isaac,
Samuel, and John the Baptist (Gen. xvi. 1, xviii. 10–14 ; 1
Sam. 1, 10, 11, 15, 16, ii. 5, 20 ; Luke i. 7)]; *but thou shalt
conceive, and bear a son* [so Luke i. 11–14, 26–37]. (4) *Now
therefore beware, I pray thee, and drink not wine nor strong
drink, and eat not any unclean (thing)* [Numb. vi. 1–21, the
Nazarite vow (Luke i. 15)]. (5) *For thou shalt conceive, and
bear a son ; and no razor shall come on his head : for the child
shall be a Nazarite unto* [literally "a separated man of"] *God
from the womb ; and* [in virtue of the power received in consequence of his Nazarite state] *he shall begin* [what Samuel
subsequently would *complete*] *to deliver Israel out of the hand of
the Philistines* [teaching Israel that deliverance could come only
in connection with Nazarite-like consecration of the priestly

nation to Jehovah (Exod. xix. 5, 6).   (6) *Then the woman came
and told her husband, saying, A man of God* [Heb., " *the* man of
God," viz., the one just mentioned : answering to " the angel
of Jehovah." She regarded Him as a prophet, like Moses
(Deut. xxxiii. 1 ; compare 1 Sam. ii. 27, ix. 6 ; 1 Kings xii. 22,
xiii. 1 ; 1 Tim. vi. 11 ; 2 Tim. iii. 17)] *came unto me, and his
countenance* [Heb., ' appearance,' as in Dan. x. 18] *(was) like the
countenance of an* [Heb., *the*] *angel of God* [*the angel of Jehovah*
(ver. 3), in whom the invisible God manifests Himself (ii. 1,
vi. 11 ; Hag. i. 13 ; Mal. ii. 7, iii. 11 ; John i. 18)], *very
terrible : but I asked him not whence he (was), neither told he me
his name.*   (7) *But He said unto me, Behold, thou shalt conceive,
and bear a son : and now drink no wine nor strong drink,
neither eat any unclean (thing) : for the child shall be a Nazarite
to God from the womb to the day of his death.*   (8) *Then
Manoah entreated the* LORD [JEHOVAH], *and said, O my Lord*
[*Master :* ADONAI, not JEHOVAH], *let the man of God which thou
didst send* [Manoah did not know that He was *the angel of*
JEHOVAH] *come again unto us, and teach us what we shall
do unto* [how we shall treat] *the child which shall be born.*
(9) *And God hearkened unto the voice of Manoah ; and the
angel of God came again unto the woman as she sat in the field :
but Manoah her husband (was) not with her.*   (10) *And the
woman made haste, and ran, and showed her husband, and said
unto him, Behold, the man hath appeared unto me, that came unto
me the (other) day.*   (11) *And Manoah arose, and went after
his wife, and came to the man, and said unto him, (Art) thou the
man that spakest unto the woman ? And he said, I (am).*   (12)
And Manoah said, Now let thy words come to pass [Heb.,
nominative plural, with verb singular : because the words form
one promise ; *and when they do come to pass*], *How shall we
order* [rightly treat] *the child* [Heb., what shall be the judgment (*mishpat*) or right of the child], *and (how) shall we
do unto him* [Heb., *and his work ?*   Not, as Speaker's Commentary explains, " his exploits :" for, in ver. 13, 14 (the
angel's answer), no mention is made of the child's work, but of
what *the parents' work* should be *to and for him.*   Also, in
ver. 8, Manoah asks solely, " teach us what we shall do unto

the child." So in Job xli. 9, "the hope *of him*," is *the hope of taking him*, not *his* hope]. (13) *And the angel of the* LORD [JEHOVAH] *said unto Manoah, Of all that I said unto the woman, let her beware.* (14) *She may not eat of any (thing) that cometh of the vine* [added to his directions in ver. 4: so Numb. vi. 3. Heb., here "the vine *of wine*," in contrast to "an empty vine" (Hos. x. 1): and the gourd-bearing vine (2 Kings iv. 39)], *neither let her drink wine, nor strong drink, nor eat any unclean (thing): all that I commanded her, let her observe.* (15) *And Manoah said unto the angel of the* LORD [JEHOVAH], *I pray thee, let us detain thee, until we shall have made ready* [the Hebrew *'asah* is equivocal: 'offer' as *food*, or as *sacrifice*, so that in Manoah's use of it, its meaning is to "*make ready*": in the angel's (ver. 16), to '*offer.*' Probably Manoah used it purposely, as being uncertain whether the stranger was human or divine: compare Gideon (vi. 18, 19)], *a kid for thee* [Heb., "before thee," "before thy face"]. (16) *And the angel of the* LORD [JEHOVAH] *said unto Manoah, Though thou detain me, I will not eat of thy bread* [food, *i.e.*, kid. So the Antitype made the glorifying of God His meat and drink, rather than earthly food (John iv. 34)]; *and if thou wilt offer a burnt-offering, thou must offer it unto the* LORD [JEHOVAH. The kid might be used either as food to be eaten by a *man*, or as a sacrifice to be accepted by JEHOVAH: I need it not as food: if you offer it as a sacrifice, offer it to Jehovah. The angel did not explicitly say, "I am Jehovah"—this He leaves to Manoah's spiritual intelligence to discover. Manoah's subsequent inquiry as to His 'name,' proves that Manoah did not understand the angel's words as directly asserting that He is Jehovah]: *for Manoah knew not that he (was) an angel of the* LORD [JEHOVAH. And therefore offered Him food to eat, as if He were a man. The angel's caution to Manoah to offer the sacrifice only to Jehovah, answers to that of the angel to John (Rev. xix. 10, xxii. 8); and that of Peter to Cornelius (Acts x. 25, 26). Still more in point is Jesus' answer to the rich ruler, who did not recognise Jesus' Godhead: "Why callest thou me good? there is none good but One, that is, God" (Matt. xix. 17). Jesus, jealous for the Father's honour, declines divine attributes when given

Him by those who know Him not as One with the Father].
(17) *And Manoah said unto the angel of the* LORD [JEHOVAH],
What [rather *Who;* for the Hebrew *Mi* means Who? *Mah,*
What?] *(is) thy name, that when thy sayings come to pass, we
may do thee honour?* [by presents, in the case of men (Numb.
xxii. 17, 37, xxiv. 11; 2 Kings v. 5, 15): by sacrifices in
the case of God (Isa. xliii. 23). Manoah does not define
which, as he is uncertain as to the nature of the angel]. (18)
And the angel of the LORD [JEHOVAH] *said unto him, Why
askest thou thus after my name, seeing it (is) secret* [rather
Wonderful; answering to "did wondrously," *i.e.*, miraculously
(ver. 19; Isa. ix. 6), "His name shall be called Wonderful."
'Name' expresses not the proper name, but the *nature:* and,
in the case of God, His character in so far as He has revealed
Himself to us]. (19) *So Manoah took a kid with a* [the] *meat-
offering* [the accompaniment of the burnt-offering (Numb. xv.
4, &c.), an *oblation (Minchah)* of flour, corn, and oil, without
leaven (hypocrisy, malice, the old nature, Luke xii. 1; 1 Cor.
v. 8): indicating the surrender to God of what was of greatest
value to man, his daily sustenance, and symbolising the Word
and the Spirit of God (Luke viii. 11; Deut. viii. 3)], *and offered
(it) upon a rock* [as the altar (vi. 20, 21, 26)] *unto the* LORD
[JEHOVAH]: *and (the angel) did wondrously* [as described ver.
20): causing fire, doubtless (vi. 21), to issue from the rock and
consume the offering: then ascending in the flame]; *and
Manoah and his wife looked on.* (20) *For it came to pass,
when the flame went up toward heaven from off the altar, that
the angel of the* LORD [JEHOVAH] *ascended in the flame of the
altar: and Manoah and his wife looked on (it), and fell on
their faces to the ground* [Lev. ix. 24]. (21) *But the angel of
the* LORD [JEHOVAH] *did no more appear to Manoah and to his
wife. Then Manoah knew that He (was) an angel of the* LORD
[JEHOVAH]. (22) *And Manoah said unto his wife, We shall
surely die, because we have seen God* [note vi. 22 (see Gen. xvi.
7–13; Exod. xxxiii. 20)]. (23) *But his wife said unto him,
If the* LORD [JEHOVAH] *were pleased to kill us, He would not
have received* [accepted] *a burnt-offering and a meat-offering at
our hands; neither would He have showed us all these (things)*

[*i.e.*, the miracle (ver. 20)], *nor would, as at this time* [*in our days;* whatever things may have possibly taken place in the days of old], *have told us* (*such things*) *as these* [the coming birth of the boy, the right treatment of him and his mother, and his destination to be deliverer of Israel]. (24) *And the woman bare a son, and called his name Samson* [derived from *Shamesh,* ' the sun :' *Sun-like* (ch. v. 31): shining with saving light on Israel in their oppression by the Philistines. But Speaker's Commentary derives it from *Shemesh,* Arabic and Syriac, *to minister,* viz., to God as a consecrated Nazarite] : *and the child grew, and the* LORD [JEHOVAH] *blessed him* [compare 1 Sam. ii. 21]. (25) *And the Spirit of the Lord* [JEHOVAH] *began to move* [*Pahan,* ' thrust ' or impel him, taking sudden possession of. So ἐκβάλλει, " *thrust* Him forth " (Mark i. 12), is the term used of the Spirit's impelling the great Antitype to His first conflict with Satan] *him at times in the camp of Dan* [Mahaneh-dan (ch. xviii. 11, 12, which refers to times long preceding Samson). The district where the 600 Danite emigrants pitched their camp ' behind,' *i.e.*, west of Kirjath-Jearim (now *Kuriet-el-Enab* in Judah)], *between Zorah* [*Sura,* seven miles south-west of *Kuriet-el-Enab*] *and Eshtaol* [in the Shephelah, or low hilly country of Judah between mountain and plain (Josh. xv. 33, xix. 41), now *Kusteel,* a conical hill, an hour's journey south of *Kuriet-el-Enab* towards Jerusalem. Allotted to Dan, on the Philistine border, between Ashdod and Askelon. The standing *camp* of the little *host* (Mahaneh-dan), as being exposed to constant warfare with Philistia, was a district well calculated to train Samson for his encounters with that people].

A QUARTER OF A CENTURY OF PEACE, FOLLOWED BY CHASTISEMENT
FOR APOSTASY : DIVINE ANNOUNCEMENT AND BIRTH OF THE
DELIVERER.

1. *Fruit of conflict.*—Ibzan ruled for seven years, Elon ten, and Abdon eight. Little is recorded of them, but that little suffices to indicate a period of tranquil prosperity. The

conflicts of Jephthah's rule for six years, secured the blessings of peace to Israel for the ensuing quarter of a century. One sows and another reaps; but both alike shall have their due reward at last from God (John iv. 36, 37). The fruit of Jesus' travail of soul, whereby He, through death, overcame our adversary that hath the power of death, shall issue in His everlasting dominion as Prince of peace. If Jephthah died without a seed to represent him, his only child being devoted to God in perpetual virginity, the next judge, Ibzan, was blessed with sixty children, and Abdon with forty sons and thirty grandchildren. So, because the Father made Jesus' soul an offering for sin, "He shall see His seed, and shall prolong His days" (Isa. liii. 10). His spiritual progeny shall be countless as the sand. Though he has no offspring by generation, he has by adoption "a multitude which no man can number" (Rev. vii. 9). This seed "shall be accounted to the Lord for a generation" (Ps. xxii. 30). Let us not be cast down, because now we have the cross and the warfare; soon our eyes shall see Jerusalem, "a quiet habitation;" and those won by us to our Lord Jesus Christ shall be our spiritual children, the crown of our rejoicing at His coming (1 Cor. iv. 15; 1 Thess. ii. 19).

2. *Sin and sorrow twin sisters.*—The history of the elect nation under the Judges moved in the same cycle throughout, and is therefore narrated in the same recurring phrases. Prosperity induced laxity: "They did evil again in the sight of Jehovah;" and as cause and effect are inseparable, Jehovah delivered them into the hand of their enemies. But, as they were His chosen people, the punishment was not destructive but corrective. Now, correction betokens love. It is a proof of a father's deep interest in his child. To be without fatherly chastisement is the note of a bastard, not of a son. So our heavenly Father speaks to His family: "You only have I known of all the families of the earth, THEREFORE I will punish you for all your iniquities" (Amos iii. 2). Israel was worse than all others, in proportion as Israel ought to have been better: "Judgment must begin at the house of God" (1 Pet. iv. 17). And as the continual repetition of their apostasy aggravated their guilt, the oppression by their Philistine enemy

was suffered to last for double the time that the longest of their past oppressions, namely that under Jabin, had continued.

3. *Grace superabounding where sin abounded.*—Before that we read of any repentance on the part of Israel, God was the first to move in mercy towards his backsliding children. God might say, "Why should ye be stricken any more? ye will revolt more and more?" (Isa. i. 5). Now He will prove them with gratuitous and unlooked-for compassion amidst their miseries. It was when the Egyptian king commanded all the male children of Israel to be killed, that Moses was born and saved from death ; and it was when the Philistine rule pressed most sorely that Samson was born. So the sorrows of His elect move our Father to remember for us His own covenant of grace, rather than our grievous backslidings. Love often melts when punishment only hardens. "Herein is love, not that we loved God, but that He loved us, and sent His Son to be the propitiation for our sins" (1 John iv. 10). This amazing love moves His redeemed to shame for their sins, and love for their Saviour ; as He saith, "Nevertheless I will remember my covenant—that thou mayest remember, and be confounded, and never open thy mouth any more because of thy shame, when I am pacified toward thee for all that thou hast done, saith the Lord God" (Ezek. xvi. 63).

4. *Peculiarity of Samson's judgeship, and its spiritual lesson.* —The history of all the former judges commences from their maturity and entrance upon office ; that of Samson from the announcement of his coming conception and birth of a mother who had been barren. No less than the Angel of Jehovah foretold all this, and directed that he should be consecrated as a Nazarite unto God from the womb. In the subsequent instruction by the Angel of Jehovah, the woman was directed herself also to refrain from anything that cometh of the vine, as well as from strong drink, and any unclean thing. In immediate connection with this imposition of Nazarite obliga- tions follows the promise: "And he shall begin to deliver Israel out of the hand of the Philistines." It is in this connection that we have the explanation of the otherwise inexplicable fact, that Samson's life and acts are described with a fulness

which seems out of proportion with the actual deliverance wrought for Israel. The small results ensuing upon his exploits disappoint the expectations which would naturally be entertained of one whose birth was so specially announced and ordered by God. His actions themselves, moreover, have the outward aspect of self-willed, foolhardy, and venturesome feats of mere strength, and these in connection with discreditable alliances with heathen women. But his very failure to accomplish Israel's deliverance, through his unfaithfulness to his Nazarite vow, in contrast to his extraordinary prowess when moved by the Spirit of God, qualified him the better to be *an embodied reproof to the Israelites, whose calling was to be a nation of priests,* though through apostasy they lost their power against the enemy. *Samson was, in his own person, a lesson to teach Israel, that her strength lay in separation from idols, and complete consecration to Jehovah.* So the Christian, who also is called to be a priest unto God, is mighty through God against all foes, so long as he makes an entire self-surrender to Him. But when once the delights of the flesh entice him, and he yields to the seductions of the world and its defilements, he becomes spiritually weak as any natural man.

On the other hand, Samson, as a Nazarite, vowed to Jehovah, was to begin to deliver Israel from the Philistines; and so, by his heroic strength, which was derived from faith in God and the Divine gift entrusted to him, he was fitted to instruct the slumbering nation how to awake and put on strength; he exhibited in his own person the might to which the people of God might attain, if only they would be faithful and wholehearted towards their God. In a word, it is *his typical aspect towards Israel* that we find the key to the character and history of Samson, the last of the judges so extraordinarily called by God, and the one in whom the power of Jehovah, exhibited so marvellously, found its culmination. His natural weakness reflected that of Israel, so continually inclined to amalgamate with surrounding idolaters, and therefore self-deprived of the Divine power whereby alone the nation could stand. He was not, like the preceding judges, leader of an army, but fought alone in the consciousness of possessing God's irresistible might,

in order to show the people how "one should chase a thousand
except their Rock had sold them, and Jehovah had shut them
up" (Deut. xxxii. 30). His 'beginning,' but not completing
the deliverance, manifested the *possibility* of it—a possibility
about to be converted into a reality under Samuel, who was
faithful to his God, and who led back the people also in
penitence to faithfulness toward their King (1 Sam. vii. 2–14).
Samson was not of giant stature and proportions, as were some
of the Philistines (compare 1 Sam. xvii. 4–7, 42–47). His
strength was not brute and natural, but spiritual; not inherent,
but imparted, in connection with his Nazarite vow to God, and
inseparably bound up with fidelity to Him. So the believer,
weak in himself, is invincible in the might of God, and His
Spirit obtained through continual, believing prayer (Isa. xl.
29–31; 2 Cor. xii. 9, 10).

5. *Significance of the Nazarite vow.*—It was of God's kindness
that he "raised up of Israel's young men for Nazarites" (Amos
ii. 11), "purer than snow, whiter than milk, more ruddy in
body than rubies, their polishing of sapphire" (Lam. iv. 7).
The vow involved three obligations—(1) To abstain from all
produce of the grape, intoxicating or not, "from the kernels
even to the husk" (Numb. vi. 4). This taught the priestly
nation of the covenant (Exod. xix. 5, 6), and teaches us also
whose calling is to be "unto our God, kings and priests"
(Rev. v. 10), that luxurious dainties and sensual enjoyments,
symbolised by the *grape-cakes* of Israelite epicures (Hos. iii. 1,
margin), as well as by the wine of the drunkard, are incompatible with spiritual consecration and consequent power (Luke
xxi. 34; Rom. xiii. 14).

(2) To leave the hair of the head uncut. This separated
the Nazarite visibly from all other Israelites, who were wont to
cut their hair; and it marked dependence on God. The
believer, "the hairs of whose head are all numbered" by God's
special Providence (Acts xxvii. 34; Matt. x. 30; Luke xxi. 18;
Dan. iii. 27), is to be separate from the world (Rom. xii. 2;
2 Cor. vi. 17), and dependent in little as well as great things
on the Lord our Head (1 Cor. xi. 3, 5, 6, 10, margin; 12), our
true position towards our Lord being that of woman-like

receptivity. Above all, the hair uncut by human hand symbolised the beauty and full vital powers which the Nazarite
dedicated to Jehovah (2 Sam. xiv. 25, 26). So the believer is
to love the Lord with all his strength (Luke x. 27). The free
growth of the hair was " the consecration of his God upon his
head " (Numb. vi. 7), like the holy crown upon the mitre of the
high priest, and the anointing oil poured upon his head (Exod.
xxix. 6, 7). Hereby the Nazarite hallowed his head to Jehovah,
so that his consecration found its fullest expression in the unshorn locks, the symbol and sacramental vehicle of his power
from God ; so the believer's head, like his heart, is hallowed
to the Lord. Heavenly wisdom gives to his head an ornament
of grace (Prov. iv. 9), even the beauty of holiness.

(3) To have no contact with any corpse, even that of the
nearest relative (Numb. vi. 6). The same rule held good as to
the priests (Lev. xxi. 11, 12). The saints as consecrated to be
a " royal priesthood—a peculiar people—separated unto the
gospel of God " (1 Pet. ii. 9 ; Rom. i. 1) are called to "arise
from the dead," to " have no fellowship with the unfruitful
works of darkness " (Eph. v. 11, 14), to " be separate and touch
not the unclean thing," so shall we be true " sons and daughters
of the Lord Almighty " (2 Cor. vi. 17, 18).

6. *Consecration must begin with parents, and thence flow to
children.*—Samson's mother too was to observe the renunciations
of this Nazarite vow during pregnancy. As the Divine promise
tested her faith, so this precept tested her obedience. The
sanctifying of the son must begin from the mother ; for from
her he draws his nourishment, both in the womb and at the
breasts. Mothers should remember how much their children's
character from the first depends on them, and should deny
themselves in all that might act prejudicially upon the children.
She who would have a holy child must herself be holy. Even
innocent things connected with evil are to be shunned. Of
all that God forbids ' beware '; all that God commands 'observe.'
They who would have Christ spiritually formed in them, must
" cleanse themselves from all whereby the growth of the new man
might be hindered (Gal. iv. 19). The ancients used to say,
The beginning is half the work. The work is one for eternity,

so none can enable us to do it for ourselves and our little ones, but He who inhabiteth eternity. God alone sees the links which connect every moment of time's little circles with the vast circumference of eternity. Every parent's prayer to God should be that of Manoah, "O my Lord, teach us what we shall do to the child? How shall we order him? how shall we do unto him?" How shall we so train him, as to be a spiritual Nazarite, and living sacrifice unto God? Manoah prayed for direction in rearing the child, even before his birth. So prayer should precede the entrance of a believer's child into the world. Grace should forestall Satan's working, which begins from the time of actual birth.

7. *Our time of need, God's time of help; and when saved ourselves, we seek to save others.*—The barrenness of Manoah's wife, which Israelites esteemed a reproach, humbled her, and so prepared her, as it did Hannah and Elizabeth, for being a vessel of grace. Had she not been barren, the Angel of Jehovah would not have visited her. The believer's sorrows prepare for his joys (Isa. liv. 1). When the glad tidings of coming maternity were Divinely announced to her, whilst in solitude and probably engaged in prayerful meditation, she hastened to communicate her blessedness to Manoah. Husbands, when awakened spiritually, should impart the blessed Gospel of salvation to their wives, and wives to their husbands (John iv. 16, 28, 29). Each should excite the other to faith, love, and good works. If the wife lead, the husband should not be ashamed to follow. And let not one devolve on the other alone the right training of the young; for the continual efforts of both are little enough for so momentous a task as that of rearing a child to glorify God here, and to enjoy Him for ever hereafter. Above all, let both pray for the inward revelations of Jesus by the Holy Ghost. The Man of God came in answer to prayer (ver. 8, 9). The Lord Jesus, when we pray in faith, will manifest Himself to us a very present help in our time of need (Matt. xxi. 22; John xvi. 23, 24; Phil. iv. 19).

8. *The angel of Jehovah the man of God.*—If we compare the name given Him, 'Wonderful' (margin ver. 18), with the name given by the Holy Ghost in Isaiah (ix. 6) to the Son of

God, Messiah, we can have no doubt who this Angel was, even
the Divine " messenger (Angel) of the covenant " (Mal. iii. 1).
His countenance "very terrible" (ver. 16), here is the same
which appeared to John (Rev. i. 16), "as the sun shineth in his
strength." He it is who went before Israel in the wilderness,
and of whom God saith, "My name is in Him" (Exod. xxiii.
21). His theophany as the Man of God was the anticipation
of His incarnation. His frequent converse in human form with
the Old Testament saints was as if He longed for the fulness of
the time, fixed from eternity to come, when He would assume
our flesh and dwell among us (Luke xxii. 15 ; Ps. xl. 7, 8). It
is true God had said to Moses, " Thou canst not see my face, for
there shall no man see me, and live " (Exod. xxxiii. 20). But
" the only begotten Son, which is in the bosom of the Father,
He hath declared Him " (John i. 18). Even in patriarchal times
Jacob saw God "face to face" at Peniel (Gen. xxxii. 30). It
must therefore have been God the Son whom he and Manoah
saw (1 Tim. vi. 16). But the full vision is reserved for the
future. The unveiled sight of God, as He is, would overwhelm
us now, just as the naked eye would be dazzled and blinded by
the sun. When the saints shall have put off the earthly and
psychical or natural, soul-animated body, and put on the
spiritual body, they shall see God, not as now dimly, and as it
were in a mirror, but without a veil and in direct vision, and
shall reflect His glory (Matt. v. 8 ; 1 Cor. xiii. 12, xv. 44, 46,
49 ; Rev. xxii. 4). As Christ is pre-eminently THE *Man of God*,
so the minister of God, as also the believer, each in his sphere,
is a man of God (Deut. xxxiii. 1 ; 1 Sam. ix. 6 ; 1 Kings xiii.
1, xvii. 18 ; 2 Pet. i. 21). He is no longer a man of the world,
but God's representative in the world. Bought with the price
of the Redeemer's blood, he is not his own. He witnesses for
God to edify the church, and to condemn those who reject
Christ's testimony (2 Tim. iii. 17 ; 1 Tim. vi. 11).

9. *God revealed especially in Jesus' sacrifice.*—It was when
the angel of Jehovah ascended in the flame which went up
toward heaven from off the altar, that Manoah and his wife,
upon beholding, fell down in adoration. They had begged to
know his name ; now He reveals it 'wondrously.' When

Jacob asked the Divine One's name, "He blessed Jacob there." *Blessing* therefore is His 'name,' that is His revealed aspect towards us (Acts iii. 26 ; Luke xxiv. 50, 51). The Lord Jesus ascended in the flame of His own offering (Heb. ix. 12). As Manoah and his wife "looked on," so did the disciples at Jesus' ascension,—fulfilling the type of Elisha, to whom his seeing Elijah, when being taken up, was the condition of being blessed with a double portion of the prophet's spirit (2 Kings ii. 9, 10, 12, 13). May we too have faith to see our Saviour ascending to be our Advocate with God our Father, on the ground of His completed sacrifice and perfect righteousness ; so that we may receive the double measure of the Spirit, and reverently and gratefully may fall low at the feet of Him who loved us and gave Himself for us.

10. *God's past grace the pledge of present and future salvation.*—Manoah had spoken with confident hope of the promise just before (ver. 8, 12). Yet now he is full of fears, just because of the revelation which ought to have strengthened his faith. We ought to guard against such unworthy fears of death, and narrow views of God. Nothing is too good, or too great, for God to give to His believing children for Jesus' sake. Even when he overwhelms us with awe-inspiring glimpses of His majesty, it is not in order to destroy, but to assure us of His power, as well as His will, to save. He hath not given us Christians, "the spirit of fear, but of power, and of love, and of a sound mind" (2 Tim. i. 7; Rom. viii. 15; 1 John iv. 18). His having given His own Son to die in our stead is ample assurance that "God hath not appointed us to wrath, but to obtain salvation by our Lord Jesus Christ" (1 Thess. v. 9).

The weaker vessel becomes the stronger ; the logic of faith forms the true inference. As Manoah here showed great fear ; so his wife, great faith. The weaker vessel proved herself the stronger believer of the two, and a true helpmeet to cheer her fainting husband. Thus "two are better than one ; for if they fall, the one will lift up his fellow " (Eccl. iv. 9, 10). The wife's trustfulness in God made her a juster reasoner than her husband ; for terror blinds the understanding, so as not to see things in their true light.

God would never mock His believing children by accepting their offerings, and promising them a Deliverer, if He purposed after all to destroy them. If He should kill them, how could His promise of a son be fulfilled? If the root should be blasted, how could the branch spring from it? Past favours are pledges of God's love, they ought therefore to be viewed as the earnest of future blessings, rather than as forerunners of ill. The Father's acceptance of the sacrifice of His Son for us is a pledge of all other blessings to them that believe (Rom. viii. 32). If we know that God has manifested Himself to us in grace through our Saviour crucified, risen, and ascended for us, then we may surely dismiss unworthy fears, and infer that He will not give us over to death, but having begun His good work in us will perform it until the day of His coming (Phil. i. 6; Ps. cxxxviii. 8, lxxvii. 7–11; compare lvi. 13 with cxvi. 8, 9).

11. *Samson the type of Messiah.*

(1) *Samson was a son born by virtue of the divine promise and faith in the promise;* and so, like Isaac, prefigured the promised seed (Gal. iv. 23; Heb. xi. 11). Our privilege too, if we be believers, and so united to Christ the Son, is, we are " children of promise " (Gal. iii. 26, iv. 28).

(2) *Samson was a Nazarite to God from the womb;* so was Jesus in deed, all that the Nazarite vow expressed in type, pure from all sin in His conception and from his birth (Heb. vii. 26). As Samson's mother for his sake was forbidden to touch any unclean thing, so the Old Testament church who was for ages in travail, and from whom in the fulness of time He was to spring, was during the long period that she waited for Him, to be a "kingdom of priests and a holy nation." Believers similarly are called to be a "royal priesthood, a peculiar people" (1 Pet. ii. 9). Moreover, their earnest prayer and effort will be, that their children may realise the Nazarite consecration to God from the womb.

(3) *'Samson' signifies* SUN; the Lord Jesus is the antitype, "the Sun of righteousness." He goeth forth in His might, infinitely above that of Samson (ch. v. 18; Mal. iv. 2). So "the path of the just is as the shining light, that shineth more and more unto the perfect day" (Prov. iv. 18); and when that

day shall come, "the righteous shall shine forth as the sun in the kingdom of their Father" (Matt. xiii. 43).

(4) But, *the Antitype exceeds the type.*—*Samson only 'began' the deliverance of Israel* (ver. 5); whereas our Jesus is not only " the *author* " (*Beginner :* Prince Leader : ἀρχηγός), but also " the *Finisher* of our faith (margin, Heb. xii. 2). Samson delivered only partially, and that from an earthly oppressor; Jesus delivers perfectly, and from everlasting death.

(5) As *the Spirit moved Samson from his youth;* so the Spirit, given by the Father without measure to the Son, impelled Him to the conflict with Satan, from whom His holy nature instinctively recoiled (note, ver. 25). Blessed are they in whom the Spirit of Jesus begins to work from early childhood! They shall be "more than conquerors through Him that loved them."

P

CHAPTER XIV.

SAMSON'S CULPABLE WEAKNESS OVERRULED TO THE INFLICTION OF
HIS FIRST BLOW UPON THE PHILISTINE OPPRESSORS.

(1) *And Samson went down* [from Mahaneh-dan (ch. xiii. 25)]
*to Timnath, and saw a woman in Timnath of the daughters of
the Philistines* [Timnath, meaning an *assigned* or *divided* part, is
the same as the Timnathah of Dan (Josh. xix. 43); haunted
by lions (ver. 5), it must therefore have been thinly peopled.
With the nice accuracy of Scripture, it is written here, " Samson
went *down* " (from Zorah) to Timnath; and in ver. 2, "He came
up " to his father and mother at Zorah. For *Tibneh*, the
deserted site of Timnath (the change of *m* into *b* occurs also
in Ata*b* for Eta*m* (xv. 8, 11) south-west of Zorah, now *Sur'ah*,
is 740 feet above the sea, not in the plain: the Shephelah,
therefore, in which it was, according to 2 Chron. xxviii. 18,
cannot mean *the plain,* but the *low rolling hills between the
mountains and the plain.* Samson, in "going down" from Zorah,
would first descend 700 feet into the valley, then would ascend
again 350 feet to Timnath. The corn which he fired grew in
the valley; whereas the vineyards and olives lined the hills.
The Philistines "came up" from the plain to Timnath]: *now
therefore get* [*laquak,* 'take' (Exod. xxxiv. 16)] *her for me to wife*
[for the custom was that parents should conduct the negotiation,
a dowry having to be paid for the bride. Presents to the bride
were called *mohar,* to the relatives *mattan* (Gen. xxi. 21,
xxxiv. 12, xxxviii. 6; Exod. xxi. 9, xxii. 17; 1 Sam. xviii. 25).
The parents' consent was asked first, then that of the bride
(Gen. xxiv. 49, 50, 58). Between betrothal and marriage
communication between the betrothed ones was carried on
through "the friend of the bridegroom" (ver. 20; John iii. 29)].

(3) *Then his father and his mother said unto him, (Is there)
never a woman among the daughters of thy brethren* [of thine own
tribe], *or among all my people, that thou goest to take a wife of
the uncircumcised Philistines* [not in Jehovah's covenant, and
therefore without its appointed token (Gen. xvii. 10): a strange
marriage for one consecrated to Jehovah (Exod. xxxiv. 16;
Deut. vii. 3, 4; 2 Cor. vi. 14, 15)]? *And Samson said unto his
father, Get her for me, for she pleaseth me well* [Heb., "she (is)
right in my eyes." His choice was to please his fancy (Gen.
vi. 2). But God's providence overruled his self-pleasing, to
subserve God's purpose]. (4) *But his father and his mother
knew not that it (was) of the* LORD [JEHOVAH (Josh. xi. 20;
1 Kings xii. 15; 2 Chron. xxii. 7)], *that he* [Samson] *sought an
occasion against* [Heb., *min*, 'from'] *the Philistines* [Samson, in
the old fleshy nature, was seeking his own self-gratification: but
the higher impulses in him from the Spirit of God, in concert
with the Providence of God, were seeking an opportunity of
quarrelling (2 Kings v. 7) with, and so delivering Israel from,
the Philistines. Whatever may have been Samson's carnal
purpose, *in effect* he sought an occasion against the oppressors.
It would hardly be fit language, to say, as the Speaker's Commentary, "*Jehovah sought* occasion." This applies to *man*, not
to God] ; *for at that time the Philistines had dominion over Israel*
(ch. xiii. 1). (5) *Then went Samson down, and his father and
his mother* [who by this time had given a reluctant consent], *to
Timnath, and came to the vineyards of Timnath* [where he
turned aside, letting his parents go forward without him]; *and,
behold, a young lion* [Heb., "a cub of lionesses"] *roared against
him* [*liqueratho*, "towards him:" "in encountering him."]. (6)
And the Spirit of the LORD [JEHOVAH] *came mightily* [Titzlach,
"came suddenly." Usually the Hebrew expresses *to prosper;*
so the additional thought here may be "came opportunely" as
well as *suddenly.* In ch. xiii. 25, the word is *pa'am*, "thrust
him," or *impelled him* to his first efforts as a youth. Here the
Spirit *comes opportunely* though *suddenly*, qualifying him for
maturer and more public exploits] *upon him, and he rent him,
as he would have rent a kid, and* [*i.e., although*] *(he) had nothing
in his hand; but he told not his father or his mother what he had*

done [so ver. 9, as to the taking of the honey from the lion's carcase. This is added to show that the solving of the riddle could only have been effected through his wife's disclosure of it. It marks also his modesty: the truly brave seldom boast. His encounter with the lion prepared him for greater feats (so David, 1 Sam. xvii. 34–37)]. (7) *And he went down and talked with the woman ; and she pleased him well* [he had only 'seen' her heretofore (ver. 1). But now that his parents had proposed for her, he 'talked' with her (1 Sam. xxv. 39 ; Song Sol. viii. 8), he was accepted, and had his first impressions heightened]. (8) *And after a time he returned to take her* [after the interval between betrothal and marriage had elapsed, the bridegroom 'took' the bride home, which was the essential ceremony (Matt. xxv. 6)], *and he turned aside* [from the road] *to see the carcase of the lion* [as he would naturally do, having killed it so wonderfully some time before] *; and, behold, (there was) a swarm of bees and honey in the carcase* [*Mapeleth*, from *naphal*, " to fall:" as πτῶμα, from πίπτω, not the mere *skeleton*, for bees would not have their hive there ; but the *carcase*, thoroughly dried up by the sun's heat, as often occurs within twenty-four hours after death, in a sultry season in the Arabian desert. Bees would not shun such a receptable, though they avoid carrion] *of the lion.* (9) *And he took thereof in his hands, and went on eating, and came to his father and mother* [who had probably gone on before to claim the bride for their son : so they knew not of his turning aside to the lion's carcase], *and he gave them, and they did eat ; but he told not them that he had taken the honey out of the carcase of the lion.* (10) *So his father went down unto the woman* [to celebrate the wedding]; *and Samson made there* [in Timnath] *a feast ; for so used the young men to do* [(Gen. xxix. 22 ; Matt. xxii. 1–11). The feast lasted for seven or even fourteen days]. (11) *And it came to pass, when they* [the bride's parents and relatives] *saw him, that they brought thirty companions to be with him* [as " children of the bride-chamber"; groomsmen (Matt. ix. 15), Samson not having brought any with him. When the Philistine relatives 'saw,' *i.e., considered* him (as 'see' is used, Gen. xxvii. 27 ; Ps. x. 14), as one capable of being a formidable foe, they thought he needed to be watched : so they gave him thirty companions, by way of honour, as if to promote the festivity of the wedding, really to watch him (but see note, ver. 19)]. (12) *And Samson said unto them, I will now put forth a riddle* [*chidah*, an 'enigma' (1 Kings x. 1); "hard questions" (Ezek. xvii. 2), often proposed at feasts to entertain the company. The wager was laid not on chance, but on the exercise of wit, very different from most wagers. Yet even this wager by its results forbids taking it as a precedent] *unto you: if ye can certainly declare it me within the seven days of the feast, and find (it) out, then I will give you thirty sheets* [*shirts*, worn within, next the skin ; סְדִינִים, *sedinim*, σινδόνες], *and thirty change of* [outer costly] *garments.* (13) *But if ye cannot declare (it) me, then shall ye give me thirty sheets* [shirts], *and thirty change* [compare Gen. xxxv. 22] *of garments. And they said unto him* [accepting the proposal], *Put forth thy riddle, that we may hear it.* (14) *And he said unto them, Out of the eater came forth meat, and out of the strong came forth sweetness* [a play on similar sounds, *Mehaokeel yatza Maakal umeʿaz- yatza Mathoqu*]. *And they could not in three days expound the riddle* [for three days they tried fair means ; for the rest of the seven days (margin, ver. 17) they urged Samson's wife to discover the secret from her husband. She of herself, through curiosity and pique at his withholding anything from her, had tried from the first day (ver. 17), but in vain. At last, on the seventh day, in desperation they threatened to burn her and her father's house—a threat which they afterwards actually executed, in spite of her treachery to Samson for their sake. In terror, then she plied him the more vehemently, till she wrung the secret from him *before the close of the seventh day*]. (15) *And it came to pass on the seventh day, that they said unto Samson's wife* [the devil has broken many a man's head with his own rib; this bait he has found to take so well, that he never changed it since he crept into Paradise (Trapp)], *Entice thy husband, that he may declare unto us* [through thee, without his notice] *the riddle, lest we burn thee and thy father's house with fire: have ye called* [invited] *us* [in order] *to take that we have* [to *impoverish us* by the loss of the wager (ver. 13)]? (*Is it*) *not* (*so*)? [they assert emphatically that the sole object of their

being invited was to plunder them, and that Samson's wife was
an accomplice in the plot for impoverishing her own countrymen, and she shall suffer for it. A vivid picture of the
unscrupulousness, barbarous cruelty, and covetousness of the
Philistines]. (16) *And Samson's wife wept before him, and said,
Thou dost but hate me, and lovest me not : thou hast put forth a
riddle unto the children of my people* [my countrymen], *and hast
not told* (*it*) *me. And he said unto her, Behold, I have not told* (*it*)
my father nor my mother, and shall I tell (*it*) *thee ?* (17) *And
she wept before him the seven days* [see note on ver. 14], *while
their feast lasted ; and it came to pass on the seventh day, that
he told her, because she lay sore upon him* [see Prov. xxvii. 15] :
and she told the riddle to the children of her people. (18) *And
the men of the city* [the thirty young men, 'companions' invited,
ver. 11], *said unto him on the seventh day before the sun went
down, What* (*is*) *sweeter than honey ? and what* (*is*) *stronger than
a lion ?* [they answer in a shrewd style, as if they had guessed
it]. *And he said unto them, If ye had not plowed with my heifer,
ye had not found out my riddle.* [His proverbial and smart reply
(*mashal*) intimates, that they had not the wit to solve his
enigma till he had disclosed it to his wife, who, he sees,
had divulged it to them, probably through the friend of
the bridegroom who supplanted Samson from the place
which he ought to have had in her heart (ver. 20)]. (19) *And
the Spirit of the* LORD [JEHOVAH] *came upon him* [see note
ch. xiii. 25). The impulses of the Holy Spirit came at intervals. The prophets had not the Spirit of prophecy always,
nor apostles the power of working miracles (2 Tim. iv. 20)],
and he went down to Askelon, and slew thirty men of them
[of the wealthy Philistines ; so that what the enemy had
devised for Samson's hurt and loss (ver. 11, 15–18) ended in
their own. The Septuagint (Alexandrine MS.) and Josephus
read in (ver. 11), " when they were *afraid* (בְּרָאֹתָם, from יָרֵא,
instead of כִּרְאוֹתָם, from רָאָה, " when they saw him ") that they
brought thirty companions to watch him "], *and took their spoil*
[' apparel,' ' clothes,' *Chalitzoth* (2 Sam. ii. 21)], *and gave change
of garments unto them which expounded the riddle* [Ps. xv. 4, end];
and his anger was kindled [against his wife for treachery ; he

therefore did not return to her for some time. That the
natural impulse of anger did not arise until after the exploit
was achieved, shows that the moving impulse had not been
carnal revenge, but "the Spirit of Jehovah" (ver. 19). Moreover, his anger was not against the Philistines to whom he had
to pay the garments, but against her], *and he went up to his
father's house* [at Zorea, without her]. (20) *But Samson's wife
was (given) to his companion, whom he had used as his friend*
[the one of the thirty companions whom he had made "the
'friend' of the bridegroom" (John iii. 29), at the marriage feast,
—the bride's escort to the bridegroom. Perhaps too, as Samson's
reply may hint (ver. 18), she already loved him too well. The
faithlessness of the Philistines,—their laxity as to the sanctity
of marriage, and the sad results of alliances of believers with
unbelievers, appear in this history. Samson, though justly
angry, had never repudiated his wife (ch. xv. 1, 2). The
parents, instead of trying to atone for the wrong done to him
by their daughter, made the evil irreparable by giving her to
another, and that other the one of all men most bound to maintain the honour of the bridegroom and the bride].

CHAPTER XV.

SAMSON'S FURTHER EXPLOITS WITH WEAK INSTRUMENTS, IN THE
FACE OF STRONG ENEMIES, AND UNFAITHFUL FRIENDS: GOD'S
STRENGTH PERFECTED IN HIS WEAKNESS.

(1) *But it came to pass within a while after, in the time of
wheat harvest* [the time suitable for Samson's device, ver. 5],
that Samson visited his wife with a kid [a customary present
(Gen. xxxviii. 17)]; *and he said, I will go into my wife into
the chamber* [the woman's apartment. His impulsive generosity
appears in his so readily forgiving his wife's falseness to him,
after the first ebullition of his anger at it]: *but her father
would not suffer him to go in.* (2) *And her father said, I
verily thought that thou hadst utterly hated her; therefore I
gave her to thy companion*: (is) *not her younger sister fairer than
she* [Lev. xviii.,18, an incestuous union forbidden by God,
(see Song Sol. viii. 8, 9); Christ redeems the younger as well
as the elder sister: the Gentiles as well as the Jews]? *take
her* ["let her be thine"], *instead of her* [the elder sister].
(3) *And Samson said concerning* [or *to*] *them,* [her father and
the surrounding Timnathites], *Now shall I be more blameless
than* [rather, "I shall be blameless before" (as in Numb.
xxxii. 22), literally, *from* (מ), *i.e.,* in respect to] *the Philistines,
though I do them a displeasure* [they have themselves to blame
for it. This wrong which the Timnathite Philistines have done
me relieves me from any obligation that I was under to them
because of my marriage to a Timnathite. That obligation
was what had made him go off to Ashkelon on a raid (xiv. 19),
now he is free in respect to all Philistines everywhere; so he
takes his revenge on the spot, appearing to avenge a private
wrong, he was really avenging the oppression of his people].
(4) *And Samson went out and caught three hundred foxes*

[*Shualim*, akin to the Persian *Schaghal*; from *Shaal*, " to burrow." The Hebrew includes also 'jackals'; gregarious animals, and easily caught. They have been seen in a flock to the number of two hundred (Bellonius, quoted by Maurer), and are found still in the neighbourhood of the Philistine Gaza. That they abounded in Palestine, appears from the names of places compounded with *Shual*, as Hazar-Shual, Shaalbim, our own Foxhayes : Shual. The fox is solitary, and therefore unsuitable for Samson's purpose. Jackals, as herding together, would readily run in couples, tied by a cord two or three yards long. Samson being the recognised judge of Israel, probably had helpers to catch and let them loose from different places, so as to consume the more of the Philistines' corn. The jackals shrinking from the flame, swift of foot, and pro- verbially oblique in their course, would carry destruction in various quarters, without compromising or injuring the Israelites with their masters, the Philistines ; nay, it would be relieving his countrymen of a noxious animal], *and took firebrands* [torches], *and turned tail to tail, and put a firebrand in the midst between two tails.* (5) *And when he had set the brands on fire, he let (them) go into the standing corn of the Philistines, and burnt up both the shocks* [the cut and bound-up sheaves], *and also the standing corn* [if he had attached the torches to the jackals singly, they would soon have been extinguished ; but when bound together in couples, they rushed wildly in different directions, and then together carried the flame into the standing corn, retarding one another by their struggles till the corn took fire], *with the vineyards* [that region was famed for " the choicest vine," called *Sorek* (Heb., Isa. v. 2 ; Gen. xlix. 11), which gave its name to the valley (Judg. xvi. 4). Eshcol was near (Numb. xiii. 23). Foxes and jackals like young grapes, and would resort to them (Song Sol. ii. 15)] (*and*) *olives.* (6) *Then the Philistines said, Who hath done this? And they answered, Samson, the son-in-law of the Timnite* [*i.e.*, Timnathite], *because he* [the Timnathite] *had taken his wife, and given her to his companion. And the Philistines came up* [incensed at their heavy losses, owing to the faithlessness of the Timnathite and his daughter], *and burnt her and her father with fire* [probably burning the house to the ground with its occupants. Burning was sometimes the penalty of adultery (Gen. xxxviii. 24); though stoning was the more merciful mode of death under the Mosaic law (Deut. xxii. 21). The vexation of the Philistines for their crops was overruled unto making them God's executioners of wrath on their own guilty countryman and his daughter. Treachery recoils on the treacherous (Isa. xxxiii. 1). The very evil which she had sought to avert by betraying her husband's secret, she brought on herself by that very treachery (ch. xiv. 15)]. (7) *And Samson said unto them, Though ye have done this, yet will I be avenged of you* [אָם כִּי אָם, "*As surely as* ye have done like this (*Kazoth*), so *surely* I will not cease till I be avenged of you.*" Or else, as English version, "Though ye have done in such a cruel way as this, and hope that I am appeased by the vengeance you have taken on those who wronged me, yet I will be further avenged," &c.], *and after that I will cease.* (8) *And he smote them hip and thigh* [Heb., "leg upon thigh," *Shoqu 'al yareek*. He cut them in pieces, so that their legs and thighs were scattered one upon another, *i.e.*, he *totally* destroyed them (Gesenius). He smote them *on the leg and thigh :* proverbial for a *great wound* (Maurer): a cruel, unsparing slaughter (Keil): the German proverb "arm and leg:" the French "back and belly :" not as Speaker's Commentary, a proverbial expression drawn from the joints of the *sacrifices*, the choice pieces, the *thigh* and *shoulder* (Exod. xxix. 22, so translates the Hebrew for 'hip'), representing the *great* and *mighty :* but there is no allusion to sacrifices in the context: and no need for so far-fetched an explanation], *with a great slaughter: and he went down and dwelt in the top* [rather סְעִיף, "the cleft"] *of the rock Etam* [he avoided towns, lest he should endanger his countrymen with the Philistines. Etam, now *Beit 'Atab*, a steep, stony, bare knoll, standing in the midst of the narrow valleys, itself without a blade of corn, but having olive groves and three abundant springs at its feet. Not far from Manoah's patrimony, from which Samson "went *down*" to it, there is a singular rock tunnel, 250 feet long, 7 or 8 feet high, and 18 feet wide, answering to the 'cleft' of Etam rock, roughly hewn in the stone, running from the midst of the

village eastward to the chief spring : its lowness, compared with
the main ridge of the watershed, accounts for the expression
"came *down.*" Here Samson could hide without any one
lighting, except by accident, on the entrance. The springs at
the foot of Etam rock were sometimes called *Ayun Kara,* akin
to En-hakkore (Lieut. Conder, in the *Quart. Statem. of Palest.
Explor.*)]. (9) *Then the Philistines went up and pitched in
Judah, and spread themselves* [they came up the narrow wadies
from their plain in close order, then spread themselves when
they reached the Judean open ground above (2 Sam. v. 18,
22)], *in Lehi* [Heb., " *the* Lechi," *i.e., jaw-bone :* the name is given
by anticipation (vers. 15–17): in Judah, between Philistia
(which is the sea-coast plain, whence the phrase correctly says
the Philistines "went up ") and the cliff Etam. Now *Beit-
Likiyeh,* a village on the north side of the Wady Suleiman : at
the entrance of the hill country of Judah, the outermost stronghold toward the south. Ramath Lehi is the *eminence;* En-
hakkore, the spring]. (10) *And the men of Judah said, Why
are ye come up against us? And they answered, To bind Samson
are we come up, to do to him as he hath done to us.* (11) *Then
three thousand men of Judah went* [Heb., *went down*] *to the top*
[rather *the cleft* (note ver. 8)] *of the rock Etam, and said to
Samson, Knowest thou not that the Philistines (are) rulers over us*
[ch. xiii. 1] *? what (is) this (that) thou hast done unto us* [the
slaughter of the Philistines (ver. 8), which might provoke them
to reprisals, upon the men of Judah]? *And he said unto them,
As they did unto me, so have I done unto them.* (12) *And they
said unto him, We are come down* [from higher uplands of
Judah] *to bind thee, that we may deliver thee into the hand of
the Philistines. And Samson said unto them, Swear unto me,
that ye will not fall upon* [*i.e.,* kill (ch. viii. 21)] *me yourselves.*
(13) *And they spake unto him, saying, No ; but we will bind
thee fast, and deliver thee into their hand : but surely we will
not kill thee. And they bound him with two new cords* [he
meekly, without resistance, notwithstanding his great strength,
submitting : so Isaac (Gen. xxii. 9): and the Antitype (John
x. 17, 18, xviii. 12)], *and brought him up* [notes, ver. 8] *from
the rock* [out of the cleft of Etam rock to Lehi]. (14) *(And)*

when he came unto Lehi, the Philistines shouted [with joy]
against [or, as in ch. xiv. 5, "at meeting"] *him* [shouting was
usual in encountering the foe (1 Sam. xvii. 20, 52). Their shout-
ing was soon changed into shrieking, their triumph into tribulation (see Job xx. 5)]; *and the Spirit of the* LORD [JEHOVAH]
*came mightily upon him, and the cords that (were) upon his
arms became as flax that was burnt with fire, and his bands
loosed* [rather, as the Heb. poetically and graphically, 'melted,'
answering in parallelism (the Hebrew mode of versification), to
"burnt with fire"] *from off his hands.* (15) *And he found
a new* ['moist,' *i.e.,* fresh, and so less brittle] *jaw-bone of an ass
and put forth his hand and took it, and slew a thousand men
therewith* [compare Shamgar's slaying six hundred with an
ox-goad (ch. iii. 31; also 2 Sam. xxiii. 8)]. (16) *And Samson said, With the jaw-bone of an ass heaps upon heaps* [Heb.,
an heap, two heaps], *with the jaw of an ass have I slain a thousand
men* [he plays on the double sense of the Hebrew *chamor* "an
ass," and "a heap"; *hachamor, chamor, chamorathaim.* In
forcing his way through the crowd of Philistines, slaying on
the right hand and on the left, he would form *two* heaps of
dead, or else he smote *one heap after another* as he overtook them. His triumphal song naturally is in poetical repeti-
tional parallelism. Speaker's Commentary suggests that he
bound the jaw-bone to his fist with the cords, and made a kind
of cestus with it. Awe of one who had burst such bonds made
the Philistines to regard him as a supernatural being. In panic
they fled headlong before him down the precipices. The Lord
of all power enabled Samson: *how* he slew the thousand is not
revealed; that he did so with so seemingly inadequate an instrument is (Josh. xxiv. 12; 1 Cor. i. 27, 28)]. (17) *And it came
to pass, when he had made an end of speaking, that he cast away
the jaw-bone out of his hand, and called the place Ramath-Lehi*
[*i.e., The height of the jaw-bone.* If the name is not used by
anticipation in ver. 9 (see note there), and if Samson does not
give the name now for the first time, he must here (ver. 17)
be playing on the name which it had already, as expressing
what he now has done, "lifted up the jaw-bone"]. (18) *And
he was sore athirst* [with the exertion of the conflict, the exhaus-

tion of pursuing the Philistines and the heat, the season being wheat harvest (ver. 1)], *and called on the Lord* [JEHOVAH], *and said, Thou hast given this great deliverance into the hand* [or else, *by the hand (beyad)*] *of thy servant, and now shall I die for thirst, and fall into the hand of the uncircumcised?* (19) *But God* [*Elohim*] *clave an* [Heb., *the*] *hollow place* [*Han-Makteesh;* which is translated "a mortar" in Prov. xxvii. 22; and is made the proper name of some place in Jerusalem, *Ham-Makteesh,* from its being a *hollow* (Zeph. i. 11)] *that (was) in the jaw* [rather "in Lehi," not in the ass' jaw-bone, just as God made the water flow at Rephidim (Exod. xvii.) and Kadesh (Numb. xx. 8–11). Some hollow among the rocks of Lehi was called *Ham-Makteesh,* "the mortar," from its shape. The spring (the Hebrew of 'thereof' is feminine, and so must refer to *the spring*) which God caused to break forth in Lehi for the supply of Samson's need, was still called in the sacred writer's days "the fount of him that cried:" this confirms the translation "in Lehi." The phrase, "that was in," would not have been used, but simply "the hollow of," if "the jaw" were meant], *and there came water thereout; and when he had drunk, his spirit came again, and he revived; wherefore he called the name thereof* [of the spring] *En-hak-kore, which (is) in Lehi unto this day* [see note ver. 8. The rocky precipice was named from its shape Lehi, "the jaw-bone;" naturally therefore the hollow gap in the rock was called (following up the figure) *Makteesh,* "the tooth-hollow." Samson cried to JEHOVAH (the God of the covenant of grace to His people), and ELOHIM (the God of creation and of nature) split the hollow at Lehi miraculously, so that water came out of it. To this possibly Ps. xxxiv. 6 alludes]. (20) *And he judged Israel in the days of the Philistines twenty years* [his exploits just recounted established his position as recognised Judge of Israel. The sacred writer sums up the record of his judgeship by briefly stating that it lasted for twenty out of the forty years of the Philistine oppression (xiii. 1). The particulars of his rule between its first establishment and its tragical close are not detailed. What follows in ch. xvi. concerns his fall, which brought to an end his judgeship; at the close the same words wind up the chapter as preceded it (compare xv. 20 with xvi. 31, end)].

CHAPTER XVI.

SAMSON'S RISK WITH ONE BAD WOMAN, AND RUIN THROUGH
ANOTHER: ROBBED OF HIS CONSECRATION, AND SO OF HIS
STRENGTH: BLINDED, IMPRISONED, MOCKED, BY DEATH HE
DESTROYS HIS CONQUERORS.

(1) *Then went Samson to Gaza* [meaning 'fortification,' the
most south-westerly town towards Egypt, and the key of the
route between Syria and Egypt. Assigned to Judah (Josh.
xv. 47), but reoccupied by the Philistines. A place hazardous
every way for Samson to visit (Prov. xiv. 16, xxvi. 11)],
and saw there an harlot [Heb., "a woman an harlot." How
degrading that a *woman*, so lovely and noble, when pure,
should become such a vile thing as an *harlot* (Isa. i. 21 ; Jer.
ii. 21). Such is the spiritual apostate], *and went in unto her*
[the same phrase as in Gen. vi. 4. It is not here said, as in
ch. xiv. 4, "it was of Jehovah." For it was wholly of his
own lust, issuing in death (James i. 13–15)]. (2) (*And it was
told*) *the Gazites, saying, Samson is come hither. And they
compassed* (*him*) *in, and laid wait for him all night in the gate
of the city, and were quiet all the night* [probably sleeping,
certainly in careless repose, relying on their having shut the
gates, and therefore apparently having secured Samson. Had
their watchmen guarded the gates, Samson could not have
lifted them out and carried them off], *saying, In the morning
when it is day, we shall kill him* [Heb., *'ad* or *ha-boquer
vaharag nuhu*, "Till the light (dawning) of the morning (we
will wait) and (or *then*) we shall kill him"]. (3) *And Samson
lay till midnight, and arose at midnight, and took* [hold of] *the
doors of the gate of the city, and the two posts, and went away with
them* [rather *tore them up*, יִסָּעֵם, *yissa'eem* : properly, *to tear up ;*
so *to tear up* the tent pegs, so as to *go away*], *bar and all* [with
the cross bar (on them)], *and put them upon his shoulders, and*

carried them up to the top of an hill that (is) before Hebron
['*Al pence*, "facing towards," "over against." If these words
be pressed strictly, some hill "before Hebron" must be meant.
But as mount Nebo is said (Deut. xxxii. 49) to be "*over
against* Jericho," though it is four geographical miles from
Jericho, and the Jordan flows between; so the hill east of
Gaza here may be said to be "facing *towards* Hebron," though
about nine geographical miles distant from it. The *Tel el
Muntar*, "hill of the watchmen," east of Gaza, at about half
an hour's distance off, is by tradition represented as the scene
of Samson's feat. It commands a beautiful view. The people
of *Ghuzzeh*, however, are ignorant of the tradition. The
mountains of Hebron are visible from *Tel el Muntar*, though
not Hebron itself. It was a prodigious feat to carry the
massive gates and bar through the deep sand of the road, and
up the hill]. (4) *And it came to pass afterward, that he loved
a woman in the valley* [*wady*, Heb., *nachal*] *of Sorek* [a name
applied to a choice vine with *dusky-coloured* grapes. The
valley was doubtless planted with this vine. Porter identifies
the valley with *Wady Surar* ('pebbles'). It separates the
rugged mountains of the 'Arkub from the low rolling hills of
the Shephelah, beyond which is the Philistine plain. The
valley of Sorek joins the great gorge which bounded Judah on
the north. On the south is Timnath; on the north are
Sur'a and *Eshu'a*, the ancient Zoreah and Eshtaol. Etam
(*Beit Atab*) is two miles westward], *whose name (was) Delilah*
[meaning "the languishing" or "pining one"]. (5) *And the
lords of the Philistines* [the five lords, viz., of Gaza, Ashdod,
Ekron, Ashkelon, and Gath (Josh. xiii. 3)], *came up unto her,
and said unto her, Entice him, and see wherein his great strength
(lieth)* [Ewald, followed by the Speaker's Commentary, translates,
Whereby his strength (is) great] *and by what (means) we may
prevail against him, that we may bind him to afflict him* [they
do not say "to kill him," lest she should shrink from this;
and their purpose was to prolong his sufferings and their
triumph by keeping him alive]; *and we will give thee, every
one of us, eleven hundred (pieces) of silver* [1100 *shekels*, or
£137, 10s. each; in all, £687, 10s., indicating how high a

price they set on Samson's head]. (6) *And Delilah said to Samson, Tell me, I pray thee, wherein thy great strength (lieth)* ["thy strength (is) great" (ver. 5) (Ewald). But Maurer supports our English version], *and wherewith thou mightest be bound to afflict thee.* (7) *And Samson said unto her, If they bind me with seven* [the divine number sealing *perfection*] *green* [moist undried] *withs* [strings; *yatharim*, as of a bow or harp; of *animal sinews*, as distinguished from *'abothim*, the 'ropes,' in ver. 11. But most Hebrew commentators translate, *withs of pliable twigs*], *that were never dried, then shall I be weak, and be as another* (one) *man.* (8) *Then the lords of the Philistines brought up to her seven green withs* [strings] *which had not been dried, and she bound him with them.* (9) *Now (there were) men lying in wait, abiding with her* [ready at hand to help her in mastering Samson, whenever it was evident that his super-human strength was gone. Heb., "the spy (was) sitting for her"] *in the chamber. And she said unto him, The Philistines (be) upon thee, Samson. And he brake the withs* [strings], *as a thread of tow is broken when it toucheth* [Heb., *smelleth*] *the fire; so* [*the secret of*] *his strength was not known.* (10) *And Delilah said unto Samson, Behold, thou hast mocked me, and told me lies: now tell me, I pray thee, wherewith thou mightest be bound.* (11) *And he said unto her, If they bind me fast* ["binding they bind me"] *with new ropes that never were occupied* [Heb., "Wherewith work has not been done with them"], *then shall I be weak, and be as another man.* (12) *Delilah therefore took new ropes* [see note, ver. 17], *and bound him therewith, and said unto him, The Philistines (be) upon thee, Samson. And (there were) liers in wait abiding in the chamber* [note, ver. 9]. *And he brake them from off his arms like a thread.* (13) *And Delilah said unto Samson, Hitherto thou hast mocked me, and told me lies: tell me wherewith thou mightest be bound. And he said unto her, If thou weavest the seven locks* [the mystical number into which his hair was plaited, implying Divine *consecration*, so as to be fastened with the web upon the loom by means of the pin or weaver's comb; or woven as a *woof* into the threads of *the warp* which was on a loom in the chamber. Supply from vers. 7 and 11, "then shall I be weak," &c.] *of my head with the web.*

(14) *And she fastened (it)* [*i.e.,* the web to the loom] *with the pin* [the weaver's comb. So Keil; but Speaker's Commentary- "She fastened the loom down with a pin, to keep it immov, able." Maurer, "She fastened (the web and seven locks inter-woven) with the pin to the wall"], *and said unto him, The Philistines (be) upon thee, Samson. And he awaked out of his sleep, and went away with the pin of the beam* [rather, "of the loom" or 'frame;' the 'beam' would mean the *roller* to which the threads of the warp were fastened, and round which the cloth was rolled when finished, a distinct Hebrew word from that here (1 Sam. xvii. 7), *Menor orgim*], *and with the web.* (15) *And she said unto him, How canst thou say, I love thee* [evidently a constant phrase in the silly lover Samson's mouth] *when thine heart (is not with me ?* [see 2 Kings x. 15]. *Thou hast mocked me these three times, and hast not told me wherein thy great strength (lieth).* (16) *And it came to pass, when she pressed him daily with her words* [see Prov. xix. 13], *and urged him, (so) that his soul was vexed* [Heb., 'shortened' (margin, ch. x. 16). Joy enlarges the heart; sorrow and worry *contract* it (Exod. vi. 9)] *unto death* [so as to be weary of life (Gen. xxvii. 46)], (17) *That he told her all his heart, and said unto her, There hath not come a razor upon mine head ; for I (have been) a Nazarite unto God from my mother's womb : if I be shaven, then my strength will go from me, and I shall become weak, and be like any (other) man.* (18) *And when Delilah saw* [from the evident sincerity of his tone] *that he had told her all his heart, she sent and called for the lords of the Philistines, saying, Come up this once ; for he hath showed me* [the oldest reading is לֹהּ, for לֹי : *to her,* for *to me;* then it is the remark of the writer, not that of Delilah : "for he *had* showed *her* all his heart"] *all his heart. Then the lords of the Philistines came up unto her, and brought money* [the promised reward of her treachery (ver. 5). Covetousness and lust often go hand in hand (Eph. v. 5)] *in their hand.* (19) *And she made him sleep* [with his head resting] *upon her knees : and she called for a man, and she caused him to shave off the seven locks of his head ; and she began to afflict him, and* [she who lulled him to sleep is the first to afflict him, just at the time when] *his strength went from him.* (20) *And she said,*

Q

The Philistines (be) upon thee, Samson. And he awoke out of his sleep, and said [within himself], *I will go out as at other times* [Heb., " as time upon time "] *before, and shake myself* [loose. from the hands of the Philistines, as in ver. 9, 12, 14]. *And he wist not that the* LORD [JEHOVAH] *was departed from him* [he had said, " If I be shaven, then my strength will go from me : " but the sacred writer here intimates that the secret of his strength lay not in his unshorn hair, as hair, but in the presence of Jehovah with him, of which presence and of the covenant between Jehovah and him, the uncut hair was the pledge. He broke away from the covenant by yielding up to a harlot the hair which he had worn in honour of Jehovah]. (21) *But the Philistines took him, and put out his eyes* [to prevent effectually, as they thought, his ever again injuring them : for even if his strength should return, he would not see where to strike. At the same time, by not killing him, they prolonged their own triumph and revenge], *and brought him down to Gaza* [which was lower than Sorek, as being nearer the sea : therefore it is said ' down.' The scene of his exploit (ver. 3) becomes the scene of his humiliation], *and bound him with* [*two*, or *double*] *fetters of brass* [*Nehushtaim :* the dual number, because *both* hands and feet were fettered with them. So Zedekiah was bound with double chains after having been blinded (Heb., 2 Kings xxv. 7] ; *and he did grind* [the Heb. participle *tocheen* expresses *continued grinding :* turning the mill : a hand mill worked by slaves (Exod. xi. 5 ; compared with xii. 29 ; Isa. xlvii. 2)] *in the prison-house* [Heb., the house of the bound " (Jer. xxxvii. 15)]. (22) *Howbeit the hair of his head began to grow again after* [Heb., *Ka-asher*, ' as ' (from the time in which)] *he was shaven* [his imprisonment till his death cannot therefore have been more than about three months, the time that his hair would take in growing again]. (23) *Then the lords of the Philistines gathered them together for to offer a great sacrifice* [consisting of many victims] *unto Dagon their god* [diminutive (expressing endearment) of *dag*, " a fish." The Babylonian Odacon, one of the four Oannes. The male god, to which the Syrian goddess Atargatis corresponds, with a woman's body and a fish's tail ; of which the imaginary ' mermaid ' is the modern relic. The Greek foam spring Aphrodite answers to Atargatis (2 Maccab. xii. 26), called Derceto at Ashkelon, from *tarag*, "an opening," in the temple, down which water brought from a distance was poured twice a year. The Philistines and Phœnicians, being on the sea-coast, naturally formed such a sea-god, combining the human form Divine with that of the perishing brute, to symbolise Nature's power of vivifying through water. At Koyunjik there was found on the doorway of Sennacherib's palace a representation of Dagon in bas-relief, with the body of a fish and a man's head under the fish's head, and a woman's feet joined to its tail. The name Beth-dagon in Judah and in Asher implies the wide diffusion of this worship (Josh. xv. 41, xix. 27). Dagon's head and hands were cut off on the threshold, before Jehovah's ark, prefiguring the final doom of idols (Isa. ii. 11–22; margin, 1 Sam. v. 46). His temples were at Gaza and Ashdod. The Israelites, not being a seafaring people, were never attracted to Dagon-worship, as they were to Baal and other of the idols of surrounding heathen. The occasion of the gathering of the Philistine lords here was probably a yearly festival, to which the capture of Samson gave extraordinary eclat], *and to rejoice; for they said, Our god hath delivered Samson our enemy into our hand* [which was especially calculated to provoke the jealousy of Jehovah for His own holy name; as in the case of Belshazzar's feast (Dan. v. 2–5), and Sennacherib's blasphemous challenge (Isa. xxxvii. 12–20 ; see Ezek. xx. 22, xxxvi. 22, 23)]. (24) *And when the people saw him, they praised their god; for they said, Our god hath delivered into our hands our enemy, and the destroyer of our country, which slew many of us.* (25) *And it came to pass, when their hearts were merry* [with wine (1 Sam. xxv. 36). "Wine is a mocker" (Prov. xx. 1, xxxiii. 29, 30 ; Hos. iv. 11)], *that they said, Call for Samson, that he may make us sport* [Heb., *Sachaqu*, "that he may play for us;" *i.e.*, *dance to music.* An usual accompaniment of idolatrous feasts (Exod. xxxii. 6]. *And they called for Samson out of the prison-house, and he made them sport* [Heb., *tzachaqu*, "sported for them," the same Hebrew as in Exod. xxxii. 6. He was made, like his

Antitype, a jest to the drunkard; suffering wanton jokes,
spittings, and mockings (Ps. lxix. 12; Isa. l. 6)], *and* [after
he had made them sport] *they set him between the pillars*
["the house" or temple of Dagon (see ch. ix. 27; 1 Cor. viii.
10), was like a Turkish kiosk, a spacious hall, opening to an
area before it, with flat roof resting in front upon four pillars,
of which two were at the ends, and two close together in the
'middle' (ver. 29), upon which latter mainly the weight rested.
The stage or area immediately in front was the scene of
Samson's sporting, and probably of the sacrifice to Dagon, to
whom there followed the sacrificial feast in the hall. From
within the hall the lords and principal persons, and from the
roof 3000 people, viewed Samson's doings].   (26) *And Samson
said unto the lad that held him by the hand, Suffer me* [*Hannichah*,
from *nuach*, נוּחַ, to rest (whence comes Noah), "cause me
to rest," "leave me in quiet," *i.e., suffer me.* He begs, as
wearied with his exertions to amuse them, for breathing time,
to be *left alone in quiet*, to lean on the pillars], *that I may feel
the pillars whereupon the house standeth, that I may lean
upon them.* (27) *Now the house was full of men and women;
and all the lords of the Philistines (were) there: and (there were)
upon the roof about three thousand men and women, that beheld
while* [הָרֹאִים בְּ, "of those feasting their eyes whilst"] *Samson
made sport* [compare the Antitype (Ps. xxii. 17; Luke xxiii.
35)].   (28) *And Samson called unto the* LORD [JEHOVAH], *and
said, O Lord* GOD [Heb., "LORD JEHOVAH," *Adonai, Jehovah:* the
vowel points are, however, those of *Elohim, e o i,* Jehovih.   The
Rabbis, from superstition, shrank from writing the name *Jehovah*,
and substituted usually *Adonai;* but here, as Adonai preceded,
they gave Jehovah with the vowels of Elohim], *remember me, I
pray thee, and strengthen me, I pray thee* [the repetition marks
the supplicating earnestness of his heart-cry], *only this once, O
God, that I may be at once avenged* [אִנָּקְמָה נְקַם אַחַת literally,
"that I may be avenged with the vengeance of one."   Keil
translates, "that I may take vengeance for the loss *of only one*
of my two eyes;" for even the terrible vengeance he was
meditating, was, in his keen sense of his loss of sight, inadequate vengeance for the *two* eyes.   But Maurer, better than

Keil, and also than English version, takes the literal Hebrew, " vengeance *of one*," as standing for " *one vengeance*," " that I may take *this one vengeance* "] *of the Philistines for my two eyes*. (29) *And Samson took hold of* [*yilpoth*, 'clasped' (Gesenius)] *the two middle pillars upon which the house stood* [firmly, *nakon*], *and on which it was borne up* [marg., " he leaned on them "], *of the one with his right hand, and of the other with his left*. (30) *And Samson said, Let me* [Heb., " my soul "] *die with the Philistines*. *And he bowed himself* [or *the pillars*] *with* (*all his*) *might;. and the house fell upon the lords, and upon all the people that* (*were*) *therein*. *So the dead which he slew at his death* (*were*) *more than they which he slew in his life*. (31) *Then his brethren* [*i.e.*, immediate *kinsmen*, for no mention of brothers of Samson occurs elsewhere (so Matt. xiii. 55)], *and all the house of his father* [the Danites; so " father's house " means a *tribe* in Numb. xviii. 1], *came down, and took him* [fear after the catastrophe prevented the Philistines from offering any opposition], *and brought him up, and buried him between Zorah and Eshtaol* [the residence of his father (xiii. 25), who probably was now dead, as the words " the burying-place of Manoah his father " imply], *in the burying-place of Manoah his father: and he judged Israel twenty years* [see note, ch. xv. 20].

SAMSON HIMSELF A RIDDLE, AND THE RIDDLE OF SAMSON.

1. *The believer's danger in affinity with unbelievers.*—Samson was a strange compound—an embodied paradox. A Nazarite consecrated wholly to Jehovah, yet in the most important of earthly choices, he chooses after " the sight of his eyes " (compare ch. xiv. 3 with Eccl. ix. 9). What a contrast to this judge of Israel is the Antitype who, when he comes to reign, " shall not judge after the sight of His eyes " (Isa. xi. 3). Commissioned by God to deliver Israel from the Philistines, he turned his back on all the daughters of Israel to go down to the Philistines for a wife. The believer who, in the selection of a partner for life, is only guided by fancy, is guilty of the most perilous folly. He must not marvel if he find a Philistine in his arms. The eye is indeed to be pleased in the choice; but

God ought to be pleased first. There is a better beauty than that of face and figure, of the hidden man of the heart, in that which is not corruptible—the beauty of holiness, "the ornament of a meek and quiet spirit," the lasting loveliness of grace. If religion be any other than a cipher, how dare we not regard it in our most important choice! (Trapp). Herein, as in war generally, one can err but once (1 Pet. iii. 4). God's warning ought to be ever before believers, "Be not unequally yoked together with unbelievers: for what fellowship hath righteousness with unrighteousness? or he that believeth with an infidel?" (2 Cor. vi. 14, 15). Let our resolution be to make a covenant with our eyes, as Job did (xxxi. 1, 7), and to obtain strength to carry out our resolution by praying, "Turn away mine eyes from beholding vanity" (Ps. cxix. 37).

2. *The believer's errors counteracted and overruled to fulfil the Lord's will.*—Samson, though guilty of dangerous folly in his choice, yet showed filial piety and wisdom in consulting his parents before proceeding further. God prospers the youth that honours his parents (Eph. vi. 2, 3). Moreover, we may learn that as the "young lion roared against Samson" at the very outset of his career, so, no sooner doth an awakened soul set out on his pilgrim journey, than Satan, in encountering him, fixes his eye upon him and roars for his prey. But Samson had turned aside from his father and mother, who went on the high road, and had wandered into the vineyards to eat grapes. Too often the young forget that in leaving the tutelage of pious parents, in order to have their so-called liberty, they are exposing themselves to the adversary, who, as a roaring lion, seeketh whom he may devour. Especially is he to be encountered in the vineyards of wine. The spiritually wise will avoid the way of danger.

But Samson's case forbids despair, even when the danger that threatens to overwhelm the believer has been the result of his own self-will. God holds out hope, when the devil would preach despair (see Jer. xviii. 12). The providence of God, if only we renounce self-confidence, and trust wholly in Him, can and will make us conquerors through Him. David had to encounter the lion and bear first, to prepare him for the combat with the giant Goliath (1 Sam. xvii. 36). God took occasion from Samson's wandering aside into the vineyards, to let him see what he could do, in the stren₅ch of the Spirit of Jehovah, in order that henceforth he might not fear to face the Philistine hosts. So God suffers the young believer to fall into temptation, in order to show him his own innate weakness, and, at the same time, the irresistible might of Jehovah's strength, made perfect in human weakness. Samson had no instrument in his hands. So the believer conquers Satan most effectually when he looks to the Saviour alone to fight for him (Ps. xxxv. 1–3), in the spirit of the hymn—

> " Nothing in my hand I bring—
> Simply to Thy cross I cling."

3. *The riddle " Out of the eater came forth meat, and out of the strong came forth sweetness," the key to the mystery of redemption.*—Samson turned aside to see the lion's carcase, in order, doubtless, to recall the remembrance of God's great goodness in delivering him. We ought at times to stop on our way, that we may wisely consider, and so " understand the loving-kindness of the Lord" (Ps. cvii. 43). God would have his children, like Moses (Exod. iii. 3, 4), " turn aside," to see His gracious doings for them. Turning aside from dearest friends and important business for this purpose, we shall often, to our surprise, find rich and sweet stores of comfort.

The Spirit had a further purpose in bringing Samson again to the place where lay the trophy of his victory—(1) To Samson himself there was a lesson of encouragement. As by his conquest of the lion he was animated to encounter the Philistines, notwithstanding their fierceness and gigantic stature; so, by dislodging the bees, he was taught not to dread the swarming multitudes of the foe compassing him like bees, because " in the name of the Lord he shall destroy them " (Ps. cxviii. 12). (2) To Israel, whose representative Samson was, the honey for food and enjoyment, drawn from the slain lion, typified that their foes, who now, because of Israel's unfaithfulness to Jehovah, were permitted to oppress the elect people, would, upon Israel's penitent return to Him, be overcome,

notwithstanding their lion-like violence, and would ulti-
mately yield a spoil to Israel, instead of being, as now, Israel's
spoilers.

(3) *Trial blessed at the time.*—Meantime the very discipline
of trial, through the violence of the Philistines, as in the case
of Samson himself, would be overruled to humble the Israelites;
so that, after the discipline was past and deliverance obtained,
they would appreciate the sweetness of God's word. How
many believers have had a similar experience : " It is good for
me that I have been afflicted, that I might learn thy statutes
—How sweet are Thy words unto my taste, yea, sweeter than
honey to my mouth " (Ps. cxix. 71, 103).

(4) Again, *to believers there is the lesson of imparting our
goods to others.*—As Samson imparted of the honey to his
father and mother, so when we have found the sweetness of
God's grace ourselves, let us invite all whom we can influence,
and our immediate relatives first, to " taste and see that the
Lord is good " (Ps. xxxiv. 8 ; compare also lxvi. 16 ; John iv.
29).

(5) *Grace precious wherever found.*—Moreover, Samson,
though a consecrated Nazarite, did not hesitate to use honey
taken from the dried-up carcase of a dead beast. Bishop Hall
wisely remarks : " Those are less wise, and more scrupulous,
than Samson, who decline the use of God's gifts, because they
find them in ill vessels." Honey is not the less honey where-
soever it is found. Let us not call that common which God
hath cleansed, but gladly discern grace, and profit by it, in
brotherly fellowship with all true Christians, though not of the
same ecclesiastical denomination as ourselves (Acts x. 15, 47,
xi. 17, xv. 8, 9).

(6) *The highest realisation of Samson's riddle is in the
Saviour's work of redemption for us.*—This is the " great mystery
of godliness " (1 Tim. iii. 16), " the wisdom of God in a
mystery," an inexplicable riddle to worldly-wise men, that God
should choose the weak and foolish things to confound the
mighty (1 Cor. i. 27, ii. 7). Christ Jesus, in the might of
weakness, and through death, destroyed the roaring lion " who
had the power of death (Heb. ii. 14, 15), and hath delivered

those, who through fear of death, were all their lifetime subject to bondage:" so out of death, the eater and devourer of all
men, comes forth that which is " meat indeed," even " the bread
of life " (John vi. 35, 55): and " the strong man " (Matt. xii.
29), Satan, who has been already bruised on Calvary, and hereafter shall be completely and finally crushed (Rom. xvi. 20;
Rev. xx. 1–3, 10), shall, in spite of himself, yield unspeakable
and everlasting sweetness to the saints; for their heavenly joys
shall be heightened by the contrast with the enemy's attacks,
then for ever past (Rev. vii. 14–17, iii. 21). It is God's
marvellous prerogative to bring good out of evil. This solves
the problem, why evil has been ever permitted. The entrance
of sin into the world, which followed the creation of beings
possessing free agency and the capability of moral choice, and
the temptations of Satan, shall prove the occasion of manifesting to all created intelligences, the infinite love, compassionate
condescension, justice, and wisdom of our God in Christ, the
Redeemer, which could never have been so manifested in the
material creation, or in an unfallen world (Rom. v. 15). The
issue of the conflict shall be to produce glory to God and
blessedness to the elect tried ones. Difficulty surmounted
becomes triumph. Rest is sweeter after toil. And heaven
itself will be the brighter for the remembrance of the dark
conflict which preceded its attainment; and angels will sing
louder praises to Jehovah, as they point to the redeemed,
" These are they which came out of great tribulation, and have
washed their robes and made them white in the blood of the
Lamb."

(7) *Sweets from affliction now.*—Even now from Jesus'
victory over Satan, there come to believers ample spiritual
provision and sweetness to outweigh their distresses and needs.
Death itself becomes the gate of life. Afflictions and temptations, and even falls from which the grace of God restores
them, are the discipline to train them for holiness, blessedness,
and glory. The conflict may be severe, but the sweeter will
be the everlasting triumph. The enemies of Christ's church
are made to promote in the end her best interests: as the
things that happened unto Paul (his imprisonment at Rome)

fell out rather unto the furtherance of the gospel (Phil. i. 12, 13): "The lightness of the affliction for the moment, worketh out for us a far more exceeding and eternal weight of glory." (2 Cor. iv. 17, Greek). God treasures up comforts for His people where they least expect to find them. When, like Jacob, we might think, "All these things are against me" (Gen. xlii. 36), God, by His Spirit, teaches us to say, "We know that all things work together for good to them that love God" (Rom. viii. 28). Let us only take occasion to turn aside, and review the marvellous providences by which God has overruled evil to good: so we shall extract the honey which His dispensations yield: and shall feel, "This also cometh forth from the Lord of hosts, who is wonderful in counsel and excellent in working" (Isa. xxviii. 29).

4. *Typical foreshadowings of Messiah in this part of Samson's history.*—Samson, in his strange combination of paradoxes, strength and weakness, consecration, yet alliance with the uncircumcised, is NOT A PATTERN TO US, BUT A TYPE OF OUR SAVIOUR. Samson's courting alliance with the Philistines has its Antitype in Him, who came "in the likeness of sinful flesh" (Rom. viii. 3), that He might "condemn sin in the flesh" (compare also 2 Cor. v. 21). Samson, in his deference to his parents, not proceeding in his suit till he has their consent, answers to Him who "went down with His parents to Nazareth, and was subject to them" (Luke ii. 51). Samson's marriage was of the Lord (ver. 4), however strange it seemed, even as Christ's entrance into this world of sin to take the church as His bride out of it was of God (Ps. xl. 7, 8; Gal. i. 4; Eph. v. 25–27). Christ could touch the unclean, yet so far from being defiled thereby, He cleansed the lepers (Matt. viii. 3), and those otherwise defiled (Matt. ix. 20): just as typically Samson took honey from the dead lion, without losing his Nazarite consecration by contact with the dead. Samson turned aside to partake of the honey out of the lion's carcase, without the knowledge of his parents; so the Antitype "tarried behind in Jerusalem, and Joseph and his mother knew not of it:" and in the temple He tasted the sweet honey of God's word from the doctors of the Jewish church, which had now become a

' carcase ' (Matt. xxiv. 28), through formalism, and afterwards imparted of the truth to His parents (Luke ii. 43–51). Christ, in beginning His public ministry, encountered and defeated the roaring lion (Matt. iv. 14); an earnest of His final crushing of the serpent's head : thus He was exalted in *His own strength* (Ps. xxi. 13), and realised the type,—Samson's victory over the lion with nothing in his hand, in beginning his career.

(1) *Further typical teachings in Samson's history : unfaithfulness of the professing Church.*—The bride of Christ is commanded to " forget her own people " (Ps. xlv. 10); but too often the professing church, like Samson's Philistine wife, is false to her Lord, and betrays His cause from regard to the world out of which He hath called her. His enemies, as in Samson's case, are they of His own household (Mic. vii. 5, 6). Satan, in assailing Christ's kingdom, could not succeed as he does, if he did not plough with the heifer of our own corruption. "Him whom the lion could not conquer, the tears of a woman conquered " (Trapp) : just as Peter, who so boldly faced the band of Roman soldiers, was overcome by the taunts of a damsel.

(2) *Disappointments in the world ought to drive us back to our Father.*—The Philistine wife's treachery stirred up Samson's anger. It would have been well, had he taken his parents' advice in choosing a wife ; but it is better to be alienated from the world, than to be in love with it, and to be ensnared by, and so perish with it in the eternal fire (ch. xv. 6 ; James iv. 4; 1 John ii. 17). Our disappointments in the world should drive us back for rest to our Father's home (Luke xv. 14–18 ; Hos. ii. 6, 7). Wrongs from bosom friends are the most poignant (Ps. lv. 12–14).

(3) *Christ's trials by His disciples.*—How keenly must Christ have felt the treachery of his own apostles, and the subsequent faithlessness of the majority of His professing church (Isa. i. 21 ; Rev. xvii.).

5. *Adverse circumstances give occasion to Jehovah to glorify Himself by destroying the enemy and saving His people.*—(1) *Forgiveness ready for the penitent.* Samson, notwithstanding his wife's past treachery, was willing to pardon and forget

the past, if she would even now return to him. But he only met with a repulse and an offer which was a loathsome insult to an Israelite and a Nazarite—

> "Forgiveness to the injured doth belong,
> He never pardons who hath done the wrong."

How much more wonderful is the love of the great Antitype, who saith to His backsliding people, "Thou hast played the harlot with many lovers; yet return again to me, saith the Lord" (Jer. iii. 1). Therefore the greater will be the destruction of all who slight such unparalleled love, and do despite unto the Spirit of grace (Heb. vi. 4–6, x. 29, 30).

(2) *Punishment by craft.*—The Philistines by fox-like craft had gained over from Samson his wife, as "that fox" (Luke xiii. 32) Herod had beguiled Philip's wife; by foxes or jackals, therefore, with crafty device they are punished. Whatever doubt self-sufficiency may suggest as to this history, faith accepts what God declares. "He that is scholar to carnal reason, hath a fool to his master" (Trapp). The weakness of the animals employed as incendiaries illustrates the power of God to confound His church's foes with the meanest agency.

(3) *Sinning through fear of man entails the suffering dreaded: the church's foes are made the church's avengers.*—The Philistines, instead of taking vengeance *upon* Samson, took vengeance *for* him upon his treacherous wife. God uses His people's foes to avenge upon one another His people's wrongs; thus He makes "the wrath of man to praise Him" (Ps. lxxvi. 10). Samson's wife, to save herself from being burnt (ch. xiv. 15), betrayed her husband's secret to his foes; retributively, the very evil which she thought by sin to escape, came upon her. "Whosoever will save his life, shall lose it" (Matt. xvi. 25; compare Prov. x. 24). Better to endure the flame that only for a time can hurt the body, than through fear of man, to sin, and so be cast into the fire that shall for ever consume both body and soul, and that shall never be quenched (Luke xii. 4, 5; Matt. x. 28).

(4) *Cruel doing entails cruel retribution: false friends worse than open enemies.*—The cruelty of the Philistines recoiled

on themselves, by giving fresh occasion to Samson to smite them with a great slaughter. But his own countrymen, the men of Judah, proved themselves ungrateful to their deliverer, and unworthy of their own once distinguished name. His meekness in submitting to be bound, and his concern for their safety, stands in striking contrast to their baseness and selfish pusillanimity. Sin it was that first had enslaved their spirits, and now debased their minds; so that they preferred indolent submission to liberty, even when such a hero offered himself as their deliverer under God—

> " Had Judah that day joined, or one whole tribe,
> They had by this possessed the towers of Gath,
> And lorded over them whom now they serve.
> But what more oft in nations grown corrupt,
> And by their vices brought to servitude,
> Than to love bondage more than liberty,
> Bondage with ease, than strenuous liberty :
> And to despise, or envy, or suspect
> Whom God hath of His special favour rais'd
> As their deliverers "—*Samson Agonistes.*

Herein the men of Judah typify the Jews of our Lord's time.—A whole army of 3000 came up against one man. So a band of armed men came to seize the one unarmed Person, the Lord Jesus. But one soldier would have sufficed, now that His hour was come; whereas myriads would have failed, had He not yielded Himself to be led bound, as a Lamb to the slaughter. Samson probably " supposed that his brethren would have understood that God by His hand would deliver them ; " but, like Moses, He was bitterly disappointed (Acts vii. 25). Instead of recognising him as the deliverer whom the Lord raised up, and rallying around him against the foe, they upbraided him with his very acts for their deliverance, for which they owed him a lasting debt of gratitude. He uttered no reproaches, but silently bore their upbraidings, being more concerned for their safety than for his own. They, moreover, were so cowardly as to bind their benefactor, in order to deliver him up to the oppressors. So the Jews, Jesus' brethren after the flesh, maligned His character and misrepresented His works of love in overthrowing Satan's kingdom (Matt. xii. 24–29), and finally crowned their wickedness and cowardly ingratitude by delivering Him up bound to their Roman oppressors, lest they should "come and take away their place and nation" (John xi. 47–52, xix. 12, 15). Hating as they did their masters (who had "rule over" them, only because they themselves had forsaken God's rule, and sold themselves to work wickedness), they yet hypocritically pretended, in their charge against Jesus, "the King of the Jews:" "We have no king but Cæsar." Yet the Saviour bore all meekly and without resistance, and would not save Himself, because He would save us, whatever suffering it cost Himself (Luke xxii. 52–54, xxiii. 35; John xviii. 3–12).

(5) *The snare broken, and the captive escaped: so the Antitype at His resurrection.*—Like the three youths in the fiery furnace (Dan. iii), which without power to hurt themselves, could only burn their bonds to set them free; so Samson, when the Spirit of Jehovah came mightily upon him, snapped the cords "as flax burnt with fire." Much more "it was not possible that Jesus should be holden of death" (Acts ii. 24), and therefore God 'loosed' from Him "the pains of death," and "declared Him to be the Son of God with power, according to the Spirit of holiness by the resurrection from the dead" (Rom. i. 4). As Samson slew a thousand, so the risen Saviour, by His Spirit in Peter, on the day of Pentecost, alone spoiled Satan's kingdom, of not merely one thousand, but three thousand souls. The instrument of Samson's victory was the jaw-bone of an ass. The feebler the weapon, the more humiliating to the enemy. The first preachers of the Gospel were mostly unlearned, and in lowly rank. "It pleased God by the foolishness of preaching to save them that believe" (1 Cor. i. 21), "that the excellency of the power might be of God," not man (2 Cor. iv. 7).

No sanction for relics and cross veneration.—Samson did not carry about the bone with him for parade, but threw it away, when it had served its use. The visible cross is not to be paraded as an ornament, much less venerated as a relic, but to be spiritually treasured in the heart (2 Cor. v. 16). Compare Hezekiah's treatment of the brazen serpent, when it was made an object of superstition (2 Kings xviii. 4).

(6) *Humbling infirmities in the hour of triumph the occasion for God's interpositions.*—Samson was sore athirst, in order to keep him lowly after such a marvellous victory, gained with such a weak weapon. His resource was prayer; a sure refuge to us also, if we believe our heavenly Father's command and promise : " Call upon me in the day of trouble, I will deliver thee, and thou shalt glorify me " (Ps. l. 15). Samson pleaded (ver. 18) his past experience of God's goodness, as his ground of praying for further grace (compare 2 Cor. i. 10): " Thou hast given this great deliverance into the hand of Thy servant." He had heretofore treated the victory as if it were due to *himself*. Now he calls it a ' deliverance,' yea, a " great deliverance " from God. Our most effectual way to gain help for the present and future is to give GOD glory for what He has done in the past. He glories only in being *God's* ' servant.' It is an excellent plea : " I am thine, save me " (Ps. cxix. 94, also 125). Further he pleads God's glory as at stake, if He should suffer His servant to " die for thirst, and fall into the hand of the uncircumcised." So we should plead (compare Jer. xiv. 21 ; Dan. ix. 19). Herein Samson manifested the real faith which animated him, notwithstanding many defects ; so that the Spirit of God, who delights to see the graces and to remember no more the sins of His people, enumerates him in the saintly roll (Heb. xi. 32).

(7) *Thirst of the Antitype.*—Jesus the Antitype, on the cross said, ' I thirst.' He who alone can give " the living waters," and who saith " If any man thirst, let him come unto me and drink " (John iv. 10, vii. 37), and made the smitten rock yield water to the millions of Israel in the wilderness, and who saith (Isa. xliii. 20), " I give waters in the wilderness and rivers in the desert," was Himself athirst. Why ? Because He thirsted for our salvation, and would fulfil all that was written in the prophecies (Ps. lxix. 21 ; John xix. 28, 29) concerning Him. As He thirsted in order to bless us, so He pronounces blessed them that thirst after Him (Matt. v. 6). He invites all such to " come to the waters " (Isa. lv. 1, xliv. 2, xlv. 13).

(8) *The thirsty ones filled : the full emptied.*—The more emptied of self we come, the more welcome we are. Samson

had called the place of his triumph Ramath-Lehi (ver. 17), "the lifting of the jaw-bone," but when he received the seasonable relief of his thirst in answer to prayer, he gives the place a name more indicative of God's grace than of his own prowess. God opens many a spring of comfort to them that pray in time of distress. Even as He opened Hagar's eyes to see the well in the wilderness (Gen. xxi. 19 ; compare xvi. 7, 14). En-hakkore, " the fountain of him that cried," should encourage us in every strait to flee to Him who saith, "When the poor and needy seek for water, and there is none, and their tongue faileth for thirst, I the Lord will hear them, I the God of Israel will not forsake them ; I will open rivers in the high places, and fountains in the midst of the valleys ; I will make the wilderness a pool of water, and the dry land springs of water" (Isa. xli. 17).

(9) *The once-rejected owned as Ruler.*—Henceforward Samson was the recognised Judge of Israel. He whom the men of Judah had bound and given up to the Philistines, became now owned by all as their ruler and deliverer. So Jesus, " the stone whom the builders refused, became the head stone" of the spiritual Israel, the church. The time also is soon coming when fully " He shall see of the travail of His soul, and be satisfied (Isa. liii. 11). The Jews who betrayed Him into Gentile hands, " shall look on Him whom they pierced " (Zech. xii. 10, xiv. 9), " and all nations shall be gathered to Jerusalem, the throne of Jehovah " (Jer. iii. 17), and He shall be " King over all the earth."

6. *Ruin by lust : recovery by penitent and believing prayer : Victory in death.*

(1) *Dallying with temptation a perilous venture.*—Fleshly lusts war against the soul. Yet men flatter themselves they can toy with the temptress, and not be entrapped. Wine and licentiousness take away the understanding (Hos. iv. 11). When we, like Samson, lay down our head to sleep in the lap of temptation, our spiritual enemies are never more wide awake. The sounder we sleep, the greater our danger. It was truly said, " Samson, when strong and brave, strangled a lion ; but he could not strangle his own lust. He burst the

fetters of his foes, but not the cords of his own passions. He burnt up the crops of others, and lost the fruit of his own virtues, when burning with the flame enkindled by a single woman" (Ambros., *Apol.* ii. *David,* c. iii.: quoted by Keil). Like a moth fluttering about a candle flame, though already scorched by it, Samson unwarned by his narrow escape from one danger which he incurred by lust, rushes into another. Herein may be seen the tempter's assiduity, Samson's security, and Jehovah's superabounding grace (Eph. ii. 7; Rom. v. 20; 1 Tim. i. 14). He who as a Nazarite, ought to have been " purer than snow and whiter than milk," blackens himself with harlotry (Lam. iv. 7).

Grace still interposing, yet he was delivered by God from the ruinous consequences of this step ; conscience roused him to a sense of his danger, as that of " one that lieth upon the top of a mast" (Prov. xxiii. 34). At midnight, under the promptings of the Spirit whom he so greatly grieved, he awoke to the sense of his guilt in defiling a temple of the living God (compare 1 Cor. iii. 17; Eph. iv. 30; Jer. xliv. 4), and of his danger in a city shut in by foes on every side. If any has been tempted to lie down in sin, it is a special grace from God, if he be aroused out of it before the trumpet call to judgment surprise him. It is better to awake late, than never, to see one's danger through lust at the eleventh hour, rather than when the season for repentance is gone, to lift up one's eyes in the torments of the lost. Samson came to the gates of Gaza, only to find himself shut in by them. But the Lord this time plucked his feet out of the net ; Samson, not staying to break open the gates, tore up the posts with them, in the face of the sentinels.

So the Antitype, at midnight long before dawn (Matt. xxviii. 1, 4 ; John xx. 1), whilst the keepers for fear became as dead men, not only rolled away the stone from the door of the sepulchre, but carried away the pillars of death, so that the gates of hell can never prevail against His church (Matt. xvi. 18 ; compare Hos. xiii. 14 ; 1 Cor. xv. 55–57).

(2) *The transgressor, though he escape often, is caught at last.* —" Can a man take fire in his bosom, and not be burned?"

R

(Prov. vi. 27, 28.) The burnt child dreads the fire. But the sinner, with the strength of a man, is far less wise than a child; for though narrowly saved from the deadly penalty of his lust before, he again plays with the flame. The gamester will play on, though often a loser, till the last throw of the dice ruins him. The libertine will *sacrifice* money, health, reputation, and soul, for the sinful pleasure of a moment (see Prov. vi. 26, vii. 26, 27). The drunkard will have his glass, though it be at the cost of drinking at last "the wine of the wrath of God poured out without mixture into the cup of His indignation." So the spiritual temptress, whether carnal wisdom (falsely so called, since it ignores the revealed wisdom of God), worldly pleasure or worldly gain, "casts down many wounded, yea, slays many strong men; her house is the way to hell, going down to the chambers of death." The law of God written in the heart by the Holy Spirit, and "reproofs of instruction are the way of life," and the only power to keep us from the flattery of the tongue of every Delilah (Prov. vi. 23, 24).

(3) *The way of sin is an inclined plane, sinking lower and lower by successive steps, till God departs from the backslider.*— Satan, like a skilful general, gains by siege many a fort which he could not carry by assault. On four distinct occasions, probably on as many different days, Delilah, the 'languishing' one (as her name means), tempted Samson to tell the secret of his God-given strength. Like a serpent, she coiled closer and closer round her victim each time; and he, with amazing infatuation, as a bird fascinated with the eye of the destroyer, ventured nearer and nearer the temptation; so much so that, in the third instance, he trifled so presumptuously with his divine gift, and so tempted God, as to propose that the seven consecrated locks, the pledge of his strength, should be woven with the web. When any ventures so near the edge of ruin, his fall is imminent. Man, with all his vaunted strength, is an easy prey to Satan, when off his guard. Our wisdom, in the case of carnal temptation, is not to meet and fight, but to "*flee* youthful lusts" (2 Tim. ii. 22), as Joseph (Gen. xxxix. 10) shunned *to be even with* the temptress. The power of tempta-

tions which, instead of shunning, we trifle with, increases by
repetition, and our power of resisting them decreases. By daily
importunity, and challenging his love, the vile harlot wrung
from Samson his secret at the last. The spring of his strength
was his dedication to Jehovah: his Nazarite locks were the
sacramental sign of God's covenant of grace with him. Let
none, therefore, slight the sign to which God attaches the grace
of the covenant, even though the connection between them may
seem arbitrary and not apparent. Laying down his head in
the lap of the temptress, he lost his locks of consecration, and
with them lost God in him, the only source of strength.
Samson said, "If my hair be cut off, my strength will depart
from me;" but the sacred writer gives the truer reason for
Samson's loss of strength—"Jehovah was departed from him"
(ver. 17, 20).

> "God, when He gave me strength, to show withal
> How slight the gift was, hung it in my hair."
> —*Samson Agonistes.*

Lust severs from God, and so reduces the strongest to feeble-
ness. Woe be to that man and that people from whom God
departs! (Hos. ix. 12.) Fallen professors are made by punish-
ments to feel this, and say, "Are not these evils come upon
us, because our God is not among us"? (Deut. xxxi. 17).
When we lose our godliness, we lose also our manliness; for
man was made in the image of God.

(4) *Declension from God is often unsuspected by the backslider.*—
"Samson wist not that the Lord was departed from him." It
is a sad but sure sign that a soul is becoming thoroughly
carnal, when the man is unconscious of the withdrawal of the
Holy Spirit, and flatters himself, amidst his lusts, that his
spiritual strength is the same still as when he was consecrated
to God. "Strangers have devoured Ephraim's strength, and he
knoweth it not; yea, grey hairs are here and there upon him,
yet he knoweth it not" (Hos. vii. 9). A secure state is often
also associated with a vaunting and fluent tongue: "I will go
out, as at other times before, and shake myself." But when
Jehovah has departed from any one, Ichabod is written upon
him, the glory is departed, and he is utterly powerless against

every foe. Oh, how we ought earnestly pray, "Take not Thy Holy Spirit from me" (Ps. li. 11).

(5) *Recovery by penitent and believing prayer.*—The chastisement was severe, but it was the very one suited to bring Samson's sin to his remembrance. His eyes had been the avenue through which lust had entered his soul; his eyes therefore are given over to destruction. Philistine women had been the objects of his lust, and Philistine men are retributively made the executioners of Divine chastisement upon him. But it is infinitefy better to lose the eyes, and save the soul, than keep them, and lose body and soul in hell (Mark ix. 47). Now, when the sight of the body was blinded by his foes, he had enforced leisure to remember how his soul had been blinded by his own lust. He had been "holden with the cords of his sins," and blinded by the god of this world; therefore he is now "holden in cords of affliction" and "fetters of brass." If we would escape the darkness of the second death, we must pray, "Turn away mine eyes from beholding vanity" (Ps. cxix. 37). Gaza was the scene of his sin, and Gaza retributively was made the scene of his punishment: he became a captive to the Philistines in the very place where he had yielded himself a captive to lust: where he had been a terror, there he is a laughing-stock: where he had displayed such amazing might, there he appears in abject weakness—a slave, and doing the 'grinding' work of a slave, even as he had been the slave of his passions. "Surely the way of transgressors is hard."

But here also began the turn to a better state. Now that he can no longer see with the eyes, his soul begins to see his sin. No murmur escapes his lips: for through grace he is led to feel God's justice in his suffering; for however unjust on the part of man, it was just on the part of God: so he meekly "accepts the punishment of his iniquity" (Lev. xxvi. 41). Then, simultaneously with his penitent return to God, by God's especial blessing, "the hair of his head began to grow again," the pledge of his renewed consecration. For "they that wait upon the Lord shall renew their strength" (Isa. xl. 31). Even a Manasseh, when "in affliction and bound with fetters, he besought the Lord his God and humbled himself greatly before the God of his fathers, and prayed unto him," was heard and restored (2 Chron. xxxiii. 12, 13). What an encouragement to all backsliders to return to Jehovah! (see Jer. iii. 12, 14, 22). Besides the penitence of Samson, another reason for God's interposition was the blasphemy of the Philistines. Whereas it was Jehovah's displeasure that caused Samson's humiliation, their lords and their people alike ascribed their triumph over Samson to their idol : " Our god hath delivered our enemy into our hand " (ver. 23, 24). Jehovah therefore was jealous for His own honour (Deut. xxxii. 27). Their triumphing was short, and soon turned into the silence of death. Nothing so fills the measure of men's iniquity as robbing God of His honour and mocking His servants ; and no means so effectually enlist God on His people's side against their insulting foes as heartfelt prayer. Samson's was necessarily secret prayer, like that of Nehemiah (ii. 4 ; Isa. xxvi. 16, margin), " O Lord *Jehovah*," who as such art *in covenant with,* and fulfillest Thy promise to *Thy people,* " Remember me, I pray Thee, and strengthen me, I pray Thee (the repetition implies his earnestness) only this once, O *God* " (*Elohim, God of creation,* having all the forces of nature and the universe at Thy command). The strength which he had lost by sin, he regains by prayer. He asked to be avenged for his eyes : Providence overruled it so that the Divine honour should be at the same time vindicated upon those who had profaned it by cruelty to His servant, and idolatry against God. His privation of eyesight, had he lived, would have been the perpetual memorial of his unfaithfulness to God, and of the foe's spiritual and bodily triumph over him. The avenging of his eyes was therefore inseparably connected with the avenging of God's cause and the deliverance of Israel ; for he was the elect nation's representative both in his faithfulness and his back-sliding. Israel, whilst faithful to Jehovah, was invincible ; but whenever she yielded to heathen seductions, she was as one blinded, a prey to every foe (Numb. xxv. 1–6, xxxi. 15, 16). When she returned to Jehovah, His honour was engaged to avenge her cause, which was His own. Of all this Samson was the embodied type. He now voluntarily chose death, since this must be the cost of avenging the cause of Israel and of

Jehovah. Jehovah herein showed that Samson's sin and shame were cancelled, the Philistine oppressors crushed, and Israel's wrong redressed. He who was the terror of the Philistines in his life, was the destroyer of their idol-temple in his death, and the vindicator of the honour of Jehovah against Dagon.

All the particulars of this last blow are significant.—*Who* were the slain? The women who had lured Samson to sin, and the men who bribed Delilah to betray him, with the Philistine lords. They assembled together only to be broken in pieces (Isa. viii. 9), whereas they had met to glory over Samson's misery. God, after chastising His backsliding people, will terribly destroy their persecutors (compare Numb. xxxi. 16 ; Isa. x. 5–13 ; 1 Pet. iv. 17). *When* were they slain? In the midst of carnal security, mirth, and treason against Jehovah, by giving His honour to Dagon (compare Dan. v. 4, &c. ; 1 Thess. v. 3, 7). *Where* were they slain? In the house of their idol, the scene of their sin becoming the scene of their punishment (compare 1 Kings xxi. 19, xxii. 38 ; 2 Kings ix. 26). *How* they were slain? By the prayer of Samson, which brought to him the might of Jehovah. This is "the weapon of our warfare, which is mighty through God to the pulling down of strongholds" (2 Cor. x. 4).

Prayer and action must go together : he first prayed, then "bowed himself with all his might." "Not only beg, but dig" (Prov. ii. 3–5), (Trapp). So the house fell, and in his death he slew more than in his life ; not only the 3000 on the roof, but the lords and the many others within the house. Though he died with them, yet not as one of them in his everlasting portion ; his was the death of the righteous, theirs was the death of the enemies of God (Numb. xxiii. 10 ; Prov. xiv. 32).

(6) *Samson the type of Messiah, especially in his death.*— Delilah, the loved one, betrayed Samson for money : the Lord Jesus was betrayed by one whom he called a 'friend' with a kiss, for filthy lucre. As they made sport of Samson, so was Messiah "the song of the drunkards" (Ps. lxix. 12), and "they smote the judge of Israel with a rod upon the cheek" (Mic. v. 1 ; Matt. xxvii. 30). The seven locks of Samson remind us of the sevenfold fulness of the Holy Spirit resting permanently on

Jesus. As Samson's arms stretched to the two pillars support-
ing the house of Dagon; so Jesus' arms, stretched out upon the
cross, shook and cast down to its basis the kingdom of darkness,
of which the earthquake, the rent rocks, and opened graves
(Matt. xxvii. 51, 52) were the sign. "Through death Jesus
destroyed him that had the power of death" (Heb. ii. 14, 15);
so He obtains our deliverance from the enemy. As Samson
voluntarily gave his life for Israel's deliverance, so Jesus freely
gave His life a ransom for us (Matt. xx. 28; John x. 17, 18).
We were strangers afar off from God, as Samson sought his
loved one among the Philistines. But the Antitype infinitely
exceeds the type: Samson prayed for vengeance, Christ prayed
for the forgiveness of His murderers. Samson died to crush
his foes with him; Christ died for His enemies (Rom. v. 6–10),
whom He would save from everlasting death, and make friends
and sharers of His eternal glory. Samson fell to rise no more;
Jesus died to rise again as the Lord of life for evermore.
Samson's blow to the Philistines by his death only in part
helped Israel: for not till blow after blow was inflicted by
Samuel and David and Hezekiah was the victory complete:
but Jesus' death issues in the full and final triumph of His
saints over the powers of darkness. "He spoiled principalities
and powers, and made a show of them openly, triumphing over
them in it (the cross)" (Col. ii. 15): and He shall put under
His and our feet the last Antichrist and Satan himself
(Rev. xix., xx.). May we, for whom the Lord of glory has done
and will do so great things, love Him with whole-hearted
consecration, shrinking from all pollution of flesh and spirit,
that we may be presented faultless before His presence with
exceeding joy!

CHAPTER XVII.

INTRODUCTION OF IDOLATRY : IDOLATRY BEGINNING FROM THEFT :
MICAH, WITH HIS GRAVEN IMAGE-GOD AND LEVITICAL PRIEST,
EXPECTS GOOD FROM JEHOVAH.

(1) *And there was a man of Mount Ephraim* [the hilly
country of Ephraim], *whose name was Micah* [Heb., *Micaiychu;*
the closing syllables containing the name of JEHOVAH are taken
away from the name, when he dishonours Jehovah by idols
(ver. 5, 8, 9, 10, 12, 13), *Micah.* Scripture does not deign
to record the name of his father and family, as he was a
dishonour to Israel by idolatry]. (2) *And he said unto his
mother, The eleven hundred (shekels)* [a shekel was about 2s. 6d.
of our money] *of silver* [the exact amount of each Philistine's
bribe to Delilah for betraying Samson (xvi. 5). The connection, *spiritually,* is suggestive. Betrayal of the loyalty due to
Jehovah is rated at the same price as betrayal of the loyalty
due to man (Jer. ix. 3–6 ; Mic. vii. 5)] *that were taken from
thee* [see Prov. xxviii. 24], *about which thou cursedst, and spakest
of also in mine ears* [*i.e.*, didst so loudly utter thy curse that it
reached my ears also, as well as the ears of others (Lev. v. 1):
"If a soul sin, and hear *the voice of swearing,* and is a witness
whether he hath seen or known of it; if he do not utter it,
then he shall bear his iniquity." Fear of his mother's curse
impelled him to confess. See the power of conscience], *behold,
the silver (is) with me; I took it. And his mother said, Blessed
(be thou) of the* LORD [JEHOVAH], *my son* ["Out of the same
mouth proceedeth blessing and cursing" (James iii. 10). Money
was the idol of mother and son alike. Therefore the son robbed
the mother, and the mother cursed the son. The passion with
which she had uttered her curse, indicated the keenness of her
love to her money, and her bitterness at its loss. "Old wood

is apt to take fire" (Trapp). Joy at its recovery turned her from cursing to blessing : " Blessed of *Jehovah* be my son ; " this she says in view of her intention to dedicate the silver to ' *Jehovah* ']. (3) *And when he had restored the eleven hundred (shekels) of silver to his mother, his mother said, I had* [or have, at this time, I hereby declare I dedicate it] *wholly dedicated* [Heb., "dedicating I have dedicated "] *the silver unto the* LORD [JEHOVAH] *from my hand* [*i.e.*, possession] *for my son* [implying he would be the gainer, not the loser, by his restitution of the money], *to make a graven image* [פֶּסֶל, *pesel*], *and a molten image* [מַסֵּכָה, *masseekah, molten work* (Isa. xl. 19). The *pesel*, ' gravenimage' of Jehovah was the principal thing (see ch. xviii. 17, 18), where it stands foremost of the four objects in Micah's sanctuary, "the graven (or carved) image, the ephod, the teraphim, and the molten image;" the separation of the *masseekah* from the *pesel*, implies they were distinct objects. In ver. 20 the *pesel*, "graven-image" alone, without the *masseekah*, 'molten image,' is mentioned; so also in ver. 30, 31. They are joined in Deut. xxvii. 15. The *masseekah* (singular), is mostly restricted to Aaron's and Jeroboam's calf, which was a representation of Jehovah (Deut. ix. 12). It is not likely that Micah's mother had two altogether distinct images made and set up in his house; Keil therefore suggests that the *masseekah* was *the pedestal* upon which the *pesel* stood. But there is no reason, in this view, why the pedestal should be ' molten,' and the image (*pesel*) ' graven.' I therefore suggest that the ' molten image ' (*masseekah*) was a miniature model of the graven image (*pesel*), and was cast in precious metal, as the silver shrines of Diana (Acts xix. 26). The graven image was the original ; the small copy was of secondary consequence as to worship, and is never again mentioned after ch. xviii. 18 (compare 20, 30, 31). A calf was probably the form of both (Exod. xxxii. 4 ; 1 Kings xii. 29)] : *now therefore I will restore it unto thee* [back again ; after that Micah had restored it to her]. (4) *Yet he restored the money unto his mother* [for his conscience would not be satisfied, if he kept the money, even at his mother's request. Extreme scrupulosity often succeeds extreme laxity] ; *and his mother took two hundred (shekels) of silver* [not quite a fifth of the whole eleven hundred which she originally had dedicated. She may have spent some more in the other trinkets and the private temple; but hardly so much as nine hundred. Her covetousness prevailed over her superstition; so she kept the old heart-idol (Col. iii. 5), as well as gained a new idol], *and gave them to the founder, who made thereof a graven image, and a molten image, and they were in the house of Micah.* (5) *And the man Micah had* [Heb., " As for the man Micah, there was to him "] *an house of gods* [Heb., *Elohim,* " an house of God," a private sanctuary or chapel; as the public sanctuary was all this time at Shiloh], *and made an ephod* [see note, ch. viii. 27. The garment of the high priest, consisting of shoulder-piece and breast-plate (*choshen*). Put on by him, when *consulting the will of God;* this was Micah's purpose in making it (see ch. xviii. 5, 6)], *and teraphim* [from *taraph,* " to cut off; " busts of human form, *cut off* from the waist (Maurer); else from Arabic *tarafa,* " to enjoy life's good things " (Gesenius). Rather from Syriac *teraph,* " to inquire " of an oracle. Heb., *toreeph,* " an inquirer " (Hos. iii. 4, 5). They were consulted for divination, and to secure good fortune to a house, as the Roman Penates tutelary, ' household gods ' (Ezek. xxi. 21; Zech. x. 2, margin). They were small enough to be hidden under the camel's furniture on which Rachel sat (Gen. xxxi. 19, 30, 34, xxxv. 2; see 1 Sam. xix. 13, margin). Condemned as idolatrous (1 Sam. xv. 23; 2 Kings xxiii. 24, margin) though worshipped side by side with Jehovah; the word is probably akin to *seraphim,* Jehovah's recognised ministers], *and consecrated* [Heb., " filled the hand of," viz., with the oblations appointed to be put in the hands of priests in consecrating them (Exod. xxix. 9, 21–24). The symbolical act of filling the hand implied putting one into possession of anything (compare Heb. viii. 3)] *one of his sons, who became his priest* [Micah's gods were a lie; his consecration and his priest could be no better (Heb. v. 4, 5; compare Jeroboam's act, 1 Kings xii. 28–31, 33]. (6) *In those days (there was) no king in Israel* [this implies that by the time when the sacred writer wrote this, there was a king in Israel (so xviii. 1, xix. 1, xxi. 15). The office of the judges was extraordinary (ch. ii. 16), and did not exercise that continual restraint over transgressors which the power of kings exercises (Rom. xiii. 3, 4; 1 Pet. ii. 13,14). Hence idolatry and licentiousness sprang up in Israel unchecked (1 Sam. vii. 3 ; Job xxxi. 26–28]. (7) *And there was a young man out of Bethlehem-Judah* [as distinguished from Bethlehem in Zabulun (Josh. xix. 15, 16], *of the family of Judah* [*i.e., tribe,* as in xiii. 2. The Levites properly had their dwelling in the other tribes, and the priests alone in Judah (Josh. xxi. 9–41). But from various causes Levites might settle in Judah, and so in *civil* matters be counted as "of the family of Judah." The Syriac, and the Vatican manuscript of the Septuagint, omit "of the family of Judah." But Alexandrian MS. has the clause], *who (was) a Levite, and he sojourned there* [the word 'sojourned' implies that he was not born there, nor was a citizen. Lord Arthur Hervey (Speaker's Commentary) suggests that the true reading for " he sojourned there " (Heb., גרשם, 'G R Sh M,' exactly the same consonant letters as in ch. xviii. 30, ' Gershom ') is "son of Gershom." But the words "And he " will have thus to be changed into " son of," whereas the Hebrew of " And he " (*vehua*) is utterly unlike that of the 'son' (*Ben*). The words are not meaningless ; they imply, that though by family residence connected with Judah, he was but a *sojourner* there]. (8) *And the man departed out of* [Heb., *from*] *the city from Bethlehem-Judah to sojourn where he could find (a place)* [that would afford him a home and sustenance. He was necessarily dependent on others. This was the ordinary state of many Levites, whence we see the force of the phrase, " The Levite which is within your gates " (Deut. xii. 12). The Levites had no lands ; and at that time especially they were in distress ; for their tithes were generally unpaid, owing to the prevalent idolatry, and the consequent neglect of Jehovah's ministers, and the absence of any permanent magistrate to enforce the Mosaic law] : *and he came to Mount* [the hill country] *Ephraim, to the house of Micah, as he journeyed* [Heb., " in making his journey "]. (9) *And Micah said unto him, Whence comest thou ? And he said unto him, I (am) a Levite of Bethlehem-Judah, and I go to sojourn where I may find (a place).* (10) *And Micah said unto him, Dwell with me, and be unto me a father* [a spiritual friend and counsellor; so Joseph is called (Gen. xlv. 8), and Elisha (2 Kings vi. 21, xiii. 14)] *and a priest, and I will give thee ten (shekels) of silver by the year* [Heb. " for the days " of thine engagement to me (margin, 1 Sam. xxvii. 7)], *and a suit* [equipment] *of apparel, and thy victuals. So the Levite went in.* (11) *And the Levite was content to dwell with the man* [so Exod. ii. 21. At the cost of his soul, for the one morsel of meat (Heb. xii. 16)]; *and the young man was unto him as one of his sons* [as well as a ' father ' (ver. 10). Better infinitely to have God for his Father, and to have been a spiritual father to others, by serving Jehovah at all costs, and separating himself from all idols (2 Cor. vi. 14–18)]. (12) *And Micah consecrated the Levite* [which none but an Aaronic priest had the right to do. One sin entails another]; *and the young man became his priest, and was in the house of Micah* [probably this Levite was Jehonathan (ch. xviii. 30)]. (13) *Then said Micah, Now know I that the* LORD [JEHOVAH] *will do me good, seeing I have a Levite to (my) priest* [How infatuated ! as if God would do him good in reward for his doing evil ! The retributive penalty followed in the loss of his idol and its appendages (ch. xviii.). Incidentally there comes out a confirmation of the authenticity of the Pentateuch, and of its date anterior to the time of the Judges, in the fact that the priesthood and the service of the sanctuary are here assigned to the Levites, as in the law of Moses].

CHAPTER XVIII.

EXTENSION OF IDOLATRY FROM ONE FAMILY TO A WHOLE TRIBE:
DAN BECOMES MASTER OF LAISH, BUT THE SLAVE OF THE
IMAGE STOLEN FROM MICAH.

(1) *In those days (there was) no king in Israel: and in those
days the tribe of the Danites sought them an inheritance to dwell
in* [in this chapter their capture of Laish or Leshem is detailed,
which had been summarily stated in Josh. xix. 47. The
Danites were straitened for room by the Amorites, and forced
from the valleys into the hilly region (Judg. i. 34), otherwise
Joshua had provided Dan with ample land and cities enough for
their numbers (Numb. xxvi. 43)]; *for unto that day (all their)
inheritance had not fallen* [Heb., "there had not fallen *in* an
inheritance" viz., *sufficient land in the character of an inheritance* to be transmitted from father to son] *unto them among*
[Heb., *in the midst of*] *the tribes of Israel.* (2) *And the children
of Dan* [*i.e.*, one portion of the tribe] *sent of their family five
men from their coasts* [Heb., "from their *ends*," *i.e., from their
whole number;* as in (Gen. xix. 4, xlvii. 2)], *men* [Heb., *sons*]
of valour, from Zorah, and from Eshtaol [(Josh. xix. 41).
Their emigration was before the days of Samson, as ver. 12, compared
with xiii. 25, margin, proves. The Danites were already settled
in these two towns allotted to them under Joshua], *to spy out
the land, and to search it; and they said unto them, Go, search the
land: who, when* [Hebrew is simply 'And,' not *Who, when*]
they came to Mount Ephraim, to [see note, ver. 13] *the house of
Micah, they lodged there* [*i.e.*, close to it. Micah's house was
probably not far from the wayside on the road leading from
Dan on the south-west northwards through Mount Ephraim,
i.e., the hill country of Ephraim (see ch. xviii. 15, note)]. (3)
When they (were) by the house of Micah, they knew the voice

[dialect] *of the young man the Levite* [that he was not a native
of Mount Ephraim, as his dialect indicated. For the Ephraimites
had so marked an accent that the Gileadites detected them by
one word alone, Shibboleth (Judg. xii. 6)] : *and they turned in
thither* [from the road to the house], *and said unto him, Who
brought thee hither ?   And what makest* [doest] *thou in this
(place) ? and what hast thou here ?*   (4) *And he said unto them,
Thus and thus* [detailing what had occurred] *dealeth Micah
with me, and hath hired me, and I am his priest.*   (5) *And they
said unto him, Ask counsel, we pray thee, of God* [the ephod
and idol being designed for the worship of *God* (!) (compare
ch. i. 1)], *that we may know whether our way which we go shall
be prosperous.*   (6) *And the priest* [after putting on the ephod
to consult God] *said unto them, Go in peace : before the* LORD
[JEHOVAH] (is) *your way* [*i.e.,* it is *approved before Him,* to
whom all men's ways are known (Jer. xvii. 16 ; Ezra viii. 21,
22).   The Levite frames his response as if from God, so as
to gratify those who consulted him.   At the same time, whilst
designing them to understand it as favourable to their enterprise, the response is so ambiguously worded as to be capable
of a different meaning, if their enterprise should fail, viz., that
it, like all other things, is before the eyes of Jehovah (Prov. v.
21)] *wherein ye go.*   (7) *Then the five men departed, and came to
Laish* [*Leshem* in Josh. xix. 47 ; the Danites who took it named
it Dan. Laish means *lion,* indicating that it was near the
haunts of lions, the jungles of lake Merom and the wooded slopes
of Bashan, Hermon, and Lebanon (see Deut. xxxiii. 22 ; Song
Sol. iv. 8 ; see note on Dan, ver. 29, below)], *and saw the people
that (were) therein, how they dwelt careless, after the manner of
the Zidonians* [who, as living by commerce, arts, and workmanship, hewing timber in Lebanon, silver and embroidery work,
neglected the science of war (1 Kings v. 6)], *quiet and secure ;
and (there was) no magistrate* [Heb., " possessor of *restraint* "]
in the land, that might put (them) to shame in (any) thing [the
Heb. *Josheleth,* 'dwelling,' is feminine, agreeing with *'am,*
masculine, *the population,* taken as a collective feminine :
masculines follow "quiet and secure." The Hebrew for
' therein ' is literally " in the midst of it ; " *i.e.,* within the city.

Keil translates יוֹרֵשׁ עֶצֶר, not 'magistrate,' but " no one *who seized the government to himself*"—" did any harm (מַכְלִים) to them." Gesenius translates with the Vulgate, and the Vatican MS. of the Septuagint, " no *possessor of wealth* hurt them." But the English version, " possessor of restraint," *i.e., ruling magistrate,* accords with the sense of the same Hebrew word in 1 Sam. ix. 17, margin; and the spiritual thought is best brought out by it, namely, their doing their own pleasure without shame made them ripe for Divine vengeance (Jer. xlix. 31; Zech. i. 15). That the vengeance was executed by the Danites, who themselves did what was right in their own eyes (xvii. 6), accords with God's principles of making bad men the executioners of His wrath against the bad (Isa. x. 5, 6 ; Hab. i. 6, 12, 13)]; *and they (were) far from the Zidonians, and had no business with (any)* [rather supply ' other,' and translate ' men ' for] *man* [Laish was doubtless a colony of Zidon; as the expression, living " after the manner of the Zidonians," implies. But the distance prevented the parent city from rendering Laish any succour; and they had no connection with the people of other towns to obtain help from them]. (8) *And they came unto their brethren to Zorah and to Eshtaol ; and their brethren said unto them* [unto the five spies], *What (say) ye?* [rather, " What have you done ? " What successes had ye ? The abrupt and curt mode of address implies their eagerness to hear the news]. (9) *And they said, Arise, that we may go up against them : for we have seen the land* [compare Numb. xiii. 18–33, xiv. 7], *and, behold, it (is) very good ; and (are) ye still* [when ye ought to be stirring (1 Kings xxii. 3]? *Be not slothful to go, (and) to enter to possess the land.* (10) *When ye go, ye shall come unto a people secure* [therefore easy to conquer], *and to a large land* [therefore worth while striving for (see 1 Chron. iv. 40, 41). The Hebrew means " roomy on both hands," affording room to dwell in, and to extend (Gen. xxvi. 22, margin)]: *for God hath given it into your hands* [they infer this from the Levites' response in ver. 6]; *a place where (there is) no want of anything that (is) in the earth* [rather " in the land," viz., Canaan (Deut. viii. 7–9)]. (11) *And there went from thence of the family of the Danites, out of Zorah and out of*

Eshtaol, six hundred men appointed [accoutred] *with weapons of war.* (12) *And they went up, and pitched in Kirjath-jearim* [meaning "city of forests," the abode of the ark after its re-, storation by the Philistines (1 Sam. vi. 21, vii. 1; 2 Sam. vi. 2–4). David and his people when in Ephratah 'heard of' the ark as a *hearsay* (so neglected was it in Saul's reign), and "found it in the fields of the wood" (Ps. cxxxii. 6), *i.e.*, in the forest town of Kirjath-jearim, and brought it thence to Zion. Its other names Baalah, Baale of Judah, Kirjath-Judah, betray its original connection with Baal-worship. Chaplin identifies it with the modern *Soba*, which means *high place*, answering to the meaning of *Baalah :* "Mount Seir" (now *Batn el Saghir*) being near, lying on the side of the deep valley which forms Judah's northern border ; *Soba* is probably akin to 'Shobal,' the name of Caleb's son who founded a new Kirjath-jearim (1 Chron. ii. 50–53). Conder (*Palestine Explor. Quart. Statem.*, April 1879, p. 98) proposes *Erma* (meaning 'Thickets,' *Jarim*) as the site on the south brink of the valley which broadens into the Sorek valley. The hills around are dense with thickets. Robinson less probably identifies it with *Kuriet el Enab*], *in Judah : whereupon they called that place Mahaneh-dan unto this day* [between Zorah and Eshtaol] ; *behold, it is behind* [*i.e.*, west of] *Kirjath-jearim* [for in taking the points of the compass *they faced the east :* so that 'before' or 'forward' means *east ;* 'behind' or 'backward,' *west.* "On the right hand," *south ;* "on the left," *north* (Job xxiii. 8, 9). Mahaneh-dan, *i.e.*, "camp of Dan," received its permanent name from the Danites' long-continued encampment here at this time. This was probably their place of assembling to equip themselves for their destination ; for they were carrying their all with them— children, cattle, and goods—with a view to a permanent settlement (ver. 21). Here it was that the Spirit of the Lord began to move Samson (ch. xiii. 25)]. (13) *And they passed thence unto Mount Ephraim, and came unto* [to the vicinity of] *the house of Micah.* (14) *Then answered the five men that went to spy out the country of Laish, and said unto their brethren* [their Danite fellow-tribesmen], *Do you know that there is in these houses* [*i.e.*, this village, including Micah's house (ver. 22) and the adjoining 'houses'] *an ephod, and teraphim, and a graven image, and a molten image?* *now therefore consider what ye have to do* [do not lose the opportunity of providing our new settlement with the means of worship]. (15) *And they turned* [aside from the road] *thitherward, and came to the house of the young man the Levite* [probably the same as Micah's house, which is called here "the house of the Levite," for it was *the latter* whom they were seeking, distinct from the house of his idol (ch. xvii. 5). But see note below (ver. 17), "went up"] *(even) unto the house of Micah, and saluted him* [Heb., "asked after his peace" or *welfare* (Gen. xliii. 27 ; Exod. xviii. 7). They talked of *peace,* whilst mischief was in their hearts (Ps. xxviii. 3)]. (16) *And the six hundred men appointed* [accoutred] *with their weapons of war, which (were) of the children of Dan, stood by the entering of the gate* [keeping the Levite in conversation outside, whilst the five went inside, to fetch the idol, &c. Without this explanation, it would have seemed strange that the priest should have stood still whilst his house of gods was being robbed]. (17) *And the five men that went to spy out the land* [Laish] *went up, (and) came in thither* [either the expression 'went *up,*' implies that Micah's idol-house was on a height ; or rather it was *an upper room* of Micah's house (see 2 Kings xxiii. 12 ; Jer. xix. 13)], *(and) took the graven image, and the ephod, and the teraphim, and the molten image : and the priest stood in the entering of the gate* [talking], *with the six hundred men (that were) appointed* [accoutred] *with the weapons of war.* (18) *And these* [five men. This verse and ver. 19 explain in fuller detail the general statement of ver. 17], *went into Micah's house, and fetched the carved* [translate 'graven ;' the same Hebrew as ver. 17], *image, the ephod,* [the absence of the article expresses the close connection of the image with *the ephod,* "the ephod-images." Arrayed in the ephod, the priest stood before the image to consult God], *and the teraphim, and the molten image : then said the priest unto them, What do ye?* (19) *And they said unto him, Hold thy peace, lay thine hand upon thy mouth* [the gesture expressing silence (Job xxi. 5, xxix. 9], *and go with us, and be to us a father and a priest* [ch. xvii. 10] : *(is it) better for thee to be a*

S

priest unto the house of one man, or [Heb., *or rather :* אוֹ] *that thou be a priest unto a tribe and a family* [*i.e.*, a considerable portion of a tribe, namely, those of the Danites who were now migrating northwards, leaving the rest of the Danites already settled on the western coast]? (20) *And the priest's heart was glad; and he took the ephod, and the teraphim, and the graven image* [*i.e.*, he took them into his charge at the hands of the five Danites who had carried them off from Micah's house (ver. 17)], *and went in the midst of the people* [the Danite emigrants. The priest with his idol went in the midst of the host, just as the priests and ark of the covenant moved forward in the midst of the Israelites (Numb. ii. 17, and x.] (21) *So they turned* [back to the road from which they had 'turned' aside to Micah's house (ver. 15)], *and departed, and put the little ones* [including the *women,* having least strength, and needing most protection], *and the cattle, and the carriage* [in the Old English meaning, not what carries, but *what is carried.* Heb., *Kebudah,* translate "the precious things," 'valuables'] *before them* [*in front,* to be out of the reach of Micah's party, from behind, if they should pursue. The mention of the little ones, the cattle, and the valuables, indicates that the Danites were emigrating with their all, on faith in the good report of the five spies (ver. 7–10)]. (22) (*And*) *when they* [the six hundred] *were a good way from the house of Micah, the men, that* (*were*) *in the houses near to Micah's house* [the men of the hamlet] *were gathered together* ["*called* together" by Micah], *and overtook the children of Dan.* (23) *And they cried unto the children of Dan: and they turned their faces, and said unto Micah, What aileth thee, that thou comest with such a company* [literally, "that thou art (*i.e.*, thy clan headed by thee are) *called* together?" the same Hebrew as in ver. 22, ' gathered ' or ' *called* together :' *niz'aquu*]. (24) *And he said, Ye have taken away my gods which I made* [his very words carry the refutation of his wicked folly (Isa. xxxvii. 19)], *and the priest, and ye are gone away; and what have I more* [*left :* Heb., "what is there still to me"]? *and what* (*is*) *this that ye say unto me, What aileth thee* [after having taken all that is most precious to me, how can you ask such an unfeeling question]? (25)

And the children of Dan said unto him, Let not thy voice be heard among us, lest angry [Heb., " bitter of soul " (2 Sam. xvii. 8, margin), for " chafed in their minds "] *fellows run upon thee* [Heb., as in xv. 12, " fall upon thee "], *and thou lose thy life, with the lives of thy household* [the retinue with him from his settlement (ver. 22)]. (26) *And the children of Dan went their way : and when Micah saw that they (were) too strong for him, he turned, and went back unto his house.* (27) *And they took the things* [*i.e., idols*], *which Micah had made, and came unto* [עַל, *upon : fell upon* (Gen. xxxiv. 25)] *Laish, unto a people (that were) at quiet and secure* [ver. 7]: *and they smote them with the edge of the sword, and burnt the city with fire* [Josh. vi. 24 ; see Deut. vii. 2, xx. 16, 17]. (28) *And (there was) no deliverer* [in its isolated position], *because it (was) far from Zidon, and they had no business with (any) man; and it was in the valley that (lieth) by* [or *stretcheth to* (Keil) לְ] *Beth-rehob* [not the Rehob in Asher, which is *near* Zidon ; for this was " far from Zidon," but in Naphtali (Keil). It answers to the modern *Hunin*, a fortress commanding the plain *Huleh*, in which the city of Dan was, and the point where the road to Hamath, through the *Bekaa* valley, begins. Rehob was one of the petty kingdoms of .Aram or Syria (2 Sam. x. 6, 8), on the way to Hamath (Numb. xiii. 21)]: *and they built a city* [Heb., " *the* city." They rebuilt *the* city Laish which they had burnt down], *and dwelt therein.* (29) *And they called the name of the city Dan* [instead of Laish or Leshem (Josh. xix. 47). The city Dan became the northern boundary of Israel, as Beersheba was its southernmost : hence the whole country was expressed by the phrase, " from Dan even to Beersheba" (ch. xx. 1). Dan means ' judgment :' accordingly, after God's judgment on Chedorlaomer, Abraham designated the *place* Dan (Gen. xiv. 14): but even then *Lasha* or Laish (Gen. x. 19) was its usual name, the north-eastern boundary of Canaan, as Gaza was its south-western boundary. This would be an additional reason, besides their own name, for the Danites calling their *city* there Dan. The thrice repeating of " the city " (ch. xviii. 28, 29), implies there was already *another* application of the name ' Dan,' namely, to Abraham's camping *ground* (see Deut. xxxiv. 1).

Le Clerc suggests that the *fountain* was called Dan, 'judge ;' as Ain-Mishpat means "the fount of justice." Now *Tel-el-Kady*, "the judge's mound :" its long level top is strewed with ruins, probably those of Dan. From its foot gushes out one of the largest fountains in the world, the main source of the Jordan, called. *El-le-Dan*, and the stream *Nahr-ed-Dan*. The district is truly "a large land, where there is no want of anything that is on the earth" (ver. 10)], *after the name of Dan their father, who was born unto Israel : howbeit the name of the city (was) Laish at the first.* (30) *And the children of Dan set up* ["raised up :" a different Hebrew word from that in ver. 31, *yaquimu- yasimu*], *the graven image* [of Jehovah] : *and Jonathan* [Heb., *Jehonathan*], *the son of Gershom* [from *Ger*, "a sojourner," and *Shom*, "a strange land," both Egyptian words (Exod. ii. 22, xviii. 3)], *the son of Manasseh* [Jehonathan was "the Levite" (xvii. 7, xviii. 3, 15, 19, 27) : for the latter was promised the tribal priesthood by the Danites, just as Jehonathan here is said to have exercised it. Gershom was his *ancestor*, not his immediate father : for "son of" often means *descendant of :* and Jehona- than being "a young man" (xviii. 3, 15), could not have been Moses' *grandson :* who at Joshua's death would certainly be *old* rather than *young*. The present Masoretic text reads, מְׁשֶׁה, *Manasseh*, with the hanging נ. The reason, according to *Rab- babar bar Channa*, on the Talmud Baba Bathr. *f*. 109 *b*, was, the sacred writer shrank from putting on Moses the ignominy of having so ungodly a descendant. The original reading, we may hence infer, was "son of *Moses*" (מׁשֶׁה), which was altered subsequently to "son of Manasseh," by inserting the one letter *n* only, to imply he was *son of Manasseh* in impiety, *son of Moses* by descent. Some MSS. of the Septuagint and Jerome read "son of Moses :" and Rabbi Tanchum calls this reading the original text (*Kethib*), and "son of Manasseh" the marginal reading (*Keri*) of the scribes. Still the Targums, the Syriac, and most MSS. of the Septuagint, have "son of Manasseh"], *he and his sons were priests to the tribe of Dan until the day of the captivity of the land* [not, as Lord Arthur Hervey (Speaker's Commentary) thinks, the deportation of the ten tribes by Tiglath Pileser and Shalmaneser (1 Chron. v. 22 ; 2 Kings xv.

29, xvii. 6). For this is inconsistent with the statement (ver. 31) "They set up Micah's graven image—*all the time that the house of God was in Shiloh;*" *i.e.,* from the time when Joshua (xviii. 1) set up the tabernacle at Shiloh, to *the time of Eli and Samuel* (1 Sam. i. 3, iii. 21, iv. 3): by Saul's time, it was no longer in Shiloh, but Nob (1 Sam. xxi.); and in David's reign, in Gibeon (1 Chron. xvi. 39, xxi. 29). Therefore the continuance of the setting up of Micah's image, and the contemporaneous priesthood of Jonathan's sons alike, cannot be here alleged by the sacred writer as extending even to Saul's reign, much less to the time of the Assyrian captivity of the ten tribes. In Ps. xiv. 7, the phrase, "bring back the captivity," means simply "restore from depression" (so Job xlii. 10): "The Lord turned the captivity of Job," *i.e.,* amply indemnified him for all he lost. So "the captivity of the land" here means *the carrying away of the ark of the covenant* (see 1 Sam. iv. 10–22), which shows how keenly the capture was felt, as that of the nation itself. This is confirmed by Ps. lxxviii. 60, 61 : "God forsook the tabernacle of Shiloh, the tent which He placed among men : and delivered *His strength* (*i.e.,* the ark, its symbol, Ps. cxxxii. 8), *into captivity, and His glory into the enemy's hand.*" The whole land seemed as carried into captivity in the carrying away of the ark, its spiritual centre and kernel. After it the Philistines treated the Israelites as subjugated captives (1 Sam. xiii. 19–23)]. (31) *And they set* ['put'] *them up Micah's graven image which he made, all the time that the house of God* [the *tabernacle* spiritually so called, even before the building of Solomon's temple of stone: so David (Ps. v. 7 ; 2 Sam. vii. 6] *was in Shiloh* [forsaken because of Israel's apostasy (Jer. vii. 4, 12). The idol of Micah continued in Dan, doubtless, only until Samuel threw down this and other idols (1 Sam. vii. 3, 4). A hint as to the date of the writing of the Book of Judges is hereby furnished : it must have been after the capture of the ark by the Philistines, and after its return and being set up at Nob (no longer Shiloh) in Saul's reign (1 Sam. xxi.). Ch. xviii. 1, implies that in *the writer's* day, royalty had been set up. Tyre is not mentioned, but Sidon oppressed Israel, and was the protector of neighbouring Canaanite cities (ch. xviii. 7); whereas in David's time, Tyre took the lead, and was David's ally, not enemy. *Not earlier* than the deliverance from that servitude to the Philistines which Samson 'began' (ch. xiii. 5), and which Samuel completed (1 Sam. vii. 9–14). See also note, ch. xix. 10. All these hints point to a date in Saul's reign. The writer was probably Samuel, or one of his school of prophets].

INTRODUCTION OF IDOLATRY: HOW IT BEGAN AFTER JOSHUA'S DEATH.

1. *Relation of the closing chapters to the whole Book.*——Chapters xvii.–xxi. form a twofold appendix to the body of the Book of Judges, which ends with the death of Samson (iii. 7–xvi. 31). As the Introduction (ch. i.–iii. 6), gave a general survey of the conduct of Israel towards the Canaanites who were left still in the land at Joshua's death; and Jehovah's consequent reproval of His people, and when this failed to reform them, His chastisement of them by those very heathen whose idolatries they had copied, their repentance, and His deliverance of them by Judges whom He raised extraordinarily; and then their sad relapse at the death of each Judge; so the appendices subjoin an account of——first, the introduction of *image-worship* into the family of Micah, and thence among the Danite emigrants to Laish-Dan; secondly, the depth of *moral corruption* into which very early after Joshua's death some portions of Israel had fallen by association with the Canaanites, as illustrated in the sin of Gibeah; at the same time also, the faithfulness of the people as a whole, shown in their earnest effort to root out the evil by taking vengeance on the guilty tribe of Benjamin.

2. *Date of the events.*——From a comparison of ch. i. 34: "The Amorites forced the children of Dan into the mountain; for they would not suffer them to come down to the valley," with ch. xviii. 1: "In those days the tribe of Dan sought them an inheritance to dwell in; for unto that day all their

inheritance had not fallen unto them among the tribes of
Israel," it is evident that Micah's commencement of image-
worship, and the Danites' carrying away of his image and
emigration to Laish, occurred in the earliest part of the period
of the Judges. It was the unfaithfulness of Dan to Jehovah's
command in not expelling the Amorites, and their being, in
righteous retribution, themselves driven out by the Amorites,
which necessitated the migration of a part of the tribe northwards. Similar evidence of the very early date of the wicked
act of Gibeah, and its avenging, is afforded by comparing ch.
xx. 28 with Josh. xxii. 13 and xxiv. 33, in all which passages
alike Phinehas, the son of Eleazar the son of Aaron, is referred
to as the priest; so that the time must have been immediately
after Joshua's death. Moreover, the origination of the name
Mahaneh-dan is given in this narrative (ch. xviii. 12); a name
which it bore in Samson's childhood (xiii. 25, margin). This
twofold narrative could not have been fittingly introduced
into the complete series of historical sketches of the Judges
which make up the body of the Book. But it is added
separately, as affording two striking pictures, drawn from the
life, of the spiritual and moral state of the times, and of the
early deterioration of Israel, out of which arose the necessity
for the Divinely-raised Judges, if Israel was to be saved. In
both alike we see Israel without a king (ch. xvii. 6, xviii. 1,
xix. 1, xxi. 25); from which we infer that by the time of the
writer of the book the kingdom of Saul had begun; furthermore, the frequent repetition of the remark implies that the
sacred writer designed to intimate the misery that flowed from
the absence of a governing power, after Joshua's death, and
the need there exists, first of Judges such as God raised, and
subsequently of a king sanctioned by Jehovah, when the
people proved themselves, by unfaithfulness to Him, unworthy
of the theocracy. In both occurrences of the appendix alike,
the will of God is inquired through the priest (ch. xviii. 5, 6,
xx. 18, 23, 27); in both the narrative is detailed with much
exact minuteness, and light is thrown on the course of events
by circumstantial clauses, implying identity of authorship, and
also that the author must have lived close to the times of the

events. The tabernacle was still at Shiloh when he wrote, and not yet moved by David to Jerusalem (ch. xviii. 31).

3. *Origination of idolatry with the people.*—The beginning of superstition is commonly attributed to priestcraft, but facts disprove this opinion. It was not Aaron who suggested the calf-idolatry to the people, but the people who "gathered themselves together unto Aaron, and said unto him, Up, make us gods, which shall go before us" (Exod. xxxii. 1). *Populus vult decipi, et decipiatur.* God is a Spirit; but the people are impatient of spiritual worship, and long for some sensible object to which they can render sensuous worship, adapted to the earthly-mindedness of the natural man; then the priests, fearing lest they should lose influence with the people, follow their leading, and carry into effect their carnal wishes. So image-worship in the case before us began with Micah's mother and Micah himself, and Micah's family; then followed his inducing the Levite to become his private chaplain and priest to his idol. The root of idolatry and priestcraft is in the human heart; and it will put forth its noxious shoots in all times, even among those favoured with the greatest spiritual privileges, such as we Christians enjoy. It is natural to our sensuous cravings; then it seeks the sanction of the church; and so sacerdotalism and sensuous ceremonialism become fully developed. The sure and only antidote to it is "to worship God in the spirit, and rejoice in Christ Jesus, and have no confidence in the flesh" (Phil. iii. 3).

4. *Idolatry associated with robbery, self-deceit, and sorrow in its beginnings, and in its issues.*—(1) *Greed the source of bitterness and cursing.* The love of money is *a* root of all evil (so the Greek in 1 Tim. vi. 10), and embitters the nearest relationships. The love of money made Micah's mother to hoard a great sum, instead of using it for the benefit of her own son, who had a grown-up family (ver. 5). The same greed of gain led the son to rob his mother (see Prov. xxviii. 24), and the unnatural mother to curse the robber, whom she suspected to be her own son, for robbing her. Loss of wealth drives the good to prayers, the bad to curses. So loud did she speak in her son's ears, when uttering her passionate curses,

that he was terrified, and under the stings of conscience restored the stolen money. It is the highest wisdom to give conscience no cause for upbraidings (see Acts xxiv. 16). It is next best, when we have transgressed, to hearken to the first monitions of conscience, and at once make all possible amends for the evil done. The mother's curses extorted restitution from the son : then she changes from cursing to blessing : where there is no grace, " out of the same mouth proceedeth blessing and cursing." But just as " no fountain can both yield salt water and fresh," " at the same aperture sweet water and bitter " (James iii. 10, 11, 12, margin), so no *real* blessing can come from a mouth given to cursing (see Ps. lxii. 4).

(2) *The only antidote to bitterness of heart and tongue.*—The grace of God alone can make the mouth that once " sent forth the bitter," to send forth the sweet. The cross of Christ Jesus can change the cursing, natural heart into the spirit of blessing (1 Pet. iii. 9) ; just as the Lord showed Moses a tree which, when he had cast into the bitter waters of Marah (Exod. xv. 23–25), the waters were made sweet.

(3) *Plausible pleas for idolatry.*—As the quarrel of mother and son proved that money was their god ; so now, when they were reconciled, they agreed to turn a part of it into a god or idol, to be openly worshipped. As covetousness is idolatry latent, so image-worship is idolatry patent. The unconverted, even when they cease from quarrelling with one another, agree in dishonouring God. Yet they do all in the name of " the Lord." " Blessed be thou of the Lord, my son—I wholly dedicated the silver unto the Lord " (ver. 3, 4). Just as Aaron's calf was in imitation of the cherubim in Jehovah's sanctuary, and was designed to be, not a god distinct from Jehovah, but the visible representation of Him who is unseen (Exod. xxxii. 4), as the people's words prove : " These be thy gods (Elohim, the plural name of the ONE God, implying His manifold power and attributes) which brought thee up out of the land of Egypt " (a deliverance which all admitted was *Jehovah's* act) ; so Micah's image was only a violation of the second commandment, not of the first. But by an inevitable necessity it led on to the violation of the first, in the worship

of Baalim and Asherah ("the groves"). Similarly Jeroboam's calves, the sin of *all* the kings of the kingdom of the ten tribes, eventuated in the Baal-worship of Ahab and his son (1 Kings xvi. 31 ; 2 Kings i. 2).

The same fatal issue has followed in large parts of Christendom from the effort to meet men's craving after sensible representations. The image and the picture set up, by way of helping the worshipper to realise the unseen world, in violation of the second commandment, have resulted not only in undue veneration of the symbol or picture, but also in violations of the first ; and gods many and lords many have usurped the prerogatives of the only true God, who will not give His glory to another (1 Cor. viii. 5 ; Isa. xlii. 8). Good intentions will never justify disobedience to God's express commands and prohibitions. Those who would please God, must come to the light of His word, that their deeds may be made manifest that they are wrought in God (John iii. 21). Men must not substitute for God's ordinance their self-devised will-worship (Col. ii. 23).

(4) *The self-pleasing of false religion.*—Women are instinctively devotional. How sad it is that devotion should be perverted to superstition ! The old mother here leads the son to false worship, which at first he declined. But when she gave part of the money, restored after the robbery, to the founder for the making of an image (see Isa. xlvi. 6), he not only consented without further scruple, but became enamoured of the made gods ; so bewitching is sensuous worship to the natural heart. As he had pleased self in robbing his mother of her money, so now he pleased self in robbing God of His honour. Children should obey their parents only "in the Lord" (Eph. vi. 1), not in disobedience to the heavenly Father, following the vanities "received by tradition from their fathers" (1 Pet. i. 18 ; Jer. xliv. 17).

(5) *The covetousness of idolatry and the idolatry of covetousness.*—Notwithstanding this woman's superstition, covetousness gained the mastery. She "had wholly dedicated the silver unto the Lord," but she makes a compromise between her love of money and her superstition by giving, of the eleven hundred

shekels, only two hundred for the fabrication of the idol, and keeping back nine hundred for herself. She gave less than a fifth to her God, and retained the rest. How many self-deceivers there are who similarly profess to give themselves and their all to the true God, and yet keep back far more than four-fifths for self. But though men can deceive themselves, God cannot be mocked: for though immediate vengeance does not, as in the case of Ananias and Sapphira, overtake him who keeps back part whilst pretending to give all, yet " whatsoever a man soweth, that shall he also reap; he that soweth to his flesh shall of the flesh reap corruption " (Gal. vi. 7, 8). Let us Christians, then, see that our giving in our Lord's name be " as a matter of bounty, and not as of covetousness " (2 Cor. ix. 5); for often there is covetousness in our very giving, and covetousness is idolatry (Col. iii. 5). Those who offer to God the refuse and leavings of their time, their strength, and their means, are offering only " the blind, the lame, and sick for sacrifice " (Mal. i. 8). God, who is the best, deserves the best at His creatures' hands: God values the widow's mite, but abhors and rejects the miser's mite.

(6) *The self-deceit of idolatry.*—" Micah had an house of gods," as he called it (ver. 5); but it was really, as the Chaldee Targum has it, " an house of error." He cheated himself fatally in thinking poison to be bread for the soul. He mimicked God's house at Shiloh with his house of idols, God's oracles with his ephod and teraphim, God's ordinances with his self-consecrated priesthood. The first error from the truth entailed the rest; for once that the transgressor has left the right path, his course is down an inclined steep, and he cannot at will stop himself. All the while " a deceived heart turneth him aside that he cannot deliver his soul, nor say, Is there not a lie in my right hand"? (Isa. xliv. 20.)

(7) *The sorrows of idolatry.*—It is significant that the Hebrew word for 'idols' [עֲצַבִּים, *'atzabim*], is akin to that for 'pains' [עַצָּבִים, *'atzābim*]. Idolatry, whether in its grosser or its more refined forms, entails on its votaries only sorrows for their pains. It was so with Micah in the end. When he lost his idol he lost his all (xviii. 24). As eleven hundred pieces of

silver occasioned the betrayal of the cause of God in the family of Micah, and then in the tribe of Dan; so retributively eleven hundred pieces were the price of the subsequent betrayal of the Danite champion of the nation into the hands of the Philistines (ch. xvi. 5). Idolatry in the church often goes along with disorder in the state. It was when (ver. 6) "there was no king in Israel," that "every man did that which was right in his own eyes : " and doing just what is right in one's own eyes, is tantamount to doing what is wrong towards one's neighbour and towards God ; and the end is, it brings bitter sorrow on one's self. Nothing tends to promote the happiness of a family and of a nation so much as a well-ordered magistracy, upholding a godly ministry. Let us pray and give thanks for both (1 Tim. ii. 1, 2) ; and let us ever remember that the way of idolatry, however refined, proves to be a "way of pain," and shuts out from "the way everlasting" (Ps. cxxxix. 24). (Marg. for "wicked way" *way of pain;* Heb., *way of an idol.*)

5. *False confidences of idolaters.*—Micah made his self-devised religion to bear some faint resemblance to the Divinely-ordered ritual of the Mosaic law. It was Judaism, so far as the use of an ephod, and the consecration of a Levite as priest, was concerned ; but it was rank heathenism in all other respects. Yet this mingle-mangle of idolatry and Judaism sufficed to give Micah an assured confidence of the Divine favour. He first presumed to consecrate his own son as priest; but afterwards, having some misgiving, it would seem, as to so flagrant a violation of God's ordinance, and having fallen in with a roving Levite, he allayed all qualms of conscience by consecrating this member of the priestly tribe to be his chaplain (compare Jeroboam's consecrating priests of the lowest of the people, 1 Kings xii. 13). Worthless gods are suitably served with worthless priests. This step was only one move further from God ; for the Levite was not of the *family* of Aaron, the only one sanctioned by God. The consecration by an unauthorised layman was a daring usurpation. The Levite was as unsettled in his principles as in his dwelling-place. God had made provision for the Levites whilst they remained

in His service, far better than that which this Levite sold his
conscience for. But he chose rather to go and seek his fortune
elsewhere. How many there are who, like him, go away from
the Father's home, " to sojourn where they can find a place "
(Luke xv. 13). If he had any of the spirit of his great pro-
genitor, Levi, and his children (Exod. xxxii. 25–28; Deut.
xxxiii. 9, 10), he would have sternly rebuked the idolater, and
warned him of God's coming judgments for his sin. But this
degenerate Levite was "content to dwell with the man," though
his office was a perpetual insult to the true God, whose minister
he was bound to be. His only concern was to secure for
himself a transitory home, the bread that perisheth, garments
that wax old, and a pittance of filthy lucre. At best, he
confesses, he comes but to *"sojourn."* At what a paltry price
men sell their souls! The pleasures and gains of sin, at best,
are *but for a season.* How infinitely better was the Psalmist's
choice, " I had rather be a door-keeper in the house of my God,
than to dwell in the tents of wickedness." " The ministry is
the best *calling,* but the worst *trade* in the world " (M. Henry).
Yet Micah confidently expected good from God, whilst doing
evil with a high hand against Him. He regarded as a special
interposition of Providence the arrival of the Levite. Per-
verters of the truth, when any unexpected event occurs, which
they can turn to their own purpose, often regard it as a token
of God's favour; whereas it is rather a token that God is
" choosing their delusions," and so " sending them strong
delusion that they should believe a lie " (Isa. lxvi. 4; 2 Thess.
ii. 11). " Now know I that the Lord will do me good, seeing
I have a Levite to my priest : " as if a Levite's presence could
bless apostates from the God of all blessing. He thought his
consecration of the Levite an act ensuring God's blessing;
whereas it was a presumptuous provocation of God, entailing a
curse. If the presence of the Divine ark (1 Sam. iv. 3–11),
and of the temple in which they gloried (Jer. vii. 4), could not
save an ungodly people without repentance, much less could an
idol and a renegade Levite bring anything but sorrow to him
who harboured them. Ignorance and sin entail their own
punishment, as the sequel proved. The Lord will do us good,

only when we are good, do good, and lay out to good account all our privileges.

6. *Growth of evil from small beginnings.*—The plague of idolatry, which began with the superstition of a doting old woman, overjoyed at the recovery of her idolised money from the son who had stolen it, and which was embodied by the latter in his image, passed thence, through the besotted blindness of Danite emigrants, and the restlessness of a mercenary Levite apostate, to a city and tribe; and so the infection spread through the nation. · Like bodily disease, originating in minute germs which, once they find a suitable lodgment, rapidly multiply and diffuse themselves; so spiritual evil begins with the small leaven, which quickly leavens the whole lump: "How great a matter a little fire kindleth." How watchfully, diligently, and prayerfully should we resist the first depravations of sound doctrine and holy practice.

7. *Wise energy of men in earthly enterprises, but recklessness as to the favour of God.*—(1.) *Wisdom of man in earthly enterprises.* The six hundred Danites had the wisdom of the "serpent by the way" (Gen. xlix. 17) as was foretold by their forefather, combined with the courage of a "lion's whelp" (Deut. xxxiii. 22). Dan "leaped" on his prey; but he looked before he leaped. The six hundred Danites took the precaution of sending spies before them to ascertain the desirability of the land for an inheritance, and the *possibilities* of their conquering the possessors. We, like them, are in quest of an inheritance; let us see that the "eternal life, which God that cannot lie promised before the world began" (Tit. i. 2), is our aim. If worldly men will make daring ventures on the report of others, shall we not, on the word of God, venture all in order to gain the heavenly Canaan. We must lay hold of it, and "strive to enter" (Luke xiii. 24; 1 Tim. vi. 12), if we would attain that "very good land and large, where there is no want of anything that is in the earth" (xviii. 9, 10), and where there are joys such as earth cannot afford; for "eye hath not seen, nor ear heard, neither have entered into the heart of man, the things which God hath prepared for them that love Him" (1 Cor. ii. 9). But though we see not

yet the heavenly inheritance, we are to send our prayers and
our believing expectations to spy out its joys even already.
Faith in the word of God, and confident hope in the promises
of the faithful One, are our spies to assure us that the inheritance is both altogether desirable and attainable to the believer.
Communion with God by the Holy Spirit and holy ordinances,
are as the grapes of Eshcol, a foretaste (Eph. i. 14) to whet our
appetites for the pleasures at God's right hand.   Above all, the
forerunner Jesus, our Melchizedek High Priest for ever, secures
our hope, which is as an anchor of the soul, both sure and
steadfast, and which entereth within the veil.   We may rest far
more securely on His word, than the Danites did on the word
of their spies ; and we may arise and go up at once and possess
the land, if we " be not slothful, but followers of them who
through faith and patience inherit the promises " (ch. xviii. 9 ;
Heb. vi. 12).

(2) *Energy of worldly men : sudden destruction of the careless
ones.*—The boldness of the Danites stands in contrast to the
luxurious apathy of the people of Laish.   The latter lived
" quiet and secure " in their licentiousness, having " no magistrate to put them to shame in anything."   Security is the forerunner of destruction : and therefore it is *thrice* mentioned (ver.
7, 10, 27 ; 1 Thess. v. 3).   It is true, the Danites were little if
any better, they too living without restraint, and doing every
man what was right in his own eyes (xvii. 6).   But God uses
one transgressor to scourge the other, and in the end suffers
neither to escape righteous judgment.   "When He hath worn
His rod to the stumps, He casteth it into the fire " (Trapp)
(see note on ch. xviii. 7).   The iniquity of the Canaanites was
now full, that of the Israelites of Dan was not yet so.   The
boldness of the Danites gave them complete success.   The
fancied security of the inhabitants of Laish was their ruin.
So it will be with the unbelieving in the great day of the Lord:
" When men shall say, Peace and safety, then sudden destruction
cometh upon them, and they shall not escape " (1 Thess. v. 3).
So also it shall be with the apostate church, the mystic Babylon : " How much she hath glorified herself and lived deliciously
—therefore shall her plagues come in one day : in one hour

she is made desolate!" (Rev. xviii. 7, 8, 19.) On the other hand, "the upright shall have dominion over them in the morning" of the resurrection (Ps. xlix. 14): "The saints shall be joyful in glory," having "the high praises of God in their mouth, and a two-edged sword in their hand—to execute upon them the judgment written: this honour have all the saints" (Ps. cxlix. 5–9).

(3) *Recklessness of men as to securing the favour of God.*—It was the accident of their recognising the Levite's voice or accent (see Mark xiv. 70), that suggested to the Danites the thought of inquiring the Divine will at all. Otherwise they would have gone forward on their perilous enterprise, without any regard to God whatever, and this in defiance of God's express command, that the leader of Israel should "stand before the priest who should ask counsel for him, after the judgment of Urim before the Lord, and at His word should go out and come in" (Numb. xxvii. 21). How many there are whose religion is a matter of hap-hazard! The irreligious recklessness of the Danites was only equalled by their ignorance. They scruple not to consult, as to the will of God, a Levite renegade from God, who unblushingly avowed himself the hireling of an idolater, and the priest of an idol! They passed by the Divinely-sanctioned oracle and high priest of Shiloh; they preferred Micah's teraphim to God's own Urim: yet they expected to obtain for their expedition the favour of God, through images forbidden by God! Such is the blind folly of the natural man! Let us, from whom the darkness is passed, seek God in the right way, by His word, by His spirit, and in the ways of His providence: so shall we go in peace whithersoever we go; all our steps shall be ordered by the Lord, and walking before Him, we shall be perfect (Gen. xvii. i; Ps. xxxvii. 23).

8. *Selfishness, ingratitude, and folly of idolaters.*

(1) *The robbers of the idol.*—The Danites, when bent on their own purpose, did not hesitate to repay the former courtesy of Micah with robbery and injury. They thought only of self, without regard to their duty to others. They were right in desiring the Divine presence with them, but wrong

in the way they took to obtain it. God "hates robbery for
burnt-offerings." As in Micah's case, so in theirs, idolatry
began with robbery. How blinding to the intellect must
idolatry be! The Danites never reflected, how utterly unable
to protect them must those gods be which could not protect
themselves from being stolen. M. Henry truly says—"Their
idolatry began in theft, a proper prologue for such an opera
[rather *tragedy*]: in order to the breaking of the second
commandment, they begin with the eighth, and take their
neighbour's goods, to make them their gods." They could
have made as good gods themselves; but superstition had
invested Micah's idols with a false halo, so that they preferred
to steal his, without inquiring into their origin. Superstition cannot bear the light of investigation. Moreover,
erroneous worship is sure to be associated with evil practice.
The sentiment of Pope is not consonant with either Holy
Scripture or experience—

> "For modes of faith, let graceless zealots fight;
> His can't be wrong, whose life is in the right."

Grapes are not to be gathered from thorns, nor figs from thistles.
A life cannot be right which grows out of a principle which is
wrong. You may hang grapes and figs on a bramble bush,
but they do not spring from it. Holy life and righteous
practice never really grow out of idolatry: its natural and
necessary fruits are selfishness and corruption. Water does
not rise above its level. Practice of holiness, purity, and truth
can only flow from faith in the holy, pure, and true God,—that
faith working by love to God and man.

(2) *The priest of the idol.*—"Like priest, like people." The
Levite was of a roving, restless disposition, like the Danites'
own. So little did he trouble himself about guarding the idol-
god entrusted to his charge, that he left it to take care of
itself, and went out to the gate to see and talk with the
strangers. Not until their messengers had stolen and brought
out the images and their belongings to the warriors, who kept
him in conversation at the gate, did he utter his faint word of
remonstrance, What do ye? A few words of the Danites

T

sufficed to silence his opposition and win him to their service. Ambition and gain were his real gods. What recked he that such a desertion of Micah was base and ungrateful to one who had given him a comfortable home, when he was a penniless wanderer! Is it not enough for him to know that he is going to be a father and priest to a tribe and clan in Israel? When once a man gives his heart up to self-seeking and covetousness, he will make no scruple of throwing away all regard to conscience or morality. Had he, through remorse of his past apostacy, left Micah and his idols to minister to the Lord at Shiloh, he would have acted rightly, and would have been entitled to a maintenance there (Deut. xviii. 6). But this renegade Levite not only forsakes Micah, but carries Micah's images with him, thereby spreading the infection of idolatry into a large portion of Israel, and laying a foundation for its perpetuation to ages to come. Not only was there no compulsion on their part, or compunction on his, but his "heart was glad." "If ten shekels won him, eleven would lose him" (Bishop Hall). The proposal of the Danites was just what suited his fickle character. He who is false to his God, will never be true to his friend. Nor can any anchor hold the man who has made shipwreck of good conscience. We know not his end. Holy Scripture draws a dark veil of silence over it. But we are sure that, however the impenitent sinner seems to prosper for a time, an awful and lasting woe awaits him; for the reward of his hands shall be given him (Eccl. viii. 12, 13 ; Isa. iii. 11). What a blessed contrast to his gladness is that of the believer, " I will be glad *in the Lord* "—" I was glad when they said unto me, Let us go into the house of the Lord " (Ps. civ. 34, cxxii. 1). This gladness has no bitter at the bottom of the cup (Eccl. xi. 9). This shall issue in everlasting "joy and gladness " (Isa. xxxv. 10).

(3) *The idol's owner.*—Micah, when he discovered the loss of his darling idols and his chaplain, gathered the whole neighbourhood. He is much excited, and raises as great a stir about his images as Demetrius in the New Testament (Acts xix. 24–28). In hot haste he pursues and overtakes the robbers. His zeal for his false gods will rise in judgment against many a

half-hearted professing worshipper of the true God. Laodicean lukewarmness ill becomes us who owe such a debt of love and devotion to our Redeemer. No force or fraud can rob us of Him, our satisfying and everlasting treasure, if only we be true to Him and to ourselves. The Danites affected not to know "what ailed Micah that he came with such a company" after them. Might is at no loss for arguments against right. But had he been wise, he would have seen that their gain was their loss, and his loss his gain. If the loss of our idols cure us of our love of them, it will be an inestimable gain. Micah's own words confute his folly—"My gods which I made": "Those 'carpenters' chips,' as Mrs. Cotismore called them" (Trapp). How could those be gods which he himself made, after having turned his back on the God who made him? His title to them, as having made them, was undoubtedly good; but what good could he expect from such gods? Yet he cries, "Ye have taken them away—and what have I more?" That object, the loss of which affects us so that, when we lose it, we regard our all as lost, is our idol. Whatever earthly thing or person we have not the heart to part with for God, is our snare. Let us rather regard the loss of the light of God's countenance as the only irreparable loss. "Woe to them, when I depart from them" (Hos. ix. 12). But, if we have Him still as ours, we may count the loss of all else as comparatively nothing worth (Habak. iii. 17, 18; Phil. iii. 7, 8). And when our Father saith, "Little children, keep yourselves from idols" (1 John v. 21), may our heart's response be, "What have I to do any more with idols?" (Hos. xiv. 8.)

(4) *Issue to the worshippers of the idol.*—The Danites congratulated themselves on their successful robbery: it was about to be a root of bitterness to themselves and their children and all Israel in the end, bearing as its fatal fruit "the captivity of the land" (Jer. ii. 19). God "gave them the lands of the heathen, that they might observe His statutes" (Ps. cv. 44, 45). They observed them only so far as suited their own wills; and in this were most punctilious, smiting the heathen with the sword, and burning their city with fire (Deut. vii. 2, xx. 16, 17); for cruelty and idolatry go together (Rom. iii. 15; Ps. lxxiv.

20). But then they followed their own delusion to which God gave them up in retributive judgment (2 Thess. ii. 10), setting up the graven image, and attributing to it (Habak. i. 11, 16), the success which they owed to God: as many still abuse the very prosperity which is God's gift, to turn their hearts from the giver (Prov. i. 32).

(5) *The idol's priest.*—The Levite, before left unnamed to mark his ignominy, is at the very close named, and the name, taken in connection with his ancestry, takes us by surprise. Jonathan means "the gift of Jehovah": yet he proved to be a curse sent from Jehovah to an apostate people. He sprung from Gershom the son of Moses, the nobly disinterested "man of God" (see note, ver. 30). But he was one who polluted God among God's people for pieces of bread, to slay the souls which should not die (Ezek. xiii. 19). He was so much the worse than others, because by his birth he ought to have been better. He was a child of Moses by descent, but of the idolatrous Manasseh by imitation. Many a good parent has a degenerate offspring; for the children of God are born, not of blood nor of the will of the flesh (John i. 13).

(6) *Permanence of the idol.*—Jonathan's priesthood continued in his family, and became hereditary. The wicked assumption was perpetuated from father to son. So much more transmissible from generation to generation is evil than good. The idol-worship lasted "all the time that the house of God was in Shiloh." How perilous it is to suffer the infection of sin ever to enter; once caught, the spiritual malady is often not cured for ages. Not till excision took place by God's judgment in suffering the Philistine captivity of the ark, as also by Samuel's abolition of idols, and the nation's return to Jehovah, was the evil remedied (1 Sam. vii. 3, 4). What constituted the chief aggravation of the Danites' sin, was, they worshipped the idol at the very time whilst God's worship was going on in Shiloh! Sinning in the face of heavenly light and great spiritual privileges is the condemnation which entails heaviest punishment (Luke xii. 47, 48; John iii. 19).

9. *The religion of worldly men, false in principle, and fatal in issue.*—(1) *The religion of unrenewed professors of Christianity*

false in principle. Micah, when he had got an idol, with an ephod, and secured a Levite to minister to it, was confident of having henceforth the blessing of the Lord: "Now know I that the Lord will do me good, seeing I have a Levite to my priest." Faint as was the resemblance of Micah's worship to that which God had ordained, it was enough, in his esteem, to secure the Divine favour. So if the religion current amongst most so-called Christians were closely examined, it would be found a mixture of heathenism and Judaism, with Christianity in the proportion that may suit the fancy of each. Covetousness, ambition, and pleasure are as truly the idols of most among us, as images were the objects of heathen worship. God, it is true, is admitted with the tongue to be One: but gods many and lords many sway the heart. THE GOD OF PROVIDENCE is ignored. Chance, luck, and men's free will are treated as the regulators of human concerns. To see the hand of God in everything, to ask and expect in faith all blessings at His hands, to fear His displeasure, to know that His eye is ever upon us, and that He searches all hearts, and will make all things work together for His people's good,—all this seems to worldly men enthusiasm and fanaticism. Then, also, God is not recognised as THE GOD OF HOLINESS, who hates all sin, and will by no means clear the guilty. If only men keep clear of crimes against the law of the land, and offences against the laws of society, it is commonly supposed that sins of heart and life against God's holy law will not be strictly judged by God. As for the Christian law of loving, whole-hearted consecration to God, and crucifixion with Christ to the world, most men think as little of aiming towards such a standard as would a heathen. On the other hand, the element of Judaism largely enters into the world's religion, in its adherence to particular forms. Each denomination has its own forms, the observance of which will, in the man's eyes, cover over his deficiencies. Attachment to some favourite preacher or leader of religious thought, is also thrown into the scale. To complete all, there must be a little Christianity as an ingredient; Christ Jesus is "acknowledged to have purchased for us such a relaxation of Divine law as we are pleased to claim, and a power to save ourselves by any measure of obedience which we choose to pay to the code we have devised " (C. Simeon). Such is the miserable and delusive ground of most men's hope; and yet to doubt that such are safe, or to fear the possibility of their perishing everlastingly when they die, is deemed the height of uncharitableness.

(2) *Such religion is fatal in its issue.*—As Micah's idols were carried away, so men's false trusts will be wrested from them in the coming judgment. Their fancied obedience will be found so utterly wanting that they will be speechless, when convicted of having presumed to appear before the King without the wedding garment. The law which they thought to bring down to their own low standard, will be found unchangeable as God its author. Then their misery will be hopeless and helpless: my gods are gone, and what have I more ? The refuges of lies are swept away, and no refuge left. In vain they call upon the rocks to hide them from the face of Him that sitteth upon the throne; they have walked in the light of *their* fire and in the sparks that they have kindled: so this shall they have of Jehovah's hand; they shall lie down in sorrow (Isa. l. 11).

10. *Vital importance of true principles.*—The Lord Jesus is " able to save them to the uttermost that come unto God by Him." If we stand before God on the ground of His meritorious obedience unto death, we cannot perish, because God cannot break His word. Eternal life, begun now and to be consummated hereafter, is unalterably ours. None can pluck us out of Jesus' hand; nor can any separate us from the love of Christ, or rob us of our portion and our great priest, as the Danites robbed Micah (John x. 28; Rom. viii. 35). Let us then resolve to take our religion from the Bible, and not from our own imaginations and selfwill, and the opinions of the world. Then having God as our reconciled Father, Christ Jesus as our only Priest and Sacrifice, and living in Him and to Him by the power of His indwelling Spirit, we can truly say, on the ground of two immutable things, His promise and His oath, in which it is impossible for God to lie (Heb. vi. 17–19), "Now know I that the Lord will do me good."

CHAPTER XIX.

AWFUL CRIME OF GIBEAH : ISRAEL'S CONSEQUENT WAR WITH
BENJAMIN, AT FIRST UNSUCCESSFUL.

(1) *And it came to pass in those days, when (there was) no
king in Israel* [(ch. xvii. 6, xviii. 1). This marks that the history
which follows was about the same time as the history of
Micah and the Danites, in chs. xvii., xviii. (compare xxi. 25).
The mention of the Levite here, and another Levite in xvii. 7,
is another connecting link between the otherwise independent
histories; also the mention of "Mount Ephraim" (xvii. 1 and
xix. 1)], *that there was a certain Levite sojourning* [*i.e.*, living
outside any of the Levitical towns] *on the side* [בְּיַרְכְּתֵי, *beyarkethee*,
"in the *recesses*" or "more remote parts": probably, *the northern
extremities* or *outermost parts* near Shiloh (ver. 18), that he might
be near the house of the Lord there] *of Mount Ephraim* [the
hilly country of Ephraim], *who took to him a concubine* [Heb.,
"a wife (*ishah*), a concubine," *i.e.*, a secondary wife, recognised
as such by usage, though against the original marriage law
(Matt. xix. 4–9); but not having the same rights as the original
and legal wife (see ver. 3, also ver. 25)] *out of Bethlehem-
Judah.* (2) *And his concubine played the whore against him*
[Heb., "beyond him" (see Prov. xxxi. 21, 23)], *and* [then] *went
away from* [Heb., *from being with*] *him unto her father's house
to Bethlehem-Judah, and was there four whole months* [Heb., "*days
(i.e.*, for a long time ; see margin, ch. xi. 4) *four months*"
(defining *how long* that long time lasted); the Heb., for 'days'
not being in the construct state forbids its being construed as
governing "four months," and being translated "days *of* four
months"]. (3) *And her husband arose, and went after her, to
speak friendly* [Heb., *to her heart* (Gen. xxxiv. 3, margin] *unto*

her, (and) to bring her again [there is no ' and ' in the Hebrew.
He " spoke to her heart *in order to* bring *her* again " (the Keri
or margin reading הֲשִׁיבָהּ?) ; or as the text reading or Chetib
(לְהֲשִׁיבוֹ) " in order to bring *it* (her heart) back " to him again :
to win back her love], *having his servant with him, and a
couple of asses : and she brought him into her father's house;
and when the father of the damsel saw him, he rejoiced to meet
him* [many will accept a reconciliation offered, who yet would
not sue for it ; will secretly wish, yet make no active effort for
it]. (4) *And the father-in-law* [this expression shows she was
the Levite's *wife* in some sense. Unfaithfulness on the part
of a wife was legally punishable with death. The levity with
which the Levite treated so grave an offence shows the utter
laxity of the times. His readiness to take her again does not
prove, as Bonfrerius and Menochius argued (Poli Synopsis), that
she did not play the whore, but only went away from him to
her father], *the damsel's father, retained* [Heb., *"laid fast hold on "*]
*him; and he abode with him three days; so they did eat and
drink* [in token of reconciliation (Gen. xxvi. 30)], *and lodged
there.* (5) *And it came to pass on the fourth day, when they
arose early in the morning, that he arose up to depart; and
the damsel's father said unto his son-in-law, Comfort* [Heb.,
' strengthen '] *thine heart with a morsel of bread* [see Gen. xviii.
5), *and afterward go your way.* (6) *And they sat down, and
did eat and drink both of them together; for the damsel's father
had said unto the man, Be content* [*i.e.,* acquiesce] *I pray thee,
and tarry all night, and let thine heart be merry* [Heb., good,
cheerful, joyous]. (7) *And when the man rose up to depart, his
father-in-law urged him; therefore he lodged there again* [Heb.,
" he *turned back* and lodged there "]. (8) *And he arose early
in the morning on the fifth day to depart; and the damsel's father
said, Comfort thine heart* [note ver. 5], *I pray thee. And they
tarried until afternoon* [הִתְמַהְמְהוּ, *linger ;* but in ver. 6, ' tarry,'
לִין?, *pass the night.* Translate as Vulgate and LXX. take it as *the
second person imperatively,* the word of the father-in-law, " Tarry
till the day turns," *i.e.,* till midday is past (Keil)], *and they did
eat both of them.* (9) *And when the man rose up to depart, he
and his concubine, and his servant, his father-in-law, the damsel's*

father, said unto him, Behold, now the day draweth ['slackeneth' in heat and light. *Raphah*, "is weakening] *toward evening, I pray you tarry* [*linu*] *all night: behold, the day groweth to an end* [חֲנוֹת, *the declining* of the day (Gesenius). "The tent pitching time of the day," according to other translators (see margin; *i.e.*, *three o'clock*)]; *lodge here, that thy heart may be merry; and to-morrow get you early on your way, that thou* [the singular is interchanged with the plural 'you,' because their stay or departure rested with the Levite alone] *mayest go home* [Heb., "to thy tent." The father-in-law, for his daughter's sake, was more than usually pressing with hospitality, in order to ensure the goodwill of the husband to the runaway wife; this is a trait in the story true to nature. These details are given to account for the lateness of their arrival at Gibeah, which was the occasion of the horrid crime that ensues. He ought either to have started in the morning, or else to have accepted hospitality till next morning. He yielded when he ought not; and was obstinate, when he ought to have yielded. So many err]. (10) *But the man would not tarry that night, but he rose up and departed, and came over against* [עַד נֹכַח, *to before, i.e.*, to the place where the road from Bethlehem to Shiloh passes before Jerusalem] *Jebus, which (is) Jerusalem* [only two hours' journey from Bethlehem, whence they had started. The occupation of Jerusalem by Jebusites still (see ch. i. 21) implies that the date of the Book of Judges was before the capture of Zion by David]; *and (there were) with him two asses saddled; his concubine also (was) with him.* (11) (*And*) *when they (were) by Jebus, the day was far spent* [Heb., *had gone down far,* רַד from יָרַד]; *and the servant said unto his master, Come, I pray thee, and let us turn into this city of the Jebusites, and lodge in it.* (12) *And his master said unto him, We will not turn aside hither into the city of a stranger, that (is) not of the children of Israel* [so utterly at this early date the aboriginal Jebusites had ousted the Benjamites and men of Judah from the city of their inheritance, assigned and in part conquered by the latter. Sad effect of compromise with the world, and of unbelief! (ch. i. 8, 21; Josh. xv. 63, xviii. 28)]; *we will pass over to Gibeah.* (13) *And he said unto his servant, Come, let us draw near to one of these places to lodge all*

night, in Gibeah, or in Ramath [leaving Bethlehem at three o'clock
(note, ver. 9), they would come over against Jerusalem about
five o'clock : at six or seven would be four miles north of Jerusalem on the Shechem road toward Mount Ephraim. Ramah
(*Er-Ram*) and Gibeah were now near: Gibeah nearest: Ramah, two
miles further north. The suddenness of sunset and nightfall
made them turn aside hither for the night. Gibeah was then a
city, with the usual open street or square, having its " 700 chosen
men," probably the same as the left handed slingers (ch. xx. 15,
16). The site perhaps answers to that now called *Tuleil el ful*,
" the hill of the beans," a conical hill, strewed with unhewn
stones and remains of a town, on the road to Er-Ram and north
of Jerusalem (Robinson): so Josephus (*Bell. Jud.*, v. 2, § 1].
(14) *And they passed on, and went their way ; and the sun went
down upon them (when they were) by Gibeah, which (belongeth)
to Benjamin.* (15) *And they turned aside thither* [being prevented by the rapidly-descending darkness from going on to
Ramah], *to go in (and) to lodge in Gibeah : and when he went
in, he sat him down in a street* [rather " in the market-place "
or *square ;* the open space before the gate, the usual place of
congregating for traffic, holding law courts, and friendly inter-
course] *of the city; for (there was) no man that took them into
his house to lodging* [how differently Lot acted, when, according
to Oriental custom, he sat in the open area within the gate of
Sodom, and saw two angels, seeming to be ordinary strangers,
come within the gates : he bowed respectfully, and pressed them
to tarry all night in his house, and offered them a feast (Gen.
xix. 1, 2 ; Heb. xiii. 2)]. (15) *And, behold, there came an old
man from his work out of the field at even, which (was) also of
Mount Ephraim ; and he sojourned in Gibeah* [the solitary
exception to the inhospitality of the townsmen was not a
citizen of the place, but a sojourner ; and his being of the
same country as that from which the Levite came, namely,
Mount Ephraim, was apparently the inducement which moved
him to offer hospitality]; *but the men of the place (were)
Benjamites.* (17) *And when he had lifted up his eyes, he saw
a way-faring man in the street* [the market-place] *of the city :
and the old man said, Whither goest thou ? and whence comest*

thou? (18) *And he said unto him, We (are) passing from Bethlehem-Judah toward the side* [the outer extremities] *of Mount Ephraim; from thence (am) I: and I went to Bethlehem-Judah, but I (am now) going to the house of the* LORD [JEHOVAH. The objection to this translation, which is that of Bertheau, is that הֹלֵךְ אֶת בֵּית does not mean "walking *to,*" but "*at* the house" of Jehovah : also the Levite was not going directly to the tabernacle at Shiloh, but (according to his own statement to the old man) to the outer extremities of Mount Ephraim. Seb. Schmidt (in Keil) rightly states the Levite's argument to be, "The Lord thinks me worthy to *minister to Him as a Levite* ("I walking at His house," as *one of His ministers:* so the phrase "*walk* before Jehovah " is used (1 Sam. ii. 30; Zech. iii. 7 "walks among these that stand by " as my ministers, iv. 14), and yet there is not one of the Lord's professing people who thinks me worthy to receive his hospitality "] *and there is no man that receiveth me to house* [that taketh me in (Matt. xxv. 35)]. (19) *Yet there is* [I want nothing that would be burdensome to my host, only house shelter, for I have] *both straw and provender for our asses ; and there is bread and wine also for me, and for thy handmaid, and for the young man (which is) with thy servants* [*i.e.,* us ; the Levite and his concubine]; *(there is) no want of anything.* (20) *And the old man said, Peace (be) with thee* [a salutation here of welcome]: *howsoever (let) all thy wants (lie) upon me* [the old host declining to allow the Levite to provide for himself]; *only lodge not in the street.* (21) *So he brought him unto his house, and gave provender* [*yabol,* from *balal,* to make a mixture, *i.e.,* fodder of grains, vetches, and other herbs mixed] *unto the asses ; and they washed their feet* [a usual kindness and courtesy to guests, whose feet, covered only with sandals, become soiled with dust in journeying (Gen. xviii. 4, xix. 2 ; John xiii. 5 ; 1 Tim. v. 10], *and did eat and drink.* (22) *(Now), as they were making their hearts merry, behold, the men of the city, certain sons of Belial* [derived from *beli,* 'without,' and *ya'al,* 'usefulness,' *i.e.,* good for nothing—our word 'naughty.' A personification of *reckless, lawless, worthlessness* (Deut. xiii. 13). Answering to Raka (Matt. v. 22) ; and "vain fellows," ha-reekim (2 Sam. vi. 20;

compare 2 Cor. vi. 15)], *beset the house round about, (and) beat*
[מִתְדַפְּקִים, *knocking with continuously increasing violence*] *at the
door, and spake to the master of the house, the old man, saying,
Bring forth the man that came into thine house, that we may
know him* [re-enacting the awful scene of the Sodomites and
Lot (Gen. xix. 4, 6; Ezek. xvi. 44–51): God's nation Israel
becoming vile as Sodom!] (23) *And the man, the master
of the house, went out unto them, and said unto them, Nay,
my brethren, (nay), I pray you, do not (so) wickedly; seeing
that this man is come into mine house* [as a *guest*, to whom
respect is due], *do not this folly* [the scriptural name for
wickedness, " shameful licentiousness;" נְבָלָה. The wicked, however worldly wise, are 'fools' before God; whilst sinning
against Him, it is *their own soul and body* that they wrong
(Prov. viii. 36; 1 Cor. vi. 18; Ps. xiv. 1). The lustful,
for the sinful pleasure of a moment, incur fearful punishment here and hereafter (Gen. xxxiv. 7; Deut. xxii. 21)].
(24) *Behold, (here is) my daughter, a maiden, and his concubine; them I will bring out now, and humble ye them, and
do with them what seemeth good unto you; but unto this
man do not so vile a thing* [the same Hebrew as that for ' folly '
(ver. 23), on which see note]. (25) *But the men would not
hearken to him: so the man* [the master of the house, ' I '
(ver. 24), *took his* [the Levite's] *concubine* [doubtless with his
guest's leave], *and brought her forth unto them; and they knew
her, and abused her all the night until the morning ; and when
the day began to spring, they let her go.* (26) *Then came the
woman in the dawning of the day, and fell down at the door of
the man's house where her lord* [husband] *(was), [and lay there]
till it was light.* (27) *And her lord rose up in the morning,
and opened the doors of the house, and went out to go his way ;
and, behold, the woman his concubine was fallen down (at) the
door of the house, and her hands (were) upon the threshold* [with
arms outstretched towards her husband, and the only shelter
from the brutality of her abusers, from whom she escaped only
to fall down dead before the door]. (28) *And he said unto
her, Up, and let us be going ; but none answered. Then the man
took her (up) upon an* [Heb., *the*, i.e., *his*] *ass, and the man*

rose up, and gat him unto his place [his home]. (29) *And when he was come into his house, he took a* [*the :* the one in the house which was used for cutting up animals into joints] *knife, and laid hold on his concubine, and divided her,* (*together*) *with* [rather *according to,* ‎לְ] *her bones, into twelve pieces* [one even for Benjamin; for it was only Gibeah of Benjamin that was guilty; the Levite might presume that the tribe generally would join the rest in punishing its guilty member (see Ezek. xxiv. 4–9). Fierce indignation prompted him to violate all natural repugnance to the mutilation of his concubine's corpse, in order by the horrid spectacle to rouse all Israel to vengeance. The appeal to the eye acts on the mind more powerfully than that to the ear. So Saul (1 Sam. xi. 7). The age was as violent in its remedies as in its diseases; such was the sad issue of the general backsliding from God's blessed law], *and sent her into all the coasts of Israel.* (30) *And it was so, that all that saw it, said* [rather the words express *what the Levite hopes* (as the effect of his thus vividly setting the crime before the nation), *that all will say,* "and so it *will be* (said he : supply אָמַר), that all that *see* it *shall say,*" &c. The Hebrew perfect הָיָה, with vau simple, exhibits the Levite's anticipation of all Israel's righteous indignation, as a *fact* sure to occur, and already *present before his mind's eye,* not as a mere conjecture : the event shows he did not deceive himself. This view of Maurer and Keil is confirmed by ch. xx. 6, 7], *There was no such deed done nor seen from the day that the children of Israel came up out of the land of Egypt unto this day ; consider of it* [שִׂימוּ, apply, viz., your mind (לֵב) to it], *take advice* [consult], *and speak* (*your minds*) [what steps are to be taken to avenge this atrocious crime].

CHAPTER XX.

(1) *Then all the children of Israel went out, and the congregation* [the idiomatic term for *the Israelite community viewed as a church, or religious body met together,* הָעֵדָה. It occurs 67 times alone in the Pentateuch, and 30 times with the addition "of the Lord" or "of Israel," 13 times in Joshua; in Judges only here and xxi. 10, 13, 16; elsewhere only 1 Kings viii. 5, xii. 20; 2 Chron. v. 6. An indication of the early date of these transactions (Speaker's Commentary)] *was gathered together* [קָהַל, the technical word for the solemn assembling of the congregation (Numb. viii. 9)], *as one man, from Dan even to Beersheba* [(see note ch. xviii. 29). Beersheba was the southern limit of Palestine, as Dan Laish was the northern; so the phrase means *the whole land from end to end* (1 Chron. xxi. 2; 2 Sam. xxiv. 2–7). 'It was allotted to Judah. Beersheba means "the well of the oath," *i.e.,* between Abraham and Abimelech (Gen. xxi. 31); also Isaac and Abimelech (xxvi. 31–33). Seven wells are there, which pour their streams into the *Wady es Seba,* and are named *Bir es Seba;* the largest is 12 feet in diameter and 44 feet deep, the second 5 in diameter 42 in depth, the other five further off], *with the land of Gilead* [the Trans-jordanic tribes, including Jabesh Gilead among its towns (ch. xxi. 8–10] *unto the* LORD [JEHOVAH. Not that the ark was taken thither; but simply the congregation met *as in the sight of the omnipresent Jehovah, and in His name* to hold a judicial court] *in Mizpeh* [(see note xi. 11). The Mizpeh here is probably not that of Gilead (though the latter was no doubt an ancient sanctuary, Gen. xxxi. 48–52); but that of Benjamin (Josh. xviii. 25, 26), where it is mentioned in connection with

Gibeon (1 Sam. vii. 5, 6). The Septuagint render its name *Scopia;* answering to the name Scopus in Josephus (Jer. xli. 6), the place of view : probably answering to Nob, Sennacherib's last stage on his march from the north to Jerusalem (Isa. x. 28–32) : " the hill of God " (1 Sam. x. 5, 10). Mizpeh, meaning ' watch-tower,' corresponds to Nob, " a high place commanding a view," the spot whence the full view of Zion breaks on the traveller from the north : akin to *Nabat,* " to view." At the present day, east of the north road, opposite *Shafat* (the Arabic for *view*), is a tell with rock-hewn cisterns and remains of a town (Conder, *Quart. Statem. Palest. Explor. and Tent Life,* ii. 116, 117). Mizpeh and Nob are never named in the same passage as distinct. They were probably either identical or close to one another. The Nob was the high place of Gibeon]. (2) *And the chief* [Heb., *pinnoth,* " the corner stones " or ' pillars ' (margin, 1 Sam. xiv. 38 ; Isa. xix. 13). The heads and fathers on whom rested the chief burden of the state (compare Gal. ii. 9 ; Eph. ii. 20 ; Rev. xxi. 14)], *of all the people, (even) of all the tribes of Israel, presented themselves in the assembly* [*quahal*] *of the people of God* [this solemn phrase implies that the purpose of the assembly was not one of worldly ambition, whence wars usually spring], *four hundred thousand footmen that drew sword.* (3) (*Now the children of Benjamin heard* [by due summons of Israel to them] *that the children of Israel* [the eleven other tribes] *were gone up to Mizpeh* [whither the Benjamites, though summoned, did not go up ; yet it was within the borders of Benjamin]). *Then said the children of Israel* [to those in the assembly whoever might be able to give evidence], *Tell* (*us*), *how was this wickedness?* (4) *And the* [Heb., " the man, the "] *Levite, the husband of the woman that was slain, answered and said, I came unto Gibeah that (belongeth) to Benjamin, I and my concubine, to lodge.* (5) *And the men* [Heb., " *Baaleey :* " a Phœnician word (see note, ch. ix. 2), " the owners," ' masters,' or ' citizens : ' perhaps the word hints at their Baal-like filthiness, such as was usual in the worshippers of Baal, not Jehovah (Isa. xxvi. 13)] *of Gibeah rose against me, and beset the house round about upon me by night, (and) thought to have slain me* [omit ' and,' and translate as

in the Hebrew order, "me they thought to have slain." The
Levite inferred this from their cruel treatment of his wife
(ch. xix. 22)] *and my concubine have they forced* ['humbled '],
that she is dead. (6) *And I took my concubine, and cut her in
pieces, and sent her throughout all the country* [Heb., 'field '] *of
the inheritance of Israel; for they have committed lewdness and
folly in Israel.* (7) *Behold, ye (are) all children of Israel* [*i.e.,*
my wrong affects not me alone, but all of you as Israelites] *give*
[the Hebrew adds " for yourselves," לָכֶם (see 2 Sam. xvi. 20)] *here*
[where you are assembled] *your advice and counsel* [see ch. xix.
30]. (8) *And all the people arose as one man, saying, We will
not any of (us) go to his tent, neither will we any (of us) turn into
his house* [until we have taken vengeance for this crime]. (9)
*But now, this (shall be) the thing which we will do to Gibeah;
(we will go up) by lot against it* [so the Septuagint supplies the
omission. The lot would determine who should go up first,
as ver. 18 implies, so ch. i. 1, 2. Speaker's Commentary suggests that the Hebrew word for "we will go up" has dropped
from the text, from its containing much the same letters as the
next word (עָלֶיהָ), *aleyah,* " against it." Keil more probably
explains "the words 'against it by lot' (we will act) contain the
resolution formed concerning the sinful town, and have all the
enigmatical brevity of judicial sentences, and allude to the
course laid down in the Mosaic law with regard to the
Canaanites, that they were to be exterminated, and their land
divided by lot among the Israelites ; so the Syriac, ' We will
cast lots upon it.' " Gibeah having degenerated into Canaanite
morals, must suffer the Canaanites' doom. The *particular* mode
of procedure, viz., as to provisioning all the assembled Israelites
(ver. 10), and as to who should begin the onslaught (ver. 18),
was a consideration *subsequent* to the first *general* resolution
here adopted]. (10) *And we will take ten men of an hundred
throughout all the tribes of Israel, and an hundred of a thousand,
and a thousand out of ten thousand* [400,000 in all, ver. 17], *to
fetch victual for the people, that they may do, when they come to
Gibeah of Benjamin, according to all the folly that they have
wrought in Israel* [retribution in kind, ch. i. 7, note]. (11) *So
all the men of Israel were gathered against the city, knit together*

['associated,' חֲבֵרִים] *as one man.* (12) *And the tribes of Israel sent men through all the tribe* [Heb., 'tribes,' *i.e.*, the families or divisions and clans (1 Sam. ix. 21)] *of Benjamin, saying, What wickedness (is) this that is done among you?* (13) *Now therefore deliver (us) the men, the children of Belial, which (are) in Gibeah, that we may put them to death, and put away evil from Israel* [war is only to be resorted to when all other means of vindicating right have failed]. *But the children of* ["children of" is an insertion of the Keri or Hebrew margin. The Hebrew text or Kethib omits the words : 'Benjamin,' as a collective noun, can be construed with the plural] *Benjamin would not hearken to the voice of their brethren the children of Israel* [this embassy of Israel to Benjamin (vers. 12, 13) must have preceded the gathering and march of all Israel "against the city" (ver. 11); for not until Benjamin, by refusing to deliver up the culprits in Gibeah, became identified with that city in guilt, did all Israel gather together against it]. (14) *But* [or *and*] *the children of Benjamin gathered themselves together out of the cities* [they had remained in them, disregarding the gathering of Israel heretofore (ver. 1–3)] *unto Gibeah, to go out to battle against the children of Israel.* (15) *And the children of Benjamin were numbered at that time, out of the cities* ["the cities" may be mentioned as the principal places, representing all the places of the tribe ; or rather, as Bertheau suggests, the cities were occupied by the Benjamites, whilst the subject Canaanites lived in the villages ; just as the Normans held the castles, the subject Saxons the open country], *twenty and six thousand men that drew sword, besides the inhabitants of Gibeah, which were numbered seven hundred chosen men* [they had fallen from their numbers, which at the first census were 35,400 (Numb. i. 37), and the second census 45,600 (Numb. xxvi. 41). The Israelites too had diminished about one-third (see note, ver. 17). The troublous times, which compelled them to live mostly in fortified cities amidst the Canaanites, may account for the diminution. The number of Benjamites now was 26,000, and 700 chosen men. But there fell, in accurate numbers, 25,100 men, in round numbers 25,000 ; *i.e.*, in the principal battle 18,000 fell, 5000 as a gleaning, and 2000 in the pursuit (vers.

U

35, 44, 45), 600 alone survived (ver. 47). The Septuagint and
Vulgate read '25,000' only; but other ancient versions 26,000.
The two statements are harmonised by supposing they lost the
900 or 1000 additional men besides the 25,100 or 25,000 in
their victorious battles on the first and second days (vers.
21, 25)]. (16) *Among all this people (there were) seven hundred
chosen men left-handed* [evidently the same 700 as in ver. 15,
the men of Gibeah. Ehud, who was left-handed, similarly
belonged to Benjamin (ch. iii. 15)]; *every one could sling
stones at an hair-(breadth), and not miss* [compare 1 Sam.
xvii. 40, 49]. (17) *And the men of Israel, besides Benjamin,
were numbered four hundred thousand men that drew sword : all
these were men of war* [a falling off from their numbers (in
Numb. i. 46), 603,550, including Benjamites; and (in Numb.
xxvi. 51), 601,730. Possibly about one-third of the men able
to bear arms were left as a guard at home against the Canaanites.]
(18) *And the children of Israel arose, and went up to the house
of God* [rather, "to Bethel." So the Septuagint, Syriac,
Chaldee, and Arabic versions. The Vulgate has "the house of
God," viz., at Shiloh. The word 'there,' in ver. 27, must refer
to a particular place. That place is Bethel, if we so translate
in ver. 18; so probably in ver. 31, as it is in ch. xxi. 19.
Bethel is in other places of Scripture (including probably Zech.
vii. 2) meant by the Hebrew *beth el;* but "the house of God,"
beth-ha-Elohim. Shiloh was too far off (15 or 16 miles) from
the seat of war to be meant. Bethel was near enough to
Gibeah (5 or 6 miles distance) for them to come and go the
same day (vers. 19, 23, 26). The ark was brought to Bethel,
and Phinehas the high priest inquired of Jehovah before it
through the Urim and Thummim. Bethel was on the northern
boundary of Benjamin, and was already a holy place, through
the revelations of God to the patriarch Jacob (Gen. xxviii. 19,
xxxv. 1–15, xxxi. 13), and Abram's first altar (Gen. xii. 8, xiii.
3; so also 1 Sam. x. 3). It was natural then to move the
ark thither, as being also near Mizpeh, the scene of the national
council (ch. i. 1)], *and asked counsel of God, and said, Which
of us shall go up first to the battle against the children of
Benjamin ? And the* LORD [JEHOVAH] *said, Judah (shall go*

up) first [so ch. i. 1, 2. They did not consult God whether
they were to war at all, or have victory, but which tribe
should lead the attack. So God answers according to their
query. Evidently their question implies there was no judge
as yet to take the lead]. (19) *And the children of Israel rose
up in the morning, and encamped against Gibeah.* (20) *And
the men of Israel went out to battle against Benjamin; and the
men of Israel put themselves in array to fight against them at
Gibeah.* (21) *And the children of Benjamin came forth out of
Gibeah* [descending on their foe from the vantage ground], *and
destroyed down to the ground* [*i.e.*, laid dead upon the ground]
of the Israelites that day twenty and two thousand men. (22)
And the people, the men of Israel, encouraged themselves, [יִתְחַזְּקוּ,
"strengthened themselves," viz., in their own strength, not in
that of the Lord God (contrast Ps. lxxi. 16)], *and set their
battle again* [Heb., "added to set," &c.] *in array, in the place
where they put themselves in array the first day* [seeking, out of
pure vain-glory, to wipe out the disgrace which their previous
defeat had brought upon them (Berleb. Bible in, Keil). We
could not otherwise account for their infatuation in choosing
the very same position on which they had just been defeated;
also God's withholding victory from them, notwithstanding their
prayers, is thus cleared up]. (23) (*And the children of Israel
went up and wept before the* LORD [JEHOVAH, *i.e.*, before the
sanctuary containing the ark of Jehovah at Bethel (ver. 26)]
until even, and asked counsel of the LORD [JEHOVAH, again through
the high priest (ver. 27, 28). Evidently they had made up
their minds to go before asking (ver. 22), and consulted
Jehovah only to obtain His sanction to their foregone con-
clusion. No wonder, then, that he answered them according
to their own self-will (Jer. xlii., xliii.; Ezek. xiv. 4)], *saying,
Shall I go up again to battle against the children of Benjamin
my brother?* [as he is "my brother," ought I to war with him?
Faith ought to have taught them, that even a brother must not
stand in the way in doing the will of God (Luke xiv. 26)].
And the LORD [JEHOVAH] *said, Go up against him)* [so 1 Kings
xxii. 13–15; Prov. xxvi. 5]. (24) *And the children of Israel
came near against the children of Benjamin the second day*

[not the day after the first engagement, as if the battles were fought on two successive days, but the second day of actual fighting—probably some days after the first fight ; the consultation of Jehovah at Bethel intervened]. (25) *And Benjamin went forth against them out of Gibeah the second day, and destroyed down to the ground of the children of Israel again eighteen thousand men : all these drew the sword* [as contrasted with the unarmed Israelites of the villages (ver. 15, 17).

THE GROWTH OF SIN IN THE ABSENCE OF LAW : ITS FATAL ISSUE.

1. *The blessings of law and civil government illustrated by the evils flowing from their absence.*—This sad history is prefaced by the significant statement that then " there was no king in Israel." So long as the civil and religious authorities ruled, there was peace in Israel. But Joshua and the elders who survived him for a time were now dead. The removal of God-fearing rulers is like the breaking down of a dam, which opens the course for sin to deluge a land, sweeping all before it. A small beginning suffices to produce a torrent of iniquity. We should hardly have expected that such overflowings of ungodliness should have taken place so speedily after the death of so godly a ruler as Joshua [see in the remarks on ch. xvii., xviii., proofs of the early date of the transactions (chs. xvii.–xxi.)] But the innate depravity of our fallen nature accounts for all. Nothing but legal checks and magisterial rule can restrain even its external outbreaks ; its inward evil needs a higher power to control it. Five times the sacred writer notices the absence of civil government and governor, as accounting for the prevalence of evil (ch. xvii. 6, xviii. 1, 7, xix. 1, xxi. 25). If even in well-ordered communities, fearful crimes are sometimes perpetrated, what a deluge of evil would overwhelm us, if good government were withdrawn ! Let us learn to be thankful for the blessings of law and order.

2. *Idolatry the parent of immorality.*—A people never rises

higher morally than their religion, however lower they fall than their profession. It is therefore suggestive, that the origination of idol-worship by Micah and his Levite chaplain, and its adoption by the whole tribe of Dan, are narrated immediately before the atrocious sin of Gibeah. Idolatry and immorality are twin sisters. " They that make idols are *like unto them*, so is every one that trusteth in them " (Ps. cxv. 8). This fundamental principle is laid down by the Divine Lawgiver (Deut. vii. 25, 26): " Neither shalt thou bring an abomination into thine house, *lest thou be a cursed thing like it.*" The servant of corrupt gods, whether material images, or the idols, self, carnal appetites, intellectual pride, becomes earthy like his idol ; whereas the servant of the holy God becomes a partaker of the Divine nature (2 Pet. i. 4), of His holiness and righteousness (Eph. iv. 24 ; Heb. xii. 10 ; 1 John iii. 2), being changed more and more into His blessed image (2 Cor. iii. 18).

3. *The evil begins in the church, then spreads in the world : Then follows judgment.*—(1) *The evil begins in the church.* The poet truly writes—

> " When nations are to perish in their sins,
> 'Tis in the church the leprosy begins."

And Bishop Hall quaintly remarks : " There is no complaint of a publicly-ordered state, but there is a Levite at one end of it, either as an agent or as a patient." It was a roving Levite that gladly accepted, for the sake of filthy lucre, the ministry to Micah's idol, and afterwards to the same image as priest for the whole tribe of Dan. It was now again a Levite who was guilty of bigamy, and whose self-indulgence and protracted feasting with his concubine's father-in-law was the immediate occasion of the late arrival in Gibeah, issuing in the awful crime of the men of that city. No tribe felt the want of good government sooner than Levi, the tribe from which the apostate to idol-ministrations came. None of the tribe of Levi, except these two, are mentioned in all the Book of Judges. Moreover, as the apostate Levite came from Bethlehem-Judah (ch. xvii. 7), so the concubine of this other Levite came from Bethlehem-Judah. Who could have conjectured that it was out of this same Bethlehem-Judah, that He was to come forth unto God the Father, whose goings forth have been from of old, from everlasting ? (Mic. v. 2).

(2) *The evil innate in the world breaks out in full malignity, when uncorrected by the church.*—The church's calling is to witness for God against the sin of the world. When the church itself becomes corrupted, the witness ceases, and universal corruption sets in. The Levite's laxity as to the marriage law of God, which ordains that each man shall be husband of one wife, and his levity in dealing with the infidelity of his secondary wife, were sure to be accompanied with more glaring immoralities on the part of Israel in general. When the world sees that the ministers and professors of religion taste forbidden pleasures, the former will drink the foul cup of carnality to the dregs, and without shame or remorse will give way to the filthy lusts of Gibeah.

(3) *Judgment then follows from God, the iniquity of His professing people being full.*—At first sight it seems unaccountable that whereas Israel's eleven tribes united against Benjamin, solely to exact justice from the perpetrators of the awful crime, and Judah advanced foremost by God's own appointment, yet forty thousand of Israel were permitted to be slain, and Benjamin, the aggressor and accomplice by connivance in Gibeah's guilt, was victor in two successive battles. But the difficulty disappears, and God's righteous government of the world is vindicated, when we remember the neglect of all the tribes to espouse His cause against the idolatry of Micah, and of his Levite chaplain, and then of the whole tribe of Dan. The presence of a Levite in both histories suggests their spiritual connection. The Israelites had joined as one man, when the interests of social order required their intervention; but they had taken no steps to vindicate God's honour against the introduction of idolatry, though His law (Deut. xiii. 12–16) had expressly commanded them to search diligently in order to ascertain the fact of such an abomination having been wrought, and then to inflict judicial vengeance on the idolaters. It was only therefore consistent with the justice of God that He should first, by Benjamin, punish the Israelites themselves,

before employing the latter as His executioners of wrath on the guilty Benjamites.

4. *Further lessons from the story of the Levite.*—(1) *The ruin of children is often due to the laxity of parents.* The father of the Levite's concubine seems to have been too ready in conniving at her sin in first "playing the whore," and then deserting her husband. Instead of faithfully reproving, punishing, and sending her back, he countenanced her sin by harbouring her in his home. The same lax character is betrayed in his protracted feasting of his son-in-law for four whole days and the best part of the fifth day. Hospitality is at once kindly and godly; but excess in pleasures of the table, at once wastes precious time, dissipates the mind, incapacitates for serious duties, and is often the prelude of bitter griefs. It is better to "welcome the coming, and speed the departing guest," when duty calls him away.

(2) *The need of resisting the solicitations of pleasures.*—The Levite, by yielding to the fond father's ill-judged importunity to stay till the afternoon, instead of starting at early morning, was unable to go further on his journey than Gibeah that evening, and so was exposed to the deadly wickedness of its citizens. He was right in wishing to go home, for "an honest man's heart is where his calling is" (Trapp); and "as a bird that wanders from her nest, so is the man that wanders from his place" (Prov. xxvii. 8); but he was wrong in suffering his good resolution to be overcome (see Gen. xlix. 4; 1 Kings xiii. 15–24). We ought to steer midway between too easy and yielding and too stern a spirit; only yielding when kindness invites and duty does not forbid, and only resisting when concession to friends would entail dereliction of duty. Well-meant kindness sometimes proves to be a real injury. Delays are dangerous. Satan always bids us defer setting out on our journey to the heavenly home till to-morrow: "be content—tarry all night" (ver. 6); enjoy life now; "in space cometh grace;" no need of haste; it will be time enough hereafter. If we would escape eternal ruin, we must peremptorily refuse, since the heavenly King's commandment is urgent: "Whatsoever thy hand findeth to do, do it with thy might; for there is

no work, nor device, nor knowledge, nor wisdom, in the grave, whither thou goest" (Eccl. ix. 10): "Arise ye, depart; for this is not your rest: because it is polluted, it shall destroy you, even with a sore destruction" (Mic. ii. 10).

5. *The sin of Gibeah.*—(1) *The profligacy of the heathen exceeded by that of the apostate from God.* As the shadows of evening began to fall, the travellers bethought them where they must lodge: a lesson to us to secure a shelter when life's day shall have ended (Jer. vi. 4 end). Jebus, the Canaanite city where the Levite's servant proposed to lodge, could hardly have equalled in atrocity Gibeah of Benjamin. The master naturally shrank from passing the night in communion with heathen strangers (2 Cor. vi. 14–18), in Jebus, and went forward to Gibeah. But this Benjamite town, by comparison, justified her less guilty Canaanite sister, in all her abominations which she did (Ezek. xvi. 51, 52). How many professors of religion live worse than the very heathen! As Sodom, so Gibeah's iniquity was "pride, fulness of bread, and abundance of idleness; neither did she strengthen the hand of the poor and needy" (Ezek. xvi. 49). This appears at the outset in that her people allowed an Israelite of God's own chosen tribe Levi to sit down in the open street, none taking him in to lodge. Lot, by his hospitality to strangers in Sodom, entertained angels unawares, who proved to be his deliverers from Sodom's doom (Gen. xix. 1–3; Heb. xiii. 2). The inhospitality of the men of Gibeah was the first step towards their destruction. Let it not be our condemnation, in the day of the Lord, "I was a stranger, and ye took me not in."

(2) *A good man found even in a bad city.*—Though there was not one *of* Gibeah, yet there was one found *in* Gibeah to compassionate the unsheltered Levite. Had there been nine more like him, as we know in the case of Sodom; if there had been in it nine like Lot, the city would have been spared (Gen. xviii. 32). The one good man in Gibeah, however, was not a native, only a sojourner. A sojourner himself, he could the more compassionate the wayfarer. All Israelites, as having been strangers themselves in Egypt, ought to have known the heart of a stranger (Exod. xxiii. 9.). The Benjamites most of all had

good reason to be good to travellers, for their forefather was born on the road side, his mother then upon a journey, not far from this spot (Gen. xxxv. 16, 17). Like this sojourner in Gibeah, the godly are *in* the world, but not *of* the world (John xvii. 14, 15). As we believers are all pilgrims and sojourners here, on our way to a better home, we ought to be kind to our fellow-travellers on the road.

This entertainer of strangers was old, and so retained some of the almost extinct graces of the old stock, such as Israel was in Joshua's days. He was an old man, and possessed of some means (ver. 21); yet not, like his self-indulgent fellow-citizens, eating the bread of indolence. *Their* abundance of idleness begat their "much wantonness" as to lusts and inhospitality to the good (1 Pet. iv. 3, 4; 2 Pet. ii. 10, 12, 18; Gen. xix. 9).. *His* honest industry all day disposed him at night to temperance in appetites and kindliness to the needy (see Eph. iv. 28). We should labour, not in order to heap up for self, but to be able to give to our fellowmen; and seek not merely in youth, but in old age to bring forth fruit unto God (Ps. xcii. 14; Rom. vii. 4).

The old man did not wait to be asked, but made the first advance to the distressed Levite. He sought opportunities of doing good, instead of staying for their being obtruded on him. The bountiful eye (Prov. xxii. 9) is quick to see a fellow-creature's need. Job (xxxi. 32) opened his doors to the traveller, and did not let the stranger lodge in the street. This old man, with a charity that "thinketh no evil" (1 Cor. xiii. 5), after hearing a satisfactory reply to his enquiries as to the stranger's destination, believed the Levite's account of himself. Then the host kindly took on himself all the charge of providing for his guests' wants. Let us Christians feel assured that in every extremity our God will provide, at His own time, and in His own way, for all our needs (Phil. iv. 19).

(3) *Man's universal depravity illustrated in the sin of Gibeah.* —The men of this city "declared their sin as Sodom," and hid it not (Isa. iii. 9). Because "they did not like to retain God in their knowledge," but "changed the glory of the incorruptible

God into an image made like to corruptible man (see chs. xvii., xviii.), God gave them up to vile affections;" so that by their unnatural lusts, they "received in themselves that recompense of their error which was meet" (Rom. i. 23, 25, 26, 27). They who begin by dishonouring God, are sure to end in dishonouring themselves. The men of Gibeah rudely assaulted the house of the only virtuous man in the city, because his goodness and hospitality were a tacit condemnation of their badness and disregard of the homeless stranger; and, unwarned by Sodom's punishment for the like sin, they sought to work their vile purpose on the latter. Who could have thought that such abominable transgressors sprang from Jacob? A depraved Israelite is tenfold more a child of hell than the heathen. The "deep corruption" of Gibeah is a typical instance of that of mankind apostate from God (Hos. ix. 9). Surely man in his natural state is vile. Good government preserves us from the savagery which otherwise would break loose: but the lion has not lost its nature: the evil heart, though restrained, is evil still. Even the otherwise worthy old man, through fear of men, was led to follow Lot's bad precedent, in offering his pure daughter to their filthy lusts. It is the glory of Christianity that it has elevated woman to her true position; so that Christian men, even in the darkest times, would have willingly sacrificed life to save the honour of a daughter. Still even now, if preventing grace were withdrawn, man's evil nature would break out into every abomination.

(4) *The sad death of the concubine not altogether undeserved.* —The men would not hearken to the old man's appeal; for lust hath no ears. The Levite's concubine was their victim. However guilty they were, God was righteous in punishing her sin in kind. Lust had been her sin, lust became her punishment. Her father had countenanced her in unfaithfulness, and her husband had lightly forgiven her; but we do not read that she had repented of her sin before God. We must not think, because we have forgotten our past transgressions, and those whom we have wronged have forgiven them, that God has forgotten and forgiven them (see Ps. xc. 8; Heb. xiii. 4). God cannot make light of sin; and, only upon our true repentance

and faith, will He remember our iniquities against us no more. " Let the guilty, that go yet unpunished, make an end of all, in God's privy chamber of mercy by repentance, that so His open judicial proceeding in court may be stopped " (Trapp).

6. *God's judicial vengeance to be executed by Israel and on Israel.*—(1) *Sin seen in its true light must inspire horror.* The patience of God appears in His not immediately striking blind the sons of Belial in Gibeah, as He smote those in Sodom. We might have expected that He would consume their city with fire from heaven, as He consumed the similarly guilty cities of the plain. But God gave to Israel the honour of avenging His cause in this present world on the city with the sword, and in the world to come He will consign those who go after strange flesh to suffer the vengeance of eternal fire (Jude 7). The saints shall share in the honour of judging the ungodly world (Ps. cxlix. 5–9; 1 Cor. vi. 2, 3). The horror of Gibeah's deed of lust and death was intensified by the terrible mode of the Levite's proclamation of it. We cannot too much loathe evil : and if sin were perceived, not in the false light that passion, the world, and Satan represent it, as sweet and attractive, but as it is in reality, viewed in the light of God's coming judgment, and in its blackness, filthiness, and deadliness to body and soul for ever, men would recoil from it with trembling fear. The wages of our sin is indeed death. How we ought to prize " the gift of God," which is " eternal life through Jesus Christ our Lord ;" and love Him who saith to each, " Thou hast destroyed thyself, but in me is thy help " (Hos. xiii. 9).

(2) *The people of God ought to be zealous in vindicating His honour.*—The only bright gleam in this sad war in Israel is Israel's holy zeal against the transgressors of God's law. Indifference to evil, easy connivance at its commission, and the absence of jealous care to clear one's self from complicity in it, are sure marks of declension in religion, as the opposite spirit characterises soundness in the faith (see 2 Cor. vii. 11). The Searcher of hearts bestows this praise on the church of Ephesus : " I know, how thou canst not bear them which are evil " (Rev. ii. 2, 20); and censures the church of Thyatira thus:

"I have a few things against thee, because thou sufferest that woman Jezebel to seduce my servants to commit fornication." The child of God must be of the same mind as his Father concerning evil and evil doers; so Samuel (1 Sam. xv. 35, xvi. 1), and David (Ps. cxxxix. 21, 22).

(3) *The appeal of the Levite speaks to us.*—"Behold, ye are all children of Israel." *Noblesse oblige.* Our high vocation is an obligation that we should in nothing dishonour "that worthy name by which we are called" (James ii. 7). A wrong committed against one member affects the whole body, for in the spiritual Israel "we are members one of another" (Eph. iv. 25). As being such, all ought to prefer the common good to individual interests; as the Israelites would not return to their homes, however personal considerations might tempt them, until they had vindicated the honour of God and Israel by exacting justice from the wrong-doer. Nor ought we to defer till to-morrow the work which can be done to-day. Strike whilst the iron is hot; for zeal is apt to cool, if the work to be done is not set about immediately.

(4) *Unity is strength.*—"The congregation gathered together as one man"—"all the men of Israel—knit together as one man " (ch. xx. 1, 11). This was their glory and power *now*, that when the common good was at stake, they were all of one mind. *Subsequently* it was their weakness and their shame, that in their ever-deepening degeneracy the several tribes became more and more disunited. Thus it is the complaint of Deborah and Barak, in their song concerning the conflict with Canaan: "Reuben abode among the sheepfolds, Gilead beyond Jordan, Dan in ships, Asher on the seashore," when they ought to have been united with their brethren against the common foe (ch. v. 16, 17). How much more ought we as believers to be associated as one man against the great enemy of Christ and mankind, and not with fatal selfishness prefer our grovelling earthly aims to the cause of the Lord and the advancement of His kingdom! Thus originally "the multitude of them that believed were of one heart and soul " (Acts iv. 32). But soon 'divisions' arose, and with them came weakness and declension from the first purity and love

(Acts xv. 1, 2 ; 1 Cor. xi. 18, 19). Let us all return back to
the primitive simplicity of the faith as it is in Jesus ; and so
"having the same love, being of one accord, of one mind"
(Phil. ii. 2), we shall be to our spiritual foe "terrible as an
army with banners" (Song Sol. vi. 4).

(5) *Judgment on all may be averted by timely surrender of
the guilty one.*—Before the Israelites proceeded to fight, they
first would treat. To arrive at a just decision, both sides must
be heard. After hearing the Levite's statement, the Israelites
appealed to the Benjamites to give up the criminals, that they
might be publicly put to death, and so the national guilt might
be removed, the infection of evil be cut off, and national judgments from God averted (compare 1 Cor. v. 6, 7). A sin so
like that of Sodom, might, if not judicially punished, bring on
all the doom of Sodom. A little concession in time would
have saved Benjamin a sanguinary war, ending in the almost
total extinction of the tribe. "Only by pride cometh contention, but with the well-advised is wisdom" (Prov. xiii. 10).
Pride will not stoop to own a wrong and to surrender the
wrong-doers. So "pride goeth before destruction, and a haughty
spirit before a fall" (Prov. xvi. 18). By screening the guilty
from their due punishment, we make ourselves responsible for
their sins. By countenancing them, or glossing over their
transgressions with soft names, we "have fellowship with the
unfruitful works of darkness," which we ought rather to
'reprove' (Eph. v. 11).

(6) *God's holy controversy with both Israel and Benjamin
accounts for Benjamin's infatuation in rejecting Israel's appeal.*—
Benjamin dared in arms to oppose both a righteous cause,
which God Himself would espouse for the honour of His
justice, and also vastly superior numbers. Self-conceit, relying
on that skill, and especially on the expertness of their slingers,
tempted them to such a presumptuous venture. Sinners,
instead of counting the awful cost (Luke xiv. 31 ; Isa. xxvii.
4, 5, 7 ; Amos iv. 12) of meeting God in battle, rush blindly
against Him who is infinitely stronger than they (1 Cor. x. 22 ;
see Job xv. 25, 26). Clever as the Benjamite marksmen were
to sling stones at an hair-breadth and not miss, they utterly

missed their mark in defending an unrighteous cause. The
Hebrew for 'sin' (*chata*) is the same as that for *missing the
mark* (ch. xx. 16). The glory of God is man's true aim.
Man's sin lies in this, he "comes short of the glory of God"
(Rom. iii. 23). It is not merely his open offences against his
fellowmen, and against his own body and soul, but all things
wherein he fails to "glorify the God in whose hands his
breath is, and whose are all his ways" (Dan. v. 23 ; Rom. i.
21 ; 1 Cor. x. 31) constitute sin ; and "the wages of sin is
death." But God permitted Benjamin's infatuated obstinacy,
so as to subserve His purpose of chastising Israel first by
Benjamin, and then sorely judging Benjamin by Israel.

(7) *Judgment must begin at the house of God* (see 1 Pet. iv.
17).—At first sight it seems strange that those vindicating a
just cause against the transgressors should be permitted by God
to suffer so severely. The Israelites were fighting Jehovah's
battles, and with His commission ; and yet the guilty Benjamites conquered them once and again. The first lesson to be
learned from this case is, we must justify God in His dealings
even before we see the reasons of them (Rom. iii. 4, ix. 20).
Next, observe "the battle is not to the strong." The Israelites
probably relied too much on mere numbers. They must be
taught that it is not by might or power of men, but by the
Spirit of Jehovah, the victory is to be won (ch. vii. 2–7 ; Zech.
iv. 6). When we lean on an arm of flesh, it proves a dis-
appointing stay, and as a reed that pierces the hand that
trusted it. Thirdly and chiefly, the Israelites must be
taught bitterly to know their own transgressions, before they
execute God's judgment upon other transgressors. It was not
for their own righteousness, but for the wickedness of their
brethren, that they were employed by God for the latter
purpose (Deut. ix. 5). Even with themselves there were sins
against the Lord their God (2 Chron. xxviii. 10). Keen as
they were to vindicate the public order and law against the
filthiness of Gibeah and their Benjamite abettors, they were
indifferent in the case of Micah and the Danites to execute the
law of God against idolaters (Deut. xiii. 12–17): they must
therefore be made to feel their own dereliction of duty first,

before they can be fit instruments of God's justice against their brethren. Lastly, we learn not to judge of the merits of a cause by its present want of success. Wait till the end, and God will vindicate the right at last (see Lam. iii. 26).

(8) *Consultation of God, in order to gain God's blessing, must be single-minded.*—The Israelites asked not, Shall we go up and succeed? They were too confident of success because of the goodness of their cause, and the greatness of their numbers, forgetting that their own hands were not altogether clean, and that success does not always attend a multitude. They slighted their adversary ; so they at first suffered severe reverses. We are then most apt to miscarry in our spiritual warfare, when we rely on ourselves, and forget the power of our spiritual enemies. Again, we may profess to consult the Lord, and all the while have made up our own minds as to our course and its issue. They did not pray for success, as if all depended on God, nor did He promise it in answering them " Go up." It is righteous retribution that God should answer the double-minded inquirer according to the multitude of his idols (Ezek. xiv. 4). When the Israelites, after their first failure, " encouraged themselves, and set their battle again in array " in the same place as before, they evidently were acting under the influence of pique and wounded pride : they will on the same spot avenge their mortification and defeat, retrieve their credit, and humble their Benjamite brethren. This vain-glorious spirit accounts for their second humiliation before those whom they had despised. It is true they had " wept before the Lord," in asking His counsel again ; but they wept more for their losses than for their sins which had caused them. Their cry was the cry of anguish, not that of repentance and faith (compare Hos. vii. 14). They " encouraged themselves," but not in the Lord their God, as David did when greatly distressed (1 Sam. xxx. 6) ; their ground of confidence still was in the justice of their cause and the numbers of their army. They needed yet to be taught by one chastisement more to humble themselves under the mighty hand of God, that He might exalt them in due time (1 Pet. v. 6). We cannot serve the Lord, unless we forsake all heart-idols, and be thorough in His

service (Josh. xxiv. 19, 20). "God *setteth Himself in battle array against* (ἀντιτάσσεται) the proud, but giveth grace unto the humble" (James iv. 6). When His people are in a fit state to bear success, God gives it; but not till then. The ways of Providence may seem dark for the time; but wait His time humbly, and all shall be cleared up.

> "Judge not the Lord by feeble sense,
> But trust Him for His grace;
> Behind a frowning providence
> He hides a smiling face."

7. *Typical aspects of the history.*—(1) *Fatal effects of the non-recognition of the heavenly King.* If such evils resulted from the absence of any civil ruler in Israel, how much more fatal must be the issue of ignoring the righteous rule of God? Social and political restraints are but external, and cannot reach the regulation of the heart. Crime and its judicial punishment by man may be avoided; yet all the while sinners are sure by the very law of human nature, to indulge their lusts, some walking in a cleaner part of the broad way to hell, others walking in its very centre and giving unbridled rein to their passions, so long as they live "without God in the world."

(2) *Blessed changes wrought by the gospel.*—When the gospel takes possession of the soul, Jesus becomes King of the whole man, inward and outward, to the exclusion of other lords (Isa. xxvi. 13). "The Lord is our judge, the Lord is our lawgiver, the Lord is our king; He will save us" (Isa. xxxiii. 22). No longer is the thought, "Who is Lord over us?" and "we will do that which is right in our own eyes;" but, we are no longer "our own," we are "bought with a price," therefore we will "glorify God in our body and in our spirit which are God's" (1 Cor. vi. 19, 20). The standard of duty is not now one of man's own making, but the unerring word of God. They are no longer "a generation pure in their own eyes," which "yet is not washed from their filthiness" (Prov. xxx. 12). Knowing their own sin by the inward teaching of the Holy Spirit, they wash every stain away in "the fountain opened for uncleanness." Knowing also the love of God, they cannot but love Him; and

loving Him, they walk in all righteousness toward their fellow-men.

(3) *The Lord's tenderness to His unfaithful people shadowed forth in the Levite's history.*—The wronged husband was the first to court the return of the wrong-doing wife. So the God, against whom we have sinned, invites us back to Himself. "They say, if a man put away his wife, and she go from him, and become another man's, shall he return unto her again?—But thou hast played the harlot with many lovers; yet return again to me, saith the Lord" (Jer. iii. 1). Nay more, the Lord in person came to bring back His lost bride, and "speaks comfortably unto her" (Hos. ii. 14), even as the Levite "spake friendly" to his erring wife. The father forgave her, and received her to his home; so God in His infinite grace deals with us. The joyful festivity of the family reconciliation is a faint picture of the gladness and rejoicing in the Heavenly King's palace, at the return of the ransomed bride (Ps. xlv. 15; Isa. xxxv. 10).

If the Levite, his wife, and her father, could have seen the tragical event before them, their mirth would have been turned into mourning; such also is the transitoriness of all earthly joys, that "they who rejoice," should be "as though they rejoiced not" (1 Cor. vii. 30). But the joy of the Lord is an abiding joy, at once satisfying and lasting for ever.

There was none found in an Israelite city to welcome the Levite: so when the virgin Mary was about to give birth to Jesus, "there was no room for them in the inn" (Luke ii. 7). "He came unto His own, and His own received Him not" (John i. 11).

Again, we have a glimpse of the loving-kindness of Jesus in the old man's care of his homeless guests. The Son of God, like him, was but a 'sojourner' here, coming in our sorest need, and, at His own heavy cost, saying to each believer, "Peace be with thee; let all Thy wants lie upon me" (see John xx. 19, 21; Phil. iv. 19; Ps. xxiii. 1; Luke x. 33–35). However, the Antitype herein infinitely exceeds the type. The old man could not save his guests from the agents of evil: the Lord Jesus both could and did save us. The Levite gave up her whom he

x

so loved to a cruel death, through the deadly lusts of the
wicked : the Lord Jesus will never give up His people (Hos. xi.
8). Nay, in order to save His elect bride from Satan and
death everlasting, He gave Himself up to an agonising and
humiliating death of shame. The Levite, with all his profes-
sions of love, forsook his wife : the Lord Jesus suffered Himself to be forsaken of God, in order that God may never
forsake us (Heb. xiii. 5). O that the effect of His love and
death for us, may be to unite us Christians together as one
man to Him, against evil and the workers of evil! If the
Israelites by their union (xx. 1, 11), in spite of failure and
Benjamin's seeming triumph for a time, secured perfect and
final victory ; much more shall the children of God, notwithstanding Satan's temporary successes now, prevail finally and
for ever over all the powers of darkness, by being knit together
in Jesus ; and to Him shall be all the glory ! (John xvii.
21–24.)

FINAL TRIUMPH OF JUSTICE OVER THE TRANSGRESSORS :
NARROW ESCAPE OF BENJAMIN FROM EXTINCTION.

(26) *Then all the children of Israel* [those engaged in the
war], *and all the people* [*i.e.*, the rest of the congregation,
incapable of taking part in the war, old men and women], *went
up, and came into the house of God* [rather " unto *Bethel* " (see
note, ver. 18)], *and wept, and sat there before the* LORD [JEHOVAH],
and fasted that day until even [they had already " wept before
JEHOVAH," the covenant God of His people, whose righteousness they were vindicating against the transgressors (ver. 23).
But even then their " encouraging " or " strengthening themselves, and adding to set in array the battle," expresses graphically their *self-reliance, because of their greater numbers.* They
did not ask that Jehovah should give them success, as if it
depended solely on Him, but only, " Shall I go up again ? "
His answer, therefore, did not promise them success ; for they
had not asked for it, but simply that they should go up.   Not

till after their second defeat, when a tenth of their whole army, 40,000, had fallen, did they humble themselves with the outward expression of humiliation, viz., fasting until even (2 Sam. i. 12)], *and offered burnt-offerings* [implying whole consecration of themselves to God] *and peace offerings* [*Shelamim*, supplicatory offerings for God's gracious aid (Lev. iii.) ; the sacrificial meal associated with these, implied their *fellowship with God*], *before the* LORD [JEHOVAH]. (27) *And the children of Israel inquired of the* LORD [JEHOVAH] (*for the ark of the covenant (was) there* [at Bethel, note ver. 26] *in those days* [before which the offerings were made (2 Sam. vi. 17 ; Lev. i. 3, 9). The words "in those days," imply that the ark was only temporarily at Bethel ; it had been brought thither from the tabernacle at Shiloh, its usual place. The holocausts or burnt-offerings were *wholly* consumed by fire ; the peace-offerings were partly eaten]. (28) *And Phinehas, the son of Eleazar, the son of Aaron* [therefore this history belongs to the period just after the death of Joshua (Josh. xxiv. 33)], *stood before it* [or Him (Exod. xxviii. 30 ; Lev. xvii. 4 ; Deut. xii. 18)], *in those days* [as the high priest]), *saying, Shall I yet again go out to battle against the children of Benjamin my brother* [the designation which Israel gives to Benjamin, " my brother," implies that their motive in warring is not hatred or jealousy, nay, that they shrink from the war. Only that zeal for God's honour impels them, even though it be against a brother (Deut. xxxiii. 9 ; Luke xiv. 26)], *or shall I cease ? And the* LORD [JEHOVAH] *said, Go up : for to-morrow will I deliver them into thine hand* [viz., the hand of the congregation, as represented by the consulting high priest. Now, for the first time, Jehovah *promises them success:* not so before (ver. 18, 23 ; compare Josh. vii. viii.)]. (29) *And Israel set liers in wait round about Gibeah* [the same stratagem as Joshua practised at Ai (Josh. viii. 4, 5)]. (30) *And the children of Israel went up against the children of Benjamin on the third day* [the first day was the fast (ver. 26), the second the day of consulting Jehovah, the third day the ' to-morrow,' on which Jehovah promised deliverance (ver. 28)], *and put themselves in array against Gibeah, as at other times.* (31) *And the children of Benjamin went out against* [" to meet "] *the people, (and) were drawn away from the city* [the manner in which they were drawn away is told in ver. 32]; *and they began to smite of the people, (and) kill* [Heb., "they began to smite of the people wounded," חֲלָלִים, *i.e.*, to smite those who pretended to flee wounded], *as at other times, in the highways, of which one goeth up to the house of God* [rather " to Bethel "], *and the other to Gibeah in the field* [*Geba'* is the masculine form for *Gibeah*, and occurs in the Hebrew ver. 10, 33. *Sadeh* means "the cultivated ground," or 'field.' Geba is now *Jeba*. The words "in the field," apparently imply a different Gibeah from the Gibeah assailed by Israel. The present road northward from Jerusalem branches off about a mile beyond *Tuleil el Ful* (*i.e.*, Gibeah) into two roads, one leading to Beitin (Bethel), and the other to Jeba (Geba). But Keil identifies " Gibeah in the field," with the chief Gibeah. At the base of the hill from which Gibeah or Geba is named, is a *cave*. The Syriac version, by a different pointing of the Hebrew for " the meadows" (ver. 33), מערה, translates ' cave,' which would seem more suitable for " liers in wait." But the " meadows " or naked treeless land (from עָרָה, *to strip*), were not the place of lying in wait, but the place whence they came to the city, after having come forth from their hiding places], *about thirty men of Israel.* (32) *And the children of Benjamin said, They (are) smitten down before us, as at the first. But the children of Israel said, Let us flee, and draw them from the city unto the highways* [viz., those named ver. 31]. (33) *And all the men of Israel rose up out of their place* [their ambush, and the " meadows of Gibeah," across which they advanced toward the city], *and put themselves in array at Baal-Tamar* [" Baal (*i.e.*, lord) of the palm tree," named *Bethamar* by Eusebius (*Onom.*), near Gibeah. The Speaker's Commentary identifies Baal-Tamar with the place which is mentioned in the later times of Deborah, as the " palm tree of Deborah between Ramah and Bethel " (ch. iv. 5). For the highway here (ver. 31), leads to Ramah, and any point north of Ramah would be " between Ramah and Bethel." But the distance from Gibeah seems an objection] ; *and the liers in wait of Israel came forth out of their places, (even) out of the meadows of Gibeah* [see note, ver. 31]. (34) *And there came against Gibeah* [rather "*from before*" or "*from opposite to,*" מִנֶּגֶד] *ten thousand chosen men out of all Israel* [these ten thousand, when the ambush had succeeded in entering and smiting Gibeah (ver. 37), now attacked in the rear the Benjamites who were pursuing the fleeing Israelites], *and the battle was sore: but they* [the Benjamites] *knew not that evil (was) near them.* (35) *And the* LORD [JEHOVAH] *smote Benjamin before Israel* [fulfilling his promise (ver. 28)]; *and the children of Israel destroyed of the Benjamites that day twenty and five thousand and an hundred men* [viz., 18,000 in the battle (ver. 44); 5000 gleaned in the highways (ver. 45); 2000 near Gidom. The whole number of Benjamin was 26,700 (ver. 15); 600 escaped to Rimmon (ver. 47); 100 more are mentioned (ver. 35), as slain in the battle of the third day. The 1000 still unaccounted for, probably fell in the battles of the two former days]; *all these drew the sword* [this is the summary account of the battles and its results, the details are next given (ver. 36–46). This is the Hebrew mode of writing history. It is simple and unartificial, circumstantial clauses affording the needed information]. (36) *So the children of Benjamin saw that they were smitten: for the men of Israel gave place to the Benjamites, because they trusted unto the liers in wait which they had set beside* [or *against,* עַל] *Gibeah.* (37) *And the liers in wait hasted, and rushed upon Gibeah; and the liers in wait drew (themselves) along* [advanced in a long-drawn train, as in iv. 6, where see note, the same Hebrew verb], *and smote all the city with the edge of the sword.* (38) *Now there was an appointed sign* [or *time,* מוֹעֵד] *between the men of Israel and the liers in wait, that they should make a great flame with smoke rise up* [Heb. " make great, so that they cause rising of the smoke to ascend "] *out of the city* [the same stratagem as Joshua practised at Ai (Josh. viii. 2–22)]. (39) *And when the men of Israel retired in the battle, Benjamin began to smite (and) kill* [see note, ver. 31, and margin] *of the men of Israel about thirty persons* [vers. 39, 40, resume what had been already narrated in vers. 31, 32]: *for they said, Surely they are smitten down before us, as (in) the first battle.* (40) *But when the flame* [see note, ver. 38, where the same Hebrew occurs] *began to arise up out of the city with a pillar of smoke, the Benjamites looked behind them, and, behold, the flame* [כְּלִיל, "the consumption:" rather, as Gesenius, "the whole"] *of the city ascended up to heaven.* (41) *And when the men of Israel turned again, the men of Benjamin were amazed* ["in trepidation" or 'consternation']; *for they saw that evil was come upon* ['touched,' 'reached'] *them.* (42) *Therefore they turned (their backs) before the men of Israel unto the way of the wilderness* [which reaches from Jericho to the mountains of Bethel (Josh. xvi. 1). The Benjamites fled this way toward the north-east, probably in order to cross the Jordan]; *but the battle overtook them; and them which (came) out of the cities* [viz., "the 26,000 men that drew sword" who "gathered themselves together out of the cities unto Gibeah" to help it (vers. 14, 15), *i.e.*, *all* the warriors of Benjamin], *they destroyed in the midst of them* [*i.e.*, in the midst of these cities, rather "in the midst of *it*" (בְּתוֹכוֹ), viz., "the wilderness:" (compare ver. 45)]. (43) (*Thus*) *they inclosed the Benjamites round about, (and) chased them, (and) trode them down with ease* [*i.e.*, *without difficulty*, מְנוּחָה. Keil explains "at the place of rest," *i.e.*, at every place where the fleeing Benjamites sought rest. So the Hebrew is translated Numb. x. 33] *over* [rather, as Heb., "*unto* over"] *against Gibeah toward the sun-rising.* (44) *And there fell of Benjamin eighteen thousand men: all these* [the Hebrew אֶת is prefixed. "So far as all these were concerned, they"] (*were*) *men of valour.* (45) *And they turned and fled towards the wilderness unto the rock of Rimmon* [according to Robinson (ii. 113), 15 Roman miles north of Jerusalem, 3 miles east of Bethel, and 7 north-east of Gibeah: distinct from Rimmon in the south of Judah (Josh. xv. 32). Now the village *Rimmon* stands on and round the top of a conical limestone mountain. But Rev. W. F. Birch suggested, the rock Rimmon might be found in the Wady Suweinit, and that the 600 Benjamites who "abode in the rock four months" (ver. 47), must have found shelter in some great *cave* with a spring adjacent. Such a cave has been probably identified by Rev. H. D. Rawnsby, viz., Mughâret el Jai, adjoining Wady er *Rumman* (which preserves the name *Rimmon*): *Jai* means an assembling together; Rimmon means 'pomegranate;' possibly that under which Saul fixed his headquarters, in Migron, *i.e., the precipice* (1 Sam. xiv. 2): the pomegranate gave its name to the rock or precipice. The cave and the spring (Ain Suweinit), are both on the south or Benjamite side of the ravine. The spring is situated halfway up the hill, and is 450 feet below the Ras el Krein (Migron?) or eastern end of the plain Jeba; the clamber from it to the cave, which is 200 feet lower down the cliff, takes about twenty minutes. The current tradition in Jeba is that the cave will hold 600 men, a curious coincidence with the Bible statement. The name Suweinit, from Sunt, *acacia-thorn*, implies that once this tree (considered by the peasantry the best for fuel) formerly abounded in the Wady, though now no big-sized bushes exist there. Thus fuel would not be deficient during the stay of the 600. Any descent to the cave from above would be hazardous. Situated in a corner of the cliff, it is so protected by outstanding ledges, that until within 10 yards of it, one would not suspect its existence in coming from the westward or Jeba end; while again the cliff to the east, curving out to the north, hides it from comers up the valley from the east. 300 could find ample room in the cave; 600 could hide there, if need be (*Palest. Explor. Quart. Statem.*, July 1879, pp. 112, 118, &c.)], *and they gleaned of them* [those slain in the principal battle being the harvest, and those slain in fleeing after the battle being the 'gleanings.' So remorseless was the slaughter, that not even the gleanings were spared (Jer. vi. 9)] *in the highways* [the one leading up to Bethel, the other to Gibeah in the field (note ver. 31)], *five thousand men; and pursued hard after them unto Gidom* [between Gibeah and the Rimmon rock, whither they were fleeing], *and slew two thousand men* [more] *of them.* (46) *So that all which fell that day of Benjamin were twenty and five thousand men* [see note, ver. 35, on the exact numbers, 25,100, for which the round number 25,000 is here given] *that drew the sword; all these (were) men of valour.* (47) *But six hundred men* [had] *turned and fled to* [*i.e.,* toward, as in ver. 45] *the wilderness unto the rock Rimmon, and abode in the rock Rimmon four months.* (48) *And the men of Israel turned again* [from pursuing the Benjamite warriors] *upon the children of Benjamin* [the unarmed inhabitants remaining throughout the Benjamite country], *and smote them with the edge of the sword; as well the men of (every) city, as the beast* [Heb., "from the city men (read מֵתִם for מתם), even to beast." The present reading means literally *wholeness;* so it is explained as "men of *full* age"; or otherwise "the whole human kind" collectively, men, women, and children], *and all that came to hand* [Heb., "even to all that was found," הַנִּמְצָא] : *also they set on fire all the cities that they came to* [Heb., as before, "all that were found." They treated Benjamin as devoted to destruction, like the Canaanite cities under the ban, as Jericho (Josh. vi. 17, 21), and others (Numb. xxxi. 17; Deut. ii. 34, iii. 6). The plague of corruption needed to be stayed by a desperate remedy (Hos. ix. 9, x. 9). Phinehas (xx. 28) consulted Jehovah; and though it is not said that Jehovah ordered Benjamin to be devoted under the ban (*cheerem,* חֵרֶם), yet certainly He sanctioned the war. Still their zeal degenerated into cruel fanaticism and personal retaliation after double defeat, so that they sought to exterminate their own brethren ruthlessly. In great national guilt the innocent suffer with the guilty (Deut. xiii. 12–17)].

CHAPTER XXI.

CRUEL DEEDS ENTAIL BITTER REMORSE: ISRAEL'S EFFORT TO
MITIGATE THE EVIL TO THE BENJAMITE SURVIVORS.

(1) *Now the men of Israel had sworn* [before the war] *in
Mizpeh* [a supplement to the account in ch. xx. 1–10 : they then,
when dooming Benjamin to the curse (*cheerem*), vowed also not
to give their daughters to that tribe in marriage], *saying, There
shall not any of us give his daughter unto Benjamin to wife* [this
is stated to explain the difficulty which the Israelites found in
providing wives for the 600 surviving Benjamites (see ver. 7)].
(2) *And the people came to the house of God* [rather "to Bethel"
(note, xx. 18, 27; also see xxi. 19), *and abode there till even
before God* [ch. xx. 26, 27], *and lifted up their voices, and wept
sore* [Heb., "wept with a great weeping;" probably they kept
a fast day too (see ch. xx. 26)]. (3) *And said, O* LORD
[JEHOVAH], *God of Israel, why is this come to pass in Israel,
that there should be to-day one tribe lacking in Israel?* [the repetition of 'Israel' twice is a virtual appeal to God as JEHOVAH,
in covenant with *Israel*, to remember that covenant in their
behalf, and show some way of averting the destruction of one
out of the twelve tribes, without which 'Israel' would not be
complete]. (4) *And it came to pass on the morrow, that the
people rose early and built there an altar* [to embody in action
their prayer. No altar is mentioned in ch. xx. 26, 27, but
only the ark. Doubtless there was one at Bethel. The one
here was an *additional* altar, as the first altar was not large
enough for the number of sacrifices now being offered by all
the tribes after their victory; not in *competition*, but in *communion* with the altar at the door of the tabernacle], *and
offered burnt-offerings and peace-offerings* [see note, xx. 26;

compare 1 Kings viii. 64]. (5) *And the children of Israel said,
Who (is there)* [from] *among all the tribes of Israel that came
not up with the congregation* [rather, " *to* the assembly," בַּקָּהָל]
unto the LORD [JEHOVAH ? This was the plan they adopted to
provide wives for the 600 surviving Benjamites, without
violating their own oath (ver. 1)]. *For they had made a great
oath concerning him that came not up to the* LORD [JEHOVAH] *to
Mizpeh* [at the meeting referred to in ch. xx. 1, &c.], *saying,
He shall surely be put to death.* (6) *And the children of Israel
repented them* ['grieved' or "had compassion for "] *for Benjamin
their brother, and said, There is one tribe cut off from Israel this
day* [" Benjamin is not, what will become of Jacob ? Benjamin
become a Benoni ! the son of the right hand, a son of sorrow "
(Henry)]. *How shall we do for wives for them that remain,
seeing we have sworn by the* LORD [JEHOVAH], *that we will not
give them of our daughters to wives?* (8) *And they said* [resum-
ing their words from ver. 5], *What one (is there) of the tribes*
[here in the sense " tribal *subdivisions*"] *of Israel that came not
up to Mizpeh to the* LORD [JEHOVAH] ? *And, behold, there came
none to the camp from Jabesh-Gilead* [the name survives in the
Wady Jabes which runs from the east into the Jordan valley.
The ruin, *Ed-Deir*, south of the Wady, probably occupies the
site of the town. It was the chief of the cities of Gilead.
Subsequently to the destruction by Israel at this time, it
recovered itself. The cruel threats of the Ammonite king
Nahash brought Saul to its rescue (1 Sam. xi.). In gratitude,
the inhabitants courageously recovered the remains of Saul and
his three sons from the walls of Bethshean (1 Sam. xxxi. 8, 13),
and were therefore blessed by David (2 Sam. ii. 5, 6)], *to the
assembly.* (9) *For* [in order to ascertain whether really there
were none present from Jabesh-Gilead] *the people were numbered,
and, behold (there were) none of the inhabitants of Jabesh-Gilead
there.* (10) *And the congregation sent thither twelve thousand
men of the valiantest* [one thousand from each tribe, as directed
in Numb. xxxi. 6], *and commanded them, saying, Go and smite
the inhabitants of Jabesh-Gilead with the edge of the sword* [utter
extermination (Gen. xxxiv. 26)] *with the women and the children.* (11) *And this (is) the thing that ye shall do, Ye shall*

utterly destroy [*tacharimu*, literally, "put under the ban," *cherem*, devote as accursed] *every male, and every woman that hath lain by* [Heb., "known the lying with"] *man* (Numb. xxxi. 17). (12) *And they found among the inhabitants of Jabesh-Gilead four hundred young virgins, that had known no man by lying with any male* [and therefore were exempted from the ban (ver. 11); according to the precedent given in the case of Midian's destruction (Numb. xxxi. 17, 18]; *and they brought them unto the camp to Shiloh, which* (*is*) *in the land of Canaan* [as contrasted with Jabesh, which was in Gilead (compare Josh. xxii. 9). After the determination had been adopted as to Jabesh-Gilead, the representatives of the congregation moved to Shiloh, which was the seat of the tabernacle, and therefore the usual meeting-place of the congregation. Shiloh was about 10 miles north of Bethel]. (13) *And the whole congregation sent* (*some*) *to speak* [or, as Heb., "sent and spake"] *to the children of Benjamin that* (*were*) *in the rock Rimmon, and to call* [Heb., "and called"] *peaceably* [Heb., "peace"] *unto them.* (14) *And Benjamin came again at that time; and they gave them wives which they had saved alive of the women of Jabesh-Gilead; and yet so they* [the 400 virgins] *sufficed them not* [not as Speaker's Commentary proposes, "But they did not find enough for them even so." But מָצָא, is properly "to reach;" German, *hinreichen, hinlangen*; Greek, ἱκανός, *sufficient*, from ἱκνέομαι, "to reach;" so "to suffice for" (Gesenius)]. (15) *And the people repented them for* ["had compassion upon"] *Benjamin, because that the LORD* [JEHOVAH] *had made a breach in the tribes of Israel* [by the extermination of Benjamin (ch. xx. 48), virtually repeating the statement (vers. 6, 7)]. (16) *Then the elders of the congregation said, How shall we do for wives for them that remain?* [the 200 of the 600 remaining, after 400 had been provided with wives from Jabesh-Gilead (ver. 12–14)], *seeing the women are destroyed out of Benjamin* [ch. xx. 48]. (17) *And they said* (*There must be*) *an inheritance for them that be escaped of* ["belonging to"] *Benjamin* [Heb., "(the) inheritance (of the) escaped remnant belongs to Benjamin;" *i.e.*, it must not be transferred to another tribe; the land of their inheritance, and the tribe (represented by the escaped remnant) must be retained as originally appointed, and therefore wives must be found for them, that they may multiply, and occupy their inheritance], *that a tribe be not destroyed out of Israel.* (18) *Howbeit we may not give them wives of our daughters: for the children of Israel have sworn, saying, Cursed (be) he that giveth a wife to Benjamin* [vers. 1–7]. (19) *Then they said, Behold, (there is) a feast of the* LORD [JEHOVAH] *in Shiloh yearly, (in a place) which (is) on the north side of Bethel, on the east side of the highway that goeth up from Bethel to Shechem, and on the south of Lebonah* [this minute description of the position of Shiloh is given to show how easily the Benjamites could effect their object; issuing from the coverts of vines in the vineyards at Shiloh, and seizing upon the dancing maidens, they could readily escape to their own territory by the contiguous high road from Bethel to Shechem, without much risk from the men of Shiloh. Shiloh, meaning ' rest,' was the place where Israel attained its rest; and the Lord rested among them (Ps. cxxxii. 14): the ark having been removed from Gilgal where it had been during the conquest of Canaan, to Shiloh upon the completion of the conquest. Here it remained till the days of Samuel (Josh. xviii. 1–10; 1 Sam. iv. 3). "The feast of Jehovah" here was probably that of Tabernacles, the feast of ingathering of fruits; appropriately to the mention of the vineyards in ver. 20 (compare ch. ix. 27). Festive dances of maidens were usual on such joyous occasions. Now *Seilun.* A tell surrounded by higher hills rises from an uneven plain, with a valley on the south side. The tabernacle on the tell would be visible on all sides. There is an excavation in the rock which may have been the spot where the ark rested, sheltered from the bleak winds. Major Wilson says, northward the tell slopes down to a broad shoulder, across which a level court has been cut, 77 by 412 feet. The rock is scarped to the height of 5 feet; this is probably the site of the tabernacle. The mosque on the summit of the hill, once a Jewish synagogue, of which the remains still exist, is called "the mosque of the Eternal." At a distance of fifteen minutes' walk, is a fountain reached through a narrow dale, and flowing into a well, thence into a reservoir, for watering flocks. Hither the daughters of Shiloh would resort, and the spectators could see their dances from the amphitheatre of surrounding hills : on these one can trace terraces distinctly marked. Lebonah north-west of Shiloh, answers to *El-Lubban*]. (20) *Therefore they commanded the children of Benjamin, saying, Go and lie in wait in the vineyards.* (21) *And see, and, behold if the daughters of Shiloh come out to dance in dances, then come ye out of the vineyards, and catch* [the same Hebrew as in Ps. x. 9, חָטַף] *you every man his wife of the daughters of Shiloh, and go to the land of Benjamin.* (22) *And it shall be, when their fathers or their brethren come unto us to complain, that we will say unto them* [in your name], *Be favourable unto them for our sakes* [rather, " *Graciously concede them* (אוֹתָם masculine for feminine, as in ver. 12 : the virgins carried off) *to us";* the Israelites, in speaking to the aggrieved relatives of the virgins, personating the Benjamite aggressors, and therefore using the first person ' us ']; *because we* [Benjamites represented by their Israelite advocates] *reserved* [' received '] *not to each man his wife in the war* [with Jabesh-Gilead, the 400 virgins taken there not sufficing, but 200 Benjamites remaining, each still unprovided with a wife]; *for ye did not give unto them* [voluntarily your daughters as wives. Here the elders of Israel speak to the relatives of the virgins, no longer in the person of *the Benjamites*, but in *their own* name ; ye did not *give* your daughters to the Benjamites ; your oath prevented you from doing so ; and it at the same time palliates the forcible means used by the Benjamites to obtain your daughters ; otherwise they must have remained wifeless : moreover the force which they used, makes you guiltless of *giving* your daughters, and so breaking your oath, though you suffer them to *remain* with their captors] *at this time* [בָּעֵת, as in ch. xiii. 23], (*that*) *ye should be guilty* [of breaking your oath]. (23) *And the children of Benjamin did so, and took* (*them*) *wives, according to their number* [200 (compare ver. 12 with ch. xx. 47)], *of them that danced, whom they caught ; and they went and returned unto their inheritance, and repaired the cities, and dwelt in them.* (24) *And the children of Israel departed thence at that time, every man to his tribe and to his family, and they went out from thence every man to his inheritance.* (25) *In those days (there was) no king in Israel:*

every man did (*that which was*) *right in his own eyes* [the sacred writer implies hereby disapproval of much of the action just recorded. Recurring to what he stated at the beginning (ch. xix. 1), he intimates that such things could not have taken place in a settled government under a king, such as existed in his time (see remarks on ch. xvii. 6, xviii. 1), as to the date and inferences from this often-repeated remark].

SELF-ABASEMENT AND PRAYER, THE SECRET OF RETRIEVING DISASTER.

1. *The saints' way of victory.*—(1) *Trust in the Lord alone.* As the Israelites failed when they trusted solely in the greatness of their numbers and the goodness of their cause, leaning upon an arm of flesh, so they succeeded when they made God their main dependence. When a righteous cause suffers for a time, it is through some fault in its upholders. The Israelites had taken for granted God's presence and blessing, and had merely asked, " Which of us shall go up first ? " (ver. 18), and " Shall I go up again ? " They were taught by their double defeat that " the race is not to the swift, nor the battle to the strong " (Eccl. ix. 11). So believers are only strong when " strong in the Lord " (Eph. vi. 10).

(2) *Humble confession of past sin and unbelief.*—Now they humble themselves before God with weeping. Their calamity elicited tears of distress, their sense of sin tears of penitence.

(3) *Waiting for the Divine promises.*—They " sat before the Lord " in His house, waiting *on* Him and *for* Him ; in the spirit of the Psalmist, " I will hear what God the Lord will speak, for He will speak peace unto His people and to His saints " (Ps. lxxxv. 8 ; compare Isa. xxx. 18 ; Habak. ii. 1). They previously had not waited for God's promise ; now they do not leave His mercy seat till they have His promise : " I will deliver them into thine hand " (ver. 28). Josephus, the Jewish historian, says, that when the Israelites inquired of God by Urim and Thummim, the splendour shining on the high priest's

breastplate presaged victory. The promises of God shine with joyous assurance on the path of the believer (see Rom. iv. 21 ; 2 Cor. i. 20 ; Tit. i. 2 ; Heb. xi. 13 ; 2 Pet. i. 4).

(4) *Coming to God through the one only Sacrifice.*—They not only wept, but also " offered burnt-offerings and peace offerings before Jehovah." We can have God's favour only in God's appointed way—through the atoning blood of the great Sacrifice. Penitently confessing our sin, believing in the Saviour once for all offered for us, and presenting ourselves in the power of the Holy Spirit a living sacrifice to God, we have His promise giving the warrant to our prayers, and therefore the certainty of victory over all our spiritual foes, the flesh, the world, and Satan. The fast which God chooses, is when men " turn from their evil way," and " turn not again to folly " (Jonah iii. 10 ; Ps. lxxxv. 10).

(5) *Presenting to God the offerings which He accepts.*—" The sacrifices of a broken spirit and a contrite heart He will not despise " (Ps. li. 17). The peace-offering which He now requires is thanks-giving and thanks-living—the devotion of the heart and life, as well as of the lips. Such thanks for past favours bring answers of peace to our prayers for favours to come.

(6) *Using means, whilst looking to God for the blessing.*—The Israelites, who previously had gone forward with such foolhardy confidence, and failed, now prepared their plan of battle with all prudence, and executed it with all energy. So God, who calls us to His eternal glory, and who promises to make us more than conquerors through Him who loved us, appoints also diligence in searching Scripture, prayer, the use of sacraments, watchfulness, circumspection, and spiritual wisdom in prudently laying out to good account our talents, as the means to the end. Though we have God's promise, we must not neglect to do our part. We must not tempt, but trust God : that would be presumption, this is faith.

2. *The way of destruction.*—(1) *Self-confidence because of temporary successes.* The Benjamites, when they had killed about thirty of the Israelites who were retreating before them, flushed with seeming success, raised at once the cry of victory : " Surely they are smitten down before us, as in the first battle."

But it is foolish to triumph till the conflict is past. Their exultation soon gave place to despair. God lifts up the ungodly for a time, that their fall may be the heavier at the last (Ps. lxxiii. 3, 18, 19). " The triumphing of the wicked is short " (Job xx. 5). They are "snared in an evil time, when it falleth suddenly upon them" (Eccl. ix. 12). So it shall be in the last days (Luke xxi. 34; 1 Thess. v. 3).

(2) *Hatred and violence towards the people of God* (Obad. 10). —The Benjamites thought to brave out their sin in screening guilty Gibeah from condign punishment, and in fighting against their own brethren who were executioners of God's righteous vengeance. But their sin found them out. It is impossible to outrun Divine justice.

(3) *Perseverance in evil, because of past impunity* (Eccl. viii. 11, 12).—This will be especially in the last days the delusion of the men of the world (2 Pet. iii. 3, 4). God's silence will be mistaken for consent ; and the continuity of the order of nature will be made the pretext for denying the God of both nature and revelation (Ps. l. 3, 21). But " our God shall come, and shall not keep silence"—" Behold, the Lord cometh with ten thousand of His saints, to execute judgment upon all, and to convince all that are ungodly among them of all their ungodly deeds which they have ungodly committed, and of all their hard speeches which ungodly sinners have spoken against Him " (Jude 14, 15).

(4) *Fatal issue to transgressors.*—The Benjamites were smitten with the edge of the sword, and all their cities were set on fire. All this fearful catastrophe sprang from one sin, perpetrated by one city, which was screened from punishment by its fellows. Flee the beginnings of evil, the first approaches of sin, and any fellowship with the unfruitful works of darkness. The awful catastrophe of the one tribe is as nothing compared with the eternal ruin of all unbelievers. Let sinners, however prosperous for their brief span of life, learn that sin, not repented of and cleansed away in the atoning blood, will surely bring its votaries to the flame that never shall be quenched.

(5) *Judgment executed by the saints.*—As the " Israelites trode the Benjamites down with ease " (ver. 43); so the saints with the Lord Jesus at His return "shall tread down the

wicked, and they shall be ashes under the soles of their feet in the day" of the Lord of hosts (Mal. iv. 3).

3. *The way of escape.*—(1) *Fleeing to the rock of safety.* Six hundred Benjamites turned and fled unto the rock Rimmon (ver. 47). So, though Israel has been rejected for a time because of the nation's rejection of Messiah their King, still, "at this present time also there is a remnant according to the election of grace" (Rom. xi. 5). The Lord Jesus is the only Rock of salvation, whither both Jew and Gentile must flee, casting down the arms of rebellion, in order to be of the saved remnant.

(2) *Abiding there* (1 John ii. 28).—Not merely for "four months," as the Benjamites did in Rimmon, but for ever we must abide in Him, our city of refuge (Numb. xxxv. 25). As the Benjamites had in Rimmon (note, ch. xx. 47) a hiding place to save them from the destroyer, and a spring of water to sustain and refresh them, and fuel to warm them; so in Christ Jesus we have perfect shelter, living water, and perpetual sunshine (Isa. xxxii. 2 ; Ps. lxxxiv. 11).

4. *The way of mercy towards the fallen.*—(1) *Phinehas' zeal, as Israel's representative, yet brotherly feeling.* "He shall have judgment without mercy that showed no mercy, and mercy rejoiceth against judgment" (James ii. 13). Such was the feeling of Phinehas. In his youth he had first vindicated Israel's *purity*, and so was given Jehovah's covenant of peace, an everlasting priesthood (Numb. xxv. ; Ps. cvi. 30, 31). Next he became mediator of Israel's *brotherly unity*, by obtaining Reuben's explanation respecting the altar of witness, and so averting a civil war between the tribes (Josh. xxii. 13–34). Now in his old age he shows the same zeal for the purity, and yet at the same time the brotherhood of Israel's tribes : "Shall I yet again go out to battle against Benjamin *my brother ?*" (ch. xx. 23, 28.)

(2) *Israel's intemperate zeal.*—The Israelites had fulfilled a sacred duty in visiting with the extremest severity the unparalleled wickedness of Gibeah, and in punishing the Benjamites its supporters; yet they were not justified by the law or the facts of the case (Acts xxvi. 7) in carrying on a war of

Y

extermination against their brethren to the degree of almost
blotting out the name of one from among the twelve tribes of
the covenant nation—the tribe from which the great apostle
of the Gentiles afterwards sprang (Phil. iii. 5). The smart of
their double defeat betrayed them into marring a righteous
cause with the bitterness of personal revenge. We should
beware of maintaining God's cause in an ungodly way. It
is bad divinity which sets at nought humanity. Zeal is, like
fire, a good servant, but a bad master. Natural passions, imported into an otherwise just undertaking, spoil all the good
of it. "The wrath of man worketh not the righteousness of
God" (James i. 20). Men like Jehu say, "Come, see my zeal
for the Lord" (2 Kings x. 16, 29), when all the while their
zeal is for self : they are glad to give their self-will a fine name,
whilst in reality they follow the will of the Lord only in so
far as it does not clash with their own. Rashness in hot rage
is sure to bring remorse in cold blood. The violent deed hastily
done cannot be at leisure undone, however we wish it. Wars
between relatives and fellow-countrymen bring no true triumph
(and therefore the Romans never allowed one in a civil war),
because whichever side wins, the state loses.

In two instances Israel exceeded moderation in wrath against
Benjamin. *First*, in the oath that no Israelite should give his
daughter unto Benjamin to wife (ch. xxi. 1)—a rash and unjust vow, and one wholly at variance with the brotherly love
which ought to have bound together the tribes. God is more
honoured in the non-observance of a wrong oath than in its
observance. Israel's right course would have been to have confessed their sin to God, and begged His forgiveness for having
taken an oath which it was unjust to keep, and then to have
allowed the Benjamites to marry their daughters. Instead of
"repenting them for Benjamin" (ver. 6), they ought to have
repented of their unlawful oath.

Secondly, the Israelites treated with unjustifiable cruelty the
inhabitants of Jabesh-Gilead. It is true, the warriors of that
city, who had wilfully disobeyed the solemn summons to join
the congregation of Jehovah in punishing guilty Gibeah, made
themselves accomplices in its guilt, and incurred the terrible

ban of Israel. Neutrality in the conflict between good and evil is high treason against God. And as the numbering of the people detected the absentees, so the great day of account will convict and condemn those who "came not to the help of the Lord against the mighty" (Judg. v. 23)—those who "knew to do good and did it not" (James iv. 17; compare Matt. xxv. 41–46). But why did not Israel show the same zeal against the heathen Jebusites as now they display against a city of Israel which had disregarded their call? It was because they were less keen to maintain the honour of God than their own authority. If it had not been for their own rash oath not to give their daughters in marriage to Benjamin, the necessity would not have arisen to find a city to destroy, in order to find wives for the Benjamite remnant. Their compassion for the survivors of this tribe was exercised at the cost of ruthless cruelty to the aged, the young, and the married women of Jabesh-Gilead, all of whom were innocent. If they had really repented of their harshness to Benjamin, as they pretended, they would not have been so bloodthirsty towards Jabesh-Gilead. "David had not yet recovered his first fall, when he dealt so cruelly with the Ammonites" (2 Sam. xii. 31), (Trapp). However the marriages contracted by Benjamin with the four hundred maidens of Jabesh-Gilead at this time were overruled by God's Providence to be a connecting link inducing Saul of Benjamin subsequently to rescue that town from the Ammonite king Nahash (1 Sam. xi.).

Thirdly, the Israelites, by their counsel to the Benjamites to carry off the daughters of Shiloh when dancing, kept their oath in the letter, but utterly violated its spirit. God will not thus be mocked. It would have been far better to break their oath, than to practise the hypocrisy of adhering to the shadow, whilst eluding its substance, and adding the sin of counselling to crime. The occasion of this crime was a public dance at a sacred feast, probably that of tabernacles—an occasion of joy, whereat Israelite virgins were allowed to dance; otherwise such a manifestation of gladness, when the nation was in trouble, would have been unseasonable (see Isa. xxii. 12, 13). The dancing of men and women together was then a thing unheard

of ; nor did married women dance : and yet with all these
limitations, the dancing of these maidens in public left them
open to the stratagems of men.   It is a precedent hardly safe
to follow.   Especially in the case of the mixed dancing of men
and women, as practised in modern times, a woman throws off
the retiring modesty which so much graces her sex, and which
is her best safeguard under God against the inroads of temptation.

So ends this sad history of sin, shame, sorrow, and slaughter.
The Providence of God alone, working in connection with His
everlasting covenant, saved for better times Israel from the
utter destruction, which Israel's own corruption deserved, and
otherwise must have entailed.   So it is still with the remnant
of the Jews which had survived so many persecutions and
desolations.   " I am Jehovah, I change not ; therefore ye sons
of Jacob are not consumed " (Mal. iii. 6).   The time shall
come, because the unchanging LORD hath said it, when, as in
the case of Benjamin, Israel's and Judah's desolations shall
cease, and her land be called Beulah, ' Married,' as Isa. lxii.
4, 5, foretells : " For as a young man marrieth a virgin, so shall
thy sons marry thee ; and as the bridegroom rejoiceth over
the bride, so shall thy God rejoice over thee."   The theocracy
of Israel in its fulness shall be revealed, as designed from the
first, and as imperfectly shadowed forth in the time of the
Judges, under Jehovah its Head and King ; and the Lord will
fulfil to Israel His promise : " I will restore thy Judges as at the
first—afterward thou shalt be called, The city of righteousness,
the faithful city."   Lord, hasten that time of blessing to Israel,
and through Israel to all nations ! (Isa. i. 26, ii. 2–5.)